D1329650

Clinical Use of Story Telling

Emphasizing the T.A.T. with Children and Adolescents

Hedwig Teglasi
University of Maryland

ALLYN AND BACON
Boston London Toronto Sydney Tokyo Singapore

To Saul and our children
Jordan and Jeremy

Copyright © 1993 by Allyn and Bacon
A Division of Simon & Schuster, Inc.
160 Gould Street
Needham Heights, Massachusetts 02194

Library of Congress Cataloging-in-Publication Data
Teglasi, Hedwig.
  Clinical use of story telling: emphasizing the TAT with children and adolescents / by Hedwig Teglasi.
    p. cm.
  Includes bibliographical references and index.
  ISBN 0-205-13938-8
  1. Thematic Apperception Test. 2. Personality assessment of children. 3. Personality assessment of teenagers. I. Title.
  [DNLM: 1. Personality Assessment—in adolescence. 2. Personality
    Assessment—in infancy & childhood. 3. Thematic Apperception Test.
  WM 145 T261c]
  RJ503.7.T45T44   1992
  155.4'182844—dc20
  DNLM/DLC
  for Library of Congress
                                                    92-10779
                                                      CIP

Printed in the United States of America
10 9 8 7 6 5 4 3 2 1 96 95 94 93 92

Contents

PART TWO
Clinical Use of Story Telling

PART THREE
Cognition and Story Telling

PART FOUR
Emotion and Story Telling

PART FIVE
Relationships and Story Telling

PART SIX
Motivation and Story Telling

Preface

Projective stories lend themselves to systematic analysis through various approaches. The narrative process, content, and structure of the protocol can be looked at through different lenses, each revealing shades and nuances pertaining to a given facet of personality. As a result, no single scoring system can exhaust the rich and diverse possibilities for interpretation. However, the various components of personality reciprocally interact. Therefore, each topic area provides a different perspective from which to view projective stories, but the general conclusions from each of these vantage points tend to be consistent with one another.

Guidelines for interpretations relevant to a specific personality domain must draw from the theoretical and empirical knowledge base regarding that aspect of personality. The initial step is the delineation of interpretive criteria in line with current understanding of the phenomenon and possibilities for its measurement. These criteria must be subsequently tested to assure their utility. One way that clinicians validate such units of interpretation is through the network of relationships of various sources of information and patterns of performance on tasks requiring different sets of competencies. Another way is through the feedback received during the therapeutic or assessment process.

Over the past dozen years, I have had the opportunity to teach practicum courses in assessment where the usefulness of interpretations of youngsters' stories was apparent through the responses of parents, teachers, therapists, and, in some cases, the children themselves. The effort to integrate multiple sources of data into a meaningful pattern also sheds light on the unique contribution of projective stories within a comprehensive assessment battery.

The interpretive enterprise involves judgment based on current understanding of the phenomenon to be measured. The organization of this book reflects the idea that professionals cannot merely follow a formula and crank out interpretations but need to be familiar with any substantive area in which interpretations are made. Therefore, a review of the relevant literature is included to provide a background for understanding the various ways in which a particular personality attribute can be expressed in projective stories. Because conclusions derived from story analysis are integrated with those drawn from the rest of the battery and from background information, the interpreter must have an understanding of how diverse sources and types of data fit together. Therefore, various chapters relate to the interpreter's concept of personality and knowledge of measurement issues that provide the integrative constructs.

The assessment of personality has to account for the interplay of its constituent parts. Thus, the concepts presented early in the book crop up later. Some concepts, such as self-regulation or object relations, draw on a combination of cognitive and affective processes delineated in earlier chapters. To the extent that personality attributes overlap or incorporate a variety of more elemental processes, there is systematic reiteration of concepts in different contexts.

Theory, empirical research, and clinical experience contribute to the development of relevant interpretive approaches for projective stories. Because the narratives are open ended, the information obtained is not restricted by prior hypotheses. Therefore, the compilation of cases over the years and protocols from research studies collected by students under my supervision at the University of Maryland have served as a continually expanding data base. The insights and questions of my students challenged me to clarify my ideas. I took inspiration from their curiosity and our common commitment to conducting faithful assessments.

Acknowledgments

First, I wish to acknowledge my debt to the many scholars whose ideas provided the foundation for my thinking. My colleagues at the University of Maryland were understanding and helpful while this work was in progress. Additionally, I am appreciative of the help and support given to me by many individuals. Two former students, Drs. Constance Locraft and Michael McGrew, generously shared extensive data collected for their dissertation research. My colleague, Dr. Henrietta Hestick, also made available numerous protocols. Individuals who provided feedback on selected chapters are Dr. Margaret Human, Mila French, Laurie Diamond, and Patricia Schmitt. Two reviewers selected by Allyn and Bacon, Dr. Lynne Kellner and Dr. Dan Philip McAdams, read and thoughtfully commented on the entire manuscript. I also gratefully acknowledge the typing and editorial assistance given by my husband, Saul Golubcow. Others who are too numerous to mention assisted with tasks such as looking up references, shuttling books to and from the library, or copying articles.

My family deserves a special note of thanks for their acceptance and support, which allowed me to keep a balance between working on this book and participating in daily household routines. Jordan, you kept your commitments and responsibilities with less than the customary guidance from me, knowing that these acts alone would give me greater ease. Jeremy, I've been working on this book for half of your life, yet you cheerfully found ways to occupy your time when you saw that I was busy at my work. Saul, thanks for keeping the family in order during the times when the balance tilted for me toward preoccupation with this effort. I especially appreciate not having to ask.

CHAPTER 1

Story Telling Projective Techniques

The defining characteristics and theoretical underpinnings of projective methods are discussed in this chapter, with emphasis on the unique contribution of projective story telling to a comprehensive assessment.

What Is a Projective Technique?

A complete definition of a *projective technique* encompasses stimulus, administrative procedure, response, and interpretation. Rabin's (1981) description of a projective technique based on the work of Lindzey (1961) includes stimulus, response, and interpretation as essential elements. The stimulus is characterized by ambiguity in that multiple interpretations are possible. The instructions and administrative procedures, along with the stimuli, set the task demands. The response generated is characterized by variety and richness, with little awareness on the part of the respondent of what the material may reveal. The task of the evaluator is characterized by its complexity in integrating multidimensional facets of responses.

Stimulus

Any task or situation that can be interpreted in more than one way is ambiguous and may, therefore, be considered a projective stimulus. The fewer the cues provided to guide the respondent's interpretation, the greater the ambiguity. Frank (1939) asserted that the greater the stimulus ambiguity, the more meaningful the personality material elicited by the projective measure. Others suggest that medium ambiguity (e.g., Murstein, 1965; Kaplan, 1967) is best for projection. Still others maintain that lack of ambiguity is necessary for personality assessment (Epstein, 1966).

Seriously impaired individuals are likely to distort and personalize even highly structured stimuli and give responses that are far out of the mainstream. Since it is easiest to establish norms for responses to structured stimuli, the interpreter can have more confidence, perhaps, in diagnosing pathology when deviance from norms can be clearly demonstrated.

Different approaches work best with different populations, and what may appear to work well in one specific sample may be less effective in another. Thus, all three positions are essentially correct depending on the purpose of the assessment. The classical approach has been that the less a stimulus is structured, the greater the projection of the respondent's personality characteristics into the themes of the story. As the stimulus pull becomes weaker, the personality and needs of the narrator become increasingly influential. Even when picture stimuli are highly structured, there are unique possibilities for responding since the response format in a story telling task is open ended.

Instructions and Administrative Procedures

In any projective technique, the degree of structure is set by the instructions and by the cues provided in the stimulus. The instructions given, the rapport established, and other factors that influence the expected response, such as queries or encouragement, must be carefully documented and accounted for in the interpretation. Any deviations from standard instructions must be noted so that modifications in the interpretation can be made. To the extent that the instructions allow for multiple interpretations in the formulation of the response, that response is less constrained. For instance, the Rorschach instruction, "What might this be?" is purposely intended to minimize cues to guide responses (Exner, 1986).

Not only verbal instructions but the format of administering a test can provide cues that shape the response. For instance, the Bender Gestalt Test of Visual Motor Integration provides less constraint for responding than does the Beery Test of Visual-Motor Integration. The Bender presents the child with a blank page and it is up to the child to plan the placement, size, and organization of the figures on the paper. In contrast, the Beery presents a space below each geometric figure, which constrains its placement and size. Thus, the format of the Bender allows for the emergence of individual variation in the organization of the response.

In administering story telling tasks, some external shaping of the response is given through questioning and encouragement. These are provided only when necessary and carefully recorded because they add relevant data about the response process. The fact that the respondent is unaware of the criteria for analyzing the responses is an important source of ambiguity in projective techniques, which has been pointed out by Bell (1948). Instructions introduce response sets and convey impressions about what the examiner is seeking to discover (e.g, creativity). The interpretation of the respondent's stories must account for these instructions.

Response

The response to projective tests is open ended and relatively unconstrained in contrast to more structured tasks. In a test battery, measures vary in the degree to which responses are constrained by either clarity of instructions or freedom to organize the response. For example, the intent of the questions on the comprehension subtest of the typical intelligence scale is clear and usually not subject to multiple interpretations. Yet, the response format is relatively open ended, allowing the examiner to make inferences about the organization of the response that go beyond assigning point values according to the content of the answer.

The Apperceptive Personality Test (APT), a story telling technique based on research with adolescents and adults, presents eight stimulus cards (Holmstrom, Silber, & Karp, 1990) and elicits responses with various degrees of constraint. In part I, the respondent tells the story. In part II, the respondent completes a series of multiple-choice questions for each card to identify the characters in each story and indicate how the characters feel toward one another. Finally, each character is rated on nine psychological scales. These ratings are then scored and compared to norms. Thus, the second procedure guides the response in a way that combines a projective stimulus with little freedom to respond.

The extent to which the response is constrained is of great importance. Responses to projective tests can be constrained in their content according to the nature of the stimuli, instructions, and form of response.

Interpretation

The manner in which responses are interpreted is considered a hallmark of projective techniques. The meaningful units for analysis are derived from the response according to the judgment of the interpreter rather than specified criteria, such as the case with multiple-choice response format. Furthermore, responses cannot be easily separated from their context, and the interpretation is based not on single elements but on their interwoven patterns. Clearly, the interpretive process for projective tests is a highly complex endeavor that requires a synthesis of information.

The nature of the scoring system and the expertise of the interpreter are essential elements of the interpretation. Responses are not reducible to a simple score but reflect a dynamic process. Performance on achievement tests are directly comparable to norms, so the higher the score, the better. Personality concepts emphasize modulation and balance among internal elements, and deviation from the norm in either direction is often viewed as problematic (e.g., Rorschach).

The more ambiguous the test, the more variable the response, the more difficult it becomes to establish norms. The more open ended the response, the more it is possible to examine formal, structural features of the response as well as the content. For instance, the comprehension items can be viewed in terms of how succinctly the respondent gets to the point. Vocabulary items can receive differential credit according to the quality of the definition, whereas information items are either right or wrong. Because of the greater leeway given for responding on the Bender in contrast to the Beery, the former can be interpreted beyond the developmental score for emotional indicators and organizational qualities.

The previous distinction drawn between the stimulus and response in connection with degree of structure can be expanded to differentiate between the amount of structure in the conditions of task performance and in the conditions of learning reflected in that performance. For instance, the conditions of learning and performance in the digit span are both highly structured. The child knows to pay close attention to the numbers because he or she will be asked to repeat them. On the other hand, the performance conditions for the test of general information are highly structured, but the conditions of learning are guided by the child's general interest in and alertness to the types of "facts" sampled on the subtest. Some individuals tune out material that is not immediately relevant and may not attend to the facts even with repeated exposure. So, tasks that represent past learning are differentiated in terms of conditions of learning and conditions of performance. These distinctions can be utilized by interpreters to identify common processes influencing responses to projective measures and other tasks included in a test battery. These processes, in turn, can be related to the presenting problem and general functioning.

The Components of a Projective Test

Task Demands	*Response*	*Interpretation*
Structure and complexity of the stimulus, as well as the instructions, set the task demands.	→ Response has two components: content and form. Respondent is not aware of scoring criteria and imposes own style for content and organization.	→ Interpretation of the response depends on purpose of the evaluation, as well as framework and expertise of the examiner.

What Is Projection?

Murstein and Pryer (1959) delineated four categories of projection after reviewing the literature. *Classical projection* refers to the view of projection originally introduced by Freud, which has pathological connotations of attributing to other people one's own unacceptable characteristics. *Attributive projection* is broader than the classical and refers to the general tendency to ascribe one's own motives and attitudes to others. *Autistic projection* represents a process by which the needs of an individual influence what is perceived. *Rationalized projection* involves an outward attribution of the responsibility for behavior. Thus, illegal behavior is justified if "everybody else is doing it."

An even broader concept of projection, encompassing all of the above, is inherent in Bellak's (1975) notion of *apperceptive distortion,* which refers to a general process of superimposing expectations based on memories of past experience to the interpretation of current experience. Rabin's (1986) view of projection as the general tendency to express unique characteristics while perceiving and responding to any kind of stimulus is consistent with Bellak's definition of apperceptive distortion. According to this broad sense of projection, individuals are projecting all the time because they are perceiving and responding to the environment in ways that express their unique style of processing and organizing information. It is this broad conceptualization of projection that provides a useful frame of reference for personality evaluation with projective techniques.

Shapiro (1965) describes *paranoid projection* as the transformation of internal tension into feelings and convictions about the external world, which is based on the individual's general style of cognitive processing and subjective state. Accordingly, an individual in a state of tension centers on an isolated clue, which confirms and perpetuates biased expectancies and provides the basis for conclusions about subsequent interactions. For example, a middle-aged woman sitting on a bench at a playground turned her head and observed two boys making faces at each other. She said in a demanding voice, "Why are you making fun of me?" She took a behavior out of context and made an interpretation which was consistent with her subjective state and confirmed a general expectation.

The following is a schematic diagram adapted from Shapiro (1965, p. 92) describing defense mechanisms such as paranoid projection:

Person is in a state of internal tension.	→ Stimulus condition or external event intensifies the state of vulnerability or tension.	→ Attention is focused on some element of the situation depending on subjective state and cognitive style which direct attention and organize information.	→ Defensive maneuvers such as rationalization, denial, or transfer of internal tension to external source.

Information-processing style is relevant to the concept of projection because the organization of current recollections bears a resemblance to the cognitive process that was originally applied to interpret the experience (Shapiro, 1965). If the original cognitions are global, diffuse, or impressionistic, an individual may not recall the details of an uncomfortable event because of a general tendency to be inattentive to detail rather than the defense mechanism of repression, which is the loss of once available ideational content from awareness.

The manner in which individuals process information determines the meaning and organization of life experiences. Responses to projective story telling tests are well suited to reveal formal qualities of thinking and perception. The manner of integrating life experiences is associated with particular subjective states and styles of personality organization. These ideas are presented here:

Response to Projective Story Telling

Individual has expectancies and biases that are outgrowths of predispositions plus past experiences.	→ Complex stimulus conditions where multiple interpretations are possible.	→ Interpretation is determined by modes of cognition, attention, and affect.

Story Telling Projective Methods

The development of personality theory, particularly the psychoanalytic perspective on projection, provided the conceptual underpinning for projective assessment techniques. The use of story telling as a projective method was spurred by the introduction of the Thematic Apperception Test (T.A.T.; Morgan & Murray, 1935), originally published to provide a methodology to investigate Murray's personality theory, but subsequently became popular as a clinical instrument. As interest in this method grew, a variety of other picture-story tests were developed.

When first introduced, the T.A.T. was valued for its ability to elicit, within a few hours, information that could be gleaned only from extended psychoanalysis (Murray, 1938), a conclusion that was subsequently reiterated by Bellak (1975). Arnold's (1962) view of what the T.A.T. reveals is as follows: "a story telling test will not reveal anything a shrewd judge of character, given intimate acquaintance over a long period of time, could not find out. . . . It does, however, make such knowledge available in the space of an hour's testing" (pp. 44–45). Feedback sessions with parents indicate that they readily recognize their child's characteristics inferred from stories told to picture stimuli. Thus, the author's experience confirms Arnold's contention.

Atkinson (1981) asserts that the analysis of thematic content is useful for probing beneath overt behavior and remains an "untapped resource" for developing an understanding of behavior. Information revealed by the Thematic Apperception Test is not easily obtained through other sources (Vane, 1981) such as direct questions or multiple-choice personality tests. Even story telling tasks that use more structured picture stimuli represent a semiprojective approach, and the information derived is not comparable.

The story telling task does not simply ask for a description of the stimulus but requires the respondent to go beyond what is depicted in the picture to tell a complete story. In so doing, individuals bring their basic approach to information processing, including intellectual and conceptual skills, attentional processes, and organizational capacities, to the interpretation of the scene and to generating the content and structure of the story.

Palmer's (1983) substitution of associative techniques for projective methods is seen as too restrictive for thematic story telling approaches. The preference for the term *associative technique* reflects an effort to elude the conceptual issues related to the word *projective*. However, focusing exclusively on the associations made between the stimulus and the individual's memories, experiences, attitudes, and feelings ignores the multitude of other processes involved, such as selecting what to say or organizing the elements of the response. For example, Rorschach content is associated to the configurations of the stimulus card, but the scoring emphasis is on the cognitive-perceptual determinants of the response (e.g., organization and goodness of fit with the stimulus) rather than the content per se. When relating a story in response to ambiguous pictures of human beings, the narrator superimposes expectations and feelings about human interactions in the setting portrayed. Simply focusing on the *content* "associated" with a stimulus ignores the fact that content is organized and expressed in unique ways, and that similar themes may have different interpretive significance, depending on the form of the response.

The ego psychology formulated by Hartmann (1951) led to an emphasis on interpreting the T.A.T. responses as being controlled by the ego (Holt, 1961; Bellak, 1975). In the absence of serious pathology, the process of producing the story reflects the narrator's attempt to deal with the demands of the task through adaptive ego processes (Bellak, 1975; Holt, 1961; Whitely, 1966). Accordingly, a primary consideration is the respondent's effectiveness in accomplishing the task requirements that are imposed by the picture stimuli and the instructions. Arnold (1962) and Holt (1961) pointed out that stories are not like daydreams; when they are, the story teller is disturbed or experiencing disruption in thought processes and cognitive organization. These disruptions can sometimes be temporary due to marijuana (Crockett, Klonoff, & Clark, 1976; West, Martindale, Hines, & Roth, 1983) or other mind-altering substances. To the extent possible, individuals monitor their self-presentation to convey a picture of themselves that is acceptable. Even under instructions to fake "bad" (Weisskopf & Dieppa, 1951), story tellers did not produce grossly unacceptable stories. Sadistic, bizarre, or regressive content is screened out unless the following characteristics associated with significant pathology are present: (1) diminished awareness of reality, (2) difficulty or inability to organize experiences, or (3) lack of desire to give an acceptable account of oneself (Dana, 1959).

The picture stimuli and instructions for administration of story telling techniques such as the T.A.T. (Murray, 1943) clearly delineate the task. Each of the pictures provides a point of departure for the narrator to construct a story. The aim of this procedure is to facilitate an appraisal of how respondents organize and experience events. If the organization of experience is faulty, the individual cannot form expectations and perceptions that are in line with current realities. These biased expectations lead to misperceptions and distortions on the story telling task.

The story is not a product of the respondent's immediate experiences nor of past events but reflects the ability to perceive and organize these experiences and to assign meaning to them. Therefore, the content of stories represents *subjective* perceptions, not necessarily reality.

What the T.A.T. reveals can be discussed separately for form and content. *Form* refers to the manner in which thematic content is organized and indicates the functional capacity of the individual to deal with the task. An emphasis on that aspect of personality that deals with adaptive functioning is consistent with the ego psychological approach. Formal characteristics of *content* refer to abstractions of meaningful units from content that have little to do with specific concerns and attitudes of the story teller, such as "adequacy of the hero" as cited by Holt (1958). Bellak (1975) points out that the adequacy of the hero in dealing with the dilemma posed is an excellent criterion of ego strength. It should be apparent that for such a conclusion to hold, the story teller should also be able to accomplish the task of telling a logically consistent and coherent story. Thus, abstractions from content should be consistent with qualities of form.

To the extent that a story teller is not aware of the interpretive significance of what is being expressed, he or she cannot effectively manipulate what is being revealed. A basic advantage of projective testing is the assumed ability of such techniques "to obtain from the subject what he cannot or will not say, frequently because he does not know himself and is not aware of what he is revealing about himself through his projections" (Frank, 1939, p. 404). Similarly, Murray (1951) emphasized the basic value of the thematic techniques as follows: "Whatever peculiar virtue the T.A.T. may have, if any, it will be found to reside . . . in its capacity to reveal things that the patient is unwilling to tell or is unable to tell because he is unconscious of them" (p. 577). This may be particularly true if the story teller is unaware of his or her motivations (Allport, 1960) or is inclined to distort self-presentation. Thus, a primary strength of projective techniques is their sensitivity to covert or unconscious aspects of behavior (Lindzey, 1961).

In contrast to projective techniques, individuals may more readily perceive the intent of direct questionnaires frequently used in personality inventories and deliberately alter their response. Hyperactive/aggressive boys tended to infer hostile intent when asked to explain a hypothetical peer's behaviors in a free-response format. However, this attributional bias did not appear when boys were asked to select explanations from among given alternatives (Milich & Dodge, 1984). It is possible that these boys can recognize appropriate solutions to interpersonal problems but cannot spontaneously generate them. Thus, differences in method of measurement tap different processes.

The issue of bandwidth and fidelity relates to the type of information elicited. The reason that projective techniques such as story telling are described as "wide band" is because the scope of the information obtained is broad (Levine, 1981). Fidelity is best when specific questions are asked, such as, "What drugs are you using?" It can be helpful to elicit such information by direct inquiry. But answers to questions like "How do you relate to people?" or "How do you organize unstructured material?" are best when they are demonstrated.

Projective methods provide information about the "larger picture" and differ from "narrow-band" methods, which are designed to obtain specific information. For instance, a T.A.T. will indicate how a child responds to lack of structure and absence of feedback. Information about the child's interaction with a specific teacher can be understood in the larger context of how the child generally deals with authorities and with structure. Similarly, although story telling methods may not give specific information about how a child feels about a younger sibling, they will provide a context for understanding such information.

Allport (1960) asserted that normal individuals "tell you by the direct method precisely what they tell you by the projective method" (p. 99). Nevertheless, individuals are reluctant to share any information that could result in criticism or punishment, or in feeling stupid, embarrassed, or humiliated. People prefer to avoid the negative consequences of disclosure, which may involve guilt, anxiety, disapproval, or punishment. Murray (1938) described the following two limitations of self-reports, which apply even when an individual is trying to be forthcoming: (1) limitations of *perceptual* ability (since reality consists of a complex stream of events, only a small fraction can be attended to at any moment, and the individual may not be aware of the relevant information); and (2) limitations of *apperceptual* ability (apperception refers to interpreting behavior in terms of its purpose, meaning, and motives, and requires the individual to go beyond the observed facts).

According to Murray, the unreliability of self-reports stems from limited consciousness of inner states, distortions, repressions of past events, rationalizations, as well as a need for privacy. Self-reports, however, are useful in giving information about how a person wants to be viewed by the examiner and, perhaps, by the public, thereby providing clues about self-presentation and willingness to share concerns with the examiner. The extent of self-awareness can be distinguished from what a person is willing to admit; self-report may tap what one *wants* to believe and/or what one wants others to believe.

Different sources of information reveal different perspectives and different levels of awareness. Direct self-report reveals the way an individual feels the self to be and/or the impression the individual wants to make. Reports of others reveal the variety of ways that others who may focus on different aspects of the person see the individual. The story telling task, which includes the presentation of a set of picture stimuli along with instructions, represents a way of securing a behavioral sample from respondents. The test responses are the products of the narrator's thought processes as stimulated by the nature of the test. The content and structure of the stories relate to how respondents select and organize stimuli in relatively unstructured situations.

Faking

Defensiveness is part of any responding, as individuals are reluctant to report or express feelings that they perceive as deviating from the norm in a particular situation. Therefore, defensiveness is a general problem in personality assessment involving self-report or projectives. Interpreters make deliberate attempts to gauge the impact of the defensiveness (Bellak, 1975).

Individuals taking the T.A.T. have some deliberate control over their response and can withold from the protocol anything they wish (Tomkins, 1947). However, to do so, subjects must have a clear and conscious idea of this aspect of themselves and be cognizant of how this characteristic might be revealed to the interpreter. Most story tellers will refrain from expressing content (sadism, bizarre ideas, sex) that they feel is not socially acceptable to share with the examiner (e.g., Clark, 1952). When such content is included, the story teller may either be unaware of the impression being created or attempting to demonstrate pathology. Incarcerated individuals with extensive criminal histories can readily withold descriptions of antisocial behavior yet still reveal the manner in which they experience the world and themselves in it. It is noteworthy that the absence of aggressive themes to aggressive stimuli is predictive of aggressive behavior (Matranga, 1976).

Awareness is a critical factor in individuals' ability to alter or fake responses. Arnold (1962) studied a multiple-choice version of the T.A.T. where high and low achievers were asked to choose one of four alternative outcomes to the stories. Both high and low achievers consistently chose positive outcomes; yet when asked to tell stories, these low achievers gave negative ones. Arnold concluded that low achievers were able to recognize one solution as more desirable than another but could not generate such stories on their own.

There are basically two aspects of faking. One is to include elements to convey a certain impression and the other is to withold elements. Holmes (1974) concluded that subjects could fake need achievement on their T.A.T. stories as well as inhibit the projection of self-revealing material. Since the instructions called for the inclusion of elements relating to achievement, one would expect an increase in such imagery. However, the warning not to be caught as fakers would pull for subtlety in their attempts to do so. That subjects will follow directions to include certain themes is no surprise. It would be important to find out how those instructed to fake had altered their response and use this information to detect faking.

Another aspect of faking is the issue of withholding information. Subjects who were asked to be "guarded" (reveal as little as possible) were less self-revealing in their T.A.T. stories than subjects who were instructed to be "open" (reveal as much as possible about themselves) (Hamsher & Farina, 1967). There was greater frequency of descriptions, stilted or stereotyped responses, and unelaborated themes in the guarded than in the open group.

Weisskopf and Dieppa (1951) studied faking of T.A.T. responses by giving subjects three different instructional sets (neutral, make the best possible impression, and make the worst possible impression). They concluded that subjects can influence the interpretations of their stories when instructed to make a good or bad impression. However, in their view, stories told to Thematic Apperception Test stimuli reflect content that is acceptable to the story teller when he or she is capable of censoring the response regardless of whether they are attempting to make a good impression on the examiner.

By reviewing some of the examples cited by these authors, it is possible to demonstrate that respondents had difficulty presenting themselves in a bad light even when instructed to do so. The following is the "worst" story told to Card 1:

> This is a young lad who has stolen a package that he found in the hallway of an apartment. This package later turned out to be a Stradivarius violin and several musical scores which were in the case. He later, not knowing the value of the violin, took a hammer and smashed it to pieces. That hurts me when I say the Stradivarius was smashed to pieces.

The "best" story of the same subject:

> This boy is about 10 years of age. He has been a child prodigy since the age of 4. He has just been given a violin by his old teacher, the violin being a Stradivarius. Although this lad is only 10, he fully appreciated the value of such a beautiful instrument of music and he resolved never to let this violin part from him and also that he would become the world's most foremost violinist, which he later did.

On the surface, there appears to be a clear difference in the attitude expressed toward the violin. The authors rightly concluded that the hero of the "best" story shows an extremely positive feeling, whereas the hero of the "worst" story portrays an extremely negative view. However, T.A.T. intrepreters draw inferences about the attitudes and feelings of the *story teller*, not the character. Even when trying to fake bad, the story teller injected that it "hurts me when I say the Stradivarius was smashed to pieces," thereby revealing a positive attitude.

Here is another example that contrasts the "best" and "worst" stories to Card 8BM:

The Worst Story:

Well, I would say that this was a young man given in two different ages. Almost like a dream. He has dreamt for a long time to bring the ending of another person, possibly his own father and that is what he has been doing for some time. He has been carrying this dream for some time and did not fulfill his wish until late in life when his father was old and decrepit. He is being helped by a friend, on the perverted side himself, who is only there to witness the pain and anguish of the man. I see in the future that he will be able to get along with society and the law but he will suffer himself because of his conscience in later life. I see him only as a murderer.

The Best Story:

Well, I see this boy is dreaming and he has just witnessed for the first time—his father who is a doctor has allowed him to witness an operation. I see him dreaming and hoping that in the future he will have the hand of his father that he may be able to prolong life as he has seen it up to this time. He may not have any appreciation for his father until he has seen him now to know the tribulations while the patient is under the knife. The operation may prove unsuccessful and the boy became confused as to whether he will be able to withstand the shock of failure that may cause death; whether the reward of lengthening the life of some will be worth the pain of failure when you lose a case.

Certain elements of the "worst" story indicate the story teller's attitude: The wrongdoer will suffer later in life because of his conscience. The story teller clearly sees him "only as a murderer." Even when instructed to fake bad, the story teller could not feel comfortable leaving antisocial actions unpunished. In addition, the sequence of events in not carrying out his scheme until later in life when the father was "old and decrepit" alerts the interpreter to the fact that the story teller is not displaying an impulsive action. Furthermore, both stories emphasize inner torment at the thought of contributing to loss of life.

One of the advantages of using projectives is that they appear to be more resistant to faking than other approaches. The story telling response is complex, and the narrator cannot attribute motives and perceptions to story characters that are not available in awareness. Furthermore, the respondent may be capable of recognizing an appropriate response but may not be able to generate one.

Using stimulus cards in story telling tasks that are so highly structured that they consistently elicit specific themes obviously sensitizes the subject to the information being sought. Yet, the presentation of stimuli that require the story teller to deal with negative situations involving tension or aggression allows for an examination of how the respondent deals with such provocation. Avoidance of themes evoked by the cards suggests the possibility of faking.

Another aspect of projective story telling that limits faking is the nature of the interpretive system. The formal aspects of story structure reveal the functional resources of the individual to deal with the task. It is likely that a person who is attempting to fake (as shown in the protocols of Weisskopf & Dieppa) will try to vary the content rather than the form of the story. In addition, formal characteristics of content refer to abstractions of meaningful units of content that have little to do with the specific themes and concerns expressed. To the extent that these abstractions are not available to the story teller, attempts to fake are generally unsuccessful. Most attempts to study faking were actually inducing instructional sets with which the respondents complied. Before accepting the conclusion of successful faking, it would be important to investigate whether the interpretive significance of a protocol by experienced clinicians was dramatically altered.

The Role of Projective Tests within an Assessment Battery

Various measures present respondents with different tasks that tap different processes. In performing a structured task, the production is largely shaped by these structuring elements that are usually absent from the daily life of an individual. The responses to the story telling task are less constrained than answers to items on intelligence tests and are, therefore, more capable of revealing how the respondent organizes and sequences ideas. Consider the following question on the Wechsler Adult Intelligence Scale (WAIS-R): In a movie theater you are the first person to notice smoke and fire. What should you do? The adolescent quickly calculates that there is an expectation to *do* something. Yelling would create a panic so it seems logical to tell someone in charge. But many aspects of real-world responding are not considered in this item, such as how long it would take to perceive the problem or whether the youngster will take responsibility for action with so many others around. How will the respondent locate the person in charge? How long will he or she vacillate before taking action? Will the youngster's emotional reaction to the event disrupt thinking? Surely the response to such a structured question reflects maximal performance, which fails to account for how long it would take to realize that something was amiss and then to decide to act or to wait for others to do so.

In real-life situations, attributes that are traditionally viewed as pertaining to the personality domain determine how cognitive abilities are utilized. Some of these attributes are recognizing the need for doing a task, setting priorities and planning toward their accomplishment, initiative, stamina, self-monitoring, pacing activities, seeking or utilizing feedback, sustaining interest and independent work in the absence of feedback, making decisions, drawing inferences, taking appropriate risks, organizational skills, and recognizing and responding appropriately to subtle interpersonal cues.

To understand further the limitation of IQ tests to approximate real-life conditions, it is important to consider what takes place during the typical administration. The one-to-one interaction between child and examiner is devoid of the usual distractions in the classroom. The examiner works very hard to maintain rapport and to motivate the child. Such efforts usually overcome low interest, lack of initiative, or impulsivity. All of this puts the examiner in the position of trying to assess the very behaviors that are controlled for by the structure inherent in the usual assessment. Of course, examiners may indicate in the psychological report that a particular child needed a great deal of redirection to stay on task. But in many cases, the nature of the task keeps the child's interest, without additional efforts on the part of the examiner, even when the youngster has difficulty persisting on independent work. The individually administered IQ test is relatively structured. The range of possible responses is highly constrained, and since items are presented one at a time, even the pacing is provided. Performance does not require a long-term plan, goal setting, or self-reliance.

The awareness and organization of cognitive and affective functions to initiate and to maintain adaptive behavior refer to some central organizer such as posited by personality theorists. Freud (1923) assumed that the ego maintained an active adaptive function. In neuropsychology, the executive function, largely attributed to the frontal lobes, comprises the capacities necessary for formulating goals, planning their implementation, and translating plans into effective actions to achieve the desired aims. Lezak (1982) describes executive functions as "those mental capacities necessary for formulating goals, planning how to achieve them, and carrying out the plans effectively." She continues that these functions are required for all "socially useful, personally enhancing, constructive, and creative activities" (p. 281). These functions are analogous to the metacognitions of cognitive psychology (Flavell, 1979). Indeed, regardless of cognitive capacities, individuals could not perform any but the most routine activities without the executive, metacognitive, or ego functions, which are responsible for the organization of self-directed behavior.

The role of metacognitions in self-directed behavior has been characterized as active monitoring and consequent regulation and organization of emotions, cognitions and behaviors. Individuals engaging in metacognition would notice that they are having more difficulty with one learning task than another and would adjust their efforts accordingly.

Grinder (1985) concluded that the focus for conceptualization of general intelligence is centering on information-processing skills such as the componential approach of Sternberg (1985), which distinguishes between the traditional psychometric approach and analyses of information-processing skills (e.g., rapid retrieval of information, efficient organization of knowledge, and higher-order thinking). Gardner (1983) identified seven domains of intelligence where ability in one area is not necessarily related to competence in another: linguistic, musical, logical and mathematical, visual and spatial, bodily-kinesthetic, interpersonal, and intrapersonal. Higher-order processing skills operate across specific domains of knowledge. Therefore, despite adequate domain-specific knowledge, an individual may be unable to solve a problem because of limited "metacognitive" behaviors (e.g., Schoenfeld, 1983).

This broader conceptualization of intelligent behavior shifts the focus from purely perceptual and cognitive abilities to less specific affective/personality factors, including temperament, which has been related to the educational achievement of children (e.g., Bender, 1987). Eysenck (1983) argued that consideration of individual differences in both temperament and intelligence are essential for education, and that different methods of teaching are effective for different temperaments. Palisin (1986) found that measures of temperament at age 4 (attention span/persistence, approach/avoidance, soothability/distractibility) correlated with cognitive and achievement measures in second grade. Learning-disabled children were rated by teachers as being lower in approach, adaptability, and persistence, while being higher in distractibility than children who were not learning disabled (Cardell & Parmar, 1988).

Projective tests come closest to assessing these attributes in the usual test batteries given by school and clinical psychologists. These tests require the individual to initiate, plan, organize, and carry out an activity independently without knowing the criteria of the performance and without feedback.

The discrepancy between performance on structured instruments such as intelligence or achievement tests and competence in everyday behaviors can be explained from a number of different perspectives. One way to account for the disparity is the identification of different components or metacomponents of intelligence that are not tapped by intelligence tests but are necessary for daily functioning. These attributes have been referred to as *executive* or *ego functions, metacognitions, temperaments,* or simply as *personality traits*. A related approach is to delineate underlying processes that are required for competent functioning in daily life and compare them with processes tapped by the tests presented. Additionally, the disparity can be approached by addressing a variety of measurement issues that influence prediction from test scores to everyday behavior. Each of these three approaches to bridging the discrepancy between intelligence test scores and daily functioning are discussed next.

Metacomponents of Intelligence

It has been argued that an individual's ability to utilize previously acquired knowledge is an important aspect of intelligence (e.g., Sternberg, 1985). The concern with the application of knowledge has led to a focus on metacognitive processes or metacomponents of intelligent behavior (e.g., Flavell, 1979; Scardamalia & Bereiter, 1985). According to this perspective, intelligence has a number of different components and IQ tests tap only a narrow portion of what is considered intelligence.

Metacomponents of intelligence include attentional processes such as focusing on the task, deciding on what problems to address, and organizing strategies and plans for how to approach the problem. Other elements are monitoring progress, eliciting feedback, and shifting strategies. Also included are motivation and the ability to regulate mood and arousal (Sternberg, 1985).

Information Processing

The notion of intelligence can be viewed as a set of information-processing strategies that respond differently to various tasks and instructional approaches. Resnick and Glaser (1976), for example, define *intelligence* as the ability to learn without direct and complete instruction. Support for this contention comes from the finding that retarded individuals need complete and explicit instruction to understand and perform a task (Campione & Brown, 1977). Emphasis on information-processing strategies has been the basis for "dynamic" approaches to assessment and teaching. Such an approach can facilitate educational intervention by seeking the optimal interplay among information processing, learning environment, and performance conditions.

Theoretically, there is the possibility that when all of the processes necessary for "intelligent behaviors" are delineated across the various situational and task domains, there will be continuities across cognitive and personality measures. Therefore, the study of underlying processes has potential to provide support for the integration among personality and ability concepts. Hunt (1978, 1983) argued that intelligence tests indirectly measure information processing by directly assessing the products of information processing. Thus, underlying processes can be explored by examining the outcomes or products of learning across various domains. Vocabulary, one of the best measures of overall intelligence, obviously taps acquired knowledge. However, the process of acquisition of vocabulary was found to be highly related to the ability to infer meaning of new words from incompletely specified contextual cues (e.g., Sternberg & Powell, 1983). Similarly, while general fund of information is based on past learning, the process of learning facts over time reflects motivation and interest.

Other processes that are related to adaptive functioning involve self-regulation of states such as moods and levels of arousal. The capacity to regulate state of arousal is a process related to modulation (initiate, inhibit, and sustain) of attention (Gardner & Karmel, 1983; Rothbart & Derryberry, 1981). Zajonc (1980) provides a rationale for viewing arousal as a primary facilitator or inhibitor of cognitive functioning. States of arousal that are too high or too low interfere with perception, concept formation, and symbolization. Thus, concepts of arousal, self-regulation, attention, and emotionality have an impact on cognitive functioning as well as social/emotional functioning.

Measurement Issues

Theoretically, prediction from test behaviors to real life would be best if the underlying processes were delineated and predictions were made for performance in life tasks that required similar processes. According to the information-processing view, what a test measures depends on what cognitive processes are employed by the test takers in dealing with the task. Sternberg (1985) argues that items to be selected for the measurement of intelligence should be based on theory such as a differentiation between fluid and crystallized abilities.

Crystallized abilities stress high-level processes that have become automatic through prior learning (e.g., vocabulary, reading comprehension), whereas *fluid abilities* require adaptation to novel problems (e.g., analogy, series completion). However, different individuals may not use the same cognitive processes to solve similar problems. Therefore, a given test may not measure the same abilities for different individuals (Sternberg & Weil, 1980; MacLeod, Hunt, & Mathews, 1978). Cognitive processes involved in taking a test are influenced by factors such as test format, situation or setting, and personal characteristics such as the test taker's level of expertise (Frederiksen, 1986). Thus, there is little theoretical explanation of what processes are tapped by specific test items.

Another distinction that has been made between ability and personality measures has been that of typical versus maximum performance (Cronbach, 1970). *Maximum performance* is associated with ability testing and *typical performance* is associated with motivation and personality testing. How an individual performs on a given measure might represent worst, average, or best efforts. It is important that this be kept in mind when making predictions. Sometimes it is difficult to distinguish between typical and maximum functioning. A structured situation such as an IQ test would generally tap maximum performance. However, the various subtests differentially tap the typical-maximum continuum. The information subtest reflects not only the individual's long-term memory but the energy and investment (interest, curiosity) in attending to and learning facts that have little immediate, practical relevance. Thus, the information score is typical of what the child has retained and organized over the long term. In contrast, the individual's score on digit span or coding may reflect a momentary increase in motivation and concentration.

It seems logical to assume that measures of typical performance would have a stronger relationship with everyday behavior than would measures of maximum performance. Individuals differ in the degree to which their behavior or performance exhibits consistency (Endler & Magnusson, 1976; Epstein, 1979). Accordingly, for some individuals, there is a small difference between typical and maximum performance, while for others there are large differences. Therefore, correlations are low between measures tapping maximum and typical performance (Sackett, Zedeck, & Fogli, 1988).

The following conditions were suggested by Sackett and colleagues as generally providing a measure of maximum performance:

1. There is heightened level of effort and attention because the task is seen as important. An individual taking an IQ test is aware of being evaluated and generally exerts maximum effort.
2. Expectations and performance standards are clear. Again, the IQ test situation is highly structured and the one-to-one administration assures that there is little misunderstanding.
3. The observation or testing takes place over a relatively short period of time where it is possible to exert an uncharacteristic amount of effort that could not be maintained over the long haul. Many of the responses to IQ tests also fall into this category.

In contrast, the characteristics of measures of typical performance suggested by Sackett and colleagues are as follows:

1. Individuals are unaware that they are being observed or evaluated, so they are not deliberately trying to perform to the best of their ability.
2. Performance is monitored over a long period of time.
3. The performance task requires skills that have to be learned through continuous past efforts. If the task is highly complex, the individual has to bring a great deal of past learning (typical performance) to the solution of a current problem.
4. Performance guidelines are not clear and, therefore, the individual has to impose his or her characteristic way of organizing and dealing with the situation. In this case, the respondent decides what to focus on, how much effort to expend, and how to evaluate performance.

Projective personality tests meet several criteria for assessing typical performance. Projective stories are based on the narrator's prior integration of past experience as well as current task demands. [Individuals are unaware of what aspects of their performance are being evaluated and, in the absence of structure, they are required to organize and plan their response according to their typical mode of functioning.]

Summary

The dichotomy between the cognitive and social/emotional domains is primarily a conceptual abstraction fostered by our measurement approaches, which does not accurately reflect their reciprocal influence on daily functioning. The inclusion of assessment techniques in the battery, which vary in degree of structure in the learning and performance conditions, is advantageous. Projective personality measures are performance tests requiring processes such as planning and organization used in everyday functioning that remain untapped by structured tasks. When administering a battery of tests, the examiner should be aware of the variations in what is being measured so that discrepancies can be meaningfully reconciled. If test-item format or one-to-one administration changes a child's performance, the reasons must be clarified.

CHAPTER 2

Stimulus and the Story Telling Task

The story telling task varies according to the content depicted in and the structural features of the picture stimuli. Therefore, the role of the stimuli must be considered in thematic interpretation. Inferences made on the basis of thematic content and structure of the story are guided by the qualities of the projective stimulus (Zubin, Eron, & Schumer, 1965). A better understanding of the stimulus pull may lead to more effective use of thematic projective instruments (Murstein, 1965).

Stimulus characteristics of the cards are often the primary determinants of the child's responses (e.g., Murstein, 1965). Stimuli can be designed to elicit themes according to a given theoretical orientation (Blackey Test, Blum, 1950; Tasks of Emotional Development, Cohen & Weil, 1975) or sample attitudes in a specific situation (School Apperception Test, Solomon & Starr, 1968; Education Apperception Test, Thompson & Sones, 1973). The thematic apperception method can be adapted for use with selected populations such as children (Children's Apperception Test, Bellak & Bellak, 1949; Roberts Apperception Test for Children, McArthur & Roberts, 1982; Children's Apperceptive Story Telling Test, Schneider, 1989), adolescents (Symonds Picture Story Test for Adolescents, Symonds, 1939), senior adults (Senior Apperception Test, Bellak & Bellak, 1973; Gerontological Apperception Test, Wolk & Wolk, 1971), or with a specific ethnic group (Thompson-T.A.T., Thompson, 1949).

Several authors introduced stimuli to compensate for what they perceived as shortcomings in the existing ones. For example, Holmstrom, Silber, and Karp (1990) introduced the Apperceptive Personality Test (APT) to address problems of the prior apperceptive stimuli that included too many cards, lack of racial diversity, and an overly depressive tone. Other problems noted were lack of objective (or semiobjective) scoring system. Another relatively recent projective story telling test is the Roberts Apperception Test for Children developed by McArthur and Roberts (1982). This test introduced card stimuli consisting of line drawings designed to elicit specific themes and provided a scoring system for children aged 6 to 15. The Children's Apperceptive Story Telling Test (CAST) was devised for children ages 6 to 13 for use in school and educational settings (Schneider, 1989). The CAST attempted to expand the range of the affective tone of stimulus cards by including cards that are affectively negative, neutral, and positive. The Education Apperception Test (Thompson & Sones, 1973) consists of 18 pictures depicting children in school or in school-related situations. The test is primarily intended for use with preschool and elementary school-aged children, though the authors have reported it to be useful with adolescents. The variety of techniques offers the possibility of systematic comparisons across stimuli and interpretive systems.

The value of the picture stimuli resides in their utility to elicit themes with interpretive meaning for significant areas of functioning. Accordingly, an ideal set of cards would sample situations sufficient to elicit attitudes toward tasks, peers, authorities, family, and the self. Another way of gauging the utility of picture stimuli lies in their ability to reveal information about how the respondent organizes experiences and processes information. The structural features of stimuli independently contribute to their usefulness in clarifying psychological functioning apart from their content. The nature of the story telling task is determined by structural elements of the stimuli such as degree of complexity, ambiguity, emotional tone, number of distracting details, or disparate elements to be reconciled.

Very young children and those whose cognitive limitations or emotional disturbance would interfere with their organization of unstructured stimuli have the most difficulty with story telling tasks. When the cognitive complexity required to tell a story is beyond the respondent's capacity, meaningful content may be scant, and the primary information gained may consist of the respondent's efforts to cope with the task demands. In such cases, a productive approach would systematically vary the degree of structure inherent in the stimulus and the amount of encouragement provided in the administration procedure. An interpretation would then include the respondent's degree of difficulty in handling stimuli with various degrees of structure.

Structural Properties of the Stimulus

There are variations in the characteristics of the stimuli from one picture to another, even within a specific thematic technique, as well as among various thematic approaches. Picture cards can vary along several dimensions:

1. *Degree of ambiguity* refers to props or cues to interpretation, such as facial expression, the presence of objects (e.g., a gun), and clarity in the nature of the situation portrayed.

2. *Emotional pull* refers to the degree of positive or negative emotions inherent in the pictures.
3. *Degree of complexity* is influenced by the number of people and nature of the implied relationships that must be integrated. Complexity also relates to the number of disparate elements or discrepancies in the details (e.g., foreground-background, discrepant emotions).

Ambiguity

Murstein (1963) distinguished between structure and ambiguity of T.A.T. pictures. He used *structure* to refer to the physical properties of the stimulus and defined *ambiguity* as having the quality of being obscure or uncertain as to the meaning or interpretation of the situation portrayed (Murstein, 1965). Thus, a T.A.T. card such as 8BM is clear about who and what are depicted but multiple interpretations are possible. The men in the background could be doctors performing surgery or they could be sadistic criminals torturing someone. Similarly, the relationship between the figure in the front and the men in the background is subject to varied interpretations. Whereas structure is the property of the stimulus, ambiguity is determined by the variations in responses to the card. The less structured the stimulus (e.g., fewer props), the less the respondent can "rely on the picture" to interpret the meaning of the situation. Part of the ambiguity inherent in picture stimuli is the degree of variation in responding to what the picture evokes.

Murstein (1965) analyzed results of studies dealing with stimulus ambiguity (Gurel & Ullmann, 1958; Kenny & Bijou, 1953; Ullmann, 1957) and concluded that pictures of moderate ambiguity yield the most revealing personality data. On the other hand, Murstein (1965) also indicated that highly ambiguous cards are least useful for personality assessment. His inspection of Eron's (1950) classic monograph listing frequencies of themes elicited by T.A.T. cards indicated that the blank card (16), the most ambiguous in the set, yielded the fewest number of themes. Highly ambiguous cards give such few cues that need to be incorporated into the story that a person could stick with pleasant content that is free of tension, conflict, or adversity. Murstein (1958) found that ambiguity and pleasantness of association were positively related, with the most ambiguous cards essentially yielding superficially positive content. At the opposite pole, if the stimulus is highly structured, the elements in the picture account for much of the story. Clearly, the more structured the stimuli, the less individual variability, the greater the ease of producing normative data. However, the value inherent in projective methods is also sacrificed. The moderately ambiguous stimulus often provides enough cues to elicit themes hinted at by the picture, yet does not preclude individual variation. Medium-ambiguous cards, as rated by students using a Q-sort technique, provided more information about personality than high- or low-ambiguous cards (Kenny & Bijou, 1953).

It is generally assumed that the greater the influence of the stimulus on a theme or story element, the less projection is involved (Lindzey, 1952; Murstein, 1965). The T.A.T. cards are highly structured as to *who* is portrayed and somewhat less structured as to *what* is happening. Therefore, the designation of characters and events are highly influenced by the stimulus. Story endings were the least dependent on the stimulus and showed the most projection. The interpretation of motives (or *why* events happened) was also less determined by the stimulus and more closely related to projection (Murstein, 1965). Murstein suggests that the stimulus be sufficiently structured as to *who* is in the picture and as to *what* is going on so that respondents may consider these cues and think along dimensions desired by the clinician.

The finding that projection depended more on those aspects of the story telling task that were free of the stimulus pull is consistent with Arnold's (1962) reliance on actions and outcomes of stories as the major source of interpretively relevant information. It is the picture that reminds the story teller about various situations and determines the general topic area. Once the stimulus characteristics are incorporated, the story teller's dominant attitudes and emotions direct the plot and outcome. Thus, the general theme and situation are expected to portray events consistent with the picture. However, the story teller's attitude guides the interpretation of motives, the formulation of plot and action, and the determination of the outcome.

The most highly structured cards on the T.A.T. portray negative scenes, and the general consensus is that the stimuli pull for sad stories. One of the criticisms of the current set of T.A.T. stimuli is aimed at their negative affective tone (Garfield & Eron, 1948; Murstein, 1963; Ritzler, Sharkey, & Chudy, 1980). However, when story outcomes of the Apperceptive Personality Test (APT) (Holmstrom, Silber, & Karp, 1990), designed to avoid the negative tone of the T.A.T., were compared with the latter, the judges rated outcomes of the T.A.T. stories as more favorable than those of the APT stories (although there were no differences in the subject's ratings of the story outcomes). This finding suggests that the affective tone of the story outcome is a function of the narrator rather than the stimulus.

A comparison of the T.A.T. and TEMAS illustrates variations in degree of structure. *TEMAS* ("themes" in Spanish) is an acronym for a projective story telling technique called *Tell Me a Story* by Constantino, Malgady, and Rogler (1988). The TEMAS manual states that "stimulus cards are structured to elicit specific responses" (p. 1). Instead of using ambiguous stimuli, TEMAS employs the concept of bipolar personality functions to elicit conflict resolution in the context of a story telling task. The stimuli present polarities of negative and positive emotions, cognitions, and interpersonal functions. TEMAS was developed to overcome the limitations of the traditional projective story telling tasks by presenting characters and life circumstances similar to those of the respondents. However, the representation in each picture of both the negative and positive poles of interpersonal functions greatly reduces ambiguity and alters the nature of the task.

Most TEMAS pictures depict a scene that portrays two conflicting situations representing an inter- or intrapersonal dilemma that needs to be resolved. If themes reflect the stimulus, then how the respondent organizes the content is more significant than the content per se. Just as with the T.A.T., it seems appropriate to emphasize the manner of resolution and the outcome to the conflict. Although both sets of stimuli provide tension or conflict, the TEMAS is more structured in that it provides clear opposites that define both sides of the dilemma, such as ice cream now or a bicycle later. Yet, these may not be the polarities that underlie conflict in a particular child. Therefore, the task is appropriately seen by the authors as a cognitive integrative task similar to Kohlberg's (1976) moral dilemmas where children are asked to deal with externally set conflicts or dilemmas rather than formulating their own.

Emotional Pull

Scenes that promote stories in which there is conflict, aggression, or adversity have a "negative pull." One of the features of the Thematic Apperception Test that has sometimes been criticized (Ritzler, Sharkey, & Chudy, 1980) is its tendency to elicit negatively toned stories. When subjects are faced with extremely ambiguous pictures portraying negative emotions that do not provide cues for interpretation, they are apt to become defensive, feeling that whatever is said will be interpreted against them. However, using such stimuli provides the opportunity to assess how the respondent accounts for the negative cues. If the task requires that conflict and the expression of negative feelings be built into stories, it is possible to observe how the respondent deals with the demand. The narrator's ability to move beyond the sadness or conflict to a more positive resolution, and to provide a realistic transition between the negative state of affairs and the positive outcome are important sources of information. Thus, the negative pull of the stimulus cards can be viewed as one of the strengths of the Thematic Apperception Test. Within the T.A.T., there are variations among cards in the degree of negative pull. Card 8BM has the combination of negative pull (depiction of gun and knife) and the presence of disparate elements (foreground-background), which seems to increase the difficulty of the task for emotionally disturbed children (McGrew, 1987) who are prone to overreact to the provocative nature of this scene and, therefore, tell more disorganized and bizarre stories to this card as compared to other cards and to a normal comparison group.

Pictures that portray more neutral or positive scenes do not compel the respondent to deal with negative emotions. Therefore, these pictures do not offer an opportunity to assess how the subject deals with such challenges. Furthermore, the cumulative impact of dealing with the negative stories allows coping mechanisms to emerge in a sequence analysis (Arnold, 1962). Variations in the degree of negative tone from one picture to another allow for intraindividual comparison of how the subject copes with various degrees of threat.

Disparate Elements

The number of disparate elements (and the number of people portrayed) that need to be integrated gives us information about the subject's response to complexity. Some T.A.T. cards, such as 4 and 7, require reconciliation of disparate elements of the stimulus into a coherent story. Likewise, Card 2 describes a busy scene that has several discrepant elements which younger children find difficult to integrate. Instead, they have a lot to say in "describing" the stimulus and often attend to the details without conceptual synthesis.

Human versus Animal Figures

In introducing the Children's Apperception Test (C.A.T.), Bellak (1954) substituted animal for human figures in the pictures on the basis of an assumption that children identify more readily with animals than with people. This view is consistent with the popularity of animals in children's stories, toys, and cartoons. The scenes in the pictures were designed to elicit material to facilitate understanding of a child's relationship to family members (parents, siblings) and developmental issues (such as Oedipus complex, defenses, sibling rivalry, feeding, etc.).

The C.A.T. consists of 10 cards and is considered suitable for children between the ages of 3 and 10. Animals are depicted in situations that range from naturalistic portrayal to complete anthropomorphism where animals wear clothes, live in homes with furniture, and generally interact as humans. Bellak considered the use of animal stimuli as advantageous because they can be neutral regarding gender. Furthermore, the portrayal of animals gives distance, which facilitates the expression of aggressive and other negative sentiments that could more easily be attributed "to a lion, than to a human father figure, and the child's own unacceptable wishes could be more easily ascribed to the less transparent identification figures, as compared to human children" (Bellak, 1986, p. 237).

The presentation of animals versus real people has implications for the degree of implicit structure or cues that guide the story. A tiger attacking a small monkey is a relatively structured stimulus. The emotions may be inferred from the types of animals and their relative sizes and ages. Attributes may be ascribed depending on the association with a particular animal. Bellak and Bellak (1965), partly in response to accumulating empirical evidence questioning the superiority of animal stimuli in eliciting children's stories (Bellak & Hurvich, 1966), introduced a human version of the C.A.T., which they called the C.A.T.-H. The reader is referred to Bellak (1986) for a further description about uses and development of the C.A.T., C.A.T.-H, and C.A.T.-S.

Studies comparing the relative merits of stories told to animal stimuli of the C.A.T. and to the C.A.T.-H (which substitutes humans in analogous situations) generally produced few differences (Armstrong, 1954; Bellak & Loeb, 1969; Ritter & Eron, 1952; Weisskopf-Joelson & Foster, 1962), but if any differences were found, they favored human stimuli (Boyd & Mandler, 1955; Budoff, 1960; Furuya, 1957; Mainord & Marcuse, 1954). Studies comparing the relative effectiveness of children's stories told to the C.A.T. and T.A.T. generally indicated that the evidence was heavily in favor of pictures with human figures (Holt, 1956; Light, 1954).

Even studies with children at very young ages (4 to 5) and kindergarten do not support the idea that children respond more productively to animal than to human pictures (Budoff, 1960; Weisskopf-Joelson & Foster, 1962). Furthermore, the contention that school-aged children are put off by animal figures was a rationale for introducing the Roberts Apperception Test (RATCE) for children ages 6 through 15 (McArthur & Roberts, 1982).

Bellak (1986) asserts that the utility of the C.A.T. does not rest on the superiority of animal stimuli but on the fact that the C.A.T. and C.A.T.-S pictures were selected to elicit themes relevant to specific issues of childhood. Similar arguments can be made for Tasks of Emotional Development (TED) (Cohen & Weil, 1975) and Blackey Tests (Blum, 1950), which are designed to elicit specific material. In this regard, the T.A.T. is more of a broad-based instrument eliciting a wide range of information on a global level, whereas stimuli structured around specific issues are designed for a different purpose. The preponderance of evidence suggests that human figures are superior to animal figures and that the T.A.T. is as good as or better than the C.A.T. for use with children.

Murstein (1963), while granting the superiority of the T.A.T. over the C.A.T. as a broad-based instrument, notes that the C.A.T. was developed to test specific problems, such as sibling rivalry or oral fixation. He stated that it is possible that the C.A.T. may be more useful with the kinds of problems the stimuli are intended to tap. In the final analysis, what is important in evaluating the relative merits of human and animal stimuli is the clinical utility of the inferences based on the stories. No matter what type of picture stimuli are used, the test of clinical utility, not type of themes or number of words, is relevant.

Similarity of Central Character to the Subject

Murray (1943) assumed that the closer the resemblance between the stimulus figure and the actual subject in age, sex, or physical characteristics, the more the story teller would identify with the figure, thereby producing more meaningful material. Accordingly, he suggested that at least one card be chosen that shows a person of approximately the same age and sex of the story teller. Tomkins (1947) proposed that the T.A.T. may be interpreted most meaningfully by taking into account the disparity between the stimulus figures and the story teller.

Murstein (1963) reviewed studies that varied the race, gender, and other physical characteristics of the stimulus figures and concluded that there is no evidence that projection is increased by the similarity of the central character to the subject. The idea that persons are more likely to identify with individuals similar in age or sex seems logically compelling. However, cultural values and other variables, such as perceived status, may complicate the matter. Indeed, similarity between the central character and the subject may interfere with projection of certain themes. Studies carried out in the 1950s, a time when achievement was viewed as pertaining to men, indicated that women projected more achievement themes to male characters (e.g., Veroff, Wilcox, & Atkinson, 1953) according to cultural expectations.

In general, research findings with apperceptive methods have shown that adaptation of stimuli for specialized populations do not necessarily elicit richer, more productive stories than the traditional T.A.T. figures (Bailey & Green, 1977; Weisskopf-Joelson, Zimmerman, & McDaniel, 1970). Furthermore, it is not possible to decide on the basis of stimulus similarity that a story teller does or does not identify with a character. Practically all children focus their stories on the young woman pictured in Card 2, although there is a male in the background. The centrality of the figure seems to be the basis for prominence in stories.

The Gerontological Apperception Test (GAT), which was introduced for use with aged patients (Wolk & Wolk, 1971) was based on the assumption that "many aged people have difficulty identifying with figures depicted in the more commonly used apperceptive devices since the stimulus figures or situations depict much younger individuals. Problems specific to the aged such as loss of sexuality, loss of attractiveness, physical limitations, and family difficulties are not usually elicited" (p. 3). A comparison of the T.A.T. with the GAT, based on 30 volunteers ranging in age from 56 to 94 (mean = 76), showed that the GAT was more successful in eliciting relevant themes in only one of five dimensions scored—that of physical limitations (Fitzgerald, Pasewark, & Fleisher, 1974). Furthermore, the motifs that the GAT cards were expected to elicit did not occur with great frequency. Both sets did elicit themes of family difficulty and dependency, but few themes relating to sexuality and attractiveness. The authors concluded that there was no major advantage to the GAT.

A subsequent study (Pasewark, Fitzgerald, Dexter, & Cangemi, 1976) tested the following assumption: If identifying with a character really does facilitate thematic production relating to areas of concern, then an apperception test that includes at least one older person in a situation associated with issues of aging should be more effective than the T.A.T. in eliciting such themes from an older than a younger population. The findings did not support the contention. References to the age of subjects did not differ qualitatively or quantitatively among the three age groups sampled. Most noteworthy is that the problems described in the stories did not seem unique to the aged and did not differ markedly from similar problems described on the T.A.T. The content of themes was related to stimulus cards rather than age of the respondent. For each age group, the GAT elicited more themes of physical limitations and reference to aging, whereas the T.A.T. elicited more stories reflecting conflict and unhappy emotional tone. Furthermore, the themes of illness and physical limitations were elicited primarily by one GAT card (GAT #11, depicting an elderly woman sick in bed visited by a gentleman of similar age). It is noteworthy that the outcome (recovery from the illness) was comparable across the age groups. In general, the superiority of the GAT cards in eliciting references to aging results from the fact that all GAT cards depict older people. Identification with one of the characters in terms of similarity did not seem to play a significant role. The essential issue may not be that of identification but the capacity to grasp the meaning of the experience portrayed.

Some investigators conclude that culturally congruent stimuli facilitate the communication of story themes and ideas (Bailey & Green, 1977). Thompson (1949) constructed a set of T.A.T. cards similar to the original T.A.T. except that black characters were substituted to test the hypothesis that the closer the stimulus resembles the story teller, the more he or she will identify with the character and produce more meaningful material. Murstein (1963) reviewed studies that had been done with the Thompson variation of the T.A.T. with black and white subjects and concluded that "the degree of similarity between stimulus and subject is of itself insufficient as an explanation of the type of response elicited" (p. 205). Murstein maintains that culture plays an important role in the interpretation and perceptions of characters depicted in the T.A.T. However, the studies to date, which relied primarily on measures such as word count and number of ideas, may not have tapped elements of stories that have meaning for personality assessment.

The TEMAS (Constantino, Malgady, & Rogler, 1988) was developed to promote reliable and valid assessment of minority children and adolescents (ages 5 to 18) by eliciting stories with stimuli depicting African American and Hispanic children in everyday events in the context of an urban setting. The TEMAS consists of two parallel sets of cards, one set for minorities and the other for nonminorities, with normative data available for each. Malgady, Constantino, and

Rogler (1984) found preliminary support for the clinical utility of TEMAS (Tell-Me-A-Story) for personality assessment of Hispanic children who respond more fluently to these stimuli than to the T.A.T. cards. As stated earlier, it is difficult to compare the TEMAS with other story telling approaches such as the T.A.T. because the task is different in the format and structure of the stimulus, as well as some of the instructions. The notion of culturally congruent stimuli must be separated from the nature of the task and overall stimulus characteristics.

A series of studies reviewed by Murstein (1963) where the central character was changed to be physically similar (e.g., obese) to the story teller led to the conclusion that when the central figure possesses characteristics that are not valued in a culture, similarity between story teller and central character may be detrimental. Likewise, subjects did not produce more meaningful responses when characters were engaged in similar occupational or vocational pursuits than to persons in differing vocations. Again, Murstein (1963) concluded that the status value of the occupation depicted in thematic cards plays a greater role than similarity.

Two questions related to the issue of identification emerge: (1) Is it necessary to know with whom the story teller identifies for meaningful interpretation of the T.A.T. story? and (2) If so, what are the implications for selection of T.A.T. stimuli?

One of the primary assumptions basic to interpretation of T.A.T. stories (Bellak, 1986; Lindzey, 1952) is that the subject identifies with one of the characters in the narrative whose wishes, strivings, conflicts, perceptions, and attitudes reflect those of the story teller. Bellak (1986) assumes that the respondent identifies with the main hero, the person whose ideas, feelings, and actions are most discussed. When in doubt, Bellak suggests that the figure most closely resembling the story teller in age, sex, and other characteristics should be considered the hero.

At the opposite end of the spectrum is the view that neither the picture nor the story per se are important. According to Arnold (1962), every story expresses a conviction or moral that constitutes the story's meaning. The essential "message" or import of the story is abstracted from the plot and outcome. Each picture has the same chance of yielding a positive or negative score and, therefore, the "stimulus value of the picture" is irrelevant. In formulating the import, the issue of whether the story teller identifies with one of the characters is also irrelevant. The identification is not with the character but with the "message" or conviction expressed in the story, which has the same implication regardless of whose point of view is expressed. Each perspective implies its complement, like opposite sides of the same coin. If a person views himself or herself as a hapless victim, then others are viewed as victimizers. The expectation of aggression from others could prompt retaliation or anticipatory maneuvers according to the dictum "do unto others before they do unto you." Just because a person *feels* like a victim doesn't mean that he or she is not an aggressor. This author's examination of T.A.T. records of inmates between the ages of 16 to 21 incarcerated for crimes ranging from armed robbery to murder indicates that many characters are described as victims.

Utility of Picture Stimuli

Rapaport, Gill, and Schafer (1975) stated the following in a footnote: "The construction of an 'ideal' set of pictures is dependent first upon gathering extensive material on one standard set of pictures . . . and second upon the exploration of a variety of pictured situations with the knowledge so gathered. Sticking to one set of pictures, therefore, is the prerequisite for future development of more comprehensive and revealing tests of this type" (p. 467). These words are no less true today. Despite a plethora of different stimuli, their parameters have not been systematically studied, thereby limiting their contribution to a common, cumulative knowledge base.

The following characteristics of picture stimuli are relevant to their utility:

1. The stimulus should suggest the cast of characters by the nature of who is portrayed and should provide some indication of what the characters are feeling. Beyond that, increased structure tailored to elicit specific "relevant" themes may alert the respondents to the areas of concern, enabling them to manipulate the impression they make by witholding material (Karon, 1981). Furthermore, pictures that do not directly pull for a specific theme permit expression of issues most relevant to the subject.

2. Pictures should have a *latent stimulus meaning* (Henry, 1956). Card 1 of the T.A.T., for example, has a great deal of latent meaning because the picture of the boy contemplating a violin symbolizes a person in an ambivalent emotional situation. Furthermore, in our society, it is usually the family that promotes a child's musical education. Although this card elicits themes of achievement (see Bellak, 1986), it is the perceived struggle with frustration and the role of parents and other authorities that enhances the depth and richness of the stories. It is the latent meaning that contributes to ambiguity and encourages unique responses.

3. Pictures should depict a variety of basic interpersonal relationships. T.A.T. Cards 11 through 20 are more "unusual, dramatic, and bizarre" (Murray, 1943, p. 2) than the first 10 cards, which represent the "everyday" series that depict human beings in more common situations, and are more frequently used. A set of pictures should vary in age, gender, and number of characters presented so that one can assess basic attitudes about various interpersonal relationships (e.g., peers, family, authorities) as well as attitudes toward tasks and reactions to challenges.

4. Pictures should be sufficiently intense in quality to intrigue the subject and provide incentive to define a problem or goal and to propose solutions to the dilemma presented. Accordingly, pictures should portray tension, conflict, or discrepancy to be reconciled. Although the T.A.T. cards have been criticized for their negative tone, such stimulus pull minimizes socially desirable and stereotypic responses and may, therefore, be a distinct advantage. Sherwood (1957) suggests that the picture must evoke associations that are incomplete so that the story teller feels obliged to exercise ingenuity and problem-solving capacity. A negative situation seems "unfinished" and something must be done to overcome adversity or to achieve closure. A stimulus showing ambivalence, a state of tension, or the presence of objects that must be explained compels an individual to integrate disparate elements.

Summary

Much information is still needed about stimulus properties, particularly in the structural features such as variation in degree of tension or number of disparate elements. There is an advantage to the development of a general set of stimuli so that clinicians can adopt a common frame of reference for interpretation through experience. Karon's (1981) point is well taken that what we really need in projective personality assessment is a better understanding of the approaches currently available than a proliferation of more techniques. A subset of the currently available set of T.A.T. cards seems quite adequate for children and adolescents. The clear implications of conflict implicit in the facial expressions and in the juxtaposition of discrepant figures and objects (the negative pull) are essential characteristics of the "productive" T.A.T. cards and is consistent with Murstein's (1965) conclusion that "a lack of ambiguity with regard to emotional interaction is facilitative of the kind of projection making for valid personality assessment" (p. 223). When the emotions are clearly depicted, the story teller constructs a rationale and a context for the emotion. If the emotion has aspects of conflict, such as anger, there is a tendency to bring the story to closure by resolving the conflict. Thus, the endings of the stories, reflecting the subject's method of coping with the tension or conflicts, are particularly revealing.

CHAPTER 3

Psychometric Issues

Approaches selected to document the reliability and validity of assessment techniques must capture the nature of the variables being measured and the purposes for which the tests are being used. Many of the attempts to document reliability and validity of story telling techniques involve inappropriate conceptualizations and methods that underestimate their usefulness (Obrzut & Cummings, 1983). Conceptualization of reliability and validity which are psychometrically sound but which are incompatible with the nature of the instrument will lead to false impressions about the measurement technique.

The Standards for Educational and Psychological Testing (AERA, 1985) acknowledges that specific statistical procedures to establish validity and reliability may not be appropriate in every case and other more appropriate methodologies that are "equivalent" should be substituted. Therefore, in validating a test, "professional judgment should guide the decisions regarding the focus of evidence that are most necessary and feasible in light of intended uses of the test and any likely alternatives to testing" (p. 9).

Story telling techniques such as the Thematic Apperception Test elicit a wide range of information. To interpret a protocol in a systematic way, scoring systems are devised to tap a specific facet of personality. Documenting the validity and reliability of a projective test is really a demonstration of the utility of the interpretive method specifically under consideration rather than a general validation of the technique (Karon, 1981).

The failure to develop a scoring system that is widely accepted has hampered the cumulative efforts of researchers to establish reliability and validity, as well as to garner empirical support of clinical utility (Polyson, Norris, & Ott, 1985). Such efforts would be facilitated by the adoption of a standard set of stimuli with standard administration and scoring principles. It has been suggested that the formulation of comprehensive scoring criteria is a monumental and perhaps impractical endeavor (Karon, 1981).

Reliability

Estimates of reliability are grounded in the notion of consistency in measurement. With regard to demonstrating test-retest or other forms of reliability for story telling methods, a critical issue concerns the unit of interpretation. A distinction must be made between the repetition of a specific story or the repetition of stories that would lead to similar inferences about personality. The latter is of primary importance (Karon, 1981). The basic attitude expressed by two stories could be identical even when their contents appear vastly different (Arnold, 1962). Conversely, stories that seem similar on the surface could lead to different interpretive conclusions.

Internal consistency is the correlation among different items in the same test. Lundy (1985) points out that internal consistency as an estimate of reliability is not appropriate to the T.A.T. because it (coefficient alpha) considerably underestimates the actual test-retest reliability. The problem lies with the fact that alpha is an appropriate estimate of reliability only within a homogeneous domain of items (Cronbach, 1970). The various cards of the T.A.T. are not comparable and are designed to elicit wide variability in thematic content. Formal or stylistic characteristics of stories, as well as interpretive conclusions that are less dependent on the stimulus than thematic content, should be more similar across cards and, therefore, might produce higher indices of internal consistency.

Themes do not speak for themselves but require translation by a competent interpreter. The essential question relevant to the documentation of internal consistency is the extent to which inferences drawn by experienced interpreters are consistent across cards for a specific phenomenon that has relevance for clinical use. Conclusions drawn from one-half of the cards may be compared with the other half. However, this approach reduces the number of stories on which conclusions are based and correspondingly decreases reliability estimates. Some interpreters (e.g., Arnold, 1962; Bellak, 1975; 1986) assert that the stories must be analyzed in sequence to note ego defenses. By artificially splitting up the stories, it is not possible to tell how individuals adapt to the task. Given the issues discussed above, it is not surprising that estimates of reliability based on internal consistency of scores across pictures (scored for similar content) tend to be low (Entwisle, 1972).

Scorer reliability is particularly relevant to open-ended tests that are subjectively coded, such as story telling. The essential question is whether two or more individuals looking at the same protocol draw the same conclusion. The answer to that question depends on whether they are looking for the same information since different people may not find the same material relevant. Obviously, the less specific the scoring system, the more clinical judgment, training, and experience are required by the interpreter. When variables are clearly and narrowly defined, scorer reliabilities generally reported in the literature appear to be high (for children and adults).

The question of whether the same scorer will draw the same conclusion after an elapsed time interval is also related to the issue of scorer reliability. Karon (1981) believes that such reliability needs to be established for each investigator since the measuring instrument is not only the test but the test plus the interpreter.

A study by Sutton and Swensen (1983) demonstrated reliability on the T.A.T. in a manner that approximates its clinical use. Raters scored T.A.T. stories and interview responses to assess levels of ego development based on previous training on protocols of the Sentence Completion Test of Ego Development (SCT) (Loevinger & Wessler, 1970). According to Loevinger (1979), experienced raters can rate responses on SCT protocols accurately, even when they are not in the scoring manual, because of a tacit understanding of the concepts. Thus, Sutton and Swensen (1983) assumed that training on SCT would enable individuals to differentiate between levels of ego development on T.A.T. stories and interviews by using ego-development theory. The authors demonstrated interrater reliability (.95) and concurrent validity (correlations across measures of .79–.89) of applying ego-development theory concepts to scoring T.A.T. stories and responses to an unstructured interview. Instead of developing a specific scoring manual for the T.A.T. and interview, these authors asked interpreters to apply their previous training to derive conclusions from responses to T.A.T. stories and to unstructured interviews. Scoring guides and manuals serve largely to help the interpreter learn to apply specified concepts. However, without a thorough understanding of what is being measured, scoring systems are tedious and burdensome.

The basic issues regarding scorer reliability are the expertise level of the interpreter and clarity with which scoring criteria are specified. Numerous studies demonstrate that scorer reliability coefficients are within the acceptable range when scoring criteria are clearly delineated.

Examples of Test-Retest Reliability

The following two stories were told to T.A.T. Card 1 by an adolescent girl. The first was told at age 15-1, and the second was told at age 16-6, but both reflect a similar orientation toward achievement despite some developmental changes.

Age 15-1:

Trying to figure out what that is. Oh, it's a violin. Before a while ago he was in music class playing the violin and he has to write a piece of music for his recital. His teacher told him to and this is the sheet of paper and there's a pen right there and he took out his violin and tried to play it and he got frustrated and he put everything down. Now he's thinking about his recital and how he's going to write his piece and what it's going to be like. (How do I want to end it? Want me to go into the future?) Little boy sitting there thinking of something to write. Gets a whole bunch of words and writes it down. Has the lyrics and writes the melody to go with it. Then he has his recital and it's really good.

Age 16-6:

Oh, that's a violin. I couldn't tell what it was. (long pause) Young Johann Sebastian Bach's apprentice, Gavroche (long pause, what are you writing?), is the, OK, next superstar of the orchestra. One day Gavroche was sitting down thinking about what he would be, do with his life. He decided that he was not only going to be equal to Bach but he was going to do this. How could he become better than J. S. Bach. But suddenly, while he was contemplating what he was going to do, a little girl walked into the room. She said, "Come quick, the house is on fire, the house is on fire. You must get out quick." So the two ran quickly out of the house. As Gavroche heard the fireman come up, he remembered that the violin was in the house. He yelled to the fireman, "You have to go quick. My violin is in there." The fireman ignored Gavroche and went to their duties. Water was coming everywhere and Gavroche wondered what would happen to his violin. The next morning, Gavroche and his parents went into the house to see the damage. Gavroche quickly ran upstairs to his room. He couldn't believe what he saw. His most prized possession was burned. Gavroche thought to himself, this was the worst birthday of his life. He was to be 12 years old tomorrow. The next day came and went. Everyone was too busy with the fire to remember Gavroche's birthday. At dinner, Gavroche's parents gave him a violin similar to the one he had before only not the same. His parents say it was the first thing they replaced from the house and they're sorry it got burned and they hope this violin will be good for him. Gavroche went upstairs to his room and put the violin down. (As a second thought) Oh, he was at his grandmother's house with the new violin. The old house burned down. He sat at his desk thinking, "They may have forgotten my birthday but they did give me a violin. Maybe this will be the violin that will help me become the best violinist in the world." Gavroche decided even though he was very sad about not having his old violin and his house burning down that it wasn't so bad.

Despite the elapsed time between the two test administrations and differences in content, the two stories have many things in common. Both stories involve high expectations for achievement but emphasize the outcome over intrinsic interest while giving minimal consideration to the actual effort involved in the process. In the first story, the boy is obliged to compose the music to play for his recital, whereas in the second, the boy aspires to outdo J. S. Bach. In the first story, the task is frustrating, yet the child successfully performs his composition. In the second story, just when Gavroche decided to become better than Bach, the plot took a sudden turn as a fire prevented instrumental action to attain the goal. The story ends with the hope of becoming the best violinist in the world, but with no plan to accomplish the goal and no intrinsic interest in the music. Interpreted in this manner, the two stories reliably indicate that the narrator has high aspirations but has difficulty doing what is needed to attain her goals.

The comparison of two other stories (Card 5) told by the same youngster one year apart also illustrates reliability when using meaningful units of interpretation. Furthermore, they illustrate consistency across very different cards.

Age 15-1:

Can you talk about someone who's not there? (Yes.) This is a little boy's room and his mom told him that he had to do his homework. He said OK mom, and he was working on the homework and he wanted to play this game—his Atari. So he started playing his Atari, playing and playing. His mom comes in, opens the door and she's very mad. She yells at him and tells him to come downstairs and do his homework at the kitchen table in front of her. So he does and he studies and he gets an A on his test the next day. (Is he mad at his mom?) Yes, he is, but he feels mad cause he didn't listen. So he doesn't argue, just went downstairs.

Age 16-6:

The mother is looking in the room to see if her son is doing his homework. First of all, the son plugs up his ears when his dad tells him to do his homework. He throws his homework in the trash and gets a fake piece of homework and puts it in his folder. He goes next door and gives it to another kid and takes his (the other kid's) homework and gives it to his high school teacher. He gets an A+ and the other kid failed. He doesn't tell his father about trading homework, just that he got a good grade and that his enemy, Jerry, failed. (Feel?) His father felt happy and so does he; his enemy feels mad. (Think?) The kid is just graduating from high school and he took all of Jerry's homework and put it in his folder. In the end, he felt happy because he got A's. He goes to computer school. The other kid, Jerry, didn't graduate.

Both stories are consistent with each other and with those told to Card 1 in that they suggest an absence of intrinsic motivation, despite a desire for successful outcomes. In the first story, success is due to effort expended in response to parental pressure and guidance. The second story, told a year later, indicates a greater emphasis on the appearance of success while minimizing constructive effort and taking the easy way out. In the second set of stories, the narrator's outlook on the possibility of attaining the high expectations through her own efforts or parental support has diminished.

These data give an indication of similarity of conclusions across cards and upon retesting. However, they also demonstrate some developmental changes that might occur within a year's time. Therefore, if the time interval is lengthy, issues of reliability are confounded with developmental considerations.

Test-retest reliability, as well as developmental influences in relation to relevant units of analysis, are illustrated by the following two stories told to Card 1 by a girl, age 6-0 and then again at age 7-1.

Age 6-0:

The boy lost his bow to the violin and his mother came in and said, "Why aren't you fiddling?" "Because I lost the bow to my violin." She said, "You look for it and if you don't find it you'll be in big trouble." Then the end. He found it and his mother said, "Good. Before you finish fiddling I'm going to give you a treat." (Feel?) (Think?) In beginning he's thinking, "Boy, I lost my bow; wait til mom finds out." He's sad. At the end, he's thinking, "Oh goodie, I'm getting a treat." End.

In the above story, the child's emotion shifts according to meeting or not meeting parental demands. Responsibility for action lies within the child, but the locus of self-evaluation and satisfaction is external (based on the immediate reward of a "treat").

Age 7-1:

You see this boy in the picture, he wanted to play the violin and he could not find his bow to the violin. And he was feeling very sad. And then he knew what was going to happen because when he got it (violin) he was pleading with his mother to get him a violin but she said that, "I will but it's a big responsibility. You'll be in big trouble if you lose a part to it or break it." He said, "I know what I'll do, I won't tell my mother but I'll search for the bow." So he searched and he searched and he searched and he searched until he finally gave up. And he also remembered something that his mother said: "This is your violin, you can play whatever you want or whatever day you want." So he said to himself, "Since she said that, I won't play it and she'll never find out." And he felt happy. The end.

Again, the child desires to play and responsibility is internal, but the emphasis is on external barriers and consequences. The moral of the above story is that a child who fails to meet responsibilities can be happy if there are no repercussions. Both stories suggest that the child has difficulty sustaining efforts without external bolstering.

The following example of internal consistency also demonstrates that the theme cannot be taken at face value. Rather, it is the judgment of the interpreter that is the appropriate unit of analysis. These two stories were told by a 14-year-old girl in a residential setting for seriously emotionally disturbed youngsters. The stories have a similar meaning, but the message is conveyed more dramatically in the second.

> Card 1: Jason was looking forward to getting a guitar for his Christmas present and he opened up his gift from his Uncle Larry. He was really shocked to see it was a violin. Larry had always wanted him to play the violin, but he wanted to play the guitar. He took the violin up to his room and just sat there and stared at it, thinking that if he could just tell his uncle that he wanted a guitar or if he could just play the violin and be his uncle's favorite. Um, so he's just sitting there thinking. Eventually, Jason decides to be honest with his uncle and tell him that he really wanted a guitar and that he can't play what his uncle wants him to. He's got to go with his own feelings.

The story conveys the message that a person can follow his or her own feelings but only at a cost. A more extreme expression of the same conviction is repeated in the story below so that what is hinted at in the first story is vividly portrayed. The message of the story is that an individual gets obliterated when others (even one's father) discover the terrible things the person thinks, feels, and does.

> Card 6GF: She looked at her father, astonished that he knew her whole scheme. Yes, she had been a maid for five years and yes she was stealing a lot of their jewelry and also yes, she was going to turn it in for a lot of money and yes, she had planned to kill their, the family's, husband. How could her father have known and how, if, he wasn't sure, could she have possibly avoided all these accusations. Thoughts are running through her head as she thought quickly of a way to deny it. Nothing could come. Her father slowly pulled out a pistol. She really got scared and afraid and ran for the door, but he was too quick. He grabbed her by the arm, knocking all the jewelry out of her pockets. Scared, she started trembling and crying down on her knees. "Please don't shoot me, please I'll give it all back. I'm sorry." But her father didn't listen. He just sat there, cold, ice in his heart, knowing that his own daughter had betrayed him and his family and one of the families he was closest to. Without thinking and without further hesitation, he put the gun to her head. Bang! That was the last sound she heard.

Validity

Whereas reliability addresses the issues of accuracy and consistency in the method of measurement, validity pertains to whether the measure is, in fact, relevant to what is being assessed. Although a test can be reliable without being valid, the opposite is not true. Validity is the most important consideration in test evaluation. The concept refers to the appropriateness, meaningfulness, and usefulness of the specific inferences made from test scores. Test validation "is the process by which evidence is obtained to support conclusions gained from the test" (AERA, 1985, p. 9).

Projective stories reflect the multifaceted concepts inherent in the abstraction referred to as *personality.* Validity can be established only if the complexities of the phenomenon being assessed are clearly understood and the manner in which the phenomenon is expected to manifest itself in the projective story is delineated. Additionally, specific relationships between the test behaviors and other appropriate criteria must be determined. The history of attempting to predict overt behavior from thematic apperception techniques provides a good example of the complexities and difficulties involved with attempts to predict behavior from story content.

Predictions from thematic content to overt behavior must differentiate between expressions of manifest and latent needs. The former are likely to be translated into action, whereas the latter are revealed only in fantasy (Bellak, 1975, 1986; Karon, 1981; Tomkins, 1947). Overt and covert needs can often be differentiated on the basis of clues such as qualifiers found within the stories, or levels of expression such as a daydream, thought, feeling, wish, or action (Tomkins, 1947).

Karon (1981) applied Tomkins's notion of level by maintaining that thoughts should predict thoughts, feelings should predict emotions, and behaviors should forecast overt action. Normal individuals would be expected to operate on many levels simultaneously; they behave, perceive, think, feel, hope, plan, anticipate, remember, and communicate with each other. These levels of functioning are expressed in thematic stories through reference to characters who think, act, react, and interact (Tomkins, 1947). The manner in which the thoughts, feelings, and actions of characters are coordinated reveals the story teller's tendency to organize the various levels of experience. The nature and source of a character's worry can be differentiated from the course of action to alleviate the distress. Actions may be deliberate, based on reflection, or provoked by the immediate circumstance. Thus, it is possible to differentiate between stylistic elements such as the degree of delay and organization of behavior from the content of the behavior.

The problems encountered in the attempt to validate thematic indices of aggression (reviewed in Chapter 21) illustrate the more general validational issues. The research highlights the need to consider the salient aspects of the phenomenon being measured, not just overt aggression. The relevant aspects of the aggressive personality, such as disturbed interpersonal relations, defective ego and superego development, or failure to identify with the values of the larger society, contribute to the prediction. Therefore, approaches to validation might consider whether a systematic scoring procedure can reflect a clinical syndrome or pattern of personality organization that is a context for viewing specific behaviors.

With these considerations in mind, selected issues pertaining to the validation of thematic story techniques are reviewed next.

Criterion validity refers to predicting or assessing functioning outside the test. To establish criterion validity, a score on the T.A.T. would be compared with some external measure or criterion that has a theoretical relationship to what the test (in this case the scoring system) is trying to assess. The criterion must be carefully selected and the attributes measured by the test must be relevant to the criterion. The problems confronting criterion validation are twofold: First is the issue of finding definable, acceptable, and feasible outside criteria that may be overt behaviors, indices of general adjustment, a specific clinical syndrome, membership in a group with known characteristics, and so forth. Second is the question of how to link interpretive units with the criteria of interest.

Selecting theoretically relevant criteria that can be tapped by the scoring units chosen is key to establishing criterion validity. The selection of very specific behaviors for criteria is problematic because of the widely accepted premise that behaviors are not only a function of the person but also of the situation. Furthermore, the behaviors of some individuals are more influenced by external circumstances than those of others. Thus, adjustment in school for some children depends on specific circumstances or match with a teacher. In fact, it is the ability of the examiner to make these conditional inferences that leads to suggestions about alternate intervention strategies and programming of the educational environment.

Conditional predictions can also be made with regard to themes of aggression. A basic attitude that violence against an authority brings punishment, but aggression against a powerless individual has no ill effects, might lead to the expectation that aggression would be expressed against persons who are perceived as less powerful. By looking at the story teller's attitudes under specific conditions, it is possible to make such situation-specific predictions. It is evident that simple frequency counts of themes such as Eron's (1950) will not work with respect to criterion validity. Variations or repetition among themes under different conditions should be carefully delineated because the essential message of a theme must include the specific conditions.

Inferences from projective stories such as the T.A.T. are related to ingrained personality or response patterns and attitudes but not necessarily to isolated behaviors. For example, one 15-year-old girl told T.A.T. stories reflecting the attitude that family members cooperate, share common interests, and can be counted on for encouragement and mutual give and take. However, this adolescent generally avoided doing household chores. Obviously, if that were the criterion to measure validity, the test would appear useless. On the other hand, her parents easily recounted numerous incidents where their daughter volunteered to do things to ease the strain on the family or to help someone. The negative pull of the stimuli elicited stories about adversity or conflict, and the themes of cooperation and family support were generated in that context. Interestingly, according to parents' reports, it was primarily during special happy occasions or during particularly difficult times that their daughter is prone to extend herself. What situational provocations will arise cannot be known in advance, but conditional predictions are possible. For example, a child's need for structure can be identified along with a range of potential behaviors in the absence of that structure. The professional is likely to have more success predicting that a child can be readily influenced by peers, or delineating the circumstances under which a child may exhibit impulsive behavior than forecasting specific behaviors.

Content validity is a judgment made by experts in the field regarding the adequacy of the items to tap the various facets or dimensions of the phenomenon. For story telling tests, content validity relates to degree of sampling of classes of situations in the pictures presented. The examiner makes choices about which cards to use to steer the respondent toward thinking about topics relevant to the assessment. However, there is not necessarily a direct relationship between the card stimulus and the content elicited. To the extent that card stimuli are oriented to elicit very specific content, the assessment departs from projective techniques and begins to resemble a guided interview. Furthermore, much interpretive material pertains to formal or stylistic aspects of stories that are not dependent on specific content. In choosing stimuli, the examiner may want to keep other relevant characteristics in mind besides "content," such as (1) degree of ambiguity, (2) complexity, (3) number of people portrayed, (4) presence of disparate elements to be reconciled, (5) emotional pull, and (6) number of specific cues provided.

An aspect of content validity unique to projective testing is the adequacy of the scoring scheme to tap the facet of personality under consideration. Accordingly, what is being validated is the *content* of the scoring system, rather than the content associated with specific picture stimuli. In general, the issue of content validity with respect to projective stories has received considerably less attention than tests of achievement, self-report, or behavioral rating scales.

Incremental validity is demonstrated when the increment of information gained by the addition of another test to the battery results in a significantly higher correlation with the criterion (Mischel, 1968). Conceptually, incremental validity is consistent with the multiple regression model advocated by Lundy (1985). The more complex and multiply determined a criterion, the more important it is to account for the role of multiple variables. Honor and Vane (1972) looked at the relative contribution of IQ scores and motivational factors measured with Arnold's (1962) scoring of the T.A.T. in accounting for school achievement. The correlation between IQ and GPA was .51, whereas that between T.A.T. and GPA was .88. Incremental validity would refer to the additional information contributed by the T.A.T. beyond that provided by the IQ score (or vice versa).

Construct validity pertains to the relationships among variables relevant to the definition of a construct. It has been argued that all questions about test validity ultimately concern construct validity. A correlation between a predictor and a criterion is limited as an index of validity because it does not provide a basic understanding of what is being measured (Landy, 1986). To determine the meaning of a test score, it is necessary to go beyond covariation to explain how and why a score indicates a certain disposition (Hogan & Nicholson, 1988). Therefore, no single criterion is sufficient to establish the validity of a measure. The process of validation involves the examination of the entire network of external correlates of the test (Cronbach & Meehl, 1955). A full definition of a disposition must differentiate it from other personality constructs and must be reliably measured. Therefore, it has been suggested that researchers obtain measures for more than one disposition using more than one method of measurement. The pattern of convergent and discriminant criteria would establish construct validity (Campbell & Fiske, 1959).

Most dispositional descriptions represent complex human qualities, and different facets are measured by different types and sources of data. Therefore, two different ways of assessing a construct such as self-concept (e.g., by self-report or teacher ratings [Marsh & Parker, 1984]) may have no relationship to each other. Likewise, concepts emerging from story telling approaches reflect different facets of a personality construct than self-report. Self-report information is limited by the informant's awareness of his or her moods, motives, bases for behavior (Wilson, Hull, & Johnson, 1981), and by efforts to influence self-presentation (Hogan & Nicholson, 1988). McClelland (1972) argues that self-report questionnaires, which he terms "opinionaires," are correlated with other measures of opinions, but they do a poor job of predicting real behavior. Inferences from story telling methods are limited by the unavailability of agreed upon and widely accepted scoring systems (Vane, 1981). An approach that combines internal consistency and construct validation might be applied to open-ended responses such as projective stories. Accordingly, aspects of a given construct such as cognitive integration may be defined and their manifestation in projective stories delineated. Subsequently, the network of interrelationships among the subcategories of the construct within and across picture stimuli could be examined.

Conceptual validity, as described by Maloney and Ward (1976), is related to construct validation in that both involve testing hypotheses about expected relationships and patterns among different measures. However, construct validation typically focuses on relationships of measures taken across many people, whereas conceptual validation refers to the patterns found within an individual. Essentially, concept validation is an approach to evaluating and synthesizing information from a variety of sources (including interview, observations, and an appropriate test battery) to produce a working model (or a set of interrelated concepts) of a person. The model is considered valid when evidence from various sources consistently and logically supports the model. Unlike construct validity, which begins with previously developed constructs, conceptual valida- tion begins with an examination of the raw data and produces constructs as its end product. The purpose of these constructs is to provide the basis for accurate inferences and conclusions in relation to the assessment of a single individual. The contribution of projective stories to the formulation of such a clinically useful model is an index of the method's validity.

The conceptual validation approach ascribes an important role to the expertise and judgment of the examiner, a view that is consistent with that of Karon (1981), who concluded that the T.A.T. is valid when the interpreters had training or experience in using the T.A.T. in predicting a criterion about which they have expertise.

Measurement theory is placing increasing emphasis on the validity and reliability of the uses of assessment data in making decisions (e.g., Cronbach, 1988; Messick, 1989). *Decision reliability* relates to the convergence of de- cisional outcomes across alternative assessment techniques, raters, and assess- ment occasions. The focus is not on the reliability of the specific instruments but on the convergence of decision outcomes with different types of data. *Decision validity* refers to the appropriateness of using particular assessment data for a specific decisional purpose (Messick, 1989). The *treatment utility* of assessment refers to its contribution to treatment outcome (Hayes, Nelson, & Jarrett, 1987) and can be considered apart from classical psychometrics. The role of projective story telling techniques in decision making and treatment outcomes is a function of its contribution to elucidating a useful model (conceptual validation) of the individual within a comprehensive assessment.

Norms

The essential feature of a projective test is *freedom to respond*, both in the content and organization of the response. Chopping up the content without regard to the eliciting stimulus or its manner of integration has a distorting effect. Norms for projective stories would be required for each stimulus and for the relevant units of inference. The absence of agreement about critical areas for scoring and of a standard set of stimuli would make this endeavor difficult. According to the Standards, "Norms, and particularly national norms, are extremely difficult and costly to construct properly and should not be produced automatically or be required of all published tests" (AERA, 1985, p. 9).

In contrast to the nearly infinite possible approaches to the scoring and interpretation of thematic content, the number of formal characteristics is limited, can be precisely defined, and has adequate scorer reliability. Most importantly, formal characteristics of T.A.T. protocols appear useful in predicting overt behavior (Hartman, 1949) and in differentiating diagnostic groups (McGrew & Teglasi, 1990). Therefore, these formal elements of stories may be more amenable to the construction of norms.

The norm is a construct representing the characteristics of an abstract person but not one person in particular. There are, for example, many ways to get an average score on an intelligence test, and the meaning of an "average" score varies with the individual. Berg (1986) made the following observations about norms with regard to the Rorschach, which seem generally applicable: "Norms are an abstraction representing the qualities of an essentially mythical figure who is supposed to describe Everyman and subsequently adequately reflects the individual qualities of nobody" (p. 115). Furthermore, Berg (1986) contends that it is questionable to assume that every personality trait or its indicator is normally distributed.

Berg acknowledges that norms provide the interpreter with the range and types of responses in the relevant population and are useful as starting points for interpretation. However, beyond that, the interpretive process relies on the professional's knowledge of development, personality theory, and psychopathology to organize and integrate the information in a meaningful way.

Summary

Many of the methods typically used to validate tests are not appropriate for evaluating the usefulness of story telling techniques such as the Thematic Apperception Test. The following conclusions emerge from the literature reviewed in this chapter:

1. Relevant units for validation should represent an inference or judgment of the interpreter rather than isolated story elements. These units should be based on clinical relevance and understanding of the phenomenon to be measured.

2. Validation studies should employ well-trained and experienced interpreters. The role of the interpreter is not likely to be diminished even if extensive age norms or detailed scoring systems were available.

3. Formal characteristics that refer to aspects of the story's structure and internal relationships among content elements should receive greater em-

phasis. These characteristics are more easily quantifiable and more amenable to group comparison and establishment of norms.

4. In clinical use, the combination of formal and content analysis with other data will prove most fruitful. More emphasis should be placed on the validation of projective stories in the context of a comprehensive assessment.

5. It would be advantageous if a standard set of stimuli and an agreed upon scoring system were available for common validation efforts of researchers. There is a proliferation of new stimuli for eliciting projective stories without a concommitant development in conceptualization of useful interpretive approaches.

CHAPTER 4

Personality Model and Implications for Assessment

The interpreter assigns meaning to the raw data of projective stories by systematically using cues to draw conclusions about the narrator. Much of the interpretation depends on the skill and experience of the interpreter whose task is to synthesize information gathered from multiple sources while focusing on the individual as an entity. Due consideration is given to a variety of factors such as gender, age, and socioeconomic and cultural background. The interpreter assigns relative weights to these variables and discerns the meaning of projective stories in relation to other data. Dana (1982) reviewed the implication of an assessor's theoretical orientation for interpretation of projective techniques. He argued that the examiner should clearly articulate the basic assumptions about personality that guide the evaluation and the writing of the psychological report.

Why do practitioners need a concept of personality? In the assessment process, the examiner obtains relevant data from a variety of sources. However, assigning the proper significance to each "fact" requires organizing concepts such as personality theory, which is a tool for drawing conclusions about different types of facts. If the "facts" and the conceptual schema do not match, the interpreter can seek additional information, become aware of alternate interpretations, or modify the concepts.

To understand human functioning, the practitioner needs information about (1) relevant characteristics of the person, (2) pertinent situational-environmental variables, and (3) theories about the linkages and interactions within and between items 1 and 2 to provide a conceptual framework for their synthesis. The interactional view of human development asserts that psychological functioning is determined by the continuously ongoing reciprocally interactive processes of subsystems within the individual and by the ongoing bidirectional interplay between individuals and environments (Ohman & Magnusson, 1987).

The study of personality cannot be based on the isolated parts but must tackle the question of how the various components relate to each other and become integrated into a functioning entity (Messick, 1987). Personality is "the integration of differentiated psychological subsystems as distinctly manifested in each individual" (Messick, 1987, p. 36). Personality theories differ in their focus of what are the essential attributes of persons, as well as the relative importance assigned to characteristics of environments in determining development. In relation to assessment, the term *personality* is distinguished from *cognition* or *intelligence* to emphasize the predominantly noncognitive aspects of personality such as temperament, motivation, affect, and style (Messick, 1979). However, the interdependence among cognition, temperament, motivation, and affect is shown in daily life. As Messick (1987) states, "In exploring the interplay between cognitions and personality, we are actually surveying a part-whole relationship and asking how some parts of the total personality influence the structure and functioning of other parts of the personality" (p. 35).

Each of the various traits of personality influences and is modified by the others. Individual differences in the integrative and organizing functions of the personality play a critical role (Murray, 1938; Murray & Kluckhohn, 1953) in how meaning is attached to experiences and in the degree of cohesion and structure of the personality. Some individuals do not care to seek information about themselves or their surroundings. Furthermore, they do not attend to seeming discrepancies in their behaviors because they do not try to formulate a consistent view of the self (see Sorrentino & Short, 1986; Raynor & McFarlin, 1986).

The practitioner incorporates knowledge of individual differences with general concepts of personality development to understanding a specific individual's style of organizing life experiences. The need for a conceptual schema in personality assessment becomes evident given the following tasks of the interpreter:

1. Select the attributes of the person and environment that are of interest relative to the presenting problem. The conceptualization of personality contributes to the initial selection of variables considered to be important.

2. Select the appropriate measures that can serve as indices of the variables chosen. The interpreter employs conceptual schema about tests and the assessment process.

3. Properly assign meaning to each of the personality attributes within the configuration of a specific individual. These attributes do not occur in isolation; each modifies the others and the resultant pattern interacts with the environment. The interpreter needs a conceptual framework to integrate the facts from various sources.

4. Make decisions about diagnosis and interventions based on an understanding of the referral issues as they pertain to a particular individual in a given family and cultural context.

Individual Differences versus Developmental Stages

With respect to individual versus developmental differences, it is pertinent to ask about the ways a child might be more like he or she was at earlier ages in comparison to similarities with same-age peers. In other words, What attributes relate to maturation plus experience and what relates to individual difference plus maturation and experience? According to Piaget's theory, young children are fundamentally different kinds of thinkers and learners than older children and adults because they think in concrete terms and are limited in their capacity to draw inferences. Developmental stages represent reorganizations of the child's conceptual framework so that there are shifts from sensory motor to representational thought, from prelogical to concrete operational thought, and finally, to the formal operational thinking of adolescents and adults. According to Piaget, these shifts are domain independent. However, Piaget's theory has come under criticism by many developmental theorists (e.g., Gelman & Baillargeon, 1983) who now believe that the young child does not think differently from the adult and is neither concrete nor illogical. Rather than interpreting phenomena according to a stage theory, an alternative view is in terms of shifts in conceptual frameworks that result from the accumulation of experience and knowledge in particular domains such as the information-processing differences found between adult experts and novices. Continuous organization and processing of life events lead to the development of schematic framework in a manner that combines individual differences, maturation, and life experience.

Traits have been criticized as static concepts that do not provide for an understanding of developmental change or of dynamic processes (Pervin, 1985). Nevertheless, the distinction between trait (structure) versus process is hazy, as indicated by Messick (1987), who puts forth the possibility that "processes are clearly identifiable only through their association with individual differences, and perhaps it is inevitable that there should be individual differences associated with any psychological process" (p. 36). Another element in the definition of a psychological *process* is the variation in behavioral manifestation under different conditions. For instance, distractibility is more likely to be exhibited when the individual's attention is pulled away by competing stimuli. The crucial question, however, relates to the manner in which distractibility shapes the individual's development through its impact on the continuous organization and reorganization of life experiences.

Personal dispositions such as temperaments or cognitive capacities give organization and continuity to experiences and lead to the acquisition of cognitive and affective styles that are self-perpetuating and difficult to modify. The characteristics that comprise the individual's personality are the "ingrained and habitual ways of psychological functioning that emerge from the individual's entire developmental history" (Millon, 1981, p. 4). Certain personal predispositions become salient at different ages and may either disrupt a previously established harmony with surroundings or overcome prior discord (Thomas & Chess, 1977): (1) because of different expectations at various age levels, (2) because certain characteristics that are expected to emerge or disappear with maturation are closely tied to these expectations, and (3) because a specific talent or interest may compensate for previous difficulties and may lead to changed expectations.

Model for Clarifying Assumptions about Personality

Figure 4–1 presents a framework for the development of personality in which a variety of theoretical positions can be represented. The schematic model is not intended to devise a new theory of personality but to serve as a vehicle for clarifying assumptions about personality that influence the interpretation of assessment data. As such, it provides a general framework for integration of data that could accommodate diverse theoretical positions and empirical findings. It is up to the individual practitioner to assign relative importance to variables seen as useful in explaining the presenting problems in a particular instance. Practitioners with different theoretical views may vary in preference for type of assessment "data." Phenomenologists are interested in subjective perceptions, whereas others emphasize behaviors, ego functions, neurochemical deviations, defense mechanisms, or interpersonal relationships. Diverse perspectives are based on different sources and types of information, all of which can be integrated into a conceptual framework.

The scheme presented in Figure 4–1 incorporates individual differences and environmental input as they relate to the organization of subjective experience and development of objective competencies. Various components of the model are described next.

Personal Predispositions

Person characteristics are inherent in the individual and comprise the essential building blocks that form the basis for individual differences in personality. These person variables are built in and exert a powerful influence on

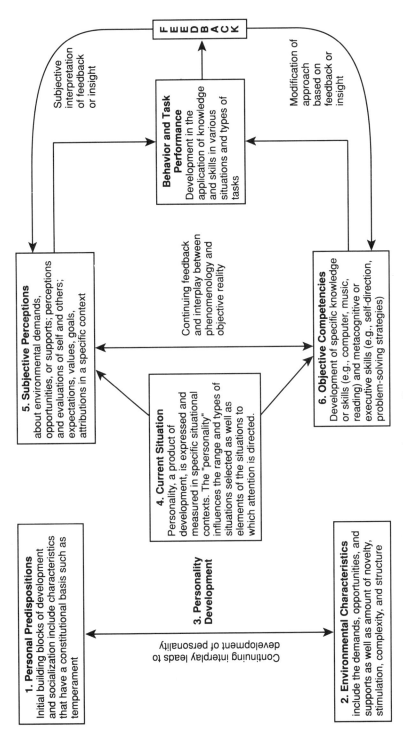

FIGURE 4-1 • Development and Measurement of Personality

Note: Measurement is always specific to the situation and measurement technique utilized; therefore, multiple measures are recommended.

development because they set the parameters for the impact of the environment. They not only determine the range of circumstances to which the individual can adapt but also shape the interpretation and selection of experience. There is wide acceptance among theorists that there is some "raw material" present in the person (e.g., the Freudian view of instincts as forces that influence the course of events), but the clarity in which predispositions are specified—what they are and how they exert their influence over time—are not agreed upon.

The basic tenet of temperament theorists is that human beings are constitutionally different in ways that play a part in shaping of attitudes and expectations (Scarr & Kidd, 1983) and in molding their personality (e.g., Buss & Plomin, 1984; Kagan, Reznick, & Snidman, 1987). Despite differences among contemporary theoretical approaches to temperament with regard to the actual characteristics to include in the temperament rubric, there is some general agreement that the term *temperament* refers to inborn predispositions that are biological in origin (Plomin, 1983).

There is ample evidence to document that children differ from each other in a variety of ways that can be measured. These early differences have implications for later development and for psychiatric risk (see Rutter, 1987). The following have been convincingly demonstrated: (1) individual differences do exist (e.g., Berger, 1985; Buss & Plomin, 1975; Campos et al., 1983); and (2) measures of children's temperament predict subsequent changes in behaviors in different contexts (Dunn & Kendrick, 1982; Graham, Rutter, & George, 1973; Rutter, 1978; Maziade et al., 1985).

Temperament is an example of a personal predisposition that is differentiated from personality but that plays an essential role in its development. *Personality* is generally thought of as a much more inclusive term than *temperament*, and it deals with broader characteristics (e.g., self-concept, social expectations, task expectations, attributions, learned strategies), which are gradually acquired through the interplay of experiences with a configuration of temperamental attributes.

According to Lewis and Michaelson (1983), temperament controls the regularity of emotional states in response to different elicitors until such time as a personality structure emerges from these states to act as an organizer of the states themselves. Cognitive processes such as expectancies, values, perceptions, or attributions (Atkinson, 1981; Bandura, 1977) that emerge as elements of personality also organize experience and mediate behavior. Individual differences in the degree of organization and structure of personality are exemplified in personality disorders (e.g., Millon, 1981).

The pioneering work of Thomas, Chess, and others (Chess & Thomas, 1984; Thomas et al., 1963; Thomas & Chess, 1977), known as the New York Longitudinal Study, set the tone for subsequent research efforts in this area. They defined temperament as the *how* rather than the *what* of behavior. Accordingly, emphasis is on *how* individuals respond to stimulation (e.g., the energy or intensity of the response) or *how* persons attend to their surroundings. Each temperamental trait represents a process or a way of approaching and reacting to experiences, which, nevertheless, has implications for the *content* of behaviors such as *what* the individual does. If temperament refers to the process of interaction with the environment, the expression of these interactive processes are represented by what the behaviors are. For instance, distractibility may be a process where individuals are drawn from their purposes by immediate stimuli. Persons who are unable to direct their effort back to their intended activity may engage in behaviors (e.g., not keeping a promise) that are described as irresponsible. Patterns of common problematic behaviors of children have been related to combinations of temperaments (Teglasi & MacMahon, 1990).

The basic focus of temperament research is on individual differences rather than normative trends in development. Most current temperament theories emphasize qualities of mood or emotionality, such as tendencies toward distress, fear, or positive affect (Buss & Plomin, 1984; Campos & Barrett, 1984; Rothbart & Derryberry, 1981; Thomas & Chess, 1980) rather than cognitive aspects of development. Cognitive style has been a separate field of study unrelated to temperament, despite the fact that the underlying assumptions bear a striking resemblance to those of temperament theorists (Thomas & Chess, 1977). Furthermore, it should be pointed out that the temperament dimensions of distractibility and persistence/attention span (Rothbart & Derryberry, 1981; Thomas & Chess, 1980) are cognitive in nature. Temperament theory and research appear to encompass affective as well as cognitive elements as they influence behavioral style.

Environment

Heritable characteristics are subject to environmental modification (Plomin, 1983; Scarr & Kidd, 1983), and temperament is no longer viewed as consisting of early emerging traits that have immutable and lasting influence on behavior due to their genetic basis (Thompson, 1986). The manifestations of temperamental attributes are likely to change as they interact with environmental demands and maturational processes. Since genetic influences change with maturation, there is no reason to believe that all personal predispositions emerge early in the life span. In fact, genetic factors may themselves be important sources of change and discontinuity in development (Buss & Plomin, 1984; Plomin, 1983). The predisposing personal characteristics in place at a particular maturational stage determine the range and types of experiences that an individual is prepared to use constructively to enhance further development.

According to Snow (1987), individual differences in aptitude "show through, or come into play, upon situational demand" (p. 12). "The term aptitude always implies prediction in some particular outer environment . . . describing the situation is part of defining the aptitude" (p. 13). A definition of traits such as aptitudes that includes the situation is basically an application of the Person by Situation interaction emphasized in personality theory (Endler & Magnusson, 1976; Magnusson, 1987; Magnusson & Endler, 1977; Pervin & Lewis, 1978). Such interactions are implied when aptitude is defined as readiness to benefit from a particular type of instruction and is inherent in the concept of Aptitude Treatment Interactions (Snow, 1987).

Likewise, the influence of temperament depends on the social context and the goodness of fit (Lerner & Lerner, 1983) or match (Buss & Plomin, 1984) between temperament characteristics and environmental expectations. For a given individual, it is reasonable to delineate the conditions for optimal functioning and comfort by specifying aspects of situations that have functional significance for relevant personal dimensions. In this sense, the defining characteristics of situations are subjective. A situation may be uncomfortable or overstimulating for some individuals and optimal for others according to their temperamental attributes such as emotional reactivity or need for stimulation.

The situational influence on behavior (Mischel, 1979; Rutter & Giller, 1983) is evident. However, the unit of importance is the person-in-context, which relates the properties of the individual with salient features of the environment. Person predispositions essentially involve process traits, and a fundamental property of such traits is the circumstances under which they become salient. Thus, adaptability or flexibility is evident in the context of changing situations. Predispositions have also been viewed as vulnerabilities that are evoked by the environment. Infants with a biologically based predisposition to develop "inhibited behavior" actualize this tendency when the environment presents stressors (Kagan, 1989). Traits are relatively stable dimensions of individual differences that may be used to describe or explain behavior in a specific context. Task and situational variations in intelligent behavior have been explained by positing multiple intelligences (Gardner, 1983), or specifying various components to intelligence (Sternberg, 1985) that are expressed according to demands of specific tasks or situations. The notion of cross-situational consistency of behavior as an important concept in personality (and intelligence) only holds if the functional significance of a situation or task remains constant.

Personality traits are predispositions to states that are evoked by situations that have a functional significance for that person and/or that trait. Situational moderators are those elements of situations that promote the development of or evoke the expression of particular personality traits. Such situational factors include but are not limited to frequency and type of feedback, the number of cues or structure inherent in a situation, types of contingencies, amount of novelty, complexity, ambiguity, or threat.

Interplay between Person and Environment

An individual's "personality" is shaped through the continuing interplay between the attributes of the person, maturational changes, and characteristics of the environment. At any time, the personality is the product of the individual's reaction to and organization of prior experience, which influences subsequent interactions. The literature on how temperament shapes and is shaped by the environment presents a prototype of the interactive process between personal predispositions and environmental impact. Temperament determines the person-environment interplay in three basic ways: (1) by influencing responses to different environments, (2) by shaping the responses of others, and (3) by promoting selective exposure to environmental opportunities.

Responding Differently to Environments
Individuals with differing temperamental characteristics respond different-ly to similar environments. Temperamental dispositions shape interactions di-rectly through their impact on behavior tendencies, and indirectly through their influence on the understanding of interpersonal events and through the learning of strategies and expectations. Those who are more emotionally reactive and less able to adapt to changing conditions (e.g., Thomas & Chess, 1977) are more extremely affected by novel or challenging situations. Temperament characteris-tics not only influence the child's susceptibility to stress but also the effective-ness of active coping methods (Lerner & East, 1984). Individual variation in emotionality shape perceptions and provide an interpretational set for how the environment is perceived by the child. Thus, children who differ in their emotionality have different interpretations of parental acceptance or rejection (Rowe, 1983). Environments that impinge differently on different children in the same family appear to have the strongest impact on development (Plomin & Daniels, 1987). Individual differences in susceptibility to signals of reward and punishment (Eysenck, 1981; Gray, 1981, 1982) are further instances of in-dividual variation in response to the environment.

The subjective interpretation and organization of experience are jointly shaped by the environment and personal dispositions. For example, caregiver sensitivity and prompt response to a child's expression of need are important environmental influences on the child's ability to organize life experiences and on the development of expectations about caregiver reliability (Lamb, 1981). However, the characteristics of the infant also determine the likelihood of perceiving a relationship between the baby's behavior and the caretaker's re-sponse (Suomi, 1981). The infant's attention to relevant social cues, interest in the environment, freedom from distress, and reaction to caregiving all play a role in the harmonious relationship where each partner develops expectations about the other.

Shaping the Responses of Others

The parent-child relationship is mutually interactive, and the infant's contribution to the socialization process is widely recognized (Bell, 1968; Bell & Harper, 1977; Sameroff, 1975; Thomas & Chess, 1981). Children's temperamental attributes influence the ways in which others respond to them (e.g., Lee & Bates, 1985; Rutter, 1978; Stevenson-Hinde & Hinde, 1986). Generally, children with adverse temperamental features are more likely to be involved in confrontation and to become the target of parental criticism or irritation. Evidence that the child is eliciting such reactions is strongly indicated by the fact that parents change their behavior toward hyperactive youngsters following beneficial drug effects (Barkley, 1981).

Sroufe (1985) argues that most parents adapt to the demands of their child and that infants who require extensive care typically receive it. Therefore, it is the combination of a vulnerable baby and a parent who cannot adapt that is the likely source of mismatch. Maternal life circumstances and attitudes (see Crockenberg, 1986) as well as cultural beliefs and expectations appear to mediate the impact of certain aspects of temperament on maternal caregiving practices (DeVries, 1984). According to Lewis and Michaelson (1983), the feedback system in terms of what is elicited from others is established at a very early age and most likely activates itself around the infant's emotional and temperamental qualities.

Promoting Selective Exposure

Individuals actively shape their environments by the situations they choose to approach or avoid (Thomas & Chess, 1977). Individuals tend to seek out environments, friends, occupations, and information according to their temperament (e.g., sociable people seek out the company of others [Buss & Plomin, 1984]). Furthermore, individuals seek or avoid situations to regulate stimulation to maintain an optimal level of arousal (e.g., Geen, 1984; Strelau, 1983). Thus, nature shapes nurture to the extent that people create their own environment (Scarr & McCartney, 1983).

Goodness of Fit between Person and Environment

Lerner and Lerner (1983) applied Thomas and Chess's (1977) goodness-of-fit model to explain the interplay between temperament and environment. According to this model, it is the match between temperamental predispositions and environmental supports and challenges that determines development. Not everyone is equally prepared to meet societal expectations in a given culture or setting. An individual who has difficulty focusing, shifting, and maintaining attention will benefit from an environment that provides cues to draw and sustain attention. A person who reacts strongly, even to mild provocation, requires a more secure and predictable environment. Some students can handle unstructured learning environments in which independent activity is required, whereas others benefit from teaching strategies that are tightly structured (Snow, 1982; Snow & Lohman, 1984). Individuals who have difficulty synthesizing events or regulating their mood states cannot maintain themselves without a highly structured, therapeutic milieu. On the other hand, there is considerable evidence of children who flourish despite adverse circumstances.

Thus, the particular ways that a child has been socialized at *any* time is a function of personal predispositions and environmental events, which jointly lead to the development of expectations, attitudes, self-evaluation standards, self-concept, goals, values, preferences, and competencies. Furthermore, the accumulation of experiences leads to the acquisition of learned strategies that may result in changes in the ways that predispositions are expressed. A person's reaction to novel situations may be altered by having had the opportunity to learn mastery in a "safe" setting. An individual who is aware of being distractible may arrange circumstances to minimize the adverse impact of this tendency.

Situational Variation

Situations or tasks that call for certain attributes come to be associated with a "sense of self" in that situation. The learned strategies and attitudes that have been formed by past transactions with the environment are not general but based on feedback from specific environments. For instance, the perceived competence of a person who is slow to adapt may vary according to the familiarity of the situation. Thus, self-concepts are specific to a particular domain or social context (Kihlstrom & Cantor, 1984) rather than being global representations of personality. Even within specific domains such as music, there are various functional elements and demands. Self as musician relates not only to proficiency in playing an instrument but to how the individual feels about practicing, performing, or composing. Over time, individuals may learn how different situations affect their moods, level of arousal, and self-confidence. Such awareness contributes to the development of insight and permits purposive, self-directed behavior. It is important to note, however, that individuals vary in awareness of the functional elements of situations in relation to attributes of the self.

Persons view situations in light of learned strategies and expectations based on past experience and predispositions. While these past experiences tend to reinforce vicious cycles, the reaction to a current situation or task demand is also based on the individual's capacity to meet the information processing and adaptive demands of the task or situation at hand. In conducting the assessment, it is important to specify the conditions under which particular traits become manifest and to make situational predictions from testing, which recognizes that different tests make different demands, and that generalizations to behavior are conditional to situations with comparable demands.

Phenomenology

Two broad categories of information determine responses to a situation. One is the subjective *perception,* which includes interpretation and organization of ideas about the situation, the feelings evoked, as well as perceived self-efficacy in that situation. The other is the person's actual *competency* and *problem-solving* approaches, which can be observed by others and by the self. There is a continuing interplay between these inner and outer levels of experience. Individuals react to an external demand or provocation on the basis of their mode of experiencing the event, which is an outgrowth of the manner in which they have organized their previous life experiences, which in turn was shaped by their endowments such as capacity for attention, memory, perception, integration, and emotional regulation. The subjective interpretation of current experiences is the product of the ability to interpret, perceive, organize, and assign meaning to them.

Johnston (1974) investigated the link between personality dimensions (active-passive, task orientation, and interpersonal orientation) and individuals' perception of the climate of their work environment. The author concluded that individuals with different personality characteristics were highly discrepant in their perceptions about the organizational environment, as well as in their behaviors. Active and task-oriented individuals perceived a more positive relationship with the organization than did passive or low task-oriented peers. Active individuals perceived fewer constraints and, when they did perceive obstacles, they generally regarded them as problems that called for constructive action. On the other hand, passive workers expressed feelings of being acted on by managers and by other impinging forces. Task-oriented individuals defined clearer goals and made more comments about specific projects, whereas the comments of low-task peers were more diffuse and expressed more general frustration and uneasiness in the workplace. Thus, Johnston's (1974) study indicated that individual differences in personality were associated with characteristic ways of defining and dealing with the realities of the workplace and that differential ability to thrive in the system was associated with different subjective perceptions.

Perceptions or subjective states are of primary importance to human beings and comprise their inner experience. Phenomenology represents the individual's subjective experiences and has a complex set of determinants, including an individual's life experiences and all of the factors constituting the capacity to organize those experiences. Emotional, motivational, and cognitive attributes play a role in information processing and subjective interpretation of events. Emotion plays a major role in perception by directing interest and attention. For example, individuals may want to believe something so much that they may refuse to accept evidence against it. Selective exposure or inexperience (e.g., young child) as well as active avoidance or selective inattention may prevent an individual from being confronted with disconfirming evidence. Peer and cultural influence on perception are demonstrated where a lot of support is given to the perpetuation of a certain belief (Baron, 1985). Escalona (1968) suggests that children's subjective experiences of social interactions may be unrelated to parental behavior. Rather, the individual's style of perceiving and organizing experience shapes phenomenology, which is assumed to be the basis for actions. For example, an individual who misperceives a situation may perform actions that lead to confrontation. The feedback received from such an encounter will be interpreted according to the individual's manner of experiencing it and influence subsequent perceptions and actions accordingly.

Generalized sets and expectations that are superimposed on specific situations have been referred to as *apperceptive distortion* (Bellak, 1975). It is important, however, to recognize that when two individuals perceive others differently, neither may be distorting because each may be eliciting different reactions, which are then interpreted through individual sets acquired through past experience. Subjective perceptions are grounded in "personality" that develops through the cumulative interaction of an individual with a particular set of endowments and the environment. An understanding of the content and organization of subjective perceptions requires a reconstruction of the historical interplay that led to a particular way of integrating experiences. The content of projective stories represents subjective perceptions evoked by the stimulus presented and by the organization of past experience.

Objective Competencies

An individual's ability to meet interpersonal and task expectations constitutes objective competencies in specific situations. These competencies also develop gradually as the maturing individual with a particular set of endowments encounters environmental opportunities, supports, and challenges (Sroufe et al., 1984). Through the feedback process, individuals may learn to modify their behavior or problem-solving approaches as well as their subjective perceptions. Feedback can be in the form of insight gained through reflection and self-evaluation or from external sources of information. Individuals differ in how they interpret or seek feedback through internal or external sources and in their ability to utilize such information to modify their perception or behavior. A useful understanding of the individual's phenomenology must incorporate the objective competencies and external feedback with subjective interpretation. Objective competencies can be assessed through a variety of observational techniques and performance measures, including the quality of the stories told to projective stimuli.

Implications for Assessment of Personality

The assessment takes place at a particular time, but the conclusions are based on multiple measures from a variety of sources that incorporate the following information:

1. Current behaviors, subjective perceptions, and objective competencies across a wide range of task and situational demands
2. Prior information gleaned from a developmental history and review of past records
3. Likely implications of the individual's functioning for future adjustment and recommended therapeutic interventions or environmental accommodations.

An assessment would attempt a comprehensive description of current functioning and a retrospective analysis of how the individual got to this point by identifying the links between the current problem and the interplay of the relevant person and environment factors. Different types and sources of information may be used to clarify various aspects of functioning in relation to task and situational demands. Test data are integrated with observations, teacher and self-reports, developmental and medical history, academic performance, and parent concerns to get a full picture of the presenting problems and their meaning to the child and family. The examiner may focus on several salient characteristics or a pattern of multiple interactive attributes to trace the development and current manifestations of the presenting problems. The result of these efforts is the elaboration of a working model of the individual that provides the basis for decisions.

Current Functioning

The current problem can be addressed by measuring cognitive, emotional, and behavioral variables as they relate to each other and to the presenting concerns. Different situations and tasks reveal various elements of cognitive, affective, and behavioral style as they pertain to the problem presented.

Phenomenology can be assessed directly through self-report or by less direct means of measurement such as projective techniques. Different levels of phenomenology can be tapped with different approaches depending on the respondents' level of awareness and willingness to share their private world. Projective tests are oriented to reveal formal qualities of thinking, perceiving, and experiencing that contribute to the development of subjective phenomenology pertaining to particular environmental contexts. Projective stories do not give a realistic account of the narrator's life circumstances but represent the subjective perceptions that are based on the accumulated organizations of prior experience.

Where the story teller perceives failure, it is appropriate to ask if the respondent is really failing, and, if so, to ascertain the causes of the failure. If the respondent is not failing, inquiries about the standards or criteria for self-evaluation are in order.

A child's phenomenology about the learning environment or tasks as revealed in projective stories can be explored by asking how these attitudes are influenced by variables such as cognitive, temperamental, or attentional processes. The overlap among these response modes is difficult to tease out because each has an impact on the others. Nevertheless, the examiner would attempt to understand the relationships among these processes and subjective experiences by seeking to explain how these attributes might affect the learning process or attitudes about school.

To understand or describe a child's current difficulties, particular traits might be identified as constitutional, learned, or as some combination. For example, a trait such as inattentiveness might have a direct influence manifested by the inability to stay on the point in a conversation. The child may inappropriately change the topic due to difficulty with monitoring the flow of the discussion. The resulting awkwardness in modulating the response to the context may elicit criticism and rejection from peers and adults. The manner in which the child organizes and integrates this feedback would be the key to the child's learning of coping strategies, which may include choices of activities that are in keeping with cognitive and emotional dispositions.

The formative bases of an individual's current perceptions are revealed through patterns of data gleaned through multiple sources. These perceptions have a developmental history and implications for future adjustment. For instance, inaccurate interpretations of current circumstances increase the likelihood of maladaptive responses that may lead to being involved in conflict. Cognitive or emotional disturbances that make it difficult for a child to organize and anticipate events impair the child's adaptive capacities and necessitate environmental accommodations. Conversely, the environment may be so chaotic as to be impossible to organize. In conducting an assessment, it is important to consider the implication of current perceptual style for development and for the possibility of making environmental accommodations to foster different perceptions. In regard to Figure 4–1, assessment of current functioning encompasses phenomenology and competencies. The retrospective analysis puts these into an historical context by tracing the interplay among person and environmental variables that resulted in the current pattern of functioning.

Retrospective Analysis

Perception reflects an individual's subjective reality developed from the interpretation of prior interactions. These subjective perceptions are jointly shaped by the nature of the experiences and the organizing capacity of the person to make sense of those experiences. It is helpful to trace possible reasons for an individual's attitudes and perceptions. For instance, a child's perception of parents as being critical may have developed because (1) the child's behavior provokes such a response, (2) the child is particularly sensitive and the parent is not actually critical, or (3) the parent is excessively critical. It is up to the interpreter to discern which of these possibilities apply. The form and content of the projective stories reveal the phenomenology of the narrator, and it is the examiner's task to determine what are the likely explanations for a given pattern of subjective experiences. Theoretically, the causal roots of these subjective perceptions, though complex and multiply determined, are possible to trace. The question of how the person has come to view the world in a particular way is addressed by examining actual experiences and the factors accounting for the organization and interpretation of those experiences. Through this process, the relationship between the developmental history (interplay between the person characteristics and environment) and the presenting problem is clarified.

Prospective

A prospective analysis of the problem addresses how the processes set in motion by history are likely to play themselves out into the future, given the expected impact of maturation and an understanding of the likely range of environmental demands and supports. Although it is not possible to predict what the individual's future experiences will be, the examiner can recognize vicious cycles and anticipate the child's ability to handle future task and social demands. A fourth-grader with excellent memory but poor conceptual abilities would be expected to encounter increasing difficulty in school as more conceptual skills are demanded.

When referring a child for assessment, parents or teachers want an explanation for the presenting problem and direction for intervention or management. Explanatory concepts that emerge from the integration of findings from the developmental history with assessment of current functioning are used to plan constructive intervention strategies.

A child who is teased by peers may have inadvertently elicited the teasing (e.g., by overreacting to events or by losing track of the "rules" of the game). Such a child may subsequently have trouble dealing with the reactions of others and perpetuate a vicious cycle. In turn, the other children may develop expectations about and reactions to this child that may be difficult to alter. The assessor's task is to recommend ways to intervene in the cycle, based on the evaluator's understanding of the contributing factors. Another aim of the assessment process is for parents to understand their offspring's actions so that they are in a better position to participate in planning and carrying out recommendations.

The Diagnostic Assessment Process

The following general assumptions pertain to the diagnostic assessment process:

1. The facets of functioning that are revealed in a diagnostic assessment depend on what instruments are used and how they are interpreted. Multiple assessments are needed because no single method is able to tap the many dimensions of psychological functioning. Different psychological tests require different processes so that the results can generalize only to tasks and circumstances that make the same demands as the particular assessment tool. Such variations in situational and task demands are incorporated in the interpretive conclusions.
2. Unique information is derived from the less structured projective story telling as part of a multifaceted assessment approach. The story telling task elicits responses that reflect how an individual selects and organizes experience.
3. A fruitful approach to evaluation combines normative comparison with an understanding of explanatory concepts. Generalizations are made from a standard test situation to the individual's life situation by understanding the process involved. There are many ways to function within the "normal" range, and individual differences in these parameters may not be evident from purely normative comparisons.
4. The primary goal of the assessment process is the elaboration of a working model of the person who is experiencing problems. This information is then used to plan interventions and make decisions.

Figure 4–2 delineates steps in the interpretive process which are summarized below:

Systematic Regularities or Patterns in Each Type of Data
Information is extracted from each data source with due consideration of the advantages and limitations. The initial focus is on the configuration of data within each measure. In the interpretation of an intelligence test, the examiner considers the pattern of scores as well as specific responses where appropriate to formulate propositions. The interpreter must have specific knowledge about each instrument to compare performance across subtests and to generate hypotheses that are subsequently cross-checked across other sources.

Systematic Regularities across Data
The interpreter seeks common elements or coherent patterns across the various sources of data to coordinate the impressions gleaned from each data source. For instance, analysis of subtest patterns of the WISC-III is compared with other information, such as performance on less structured tests like pro-

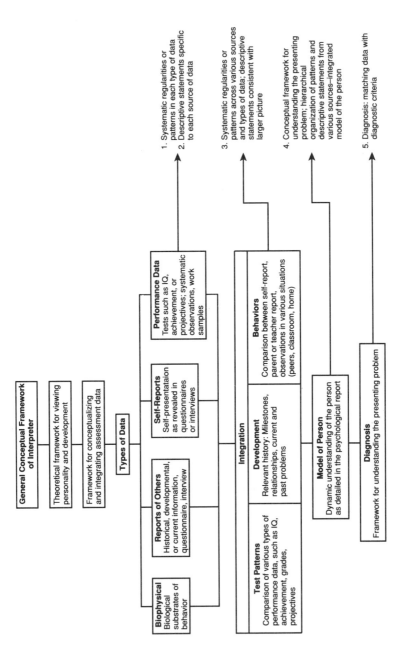

FIGURE 4-2 • Steps in the Assessment Process
Source: Adapted from Dana (1982, p. 60).

jective stories. Discrepancies and similarities in functioning in various environments and types of tasks are noted as data from various sources are integrated. Likewise, the assessor incorporates the multiple sources of historical data to form an impression of the developing individual in relation to the home, peer group, and school.

Interpretation

The pattern of observations described in the first two steps are translated into constructs or traits that explain the presenting concerns. The interpreter uses a broad knowledge base to link the concepts emerging from the integration of the data to coherent patterns of generalizations relevant to a theoretical area (e.g., thought disorder or defense mechanism) and pertaining to current functioning. For instance, the interpreter would delineate how distractibility or associative thinking style relates to the individual's presenting problems.

Since manifestations of a trait are specific to a circumstance, agreement across measures is not required. In fact, multiple methods of assessment yield information that helps identify the relevant processes because systematic regularities or variations in the data allow for generalizations of traits. Conclusions are compared across data sources to verify or refute the hypotheses bearing on the conceptualization of the presenting problem. Interpretive conclusions explain the pattern of similarities or discrepancies in performance across measures (e.g., structured versus unstructured) and data sources (e.g., parent reports, teacher reports, previous tests, medical or school records) and permit conditional or situation specific descriptive statements.

Model of Person

At this point, the concepts that emerge from the various measurement procedures are hierarchically organized and related to the presenting problems, which are understood in the context of all the relevant attributes including cultural influences and family patterns. A model of the individual is formulated that includes subjective phenomenology and actual competencies in various contexts and that incorporates the restrospective, current, and prospective views discussed earlier. This conceptualization promotes the delineation of the conditions (environments, tasks, teaching strategies) for optimal functioning and specification of recommendations for intervention.

The working model includes a description of the relevant processes within the individual in relation to a comprehensive definition of the presenting problem. The model should specify how each response system, such as cognitive, motoric, physiological/emotional, or behavioral, contributes to the problem. Any trait is expressed through the cognitive, affective, and behavioral response systems, which are interconnected. Consequently, a trait such as anxiety or fear can be expressed in several ways: (1) cognitively through thoughts relating to expectations of bad events, loss of control, inability to concentrate, excessive focus on the self or on threatening aspects of the environment; (2) behaviorally by a tendency to avoid uncomfortable situations; or (3) emotionally or physiologically by sweating, trembling, crying.

Likewise, a trait such as distractibility is expressed differently across a variety of tasks, situations, and response modes as follows: (1) cognitively by the tendency to be drawn to the most compelling stimulus, by difficulty focusing on the most relevant pieces of information, or by difficulty sustaining attention; (2) behaviorally by engaging in undirected activity, not following through on intentions, or by being easily provoked; or (3) emotionally, by displaying increased activity or fidgetiness, or by intense reactions that are out of proportion to the provocation.

The manifestations of a trait across the three response domains vary according to the individual and the configuration of other traits. Furthermore, within a response system such as cognition, a variety of processes can be identified. Therefore, the working model of the individual explains consistencies and variations within and across response domains.

Description of problem behaviors includes the specifications of the conditions for occurrence and delineation of such features as frequency, duration, and intensity in relation to normative expectations. The conditions or situations that exacerbate or ameliorate the problems in each of the response domains are indicated. The developmental history of the problem and impact of previous interventions contribute to the conclusions drawn and to the recommendations offered.

Diagnosis

Diagnosis refers to matching the behaviors and symptoms exhibited to the criteria specified by a diagnostic label within a given classification scheme. Diagnosis requires knowledge of psychopathology as well as familiarity with the classification system. Blashfield and Draguns (1976) set forth five purposes of psychiatric classification: (1) communication among professionals, (2) information retrieval (key words for literature search), (3) descriptive value, (4) prediction, and (5) source of concepts for scientific theory.

The working model of a person as described above focuses on the internal structure and coherence of patterns of attributes within an individual. Diagnosis refers to distilling these characteristics to match the diagnostic categories. Theoretically, the symptom clusters in a diagnostic system also have a coherent structure in terms of intercorrelations of symptoms, time sequence of appearance, etiology, and response to treatment (see Robins & Helzer [1986] for a review). A diagnosis implies a host of other associated features that can be inferred especially if a great deal is known about a particular syndrome. In this way, theoretically sound diagnostic entities can function somewhat like the key concepts in formulating the model of an individual. Diagnosis in terms of a nosological categorization should not be made on the basis of a single test.

However, if a diagnosis is required, Bellak suggests that the following "formula" be used: "The data represented in the TAT are consistent with the diagnosis of. . . ."

Summary

The professional's view of personality and of assessment influences the process and outcome of the evaluation. Therefore, it is necessary for the examiner to explore the assumptions and purposes that guide test selection and interpretation. Accordingly, this chapter presents a schematic model intended for use as a tool to clarify the basic personality concepts and their interplay within an organized context. A framework for a comprehensive assessment is also described.

CHAPTER 5

Orientation to Interpretation

The parameters for the story telling task are set by the picture stimuli and instructions. The narrator is expected to deal with the realities of the stimuli and incorporate the elements indicated in the instructions. Interpretation is based on an understanding of the task to be accomplished and the differentiation of meaningful content from that which is pulled by the stimulus or constitutes fleeting associations. Form, content, and process elements of the narrative provide parallel indices of task accomplishment. At the level of story structure, the narrator is expected to include and realistically resolve tensions depicted in the stimulus. In terms of content, the story characters are expected to cope with the dilemmas set before them. The extent to which the characters are able to deal realistically with the challenges built into the story as a result of the stimulus pull parallels the ability of the story teller to negotiate other unstructured tasks (Bellak, 1986). Finally, in the process of telling the story, the respondent should have a plan and monitor the expression of ideas.

Competencies Needed for the Story Telling Task

An analysis of the competencies required for successful completion of the story telling task provides clues about individual differences in sources of difficulty in meeting task demands.

Self-Monitoring

The story teller needs to be relaxed enough to allow a free flow of ideas yet must keep enough distance to monitor and organize the stream of thoughts. Persons who cannot observe the quality of their production may respond by verbalizing thoughts as they are evoked by the stimulus, by previous story elements, or by personal associations without utilizing a strategy to produce a conceptually integrated story. Such respondents may have difficulty monitoring the inner logic of the story and may introduce contradictory details. The narrative may proceed without a plan and meander tangentially from one idea to another, with little or no connection to a main theme. Stories may be told at a fast pace because the child doesn't slow down to organize ideas or to calibrate responses with the examiner's writing.

Children who do not have a strategy for telling the story may react to various elements of the stimulus as points of departure rather than organizing the entire stimulus configuration. The narrator may distort or disregard parts of the stimulus because of inability to coordinate the picture with the flow of ideas. It is difficult to tell a coherent story if the narrator cannot focus on the relevant aspects of the cues provided in the picture, gets lost in story details, is unable to shift from the previous idea expressed, or cannot back away from the pull of the picture stimuli. Perseverative content is a product of attentional and organizational problems stemming from difficulty shifting focus from one idea to another without external input.

Children with difficulty monitoring their behavior may perform relatively well in structured tasks such as an individually administered intelligence scale. Nevertheless, the answers to the more open-ended subtests like vocabulary or comprehension may reveal a rambling style or difficulty getting to the point. On these subtests, the respondent may simply tell everything that comes to mind, without prior organization or ongoing monitoring of the adequacy of the performance.

Self-Direction in the Absence of Feedback

Constructing a story is a complex response requiring initiative and inner directedness to coordinate a sequence of responses in the absence of feedback. The story is made up through a combination of external constraints set by the stimulus and instructions and the ideas or constructs available to the story teller. The narrator must make a decision about a story line and then develop the plot without vacillation, indecision, or overemphasis on detail. The narrator is required to overcome the "immediacy" of the stimulus pull to generate a realistic solution that is not apparent from the picture. From a task-performance perspective, responses that fail to resolve adversity might suggest that the narrator was unable to use self-directed effort to move beyond the pull of the stimulus or the immediacy of the circumstance. Likewise, positive outcomes where obstacles are overcome without adequate transition or explanation also suggest that the narrator cannot direct efforts.

Individuals who have difficulty directing their actions without external guidelines approach the story telling task without a plan. They tend to react to the stimulus provocation, describe characters who act without a plan, and fail to incorporate long-term purposes, time frame, or interpersonal considerations. Actions are provoked rather than directed by goals or convictions. The thematic content is pulled from the stimulus without embedding events into a broader context. The story emanates from the stimulus just as behavior emanates from provocation.

Affect Modulation

Successful task accomplishment requires that the story teller cope with the emotions generated by the task. The negative, threatening aspects of the picture stimuli dictate that the story teller build tension and conflict into the narrative. An individual who cannot tolerate anxiety or anger will have a hard time when confronted with the necessity of incorporating such emotions into the story. The person may overreact to features of the stimuli, particularly to the emotional or threatening elements. Additionally, the unstructured story telling task that provides minimal guidelines may be a painstaking experience accompanied by discomfort, frustration, or anxiety.

The disorganizing impact of the respondent's emotional reactions is one of degree. Accordingly, the task may provoke different levels of disruption, ranging from mild vacillation or dysfluency to the production of aimless verbiage. Respondents may keep changing the story line (indecision), become overly invested in a particular story element, or may even become confused. The emotional reaction or cognitive disorganization (e.g., overelaboration, vacillation, or non sequiturs) may be related to specific stimuli or themes or may be more generally manifested. Sometimes, the respondent does not recover from reactions provoked by a threatening stimulus or from the cumulative impact of the previous cards.

Cognitive Integration

The task requires the respondent to coordinate multiple perspectives to develop the story line. The instructions ask the narrator to: (1) superimpose a time frame on events by indicating what happened before, what is happening in the picture, and how the story turns out; (2) integrate inner and outer elements of experience by describing what the characters are thinking and feeling in relation to external events and to the actions taken. Furthermore, the task implicitly demands the respondent to: (3) reconcile perspectives (inner and outer experiences) of the various characters; (4) link actions and outcomes in ways that properly connect causes with their effects; and (5) coordinate stimulus features with story content.

Characteristics of thinking (e.g., abstract, concrete, stereotyped, dichotomous, or disorganized) are revealed in the conceptual level of stories that parallels the level at which experience is organized. An integrated story establishes significant linkages among multiple levels of experience by incorporating time frame, connections between actions and outcomes, coherence among thoughts, actions, and feelings, and coordination of give and take among characters. Such integrated stories go beyond the stimulus and everyday concerns to deal with long-term issues and general principles.

Insight and Reflection

The task requires the respondent to generate a story that incorporates the inner framework of the characters. The degree of reflection and insight is evident in the elaboration of characters' thoughts and feelings in relation to their circumstances, actions, and outcomes. The richness of the story teller's inner life and interpersonal experiences is reflected in the themes. When the narrator has little depth to draw on or has no basis in real-life experiences to describe the interpersonal relationships as depicted in the stimulus, the plots may be borrowed or have a "soap opera" quality. Events and feelings are described in terms that are vague, and relationships are stereotypically portrayed. The story teller may be working very hard to comply with task demands but cannot produce themes that reflect genuine concerns. The structure of the story may be adequate, but content may be highly superficial. The ability to look inward and to coordinate the internal and external worlds requires the integration of cognitive and emotional components of experience.

Form, Process, and Content Characteristics of Stories

Form and content are two broad aspects of T.A.T. protocols that have been distinguished (e.g., Bellak, 1986; Dana, 1959; Henry, 1956; Holt, 1958; Neman, Brown, & Sells, 1973; Rapaport, 1947). Form relates to *how* the story teller organizes efforts to accomplish the task, whereas content refers to *what* the specific themes express. Formal analysis emphasizes how the narrator approaches the task and develops the themes as reflected by the structural elements of content such as internal logic or compliance with instructions. Content analysis is focused on the concerns, sensitivities, or convictions of the story teller. The process of telling and organizing the story reflects the respondent's mode of thinking and reacting, which is inherent in story structure and content.

Holt's (1958) definition of *form* includes structural characteristics of content. He notes that a general variable such as "adequacy of hero," which refers to the success of the protagonist in achieving goals, is part of the story's substance as well as its form. This variable is considered a formal aspect of the story because it is not necessary to refer to any particular way of being adequate to make an interpretation. Similarly, other elements of stories, such as the expression of bizarre or socially inappropriate themes, touch on content but do not require specific thematic interpretation. If the expression of content stretches the constraints of conventionality, then such verbalizations reveal something about the story teller's approach to the task, which is independent of content (McGrew & Teglasi, 1990).

Although both content and form contribute to diagnostic understanding, some researchers (e.g., Hartman, 1949) have suggested that formal characteristics of T.A.T. responses be given increased emphasis because they can be more objectively determined and may be more revealing of certain aspects of personality. Leitch and Schafer (1947), working with children ranging in age from 5 to 17, concluded that for the purpose of diagnosis, the analysis of the formal structure of the stories and the formal characteristics of their content is more useful than an analysis of their thematic content. Furthermore, formal aspects of T.A.T. stories may be more readily amenable to group comparisons and standardization than content analysis (e.g., McGrew & Teglasi, 1990).

The narrative process can be distinguished from structural or formal features of stories. The *process* refers to how the story evolves and reflects the narrator's reaction to the task and organizational strategies to accomplish the task. The sequence of reactions and variations in task performance reflect changes in the process that may be associated with stimulus characteristics, inquiry, story context, or emotional reaction. The examiner discerns what seems to be provoking the respondent's vacillation or indecision and gauges the narrator's tendency to return to the main ideas after digressing.

Analysis of the story telling process reveals stumbling blocks or strengths that the individual brings to ordinary life experiences. The story telling process is closely tied to the quality of the story. The manner in which the story develops (process) leads to how it is structurally organized. Thus, *form* is a reflection of the story telling process. The analysis of the structural characteristics of the story includes the internal logic and sequencing of story elements. Other aspects of form may relate to how the story is expressed (e.g., long sentences, many adjectives, emphasis on detail, originality, rhythm, sequence).

Interpretive meaning emerges from an integration among form, narrative process, and content of stories, which should provide complementary data. The nature of the individual's experiences and concerns (content) is influenced by how those experiences or perceptions are organized (form). Information provided through an analysis of form and process greatly enhances the interpretation of content and, indeed, may be the chief source of interpretive conclusions when stories contain meager content. Themes do not speak for themselves; their meaning is derived according to the skill and knowledge of the interpreter who determines whether content reflects genuine concerns versus momentary associations to the stimulus or to previous story elements. Themes of violence, hostility, death, restriction, guilt, and frustration are commonly included in stories told to

T.A.T. stimuli by respondents of all types and all ages and are not peculiar to any clinical group (Eron, 1950). Such themes are pulled by the stimulus and are not necessarily indicative of the story teller's concerns or preoccupations. The story teller's organization of the narrative and the manner in which themes play out hold the key to their message.

The following are specific examples illustrating how inferences are made based on a combination of the formal and content characteristics of the story:

1. *Decision Making*   The narrator's decision making can be inferred from the extent of vacillation about what the stimulus is and from the ability to depart from the stimulus to maintain a story line. Likewise, information about decision making is revealed through content by looking at how characters make decisions and actively solve problems.

2. *Volitional Control*   Formal elements relate to the story teller's deliberate efforts to accomplish the task by incorporating the directions and the stimulus and by monitoring the progress of the story. Content elements relate to characters' intentional pursuit of goals or thoughtful resolutions of dilemmas versus being subject to uncontrollable external forces or negative circumstances that are not surmountable through realistic, constructive means.

3. *Specific Sensitivities*   The narrator's concerns are gleaned from thematic analysis. However, formal elements permit the interpreter to discern whether content reflects durable concerns or immediate reactions provoked by the stimuli. The pull of the stimulus must be clearly differentiated from the particular interests or concerns of the respondent.

4. *Emotions*   Intense emotions can be evident in the story teller's overreaction to the stimulus or cognitive disorganization in response to the task. Emotional attributes are also revealed by the characters' expression of apprehension, worry, fear, self-doubt, or inability to cope with the task or problem at hand.

Interpretation of Form and Process

Reaction to the Story Telling Task

The reaction to the story telling task provides information about how respondents deal with ambiguity and how they utilize the available cues. Some individuals immediately say, "I can't do this!" or insist that "It doesn't give me a story." Others may say, "This card is easy." Such comments usually indicate that the subject does not have the sense that the story is actively constructed. Rather, the individual is looking for cues from the picture or the examiner to provide guidance. An individual may cope with the task by deliberately searching for familiar stories (fairy tale, movie, or recent event) to superimpose on the picture rather than flexibly constructing a story by drawing on experiences relating to the stimuli.

The interpreter can distinguish between the initial reaction to the task or stimulus and subsequent coping style. Some respondents ask a lot of questions at first but make fewer inquiries as they get their bearings. Some begin by describing the stimulus before proceeding with the story. Some closely follow the four questions, giving themselves cues, whereas others pause to be led by the examiner. Some respondents give self-critical comments when they perceive that their stories are inadequate, yet others who tell bizarre or poorly integrated stories seem totally unaware of the quality of their performance. Still others blame the card or the examiner for the discomfort they feel in having to produce stories. It is important to keep in mind not only the formal aspect of a break in the internal logic of a story but also the process by which it was produced. For example, when asked a structuring question such as "What happened before?" respondents may provide details that are not logical because they have not been able to monitor the evolving story or because they have difficulty shifting to a different idea.

The formal characteristics of process and structure (approach to the task and the product itself) reveal the extent of anxieties produced by the task and methods of dealing with the discomfort. Verbalizations indicating anxiety or sensitivities, (e.g., "Oh my gosh" or "Oh boy") may be related to specific stimuli or may represent a generalized tendency to overreact to threatening elements of the stimulus. These reactions are also manifested in variation in language, narrative form, spontaneity, and fluency across cards or thematic content areas. Deviations from the usual pattern, greater restlessness, or other changes in demeanor are noted when confronted with different story telling cards as well as when responding to different tests within the battery (e.g., story telling versus intelligence test).

Sequence of Ideas

The meaning of the story is not only derived from the ideas expressed but also from how they are generated and organized: (1) Are ideas organized around a central theme? How are elaborations and details produced? Do they enhance the story, build suspense, or interrupt the flow of ideas? (2) What drives the progression of thoughts expressed? Are themes pulled directly by the stimulus? If so, does the narrator respond to isolated elements of the stimulus? Does the story progress in response to global affect generated by the card? Are ideas triggered by association to a previous idea? Does the next event occur simply because time passes? Does the narrator justify every word by referring back to the card or smoothly incorporate stimulus elements?

Problem Solving and Judgment

The following aspects of stories were considered as being indicative of the narrator's judgment and problem solving (McGrew & Teglasi, 1990): (1) action-outcome connection, (2) freedom from bizarre or highly unlikely content, (3) coordination of story content with stimulus, and (4) freedom from gross contradictions in the internal logic of the story.

Action-Outcome Connection

Adequacy of judgment is evident in the relation between characters' actions and their outcomes. The story teller's ability to incorporate actions to produce realistic solutions to predicaments depicted in the story reflect quality of judgment. Moreover, adequacy of judgment is indicated by the way the problem or goal is defined in relation to the stimulus. The appropriateness of instrumental actions taken to attain a goal, meet a need, overcome adversity, or to deal with some kind of problem depends on the nature of the dilemma. The key indicator of judgment is the relationship among goals, actions, emotions, and attitudes of the characters in their contribution to the outcome.

Story endings involve more projection than any other parts of the narrative and are most free of stimulus characteristics (Murstein, 1965). Arnold's (1962) emphasis on means-to-ends relationships in evaluating outcomes is consistent with the view that story endings represent projection beyond the stimulus. Likewise, Eron (1950) found few differences between subject populations of varying psychiatric health with regard to emotional tone of stories told to T.A.T. stimuli but found considerable differences when endings were compared.

Social Acceptability of Content

Bizarre and socially unacceptable responses represent poor judgment. Similarly, unusual verbalizations unrelated to the story, such as extreme self-derogation or expressions of content that are outside of the norm, reflect some disturbance in functioning or loss of deliberate control over behavior. The expression of bizarre content or atypical verbalization is more common among disturbed children and contributes to the distinctions between those classified as exhibiting serious emotional disturbance and normally adjusted peers (McGrew & Teglasi, 1990).

Coordination of Story Content with Stimulus

Quality of judgment is also revealed in the coordination of story content with the stimulus presented. The narrator's response can range from excessive dependence on the stimulus elements to total disregard for dealing with reality demands posed by the stimulus. Integration among the characters' affect, cognitions, and behaviors with the stimulus represents the respondent's mode of dealing with reality demands in an unstructured context. It is important to note how the narrator deals with the negative features of the stimulus (ignore, overreact, copes realistically). Furthermore, it is relevant to note what stimulus features are not recognized, as well as what elements are emphasized. A complex stimulus requires the narrator to decide what elements to focus on, whereas a picture that has many disparate elements requires a meaningful conceptual integration of those discrepancies. Respondents who cannot manage the stimulus complexity may focus narrowly on one stimulus element while ignoring the others or may deal successively with all of the elements by zeroing in on one aspect at a time without meaningfully relating them. The following questions pertain to the stimulus: Is the story predicated on the essential aspects of the stimulus in a way that captures its meaning? Is the narrator overly bound by the stimulus to justify the story? Are there areas of overelaboration or overinvolvement with the stimulus? Are there misperceptions or omissions of major stimulus elements? Is there a minimal relationship of the story to the stimulus or is the stimulus irrelevant?

Internal Logic

The organizational structure of the story is examined through the following: (1) *Logical sequence of events*—is the sequence of events free of contradictions? Is there inner logic and focus to the story? (2) *Connections among ideas*—Do story details relate to the central themes? Are there areas where the story teller got "carried away" by emotion or by loosely connected, associative cognitions?

Interpretation of Content

Framework for Content Interpretation

With the emergence of ego psychology, content analysis of projective stories focused on the organizing and integrative functions of the ego as they guide behavior (Arnold, 1962; Bellak, 1975; Wyatt, 1958). Accordingly, the story is not viewed as a patchwork of memories, string of images, or personal associations, but as a creative reorganization of experience evoked by the stimulus. Therefore, the meaning of the narrative cannot be extracted by segmenting individual themes from their context (Arnold, 1962). Furthermore, impairment in the integrative functions is indicated when the story content is a series of loosely related or disconnected thoughts.

The study of human thinking through narrative approaches has received increasing attention in several areas of psychology (Howard, 1991). Ethnographic studies have found that cultures are defined by organized, coherent belief systems, and that customs or discrete cultural traits cannot be isolated from the context that gives them meaning (LeVine, 1984). The organized nature of each culture is expressed in the dominant stories shared by members of that culture. Cross-cultural differences are viewed as being rooted in variations in the stories and in roles within stories. An individual's subjective culture (Triandis, 1972) represents that person's orientation toward life (story), including plans and goals as influenced by the societal and family milieu. Narratives elicited by story telling approaches to personality assessment represent the subjective culture. However, personal stories are embedded in a larger cultural context, which interpreters must consider when extracting their essential meaning.

Unit of Interpretation

The subjectivity or objectivity of the unit of analysis refers to whether the unit represents an inference or is coded directly from phrases of the story. The latter breaks the story into component parts; the former expresses the interpreter's synthesis of story elements. A completely objective unit of interpretation, such as counting the frequency of something specific (number of words, certain detail, type of thematic content), does not require interpretive judgment because it gives equal importance to every utterance without respect to context or evoking stimuli. Bellak (1986) indicates that breaking down responses to component parts detracts from meaningful interpretation. A sentence-by-sentence, word-by-word dissection of T.A.T. stories (Ritter & Eron, 1952; Rotter, 1946; Stein, 1955) has not been useful in differentiating normal from abnormal groups. Validation of units for diagnostic purposes and normative expectations go hand in hand. Given wide variations in content and the fact that no "correct" answer can be easily identified, then structural elements and the organization of the content is the most obvious basis for norms.

The Import

The import condenses the entire story into its essential message that expresses the narrator's conviction (Arnold, 1962). This basic unit of inference is based on careful consideration of all the story details, with particular emphasis on the nature of the actions in relation to the problem resolution. Two stories with similar plots and actions but with differing outcomes have different morals. Likewise, two stories with similar plots and outcomes, but with different actions, would convey different messages. For example, Arnold indicates that the story of a man who tries to rob a bank but is caught and sentenced to a long prison term expresses the conviction that crime does not pay. On the other hand, the story of a clever bank robber who gets away with the loot and lives in affluence expresses the conviction that crime does pay. The first moral suggests that the story teller would reject such antisocial action. The second narrator may never rob a bank but would generally expect to profit from luck, tricks, or clever deceit rather than from hard work.

According to Arnold, scoring imports rather than individual story elements eliminates undue emphasis on the picture and equalizes for story length, which is particularly advantageous for testing children with low verbal skills. Nevertheless, the manner of incorporating the stimulus features in the definition of the problem, goal, or dilemma plays a crucial role in the interpretation.

Bellak's (1986) analysis of the content is also an "attempt to restate the gist of the story" (p. 75) by reframing the main theme into five levels: descriptive, interpretive, diagnostic, symbolic, and elaborative. Bellak's interpretive level is similar to Arnold's (1962) import; both recast the story into a general statement of the convictions, beliefs, and attitudes held by the story teller. The import incorporates all the nuances in the story without introducing extraneous information. Arnold points out that such an attempt to abstract the essential meaning of the story from the narrator's point of view is analogous to the interpretations of a nondirective counselor who suspends judgment and reflects the essential message behind the client's words. Arnold gives the following guidelines for formulating a story import: (1) set aside theoretical preconceptions, (2) do not assume that everything is rooted in a specific childhood experience, (3) abstract the essential message from the details of the story as it applies to the story teller's life situations, and (4) write the import from the point of view of the main character, though whether or not the story teller identifies with that character is irrelevant.

The import expresses what is implied in the story from the point of view of the narrator, not the characters. However, the hero is frequently the point of reference for scoring categories (e.g., Bellak, 1986; Cox & Sargent, 1950). Stein (1955) proposed the use of one or more of the following criteria for identification of the hero in T.A.T. stories:

1. The first character about whom the subject chooses to speak
2. The character who occupies the story teller's attention throughout most of the story; the character whose thoughts and feelings are emphasized
3. The character who initiates the important activities
4. The character about whom the story revolves
5. The character who is being acted upon by most of the other individuals
6. The character who is most like the story teller in terms of age, sex, physical appearance, or psychological makeup

Arnold (1962) indicates that it may not be necessary to identify the hero to discern the meaning of the story. Relationships are reciprocal so that a victim implies a victimizer. Therefore, regardless of whose perspective is emphasized, an interaction between a bully and a helpless victim represents a view that relationships are unequal or that might makes right. The import of the following story, told by a girl age 15-4, expresses the same conviction regardless of whose perspective is taken. The narrative can be recast into its essential message from the point of view of the mother or child.

> Card 5: It looks like a mother going into a children's room, and she sees her child's gone. She's kinda surprised. I can't think of anything else really. (To?) I guess she gets her child back.

The import would ordinarily be written from the mother's perspective because she is the main character. From the mother's vantage point, the import would read as follows: A mother is surprised when her child is missing but eventually gets the child back without taking constructive action. The import from the child's perspective is: If a child goes away from home, she assumes that her parent (mother) will do nothing and returns. In both instances, the essential message conveys that neither the mother nor the daughter engages in purposeful behavior to understand, communicate, or resolve their interpersonal dilemma.

Positive and Negative Imports

The conviction or basic attitude determines whether the message is positive or negative, not the nature of the outcome or the prevailing mood of the characters. The actions that lead to success or failure express the narrator's convictions. Happy outcomes are positive when such outcomes are realistic, socially acceptable, and when actions and events leading to the happy endings are constructive and appropriate. Unhappy outcomes can also express a positive message, depending on the attitudes and actions leading to unhappiness. For example, failure that is attributed to lack of effort conveys a positive conviction.

Arnold (1962) developed an empirically based scoring system for imports that predicts success in various occupations. The formulation of the import emphasizes the central issue of the story, which can be: (1) task to be accomplished or goal to be reached; (2) an interpersonal conflict to be reconciled; (3) loss, setback, or adverse circumstance to be overcome; and (4) moral dilemma to be decided. Within these four content areas, the interpreter focuses on how conflict is resolved or goals are attained in terms of the characters' intentions and actions.

Positive and negative convictions are also distinguished according to the following formal considerations, which expand on the content emphasis provided by Arnold: (1) *The nature of the problem or conflict*—Positive imports account for the stimulus in the problem definition and clearly delineate a goal or dilemma rather than being vague or comprised of mere association to the stimulus; (2) *The type of action and intentions*—Imports are positive when characters' actions are deliberate, planned, and proactive rather than reactive, aimless, or haphazard; (3) *The outcomes in relation to the problem set and efforts expended*—Imports are positive when the outcome is reasonable in relation to the conflict posed and actions taken; (4) *Welfare of all relevant characters*—Imports are positive when the outcome presents a meaningful resolution for all concerned; and (5) *The story structure*—Imports are positive when the story is organized and coherent.

Combining Form, Process, and Content to Formulate the Import

Not everyone tells a story. However, the production can still be meaningfully interpreted based on the process and formal elements. Arnold did not consider formal elements in formulating the import. However, it is apparent that the meaning of the story cannot be based entirely on content. Sometimes, content is so disorganized that the stories do not express a conviction but reflect the respondent's struggle to cope with the task. In these cases, the import is based almost exclusively on the process of telling the story or the manner of refusing to engage in the task. The following three stories told by a boy, age 7-1, with low-average intelligence illustrates this point.

> Card 2: Two ladies and two wives. Two books and none looks on the lady and a man and a cemetery. (Q) One day the man has a horse. He was a farmer. Was a cemetery made out of rocks? These two big mountains were here. They might explode.

The following import incorporates the process and content of the story: When a person looks around and takes stock of the scene around him (concrete card description) but can't make sense of what is seen, he worries about unpredictable catastrophies.

> Card 6BM: Father and mother in a house. They have drapes and windows. Had hands. One day they went in this house. Didn't like this house. It was spooky in it. (Q) That's all.

Again, the import is based largely on the form of the narrative and process of story telling: One (parents) can only see what's on the surface and feels "spooky" without understanding what's happening.

> Card 13B: Boy sitting down in the barn—no shoes. One day he was in this old house. He didn't like it in there. Because there were robbers. (Q) Some men in the house. (Q) Nothing else.

Again, the following import extracts the essential message from the process, form, and content: It is difficult for a boy to understand what's going on, and he doesn't know what to do, though he expects bad things to happen. The cast of characters differs in all three stories (in keeping with the stimuli), but the story telling process, the form, and the essential message remain the same.

Explanatory Concepts

The interpretation seeks to go beyond the import to the formulation of explanatory concepts. For instance, if the respondent expresses the conviction that relationships are unequal (e.g., others are domineering), the examiner tries to discern the reasons for the development and maintenance of such a conviction, which may be attributed to one or more of the following: (1) lack of empathic connection, (2) inability to incorporate different viewpoints, (3) difficulty dealing with the unstructured task in which case relationships might be difficult since they are also unstructured, and (4) impulsivity or nonreflection to inner experience.

The association between story themes and explanatory concepts is evident through an understanding of attributes such as distractibility and their likely impact on subjective perceptions of life events that are expressed in the narratives. The impact of distractibility is also evident in behaviors and interpersonal interactions, as well as variations in performance across tasks with differing demands for concentration and organization. The relationship of response patterns to theory also provides the basis for explanatory concepts. A full understanding of the story is possible only when process, structure, and content are analyzed in relation to one another and in relation to other data.

Interpretive Issues

The import is a judgment of the interpreter about the story teller and not about the character or story per se. When abstracting the essential message of the story, the interpreter makes decisions about the following: (1) What should be emphasized in the interpretation? (2) How much of the content can be taken at face value? (3) Is the conviction expressed in a particular story highly situation-specific or more general?

What Should Be Emphasized?

Stories reveal preoccupations, motivating attitudes, and convictions that are acquired through organization of past experience (Arnold, 1962). For example, if an individual has come to believe in the efficacy of self-determined effort, then such content is included in the stories. But what aspects of stories should be emphasized in attempting to distill the story teller's ideologies?

Murstein (1965) indicated that the *who* (characters) and the *what* (events) aspects of the stories are most dependent on the stimulus and least related to projection. Story endings have more projection beyond stimulus demands than any other part of the story. Next is the story teller's interpretation of why events happened. Accordingly, Murstein (1965) suggested that in the interpretation, emphasis should be placed on story endings and on the reasons why events happened. This approach is consistent with Arnold's (1962) assertion that story actions and outcomes are shaped by the narrator's motivating tendencies.

Lindzey (1952) made two assumptions relevant to the interpretive significance of particular story elements. First, themes that are clearly related to the stimulus material are less likely to be interpretively significant than those that do not appear to be directly determined by the stimulus cues. And second, recurrent themes are likely to reflect the preoccupations of the story teller.

Should Content Be Taken at Face Value?

As stated previously, a full understanding of the story content includes the interpretation of process and structure. Thematic content is evoked from memory and may not reflect ideas that preoccupy the story teller. Rather, themes may represent reactions to the immediate stimulus or express stereotypic ideas that are "borrowed" rather than some inner representation of actual experience (Lindzey, 1952). On the other hand, elements that seem to be missing from the story shed light on components of experience that have not been integrated. Therefore, a pure content analysis without consideration of form and process could be highly misleading. Silliness, superficiality, or phony sentimentality, as well as ostentatious use of language or knowledge, must be interpreted in relation to the content.

If a hopeless, negative tone pervades stories told to T.A.T. cards, the interpreter cannot assume that the narrator is depressed or unhappy. If the feelings expressed are directly tied to the stimulus, the conclusion may be that the narrator could not get past the immediate pull. The narrator's inability to describe characters who alter their circumstance through constructive action suggests that feelings are reactions to immediate occurrences rather than to more inner-directed considerations. Such a person is easily swayed by appearances and makes decisions without weighing all the relevant information. Likewise, a protocol portraying stereotyped or vague but socially appropriate interactions may not represent genuine intentions.

The following stories told by a sixth-grade boy do not reflect the narrator's inner convictions or actual concerns. The narratives evolve without meaning attached to the words and represent a glib, superficial effort to get through the task.

> Card 1: There's not much going on in this one. He's planning on committing suicide. But then his mother comes in and makes him play his violin. He's getting better, now he's happy. When the picture was taken was when he was planning to commit suicide; now he's very very happy. He's a good violin player and he's a professional and he plays in a recording studio and makes a lot of money and he's very happy and he didn't commit suicide.

The import has to account for the extreme fluctuation of prevailing mood states that hinge on rather unrealistic changes in external circumstances rather than emanating from within the individual. An import combining process, form, and content might say: If the demands of your current situation are intolerable, you are devastated (contemplate suicide) but then your despondency is quickly overcome when you imagine an unlikely turn of events that leads to fame, fortune, and happiness.

This import implies that the content reflects momentary whims, unrealistic wishes, or superficial connections rather than being based on actual experience. It is not likely that the narrator is contemplating suicide, as suggested by the distinction between latent and manifest content (Karon, 1981; Tomkins, 1947). Since the mention of suicide did not refer to behavior but only to a passing thought (probably feigned), the probability of carrying out a suicide is remote. The content of the following story told by the same child has an unreasonably happy ending, which also cannot be taken at face value.

> Card 4: This man is, umm, a cowboy. He wants to go camping in the desert catching cows. This is his wife and she doesn't want him to go. So his wife threatens to kill him; then he threatened back. Then they decide she can go to the desert with him. From now on they live happily ever after in the desert catching cows.

Again, feelings, actions, reactions, and relationships are exaggerated. Individual differences leading to conflict are neither accepted nor realistically resolved. Intrusive threats force a glib compromise where characters disregard each others' wishes yet "live happily ever after."

The import might be as follows: A husband and wife threaten each other to get what they want and finally compromise in ways that don't deal with their differences.

Story interpretation includes the consideration of elements that are missing based on what is presented in the stimulus. Therefore, exclusion of feelings or content portrayed by the stimulus needs to be interpreted. Similarly, omission of expected content based on the plot also requires interpretation. The following story told by a 19-year-old incarcerated male (below average WAIS-R IQ) incorporates the characters and feelings depicted in the stimulus but has a glaring omission in the content.

> Card 10: Looks like father and son. Umm, looks like they had a death in the family and the kid, son, mother died. Him and his father are hugging. The father's telling him everything is going to be alright and the son is happy he has someone to depend on and tell him everything will be alright. The son feels good that he has someone to depend on. (End?) Like a happy story cause they look like they love each other and they're just hugging that they got each other.

What is clearly missing from the story is the continuity of the inner life of the characters who react to the loss on the basis of their immediate need. As long as the boy has someone to depend on, the death of his mother is irrelevant. The story is "happy" because the people in the picture "look like they love each other." The reaction of the characters and the resolution of the tensions are externally determined (by the stimulus and by the support available). Relationships are not reciprocal but judged according to one character's feelings in the moment. The lack of inner continuity to relationships suggests that the narrator's need for external support and guidance is excessive.

According to these considerations, the import of this story is as follows: When a child loses a parent, he can be happy as long as others provide constant reassurance and support.

Is the Conviction General or Specific?

A conviction can be general or can apply under specific conditions or in the context of certain types of relationships. The level of generality of an interpretation is greater when there is: (1) absence of qualifying statements or special circumstances, (2) repetition of themes across cards, or (3) convergence of process, form, and content.

The issue of qualifying elements or special conditions relates to two factors. First is the fact that different stimuli portray different circumstances and relationships so that the convictions expressed may be peculiar to the relationships and situation depicted in each card. Perceptions about peer relationships could differ from attitudes toward authorities, and these differences can be gleaned from patterns across cards depicting various types of interpersonal interactions. Likewise, the story teller may display different attitudes toward academic work or achievement in other areas. Second, the narrator may qualify or explain a character's actions as being unique to specific circumstances (e.g., the character was provoked) or may otherwise distance the self from the story content.

The *principle of redundancy* has been articulated by Lindzey (1952) in terms of recurring thematic content. However, redundancy is even more apparent in the process of telling the story and in the formal features or structure of the narrative because they are not as dependent on the stimulus as is the content. Although specific content varies across cards, meaningful inferential units that incorporate the form and process tend to be more consistent.

The *principle of convergence* assumes that different ways of looking at stories should yield complementary conclusions. The narrator's mode of information processing, affective reaction, and manner of interpreting situations are revealed in many ways that converge. This idea was alluded to by Arnold (1962) when she indicated that similar convictions are evident regardless of which of the four thematic categories the interpreter chooses, and regardless of which character's perspective is emphasized. Different vantage points for scoring should yield the same conclusion. The principle of convergence is based on the assumption that the content of experience is linked to the emotional and cognitive process employed in their perception and organization. Therefore, one goal of thematic interpretation is to uncover the bases for particular preoccupations or convictions indicated by the systematic convergence of formal and content elements.

The issue of situational-specific conclusions relates to the entire testing process and organization of the psychological report. To obtain corroboration for a general inference, the interpreter looks for repetitive or consistent patterns of relationship with other tests and with information obtained from teachers, parents, history, and educational records. To obtain corroboration for situational or conditional interpretations, the evaluator looks for systematic variations in responses to different types of card stimuli, tasks, and other sources of information. A test-by-test interpretation may yield conclusions that are task specific. However, the integration of the patterns of convergences and discrepancies will reveal the conditions under which an interpretation is relevant.

Summary

The content of projective stories reflects the subjective world of the respondent, which is the product of the manner of organization and integration of past experience. The convergence of form, process, and content within the stories provides a basis for extracting the essential meaning of the narrative. A practical approach, emphasizing quality of cognitions, reality testing, and integration, rather than symbolic interpretation, is consistent with the ego-analytic orientation.

CHAPTER 6

Administration

Any unstructured task is sensitive to deviations from the usual administrative context and procedures. Even minimal cues can guide responses so that inadvertent reinforcement or instructional sets can influence the production (Dana, 1982). Therefore, examiners must be able to evaluate their impact on the composition of each protocol.

The T.A.T. is anxiety provoking for both adults and children because of its ambiguity (Newmark, Hetzel, & Frerking, 1974; Newmark, Wheeler, Newmark, & Stabler, 1975). To make the respondent as comfortable as possible, it is necessary to establish rapport prior to administering such tests. Furthermore, flexibility is required for the examiner to respond when something has the potential to disrupt the administration. A child may become upset by a card, refuse to continue, and even toss it aside or stomp on it.

General Procedures

It is best to administer the projective measure toward the end of a battery for three reasons: (1) the respondent's concerns about the testing and about the relationship with the examiner can be clarified in the context of relatively less threatening tasks, (2) the respondent will feel more comfortable about the task after having established rapport through earlier interactions, and (3) any anxiety or resistance generated by the projective test will not interfere with subsequent tasks.

Directions

The original directions for T.A.T. administration (Murray, 1943) presented the task as a "test of imagination, one form of intelligence" and prompted the subject to "make up as dramatic a story as you can." Some respondents feel at a disadvantage with these instructions because they don't view themselves as imaginative, whereas others are concerned with the idea that a *test* should have "correct" answers. Furthermore, encouraging stories to be dramatic makes it difficult to evaluate the child who displays "unbridled spontaneity" because the directions have given implicit permission. Concepts like creativity and intelligence, or even tests may have differentiated impact and thereby complicate the interpretation. Peterson (1990) points out that such instructions are dishonest since neither intelligence nor creativity is of particular interest. The directions are usually modified to exclude reference to creativity and intelligence.

Peterson (1990) argues that the instructions for T.A.T. administration should give as few cues as possible. He suggests the following: "Tell me a story about what might be happening in this picture" (p. 194). The absence of any further guidance is designed to permit greater leeway for narrators to reveal their conception of self and other. For instance, some individuals may dwell on the immediate present and ignore the past or future. However, the more structured instructions proposed by Murray are advantageous with children and adolescents because they facilitate the narrative process and provide a vehicle for subsequent queries by the examiner. Such prompts are frequently necessary to obtain sufficient material for interpretation.

Murray's (1943) basic instructions require the incorporation of four elements into a complete story that has a beginning, middle, and end: (1) current situation, (2) past circumstances, (3) feelings and thoughts of characters, and (4) outcome. As long as these basic elements of the instructions are included, the examiner can alter the wording of the instructions to suit the cognitive level of each individual respondent.

General instructions for younger children are as follows (Murray, 1943):

I am going to show you some pictures, and I would like you to tell me a story for each one. In your story please tell: What is happening in the picture? What happened before? What are people thinking and feeling? How does it all turn out in the end? So I'd like you to tell a whole story with a beginning, middle, and ending. You can make up any story you want. Do you understand? I'll write down your story. Here's the first card.

The examiner can repeat parts of the instructions if the child looks puzzled. If the child seems hesitant, the examiner may show the first card and ask what is happening in the picture. Further prompting can be more general, such as "Go on." If needed, the examiner can prompt with, "What happened before?" Inquiries are given only as needed to assure the inclusion of all elements requested in the directions.

The directions for older children are as follows (Murray, 1943):

I am going to show you some pictures, one at a time, and your task will be to make up a story for each card. In your story, be sure to tell what has led up to the event shown in the picture, describe what is happening at the moment, what the characters are feeling and thinking, and then give the outcome. Tell a complete story with a beginning, middle, and end. Do you understand? I will write your stories verbatim as you tell them. Here's the first card.

If a child asks a question requesting more structure, such as "Should I give people names?" the reply should be "It's up to you." Similarly, if a child points to an object in the picture and asks what it is, the examiner should give essentially the same response.

Seating

It is helpful if the child cannot see what the examiner is writing. The examiner should show interest in the child's story but generally keep a low profile and minimize cues conveyed by facial expressions or verbalizations. Side-by-side seatings would tend to minimize such clues. However, it is advisable to keep the same seating arrangement utilized during the administration of previous tests in the battery unless the test is introduced at a different session.

Encouragement

Even though Murray (1943) considers the T.A.T. suitable for children as young as 4 years, many youngsters have difficulty going beyond simple card description. Children may hesitate because they need direction and cannot maintain a sequence of behaviors without feedback or guidance from adults. The task of the examiner is to encourage the child to comply with the instructions to include the four major story elements. Children are not admonished by statements such as "Don't just describe the card." Rather, after having produced a description, they are prompted by specific questions such as "What happened before?"

After having given a prompt, the child's response is accepted even if it seems to miss the point. For instance, no further inquiry is given when a child, having been asked how things "turned out," replies with "Good." Another example is that of a child who was asked what the person was feeling. The response was, "The table." This response was quite literal, and it is important to note this conceptual level. It may be helpful if subsequent inquiries begin with "How is he or she feeling?"

The child is given a chance to reveal how he or she approaches the story telling task with a minimum of cues. Thus, the examiner must avoid leading questions that provide sets for subsequent responding. Rapaport, Gill, and

Schafer (1975) defined a *suggestive question* as an inquiry that makes the respondent realize that there are other possibilities besides the ones spontaneously given. If a child tells more than one story or something doesn't make sense, the examiner doesn't say anything. Similarly, the examiner does not ask what the story teller saw in the picture or what part of the stimulus is being responded to. Occasionally, when a pronoun reference is unclear, the examiner may ask to whom the pronoun refers.

Children sometimes ask what the violin in Card 1 or the gun in Card 3BM might be. The best reply is something like: "You can make it whatever you like in your story." Similarly, a child who uses the instructions as an outline and gives very barren stories that still include all of the elements is allowed to proceed.

When a child asks questions or requests assistance, the examiner must be careful not to change the rules of the game and to resist giving extra cues beyond those indicated by the instructions. The reasons why a child is having difficulty are important to consider. Is the child overly cautious, concrete in thinking, or immobilized by anxiety? Some children do not catch on to the idea that they are creating the story. They expect the picture to bring to mind a prefabricated story. Thus, they may say, "I don't know a story to that one" or "This one is hard." The examiner may remind the child, "Remember you are to make up the story about the picture. The story is not in the picture. You decide what's going on and what will happen. Let's begin by your telling me what's happening now." The examiner must avoid the temptation to help the child by starting off a story even with something as innocuous as "Once upon a time."

Generally, if the child merely hesitates, an encouraging statement such as "Go on" should be given in lieu of a specific prompt, which is offered only when necessary. The examiner uses discretion to provide encouragement as the situation warrants, with the understanding that the stance typically used in more structured tests is altered when administering a projective technique. For instance, when giving an IQ test, the examiner clarifies misunderstandings and, within limits allowed by standardization, offers support and structure to encourage optimal responding. In contrast, the child's typical response to an unstructured situation is allowed to emerge during administration of projective stories.

The Standards for Educational and Psychological Testing (AERA, 1985) specifically state that, in administering tests with open-ended responses, "special care is needed [with such approaches] to ensure that the instruments are administered in a facilitating atmosphere without suggestions or cues that might influence the response given, unless such prompting is specifically planned as part of the test" (p. 46). On rare occasions, the examiner feels quite certain that the child has been given ample opportunity to demonstrate his or her response style and that no further material will be obtained without additional inquiry. In such cases, prompts that depart from the usual procedures, such as questions about why a character does something or how another character may feel, could give significant information.

Recording Responses

The examiner writes verbatim the child's story and any incidental comments. Questions or encouraging comments made by the examiner are also recorded. Rapaport, Gill, and Schafer (1975) suggest that hesitations or long pauses in relating the story should be indicated by dashes or by the number of seconds elapsed. Thus, the record reflects not only the content of the story but also the manner in which it was told. The process by which the story evolves reflects the child's style of coping with the unstructured task and becomes an important ingredient in the interpretation. Where story content is meager, process and formal characteristics can be quite revealing of the sources of a child's presenting problem.

The biggest challenge in producing an accurate written record of the story is difficulty keeping up with the youngster's rate of delivery. A helpful technique is to develop abbreviations for frequently occurring words. Still, if the examiner has fallen behind the child's pace, reading aloud what is written clues the child to slow down (Rapaport, Gill, & Schafer, 1975). It is important that the examiner read aloud in a neutral voice. For example, a student examiner typically gave a questioning inflection at the end; the child responded by changing the response every time the examiner read aloud. Children are quite sensitive to an adult's tone and may feel that their response is being questioned and that a correction or clarification is being sought.

Children may ask, "You're writing down everything?" The response might be, "Yes, I am so that I can remember what you say." When asked, "Are you going to show these to my mom?" The answer is usually "no." Children are apt to say, "Don't write that," when they are making incidental comments or when they change their mind about part of the story. Lightly cross out the offending parts so that they are still legible, and continue. Generally, it is best to write in a notebook or clipboard with the examiner positioned in a way that the child cannot see what is being recorded. This will minimize concerns about what the examiner is writing.

The T.A.T. was intended for administration in an interpersonal situation that dictates that the pacing of the stories be responsive to the examiner's writing speed. Furthermore, such a procedure leaves the respondent without time to censor or polish stories. On very rare occasions, a child who has difficulty narrating stories may do better when permitted to write them down. According to research reviewed by Dana (1982), stories given orally differ considerably from responses dictated into a recorder. Furthermore, group responses differ from responses to an individual administration.

At times, it is difficult for examiners to keep up with the respondent's pace. The use of a tape recorder may facilitate the session and provides a helpful adjunct to hand recording, particularly when the examiner continues to write as much of the child's verbatim responses as possible. Sole reliance on the tape recorder has the following disadvantages: (1) the child's ability to modulate the speed of delivery to the interpersonal requirements cannot be assessed; (2) since a written or typed form of the T.A.T. protocol should be available in the child's record, using the tape recorder usually entails the examiner's spending more time later transcribing the responses; and (3) tape recorders may not work. Background noises or the child moving about may preclude a comprehensible recording.

Card Selection

In developing the T.A.T., Murray (1938) selected 30 pictures and included one blank card. These cards were organized into four parallel sets of 20 pictures, individualized according to age and gender of the subject. The cards are numbered from 1 to 20, with some containing letter suffixes to designate them as appropriate for boys (B), girls (G), females over 14 (F), males over 14 (M), or combinations (GF, BM). Cards that have numbers but no letters are considered suitable for any age (4 and up) and either gender. The primary basis for inclusion in each set was the assumption that individuals relate best to characters who are the same sex, comparable age, and face similar interpersonal issues.

The original instructions required the administration of 20 cards over two sessions. However, most examiners use fewer cards because the T.A.T. comprises only a part of a typical test battery. Examiners should administer enough pictures to ensure high reliability and maximize confidence in their inferences, while avoiding tedium and using time effectively. The number of cards considered optimum by most clinicians varies between 10 and 12 (Bellak, 1986). The most common approach is to select a basic set of T.A.T. cards that is generally useful (for any age and gender) and then to supplement this set with 2 to 4 cards particularly suited to elicit themes relevant to understanding of a particular respondent.

Some T.A.T. cards elicit more useful material than others, and clinicians tend to select cards that bring out the most relevant material (Gurel & Ullman, 1958; Ullman, 1957). The selection of cards by clinicians is generally not in accord with their original designations regarding their suitability for specific ages or gender. In clinical practice, cards such as 3BM, 6BM, and 7BM, which were originally intended for boys and older males, are considered equally meaningful and appropriate for girls and women (Arnold, 1962; Bellak, 1986; Henry, 1956;

Karon, 1981). The present writer agrees with Arnold's (1962) statement that many of the male pictures are preferable for both sexes because they elicit richer and more complex themes. Six of the nine cards considered by Bellak (1986) as essential for testing males were included among the cards he deemed essential for females (6BM, 7BM, and 12M were substituted for 6GF, 7GF, and 9GF). Karon (1981) found 3BM the single most useful card for both men and women. Bellak (1986) also indicated a preference for 3BM over 3GF.

There is considerable agreement among clinicians in their preferences for specific T.A.T. cards. For instance, Arnold's list of preferred cards (1, 2, 3BM, 4, 6BM, 7BM, 8BM, 10, 11, 13MF, 14, 16, and 20) include all but one (12M) of Bellak's (1986) *essential* and *male* cards (1, 2, 3BM, 4, 6BM, 7BM, 11, 12M, and 13MF). The preferences indicated by Rabin and Haworth (1960) for children between the ages of 7 and 11 (1, 3BM, 7GF, 8BM, 12M, 13B, 14, and 17BM) and for adolescents (1, 2, 5, 7GF, 12F, 12M, 15, 17BM, and 18GF) include many of the cards favored by both Arnold and Bellak. What is important to note is that with some exception (e.g., 13MF), the productive cards seem to work equally well for all ages and both sexes. Furthermore, cards with more bizarre content and cards such as 3GF, which depicts a person immersed in thought with no additional cues, are not as useful. This writer has found the following cards highly productive for children and adolescents of both genders: 1, 2, 3BM, 4, 5, 6BM, 7GF, and 8BM. Others that are used frequently, depending on age and the referral issues, are: 7BM, 10, 12M, 13B, 13MF, 14, and 17BM. Table 6–1 summarizes selected studies on the utility of T.A.T. cards.

There is a logic to the sequence of cards, and they should be administered in numerical order (Arnold, 1962; Bellak, 1986; Karon, 1981). For example, Cards 1 and 2 are relatively benign, whereas cards 3BM and 4 depict more threatening scenes. Card 2 has more disparate elements, and younger children, individuals functioning at lower conceptual levels, or those experiencing difficulty focusing on the most relevant aspect of a complex stimulus have considerable difficulty integrating these discrepant pieces into a coherent and logical story. Instead, they may describe the card or focus on one element at a time. Card 4 requires children to grapple with discord in adult relationships and reconcile the physical proximity of the characters with their disparate emotions. Card 8BM portrays a scene that is also difficult for some respondents to integrate. In addition, this card depicts threatening elements that have a disorganizing impact on vulnerable individuals. It was the most useful card in differentiating emotionally disturbed youngsters from a normal comparison group (McGrew & Teglasi, 1990).

The reader is referred to the following authors who provide descriptions of each card (Murray, 1943) and some general comments pertaining to their usefulness: Bellak, 1954; 1975; 1986; Dana, 1982; Eron, 1950; Henry, 1956; Karon, 1981; Rapaport, Gill, and Schafer, 1975; and Stein, 1955.

Table 6–1 • Summary of Most Productive T.A.T. Cards

Author(s)	Subject	Method	Cards
Weisskopf (1950)	Undergraduates	Compiled list of 5 cards that elicited most and least projection	High transcendence: 6BM, 4, 7BM, 7GF, 2. Low transcendence: 12M, 13G, 17GF, 20, 9BM
Hartman (1970)	Over 200 psychologists	To select the most "valuable" T.A.T. cards on the basis of clinical experience with adults and children	Adults: 13MF, 1, 6BM, 4, 7BM, 2, 3BM, 10, 12M, 8BM, 18GF. Children: 1, 3BM, 6BM, 4, 7BM, 2, 3BM, 10, 12M, 8BM, 4, 10, 12M, 16, 18GF. Overall: 1, 2, 3BM, 4, 6BM, 7BM, 13 MF, 8BM.
Irvin and Vander Woude (1971)	25 male undergraduates with history of military service	Authors rank-ordered all 20 T.A.T. cards on the basis of number of themes elicited and suggested a basic set.	Basic set: 13MF, 1, 6BM, 4, 3BM, 7BM, 9BM, 2, 20, 14, 11.

Study	Sample	Method	Results
Haynes and Peltier (1985)	107 psychologists in 35 juvenile forensic centers were surveyed. Their responses were based on practice largely with male adolescent delinquents who were given a complete psychological evaluation.	Frequency of usage was indicated for each T.A.T. card.	Rank order of frequency of use: 1, 6BM, 3BM, 13MF, 8BM, 4, 7BM, 2, 5, 12M, 14, 10, 17BM, 18BM, 16, 9BM, 11, 20, 15, 19. The majority of subjects reported using between 6–10 cards.
Cooper (1981)	25 11-year-olds, 25 14-year-olds, 25 17-year-olds	10 most valuable cards were selected at each age based on criterion of thematic frequency.	Suggested basic TAT: Age 11: 3BM, 4, 8BM, 10, 15, 6BM, 7BM, 1, 17BM, 18BM. Age 14: 6BM, 4, 3BM, 8BM, 10, 15, 13B, 18BM, 7BM, 1, 20. Age 17: 6BM, 4, 18BM, 3BM, 7BM, 10, 8BM, 20, 13B, 1. Overall: 4, 6BM, 3BM, 8BM, 18BM, 15, 7BM, 1, 13B.
Newmark & Flouranzano (1973)	30 white-male, hospitalized, psychiatric patients between ages of 26–49 (M = 34.2; S.D. = 4.8) with at least average intelligence. All diagnosed as psychoneurotic with absence of cultural dysfunction.	Similar to Irvin and Woude (1971). All 20 cards for adult males given individually. Criterion was number of themes elicited.	Rank order of cards deemed most valuable: 4, 1, 3BM, 13MF, 12M, 18BM, 8BM, 2, 6BM, 7BM, 14, 10, 5, 20, 17BM, 9BM, 15, 16, 19, 11.

Table 6–1 • *(Continued)*

Author(s)	Subject	Method	Cards
Ullman (1957)	5 most recent T.A.T. protocols administered by each of 35 clinical psychology trainees at a VA neuropsychiatric hospital. 175 were males between the ages of 19–59 who were hospitalized and referred for diagnostic evaluation.	Selection of cards was done by each examiner. All subjects dictated their response to the examiner.	Top 10 in frequency of use: 6BM, 1, 4, 13MF, 3BM, 7BM, 12M, 2, 8BM, 18BM. Top 10 in frequency of emotional words: 6BM, 4, 7BM, 3BM, 1, 13MF, 18BM, 2, 15, 8BM. Conclusions: The two sets are remarkably similar. Clinicians select cards on basis of productivity.
Eron (1950)	Groups of normal individuals hospitalized, nonhospitalized neurotics, and psychotics	Rank order of T.A.T. pictures on the basis of number of themes each elicits.	13MF, 20, 18BM, 6BM, 3BM, 4, 12M, 15, 7BM, 10, 17BM, 8BM, 9BM, 14, 1, 2, 5, 11, 16, 19.

Summary

Administration procedures for eliciting projective stories warrant careful scrutiny. The ambiguity of the task makes it likely that the respondent will use subtle or unintended cues to guide the production. To produce a record that reflects both narrative content and story telling process, responses are recorded verbatim with any incidental comments, hesitations, gestures, or other behaviors. Likewise, all probes or encouraging remarks made by the examiner are included.

CHAPTER 7

Cognition

Cognitive styles and perceptual patterns have been viewed as the basic organizers of experiences that shape the development of personality structure (Forgus & Shulman, 1979; Messick, 1987; Shapiro, 1965). According to a cognitive view, maladjustment is due to the misperceptions of the self in relation to the environment and to other people. Some personality theorists emphasize the control of basic cognitive categories over person perception and affective reaction (e.g., Kelly, 1963; Lewin, 1935). Problems with attention, cognitive organization, and conceptualization are reflected in personality development (Millon, 1981; Shapiro, 1965). Sullivan (1953) refers to *selective inattention* as the failure to perceive significant details in the surroundings in a manner that impedes reality testing. It should be noted that selective inattention can be adaptive as well as maladaptive (Rothbart & Derryberry, 1981).

The connection between personality and cognition is also evident in the componential subtheory of intelligence (Sternberg, 1985), which includes both cognitive and noncognitive variables as inherent to the concept of intelligence. This conceptualization casts traditional psychometric approaches to measuring intelligence into information-processing terms and provides links between cognition and personality. Three components of information processing are: (1) *metacomponents* (qualities of planning, monitoring, organizing, or restructuring information); (2) *performance components* (specific skills used to execute the plans); and (3) *knowledge-acquisition components* (incorporation of new knowledge that is driven by the metacomponents).

Responding to the environment is a matter of information-processing (cognitive) style and not ability in its narrow, classical definition (Messick, 1984). The componential approach incorporates personality, motivation, and values as aspects of cognitive style. Cognitive psychologists have become increasingly interested in projective techniques as a method of assessing cognitive functioning such as problem-solving strategies (Sobel, 1981) and cognitive style, which are revealed in the form and content of responses to ambiguous stimuli. Projective stories are not fantasies or loose associations but are products of deliberate cognitive operations (Arnold, 1962; Holt, 1960, 1961). These aspects of thinking can be gleaned from the manner in which the stimulus is used, the elements of the picture to which the story teller attends, approach to reconciliation of discrepancies, logic and complexity of the plots, integration of different levels of experience, and the ability of the story teller to monitor the evolving story.

Whitely (1966) viewed the T.A.T. as a behavioral task that requires planning and organization. He based his scoring system of the T.A.T. on a definition of *adaptive ego functioning,* which includes "each individual's capacity to perceive subtleties and nuances in situations, then act in response to these perceptions" (p. 4). Adaptive skills can be viewed from two vantage points: the formal characteristics of the story and the problem-solving skills exhibited by story characters. Accounting for stimulus subtleties in problem identification is important for adaptive behavior. Leitch and Schafer (1947) reported that psychotic children distort T.A.T. stimuli more than nonpsychotic children. Whitely incorporated the following as important aspects of ego functioning into the scoring criteria: acceptance of responsibility for actions, governing one's impulses, directing energy to pursue activities, and planful considerations of long-range consequences by the connection over time between means and ends. Adaptive skills are inferred when story characters act in terms of long-range interest and accurately anticipate the future consequences of their actions. These ego capabilities of characters require the metacognitive skills described by Sternberg (1985) and others.

Characteristics of thought processes are reflected in the stories. The two areas of cognition covered in this chapter include perceptual integration and concrete versus abstract thinking. Subsequent chapters deal with attentional and integrative processes.

Perceptual Integration

Telling stories to picture stimuli involves the integration of perceptual and conceptual processes. How well the story content, structure, and process are integrated with the perception of the stimulus is a key element in understanding the story teller's approach to the task. Perceptual integration refers to (1) accounting for major features of the stimulus, (2) accuracy in interpreting subtleties in the interpersonal cues, and (3) positing of conceptual relationships among the perceptual features rather than focusing on stimulus elements in isolation.

Piaget emphasizes the distinction between perceptual and conceptual processes (Flavell, 1963). Individuals with intact sensory systems often arrive at different interpretations of seemingly identical sensory input. With development and increasing experience, individuals learn to rely on acquired conceptual structures such as sets, expectations, or schema to organize and integrate perceptual inputs into meaningful information. Object permanence and the various conservations are common examples of such structures (Flavell, 1963; Piaget, 1954). Thus, the ratio of sensory to symbolic/conceptual processes decreases with development. Piaget reasons that due to *centration* in perceptual processes (focusing on a narrow aspect of the object), the perceiver distorts the object by formulating partial impressions apart from the context. Centration is not a purely developmental phenomenon and can occur at any age because of cognitive or attentional limitations that interfere with reflection or conceptual integration. In relation to projective stories, the question is whether the narrator responds to direct perceptual input or posits a conceptual relationship among the various perceptual elements. A smoothly operating conceptual framework permits the narrator to incorporate the stimulus and instructions to produce a story that includes all of the required elements in a way that captures the "gist" of the entire stimulus configuration and complies with the directions.

Degree of congruence with the stimulus is on a continuum that has two dimensions: (1) accuracy in defining stimulus properties, and (2) positing a meaningful relationship among relevant stimulus features. Dana's (1959) concept of perceptual range refers to the inclusion of expected elements of a stimulus, and scoring is based on adherence to norms for mentioning designated stimulus and story elements available for several T.A.T. cards (male and female versions of 2, 3, 4, 6, and 7). The following story told to Card 2 of the T.A.T. by a girl in kindergarten illustrates centration on one element of a stimulus and, therefore, would be scored low on Dana's perceptual range.

Card 2: That's the mother. Think she feels sick. A bug made her sick. She goes to the doctor. She gets better.

The expectation is that an individual would mention the following: a family, a young girl, a woman, an adult male, a specific activity, fields or farms, and books or school.

Perceptual integration as proposed here does not merely involve inclusion or exclusion of stimulus elements but considers the relationships among them. For Card 2, perceptual integration would refer to the relationship among the characters and activities described so that mentioning each character in an isolated activity is not sufficient. Furthermore, the emotions must be accurately described. For example, the expectations according to Dana (for an adult) regarding Card 4 is to include a male and female (noting emotion and specifying activity for both) as well as conflict or cooperation. The following story told by the same kindergarten girl as earlier mentions all of these elements but does not integrate the disparity in the characters' emotions as depicted in the stimulus.

Card 4: A mother and father. They're hugging. They're happy. (Thinking?) I don't know. (To?) Don't know.

Thus, perceptual integration involves making distinctions and inferring relationships among the characters in accordance with the scene depicted, as well as the inclusion of major stimulus elements. The following story told by a fourth-grade boy, aged 9-11 with average intelligence, makes no distinction between characters who are in fact quite different in the picture.

> Card 6BM: . . . um . . . Let me think. Probably wondering what the day's going to be and it's sunny so in the end they go out and do something. (Before?) Just get up from bed and want to know what it would be like. (Thinking and feeling?) Happy, it's a sunny day.

Omissions or misinterpretations of stimuli can range from gross to very subtle as follows: ignoring the stimulus altogether, misreading emotions so that relationships or interactions are at odds with cues presented, failure to identify major conflict or tension, only attending to one area, misperceiving major objects in the stimulus, failure to account for role and age differences of characters, emphasis on background features or less relevant aspects of the stimulus, leaving out subtle features, or overincorporation of every nuance. Subtle perceptual distortions may be revealed by leaving out some less important aspects of the stimulus, such as the gun in Card 3BM, whereas a more significant distortion is indicated when emotions or relationships among the characters are not congruent with the stimuli, such as a description of Card 4 as "two people in love" (which misses the central conflict).

The posture and facial expressions of the characters depicted suggest some relationship among them that must be accurately incorporated into the story. All of the relevant characters should be included in accord with their age, emotion, and seeming relation to one another. Lack of perceptual integration is shown when separate vignettes are told to each major area of the picture without positing a relationship. This is not uncommon on Card 2 of the T.A.T., which is a complex stimulus and difficult to integrate for young children.

Perceptual emphasis refers to the part of the picture that receives the most attention. The usual emphasis is on the foreground or on the major stimulus elements. For instance, in Card 2 of the T.A.T., the story is typically focused around the girl. However, some respondents focus on the horse, mountain, or other background features. Other cards, such as 8BM, also have distinct foreground and background elements.

If an unambiguous picture is distorted, the narrator's ability to calibrate responses to the situation is poor either because of intense preoccupations or faulty information processing and judgment. Such distortions must be examined closely (e.g., Tomkins, 1947; Rapaport, Gill, & Schafer, 1975) particularly in relation to stimuli such as the T.A.T., which are not ambiguous as to who the characters are and what they are doing in the picture (Murstein, 1965). The posture and facial expressions suggest some conflict or negative feeling, the nature of which is defined by the respondent.

Deficits in perceptual integration are placed on a continuum that assigns point values according to the degree of severity of perceptual distortion. Four levels of perceptual integration are described and illustrated next. Scoring must be done by individuals with extensive experience with the stimuli.

Level of Perceptual Integration

1 = Extremely Poor

The story is not appropriate to the overall stimulus configuration. It is based on a misperception of the emotions and relationships depicted in the stimulus, leaves major characters out of the story, or emphasizes minute stimulus features (e.g., eyebrow) without perceiving the gestalt (e.g., the emotion). An obvious tension state is not recognized, so that characters looking in different directions or having different facial expressions such as in Card 7GF or in Card 4 of the T.A.T. are identified as doing or feeling the same thing.

The following story told by a 9-year-old boy distorts the emotions, fails to recognize the conflict, and includes irrelevant detail:

Card 4: He looks sad, and she looks happy. They're both holding each other. She has brown hair, and he has red hair. That's all. (Before?) They were running from each other. (To?) Good.

The following story told by a kindergarten boy not only ignores the object but also the central tension.

Card 1: He's thinking. (Q) Don't know. (Feel?) Sick. (Q) Don't know. (End?) He'll get up and sit down and watch TV.

A boy, age 6-10, told the following story in which the departure from the stimulus was silly and illogical:

Card 1: I don't know anything to go with it. (Try). OK, a cat lived with this kid who was real lonely. He gets married. Meow went the cat, bark, bark went the dog, and meow, meow went the hamsters. Do hamsters meow? My sisters do. They meow at each other. (Thinking?) I don't know, it's just meowing. (Feeling?) Meows from the hamster and the cat. (Child begins to make noises.)

Since the child was floundering with the T.A.T., the more structured Tasks of Emotional Development (TED) cards were administered the following week. Again, there was stimulus distortion, as shown by the following story to Card 1 (LB1), which depicts a realistic photograph of four boys apparently interacting (facing each other) in a group (bat and baseball gloves) with a fifth child looking at them from a distance. The story does not incorporate the boy standing off by himself and does not deal with relationships among peers (as intended). As with the response to T.A.T. Card 1, the central tension was not incorporated in the story to the TED card (peer group versus boy standing alone).

> TED Card 1: They're playing baseball. They're feeling bad. (Q?) Because their baseball got sunk in the mud. (Q?) They're thinking about the ball sinking in the mud before they come back. (To?) They buy a new ball.

The following story told by a fourth-grade boy, age 9-11, focuses on *one* character when the stimulus depicts more than one person. Only the girl in the foreground is included in the story, while other characters and stimulus features are ignored so that the overall context implied by the stimulus is disregarded.

> Card 2: She's probably thinking about she has a test and thought what she was going to make on it. And when they give it out, she's really worried and after they give it out she worked really hard and gets an A.

2 = Poor

The distortion primarily involves the failure to grasp the implicit meaning of the stimulus configuration. Relationships or emotions are not grossly incompatible with the stimulus nor are prominent characters omitted. However, major objects may be omitted or misidentified (e.g., focus on background features while ignoring more major stimulus elements). Age and role differences may not be recognized (e.g., adults are seen as playing childish games). Difficulty with perceptual integration is conveyed by responses that do not coordinate major stimulus elements but produce separate vignettes about each component of the picture without indicating relationships implied by the stimulus. Thus, major elements of the picture may be recognized but not integrated.

In the following story told to Card 2 of the T.A.T. by a girl aged 6-3, the characters are not related to each other; no common concept (e.g., family) glues the descriptive statements together. To the child's credit, she realized that she did not accomplish the task of telling a story.

> Card 2: Can I tell what's in the picture? In the picture there's a beautiful school girl with a braid and a man taking care of the horse with no shirt on and there's a farm. The girl is thinking how will I do in school. She looks

like she's about 13. There's a pregnant woman and you can see the man's underwear. The woman is standing on a tree like an Indian. The girl is staring. Can't make up a story. End.

3 = Medium

Basic feelings and relationships are compatible with the stimulus configuration, even if minor objects are left out, overly elaborated, or misidentified. However, a subtle tension state may not be recognized, or there may be indecision about who the characters are or what they are doing or feeling (e.g., 3BM crying or sleeping) as illustrated by the following story told by a girl, age 6-1, with high-average IQ.

Card 7GF: The little girl is sitting on a chair with her mother. No, it looks more like an aunt. Well, either one, it looks like some sort of lady. And it looks like they're both thinking about some things, not doing anything. Looks sort of old fashioned, the picture does. (Q: what are they thinking about?) Things they usually think about. For example, maybe the girl is thinking about make-believe.

The distortion is subtle because characters are described as thinking without a sense of tension. The distortion is not so blatant as to describe them as interacting happily or as thinking about the same thing.

In the following story told by a sixth-grade boy, the narrator ignores a major portion of the stimulus (the violin), but the story content is consistent with the emotions and central tension depicted.

Card 1: It's a little boy, and he found out he was going to be having a test. And he has to study real hard for it. He doesn't study a lot so he has to cram a lot of it at night now. He studies all night and he thinks he's going to pass the test. The day the test comes, he feels different. He looks at the test and he doesn't remember anything. He looks at it some more and some of it starts to come back. And he ended up getting a passing grade on the test. (Feeling?) When he gets the test he wasn't feeling that well because he doesn't remember anything.

Similarly, the story told below by a kindergarten girl ignores the violin but doesn't contradict the emotions portrayed.

Card 1: He's sad because nobody is playing with him. (Think?) He doesn't have anyone to play with. He goes and finds somebody to play with. They have fun. They play to dinner time.

4 = *Good*

The story smoothly incorporates the cues provided in the picture, accounting for subtle nuances of relationships despite possible omission of minor details. Even if there's some overincorporation of details, it does not interfere with flow or content of story.

The story below, told by a boy, age 5-0, with very superior IQ illustrates good stimulus integration. The tension state is recognized (the girl is looking away) and characters are identified without vacillation.

Card 7GF: Once upon a time (sigh), a little girl went to her grandma's, and her grandma was sewing all day, and she was alone.

Concrete versus Abstract Thinking

Abstractness, as defined by Bruner (1966), is the degree to which the internal representation of perceived objects (schemata) are detached from their concrete form. Thus, abstract thinking involves relative freedom from context, whereas concrete thinking is constrained by immediate cues. Behaviorally, abstractness is manifested as independence from the situation in which a given behavior takes place. The individual behaves according to inner principles or convictions rather than being compelled by the situation.

Since concrete thinking is tied to the immediate circumstance and does not incorporate time perspective, it fails to integrate past experience and future considerations. If a behavior has meaning only in the present, there is little incentive to tolerate frustration, and external sources of motivation are needed continuously. A person is unprepared to deal with new events or circumstances when experience has little relationship to that which preceded it and to that which will follow. If thought processes are constrained by the immediate context, the individual tends to focus on immediately present stimuli and interprets information literally.

Some aspects of cognitive style, such as field dependence-independence and impulsivity-reflection, appear to be related to how directly the individual responds to immediate stimuli versus directing behavior from an internal context. *Field dependence-independence* (Witkin & Berry, 1975; Witkin, Moore, Goodenough, & Cox, 1977) refers to the ability to separate a stimulus from its context, whereas *impulsivity-reflection* (Kagan, 1966) refers to the tendency to evaluate thinking and actions. Reflective children gather information more systematically and more critically evaluate alternatives (Messick, 1976).

The story telling task such as the T.A.T. requires the narrator to draw inferences and conclusions based on stimuli presented. Conclusions may be drawn directly from the picture or can encompass more abstract interpretations of the stimulus. For example, the first description of the boy on T.A.T. Card 13B is more concrete than the second: "He has no shoes, so he must be poor" versus "This boy's an orphan." Concreteness is expressed in projective stories in a variety of ways such as interpreting T.A.T. stimuli or instructions literally. The following story illustrates that the directions can be taken quite literally.

Card 1: The boy got a violin. Now he's deciding to play. He feels fine, and in the future he will play.

When responses are closely bound to the stimulus or instructions presented, the story teller is looking to the environment for structure. Content may be purely descriptive of stimuli and may contain little expression of thoughts, intentions, feelings, or conflicts. Stories that are formulaically structured around elements of instructions represent a fairly concrete strategy for the task, which results from focusing on a narrow aspect of the task demand. Stereotyped content often doesn't ring true because it is borrowed rather than based on the respondent's integration of real experiences or convictions. Individuals with highly limited intellectual capacity may not be able to translate a representational stimulus into a hypothetical story consistent with the picture. The narrator may be unable to grasp the idea that the detail of the story emanates from the respondent rather than from the stimulus picture. A different kind of concreteness, which is the overuse of detail to justify every feeling or statement on the basis of the stimulus, may be related to a variety of factors such as reluctance to take risks (possibly due to anxiety or not trusting one's judgment), desire for external cues to bolster one's judgment, or difficulty inferring inner states.

An individual who is functioning concretely will act on the moment and will need to relearn responses for each situation rather than gradually learn to act on generalized accumulated concepts. In the absence of such internal representations, the quality of inferences and subtlety in processing stimuli are diminished. An individual who is threatened by the stimulus or the task or who is perhaps a low-risk taker may have the cognitive capacity to think abstractly in more structured tasks but vacillates and looks for cues in the picture to justify responses.

Abstraction-Concreteness in Projective Stories

Three broad indices of abstract thinking in relation to the stimulus are described:

Meaning of the Picture
One of the most important elements of abstraction is an understanding of the task to tell a story that interprets the scene presented by accounting for the stimulus features without making direct reference to it (e.g., Card 6BM: "This

woman has a window"). An abstract attitude is required to understand that the story teller makes up the story from an inner frame of reference rather than discovering the story from the picture. Children who are limited in their ability to think abstractly may attempt to describe the stimulus in an effort to tell a story. They may have difficulty grasping that it is they who are generating the story and the answer doesn't come directly from the picture. Abstraction in the expression of feelings is shown when emotions are tied to the internal state of the character rather than emanating directly from the stimulus.

Intervening Processes

Another index of abstraction is the ability to include transitional events to formulate resolutions to the tensions or negative situations depicted in the cards. Concrete thinking is suggested when the change or resolution in feeling is tied directly to a sudden change of event without an intervening process. If the final feeling state refers back to the picture rather than to the story, this may suggest that the story teller cannot get away from the negative feeling tone of the picture or cannot coordinate changing feelings with changing circumstances.

Context for Events

Abstraction requires conceptual integration of ideas and of disparate elements of the stimulus by incorporating them into a common context. Description of specific stimulus elements that cover every area of the picture without meaningful integration of the perceptions indicates difficulty organizing the stimulus details into a conceptual framework. Likewise, a narrator who juxtaposes story details by the association of ideas is not organizing details according to central concepts.

The absence of these three elements is illustrated by a story to card 3BM told by an 18-year-old incarcerated male:

> Card 3BM: She's sad. Seems like she feel. She's not feeling too good. (happened before?) She's been in a small room. What's this supposed to be? (up to you) I'm not sure if it's a gun or not. She might have been shot. (by who?) Who knows, somebody. (To?) No one is dead but her.

The picture is taken at a literal level. As soon as the narrator notices the gun, he simply decides that the character is shot. Rather than describing a context or intervening events, the narrator points to stimulus elements. When themes expressed are determined in a direct way by the stimulus, they cannot be judged to reflect typical concerns because they are immediate emotional or cognitive reactions evoked by the picture or by the struggle to comply with task demands.

Abstract thought process is evident in (1) relation of the picture to the story—as described above (e.g., meaning, intervening process, context); (2)

thematic content—level of abstraction of concepts and level of awareness attributed to characters (e.g., awareness of intent, time frame, consequences); (3) structure of the story—internal logic and complexity of plot as well as the relative emphasis on details versus concepts; and (4) the story telling process—the narrator's approach to telling the story (e.g., planned, haphazard, or structured around the four elements).

Degree of Abstraction in Card Description

Sometimes, children do not go beyond card description when faced with a story telling task. Even when only card descriptions are available, one can distinguish variations in the level of abstraction that relate to whether the individual names, describes, or interprets elements of the picture. Eron (1950) refers to several different types of stories as being symbolic, descriptive, or comprised of themes or comments.

Enumerative Description

There is no story, but only naming or some elaboration of parts of pictures without integrating the stimulus components. Simple descriptive statements do not cohere and apply to isolated features of the stimulus. Feelings do not depart from the stimulus.

The following story told by a boy, age 7-1, with below-average intelligence is an example of enumerative description.

Card 3BM: This man has a head in his arms. He has two feet. He has a bed. He's leaning on the bed. One day this man lived in a far away place. His mother and father were dead. He had nothing to eat in his house. That's all. (Feeling?) Nothing.

The following story told by a 9-year-old boy also enumerates aspects of the stimulus that are concretely tied to what is happening in the moment.

3BM: (off-task remarks) She got hurt. . . . She's crying. . . . She's bleeding really hard and she's laying down. . . . (Think?) She's crying. (Feel?) Sad. (To?) Bad. . . . I don't know how it will turn out.

Concrete Description

Content is not narrowly tied to the specific stimulus elements but rather to a more holistic view of the picture. Actions or events do not incorporate inner purpose or motives but are reactions to provocation (e.g., stimulus, preceding events, emotion). Queries about thinking and feeling are answered in a superficial manner. The story progresses by moving to the next time frame or by successively describing different characters or as a reaction to the previous story content. There is little or no logical integration of inner states with the stimulus or sequence of events.

The following story told by a girl age 6-1 begins as a personal reaction to the stimulus. The first ending was not acceptable to the story teller, so the second ending was made up as a reaction to the first. The concreteness is evident by the child's reaction to the stimulus, the story telling process, narrative structure, and character's actions.

> C.A.T. Card 7: This picture is scary. I think I would be scared like the monkey if a tiger just jumped up and growled or could say roared at me. (Then what?) The monkey can't do it as fast as he has to do it. The monkey has to do it very, very fast. (What can't he do?) Climb up it fast enough. (How does it end, turn out?) The monkey gets eaten. Poor little monkey. But the monkey gets out of the tiger's mouth and locks him up in a cage. That's the end.

The following story told by a 9-year-old boy shows no connection between causes of events and consequences of actions. The narrative consists of a series of associations to the stimulus or previous idea rather than progressing conceptually.

> Card 2: Can you repeat it? (Examiner says can play tape again when they're done). Can I stop it? . . . She just walked in the garden and got in trouble for, uh, running away and she went home and her mother spanked her. That's all. (Think?) I don't know, that she's gonna get in big trouble (Feel?) Bad . . . sad, that's all (To?) Bad . . . she got punished. That's all. That's all I can think.

Interpretive Description

The scene is interpreted by incorporating inner states as explanations of the picture and of the events in the unfolding story. Interpretive description of the stimulus is shown by the following two stories told by a boy aged 5-0.

> Card 1: This boy is sad because he can't play the violin.

> C.A.T. Card 7: Looks like a tiger is growling at a monkey cause he's climbing his tree. (Then what?) Let me see. Then the monkey slid down the tree because he was scared.

In both stories, the narrator describes the event as well as the reason for it. The first response is not a complete story, but it interprets the scene by providing reasons for inner states that match the stimulus. In the second story, the tiger growls because the monkey is climbing the tiger's tree; the monkey slides down the tree because he's scared of the tiger. Thus, there is a relationship among the ideas expressed which is not apparent in the stimulus. The interpretive description gives motives, reasons, causes, or antecedents of events so that the characters' feelings, thoughts, and actions are explained within a context.

Summary

Information-processing style determines the manner in which experience is organized and is revealed by narratives elicited through projective methods. This chapter describes various manifestations of perceptual integration and of abstract-concrete thinking styles in projective stories.

CHAPTER 8

Regulation of Attention

Cognitive operations like judgment, problem-solving, and planning require the individual to direct attention to weigh alternative possibilities. The ability to make conceptual shifts or to avoid preoccupation with a thought depends on active control of attention to change focus from one idea to another. Intrusion of affect into the attentional process may pose a threat to the integrity of cognition. High levels of anxiety or arousal reduce the range of attention or cue utilization and tend to restrict and bias the process of memory retrieval (Bacon, 1974; Hockey, 1979). Difficulty with focusing, shifting, and sustaining attention interferes with the capacity to consider the most relevant aspects of situations and to develop a systematic, deliberate approach to processing information. Focusing on less relevant detail while missing the main point may lead to a tendency to react emotionally to minor events without considering their context. Cognitive attentional problems, behavioral problems, and emotional problems are thus interrelated.

Attention is a multifaceted process that is defined and expressed according to characteristics of a task (e.g., novelty, ambiguity, complexity), situation (e.g., guidelines, individual attention, contingencies), and a person (e.g., emotional reactivity, cognitive style, distractibility, persistence.)

Characteristics of Tasks

Tasks make different demands on attention. Some tasks require focused attention or the ability to attend to relevant material while ignoring irrelevant stimuli. Others require sustained attention or concentration over time. Various conceptions of attention are tied to the specific tasks employed in their measurement. Conclusions and generalizations from tasks to behaviors are limited to tasks with similar attentional demands and not treated as generic constructs.

Characteristics of Situations

Situational demands can vary according to guidelines available for accomplishing a specific task or in the interpersonal context. Relevant situational factors are novelty or familiarity, degree of structure, clarity of expectations, amount and type of feedback, balance among supports and demands, and range of options to select tasks or activities.

Two types of attention have been described in relation to novel or familiar stimuli (Brimer & Levine, 1983; Tucker & Williamson, 1984). First, exploratory attention in novel situations consists of searching the environment for stimuli that are intense, complex, novel, or incongruous. This type of attention increases stimulation. Second, sustained attention processes that are organized and goal directed come into play in more familiar situations. These require selective focus of attention and inattention in a search for environmental regularities. According to Brimer and Levine (1983), it is the continuous scanning of the environment, the distraction by stimuli, that accounts for the attention deficits and impulsive behavior of hyperactive children.

The application of knowledge requires the ability to assess the parameters of a task or situation prior to making a judgment about appropriate behavior. Individuals with poor attention cannot observe features of the task from which to infer task difficulty (Feldman, Levine, & Fenton, 1986). Such children are unable to estimate their performance on tasks because they cannot assess the demands of the task in relation to a realistic appraisal of their coping skills. Therefore, they require more frequent feedback and greater environmental support. Mischel (1984) contends that emotionally disturbed children have difficulty sizing up new situations and cannot see the negative impact of ineffectual solutions.

The execution of a complex sequence of behaviors requires active attention and self-monitoring to modulate actions to changing cues (Wallander & Hubert, 1987). Different situations require different attentional demands. Routine, structured situations requires (1) generalization from previous experience, (2) regulation or modulation of a sequence of actions, and (3) inhibition of inappropriate impulsive behavior. An unfamiliar or complex situation requires (1) emotional/cognitive capacity to rapidly size up and react to novelty, (2) ability to focus on what's essential, (3) flexibility to shift attentional focus, and (4) internal self-regulation to sustain and guide attention in the absence of clear external cues.

Situational differences in the manifestation of attentional disorders depend on which functional processes are required by a particular task in a given situational context.

Characteristics of Persons

Attentional processes are located within a person but are manifested as the joint function of person, task, and situation. It is not helpful to describe a child as inattentive without specifying precisely what conditions influence the degree of attentiveness or inattentiveness, as well as the type of attentional processes involved. A child with attentional deficits can watch TV or play computer games for a long time and resist parental efforts to disengage. Such a child can sustain attention when it is riveted on highly compelling stimuli. However, if attentional processes are externally rather than internally controlled, then the nature of the task and availability of cues can greatly influence task performance. Furthermore, if the flexibility and voluntary control of attentional processes are deficient, then the child cannot coordinate behaviors and responses according to changes in task or situational demands.

Distractibility

A person is said to be distracted when attention is captured by extraneous stimuli, rather than deliberately shifted (Thomas & Chess, 1977; Thomas et al., 1963). High distractibility may reflect a process whereby attention and arousal are regulated by changes of input from the environment rather than internally directed. Difficulty filtering out sensory input makes distractible children vulnerable to loss of control over attentional processes (Rosenthal & Allen, 1978).

It is important to distinguish between two essentially different sources of distraction: stimuli that are external to the task and stimuli within the task. Rosenthal and Allen (1978) have argued that distractibility should be defined in terms of ability to ignore irrelevant stimuli in the context of the task at hand. An individual may be distracted by various details of a complex task because of inability to selectively tune out some components to maintain focus on others.

Distraction by Extraneous Stimuli

Stimuli external to a task capture attention so that what is happening now draws the person from his or her purpose or from the task at hand. The impact of extraneous variables (e.g., noises) on ongoing activity has been described as the temperamental attribute of distractibility (Rothbart & Derryberry, 1981; Thomas et al., 1963).

Individuals can also be distracted by extraneous stimuli that are internal, such as thinking about a forthcoming reward or party. For some individuals, thinking about watching TV (when a favorite show is on) can be as distracting as the actual sound of the TV. The performance of hyperactive children is impaired by providing or withdrawing contingent or noncontingent praise or reward but these have no detrimental effect on the performance of those in normal comparison groups (Douglas, 1983; Douglas & Parry, 1983; Douglas & Peters, 1979). Thus, for hyperactive children, the anticipation of rewards may serve as distractors that draw attention away from the task at hand.

Difficulty with voluntarily directing or withdrawing attention is the essential process of distractibility. The child cannot back away from the most compelling stimulus that captures attention. A child exhibiting this style may feel most comfortable in situations where he or she is expected to attend to stimuli that are highly compelling and interesting or in novel situations where exploratory attention is warranted. The most difficult situations are those that require the child to withdraw attention from highly stimulating events or thoughts (anticipating a big party) to routine tasks or activities.

Distraction by Stimuli within a Task or Social Interaction

Another type of attentional difficulty relates to a process whereby less relevant details distract the individual from the most essential components of a complex task or social situation. This aspect of distractibility relates to difficulty identifying the appropriate focus of attention. If the person cannot exercise selective attention to focus on the main idea, then he or she will inevitably get lost in the details. A child experiencing difficulty focusing and shifting attention can't keep up with the natural flow of conversation and may react to details that are out of context or tangential to the main points. Perseveration reflects an underlying deficiency related to the attentional control process that monitors stimuli and separates relevant from irrelevant sources of information. In relation to projective stories, the narrator may perseverate or keep harping on the same themes because the respondent cannot shift to an alternative idea.

Deficits in selective attention or in the ability to focus on the most essential features of a task are particularly handicapping in more complex, less structured situations. Individuals who have difficulty utilizing conceptual and organizing strategies to select the focus of attention do not integrate the essential elements of the entire situation and may be prone to quick decisions without incorporating the relevant facts or fully anticipating the consequences. Deficits in selective attention may lead to arbitrarily shifting focus and difficulty monitoring behavior according to changes in demands. The child may not attend to small differences in stimulation because attention is drawn to the more compelling components. On the other hand, small, less significant details may capture attention, but the child may not be able to coordinate these into larger, more meaningful units by attributing priority to the details. Thus, shift or flexibility of attention is needed to deal with complex tasks and many social situations.

Hyperactive children react to the salient aspects of a stimulus complex and fail to process the more subtle aspects (Douglas, 1980). Such children did not learn vicariously from a model, whereas their normal counterparts used the opportunity to improve their subsequent performance (see Whalen & Henker, 1985). Apparently, the hyperactive youngsters did not shift their attention from their current activity to observe others to obtain information necessary for a future task.

The coordination of task and interpersonal demands of a situation also requires the capacity to shift the focus of attention according to priorities. Children who cannot regulate attentional processes have difficulty coordinating task demands with interpersonal considerations; they can focus on one or the other but have difficulty balancing the two. They may have problems waiting their turn or inhibiting their response because they can't alternatively shift focus from their internal state to the flow of external events. The application of social skills requires modulation and shifting attention to keep track of conversation and put events into context. This process allows the individual to respond to the main points rather than to the most immediate provocation.

A distractible person may be unable to exclude irrelevant features of the environment or of a task to permit self-monitoring of ideas or activities. The intrusions of environmental and task stimuli are not evaluated in terms of priorities and consequently compete for attention. Thus, distractibility can interfere with the conceptual organization of ideas. An individual whose attention is diverted by stimuli extraneous to the task may need to be physically separated from the sources of distraction. However, if elements of the task are distracting, then the individual may need more structure, guidelines, clues, or one-to-one assistance. Children who are distracted by various stimuli within the task cannot identify what is most relevant, but may improve their performance when the main ideas are provided.

Active versus Passive Attention

Some children fail to apply sufficient, organized, and strategic effort to information processing (Torgesen, 1977). The attentional deficits of such children may actually reflect problems with active organization and restructuring of information (Keogh & Margolis, 1976; Kistner, 1985). Hyperactive children may possess the skills to learn but do not apply organizing strategies in a spontaneous manner (Douglas, 1980). For example, they did not generate an organizational strategy to aid their effort on a recall task, but when such a strategy was provided, their performance approximated that of a normal comparison group (August, 1987). While the immediate effect of providing the organizational format to the hyperactive boys was to raise their performance to the level of the normal group, they were unable to sustain their efforts over successive trials. Their difficulty maintaining performance over time is consistent with complaints of tasks being "boring." Effortful processing over extended periods of time requires investment and absorption in the task.

Individuals may attend to and encode incoming stimulation as it is presented or may actively restructure or organize that information. Demands of tasks and situations differ in the degree of active restructuring required. Recall of digits (a subtest on the Wechsler Intelligence Scales) requires some strategic effort (rehearsal) but does not require much active reorganization. In contrast, recall of digits backward entails more concentration in restructuring the information while retaining it in short-term memory. These processes have been differentiated as *attention* versus *concentration*, respectively. The ability to strategically break down and organize learning tasks as well as active rehearsal aids learning and retention. Organizing effort facilitates reading comprehension as well as math computation. Passage comprehension is significantly increased if the reader organizes the information according to key concepts. However, memory for isolated facts and details may not be facilitated by this strategy.

The continuous organization of information is related to the ability to regulate attention to the task demands and involves active effort in the processing of information. Passive attention relates to boredom, lack of investment, and absence of active, effortful, strategic processing. Inactive processing relates to difficulty making inferences because the individual is attending to the flow of information without interpreting or reading implicit cues. Children with inactive style may have difficulty performing tasks such as projective story telling that require focused, directed, and organized effort and may do better with concrete tasks that do not require reflection.

Continuous or Sustained Attention

Sustained attention or the ability to continuously process information without being distracted by competing stimuli underlies complex thinking. If an individual is able to regulate attention and tune out extraneous or less relevant stimuli, then at a very *basic* level the person maintains an internal locus of control. For temperament researchers, *attention span* refers to duration of sustained attention or continuous processing of information given a particular type of stimulus (Rothbart & Derryberry, 1981). *Persistence* (Thomas et al., 1963), which is also viewed as a temperamental trait, refers to the continuation of attention on an activity, object, or task by resisting obstacles or interruptions.

Sustained attention can be assessed by two different approaches: (1) short-term measures of maintenance of task performance, encoding, alertness, vigilance, or freedom from distraction; and (2) attention or persistence over time on performance of tasks that require organizing effort and sustained interest. The capacity for short spurts of sustained attention that has been related to neurological status is typically measured by routine tasks given under (for most people) highly motivating circumstances (e.g., various versions of the Continuous Performance Task [CPT]: Rosvold et al., 1956).

Vigilance is an element of sustained attention because temporarily tuning out during ongoing presentation of stimuli will cause the respondent to miss some significant pieces of information. The speed of reaction to a signal stimulus has been viewed as an index of alertness or vigilance, and the typical approach to measuring this quality of attention has been speed of response to a simple task (e.g., Samuels & Edwall, 1981). A number of studies have shown that hyperactive children are slower, show more intraindividual variability, and are less persistent across trials on various tasks that measure simple reaction time in comparison with controls (Cohen & Douglas, 1972; Porges et al., 1975; Spring et al., 1974).

Sustaining attention on tasks for longer durations is more typical of real-life circumstances than the relatively short spurts of attention. Such persistence requires interest and active organizing effort, as well as cognitive capacity compatible with the information-processing demands of the task to be accomplished.

Emotion, Interest, and Arousal as Regulators of Attention

The "facts" that dominate awareness are obviously those that command attention. Since individuals direct attention to that which is interesting or relevant, emotions have an organizing influence on information processing. Stimuli have both arousal value, which relates to emotions and interest, and cue value, which relates to the relevance of the information to cognitive processing and problem solving. Some individuals may be relatively more compelled by the arousal value and others by the cue value.

Functional relationships have been described among the temperament processes of arousal, emotion and, attention (Derryberry & Rothbart, 1988). Rosenthal and Allen (1978) suggest that activity level, arousal, and attention are interrelated constructs that focus on different dimensions of human functioning. *Activity* consists of overt behavior; *arousal* refers to the quality and quantity of control of autonomic activation; whereas *attention* is a cognitive construct. They argue that both activity and features of attentional processes are dependent on aspects of physiological arousal. Sensitivity to reward or punishment is reflected in what draws an individual's attention. For instance, introverted and anxious subjects who have higher arousal more readily direct their attention to a negative stimulus than do extroverts who have lower arousal (Derryberry, 1987) and nonanxious subjects (MacLeod, Mathews, & Tata, 1986). Extroverts are more sensitive to signals of reward, are more prone to the emotions of hope and relief, and have a greater tendency to engage in impulsive behavior. Introverts are more sensitive to signals of punishment and nonreward, and are predisposed to feelings of fear, frustration, and anxiety (Gray, 1981, 1982). Individual differences in the trait of sensation seeking (Zuckerman, 1979) are assumed to be related to the balance between reward and punishment systems. It has been argued that the

Attention Deficit Hyperactivity Disorder (ADHD) is associated with decreased activity in the brain's behavioral inhibition system so that the threat of punishment is less effective in the regulation of behavior than in normal children (Quay, 1988).

Individuals who believe they cannot manage potential threats experience high levels of stress and anxiety arousal (Bandura, Reese, & Adams, 1982; Bandura et al., 1985). They tend to dwell on their deficits and view the environment as threatening. Cognitive theorists posit that such thoughts amplify their distress and further constrain or impair their level of functioning (Lazarus & Folkman, 1984; Meichenbaum, 1977; Sarason, 1975). The perceived inability to tune out aversive cognitions is a major source of distress (Kent, 1987; Kent & Gibbons, 1987; Salkovskis & Harrison, 1984). Perceived inability to control depressing ruminations increases the occurrence, duration, and recurrence of depressive episodes (Kavanagh & Bower, 1985; Mathews, 1986).

Attention and Projective Stories

Aspects of attentional processes reviewed above are evident in responses to projective story tasks in four areas: (1) *Use of stimulus properties*—What features of the stimulus capture attention? (2) *Planning and monitoring*— Is there evidence of a plan for the story details? Does the respondent monitor the story to avert gross inconsistencies? Are characters planful, basing their actions on goals, purposes, or motives rather than on external provocation? (3) *Reflection*—Is there an active, organizing process in the construction of the story so that events, actions, and outcomes are realistic and compatible? Is the narrator aware of implications beyond the surface or is the content stereotyped, glib, or nonreflective? and (4) *Production of ideas*—How are ideas generated? Are story details triggered by an associative process or guided by active conceptual integration?

These four areas are elaborated below:

Use of Stimulus Properties

Picture stimuli such as the T.A.T. have numerous details that can draw away attention. Therefore, it is possible to examine how the story teller incorporates some of the card clues while excluding others, as follows: (1) *Most salient aspect*—The story teller is tuned in to the most obvious (e.g., foreground), compelling, or personally relevant aspects of the stimulus but not to the more subtle features; (2) *Isolated element*—The respondent centers on only part of the picture, failing to see the whole; the narrator may be caught up in the more trivial aspects, narrow elements, or minor features of the stimulus (e.g., most emotionally relevant, most novel, or most threatening component); (3) *Flitting from one element to another*—The story teller responds successively to fragments of the stimulus without capturing the complex gestalt; and (4) *Vacillation*—Indecision about what is depicted in the picture.

Planning and Monitoring

The formal characteristics of the story structure as well as elements of content provide clues about the planning and monitoring capacities of the respondent. The narrator's planfulness in organizing the story and maintaining its focus by keeping track of the unfolding plot is revealed in the structural elements of the narrative. The main ideas emerge clearly without being cluttered with details. With respect to story content, the key issue is the degree of planfulness of the characters.

The following elements are noteworthy with respect to story structure and narrative process:

1. Vacillation about what is happening (such indecision can relate to the inability to stay on one track of thought by screening out other possibilities)
2. Irrelevant responses, silly content, and extraneous chatting while narrating a story
3. First-person stories or personalizations that reflect an inability to distance the self from objective demands of the task
4. The narrator is drawn away from initial focus by inquiry or personal association
5. Arbitrary shifts in perspective, inconsistencies, or contradictory details in the story
6. The story teller complains about being bored, expresses a desire to stop, or keeps asking how many more
7. Outcomes fail to integrate previous story content or shift focus without adequate transition

Formal aspects of story content relate to characters' problem-solving deficits that may pertain to the narrator's attentional difficulties:

1. Story characters are burdened with feelings of boredom or disinterest that spur short-term resolutions or wishful thinking.
2. Content emphasizes immediate gratification, not long-term aims. People want external things, money, and material items without realistically working to obtain them.
3. Characters just react without sizing up the situation or clearly defining the problem to be resolved or goal to be accomplished.

4. Characters don't plan ahead, don't anticipate, are forgetful, and are surprised or even baffled by consequences or reactions of others. They engage in trial-and-error problem solving where actions are unsystematic, unplanned, ineffective, careless, or unrealistic.
5. Characters jump to inappropriate conclusions, can't figure things out, misinterpret facts, fail to consider all of the alternatives, change their mind without basis, or overreact to minor events.
6. Characters react to unfair or incomprehensible demands made by authorities (e.g., parents or teachers). They are angry, rebellious, and desire to avoid or escape restrictions, responsibilities, or tasks.

Reflection

Reflection is evident when there is a context for actions that considers both inner motives and purposes along with realistic external constraints. Reflection is also shown by clarity of purpose in the manner of delineating the motives, intent, or aim of an action. Nonreflection refers to emphasis on action, appearances, or outward events without elaborating inner concerns. There is an absence of context indicated by description of immediate states of the characters without articulating the reasons for the predicament or purpose for action beyond the immediate dilemma. Characters make quick, impulsive decisions rather than display rule-bound or purposive behavior. For example, the description of the scene portrayed in Card 2 of the C.A.T. as "playing tug of war" shows more reflection than "they are pulling a rope" because it implies a purpose to the action.

The key question is whether the unfolding story is organized around a balance of inner states and incorporates a context for action rather than evolving through reaction to the stimulus or previous story content. Absence of reflection is indicated when (1) inner purposes are not well delineated or the impetus for action comes from external demand rather than inner motives (e.g., primary emphasis on consequences of actions); (2) there is a direct relationship between stimulus and action which bypasses inner motive (e.g., "The girl has books, she's going to read"); and (3) actions are not guided by realistic considerations but triggered by emotions or dominated by wishful thinking where the story teller does not adequately distinguish between possibility and probability, and, therefore, produces an unlikely or unrealistic sequence of events. In this case, there is selective attention to facts that are provoked by wishful thinking rather than guided by an active organizing process.

Production of Ideas

The unfolding story can progress as a result of the planful, organizing effort of the story teller, or ideas may be produced by associating to (1) features of the stimulus, (2) previous story detail, (3) emotional pull of the stimulus, or (4) particular sensitivities triggered by the task.

Associative thinking is the production of ideas that are not concisely, logically, and planfully related to a central focus. Story elements are not structured around a main idea but evolve from detail to detail in a linear manner. Ideas may be produced by associations to various parts of the picture or through an elaboration of one side of an issue rather than integrating multiple perspectives into a common context. Such linear thinking may be due to problems with selective attention or with ability to screen out impinging stimuli. Other factors include conceptual limitations that interfere with the ability to grasp the main point, as well as disinterest, which results in deficits in the motivation to exert the organizing effort required to maintain selective attention. Associative thinking is produced by an inactive approach where information processing addresses only what is immediately apparent without active restructuring. Disruption in the logical organization of thinking in response to emotional provocation can also result in an associative thought process.

Strategy utilization in general requires the active focusing and shifting of attention to engage in the process of reflection (active mulling over) and organization of ideas required for self-directed behavior. Such inactive thinking can also be manifested in vagueness and imprecision in processing information as reflected in projective stories by global, poorly differentiated or stereotyped descriptions of characters, problems, or actions. Stories may also suggest a lack of awareness of implications beneath the surface, poor time perspective, and fuzzy connection among motives, efforts, and outcomes. The narrator may focus on one character only or be unable to coordinate viewpoints among characters.

Associative Thinking in Projective Stories

An examination of what drives the sequence of ideas in the story and how the narrator monitors those ideas provide clues about the cognitive and attentional processes related to associative thinking.

In the most serious instance of attentional difficulties, the individual cannot select the most important element on which to focus but is diverted by the stimuli haphazardly without an ability to prioritize or to monitor events in the story. Irrelevant or subtle aspects of the stimulus demand attention in a way that suggests personal associations or lack of distance from the stimulus or, perhaps, loss of focus as attention wanders. The story is not constructed according to a plan but progresses by meandering from one idea to a loosely related one. Such a story may be provoked by the stimulus so the story teller jumps from one stimulus characteristic to another (associating to the stimulus) or as a reaction to previous story content or as aimless verbiage. An associative process may be operating regardless of the relationship of the story of the stimulus. One story teller may be reluctant to depart from the stimulus, whereas another may wander further and further from the stimulus as one idea triggers another.

Associative thinking related to attentional difficulties is frequently accompanied by a need for externally imposed structure due to problems maintaining self-directed sequences of behavior. Therefore, it is also important to note the narrator's ability to return or to be directed back to the task or central concepts. A comparison of the respondent's performance on more structured tasks (such as IQ) and observations of behavior in situations with varying degrees of structure can be enlightening. A child who exhibits an associative, distractible thinking style on the story telling task may perform quite well on more structured tasks. Nevertheless, difficulties become apparent when such a child is in a less structured situation as during class discussions (e.g., makes comments that are not directly related to the point and may be perceived as disrupting the flow of the lesson).

Associative thinking is often evident in responses to the more open-ended questions on the intelligence tests such as Vocabulary or Comprehension where the child may associate to the question rather than giving a precise answer. For instance, the child may state that a parrot has many colors, talks, has feathers, but never says that it is a bird. Some children give every answer they know or continue to respond by adding irrelevant details because they get caught up in the associative process and/or because they can't judge the quality or sufficiency of the answer. Associative thinking appears less integrative and, therefore, has to be differentiated from concrete thinking where the story appears to ramble because of the narrator's conceptual limitations. Likewise, the examiner must also differentiate between indecision and associative thinking and recognize when language dysfluency interferes with the organization and momentum of the story.

Thematic content reflects the degree of disorganization related to the attentional difficulties or associative thought process. An individual who is extremely distractible or inattentive is not likely to develop an organized, integrated frame of reference. The story teller may be unable to infer motives (thoughts or feelings) or to make a decision about what is happening in the picture. The story content may reveal the boredom or the conflict with authorities. Passive attentional process is suggested by vague, global, undifferentiated, unintegrated responses. The content and structure of the stories reflect how the attentional difficulty or inactive thinking style plays into the organization of experiences. Stories may be characterized by (1) emphasis on external influence, hindrances, and obstacles to adequate performance; (2) lack of sophistication in describing inner states and in making inferences about character's motives and feelings; (3) difficulty anticipating people's feelings and reactions (e.g., getting into trouble without understanding the cause); and (4) lack of sustained interest, boredom, frustration, or aggression.

Levels of Associative Thinking

The proposed scaling of associative thought process emphasizes the manner in which the narrator produces and organizes ideas. Using the T.A.T., Tarvin (1989) found interrater agreement of 87 percent for the scoring categories described below.

Level One
The story is driven by the association of ideas rather than conceptually organized.

1. The story rambles from one idea to a loosely related one rather than being organized around a central theme.
2. The story teller can't focus on what is important and reacts by associating directly to the stimulus, to the previous story elements, or to emotions evoked by the task.
3. The narrator builds on the same idea over and over without a conceptual shift (e.g., a series of actions designed to accomplish the same purpose), like a tall tale that grows and grows by elaborating on the same idea.
4. There is evidence of lack of distance from the story or stimulus such as personalization or first-person stories.
5. References to details or ideas are irrelevant or tangential to the story so that the main ideas are lost and the story appears disorganized.
6. The story teller talks excessively about irrelevant topics and cannot be refocused by examiner.

The following story told by a 9-year-old boy with very superior intelligence (IQ = 133) and diagnosed as ADHD progresses through actions without reflection or purpose. The stimulus serves as a point of departure for the story, which proceeds by association to the previous idea. The sense of humor is noteworthy.

> Card 13B: I came out of a barn and see a goat. Goat is cold. I went up on a monorail for the hay, but there was a monkey up there and he turned on the lever. I started going across the barn which was three stories high and went out to the haystack. The monorail clip let me go, and I fell three stories in a haystack. I said there's nothing easier than finding a needle in a haystack. Ow!

The following story told by an 8-year-old girl with above-average intelligence, also manifesting attentional deficits, is qualitatively similar.

Card 13B: I live in a farm house with all the chickens going cock-a-doodle-do, and I help out with my father with his tractor. Sometimes we go for a hayride and sometimes we fetch a lot of crops. Then we have a little beans in our garden. We pick them out and put them into cans. Then we pick corn cause we like corn a whole lot. When I go play with horses and sheeps and get them water and give them beans. Sometimes cows run away and they get lost. I call "cows ahoy" and then they come after you and go back to your house. I have to put pigs in the pigpen. They run all over in pig poop. They get all muddy and look disgusting.

The following story told by a 9-year-old boy in a self-contained class for emotionally handicapped children is generated by associating to the stimulus rather than rambling from one story event to another.

Card 4: He looks sad and she looks happy. They're both holding each other. She has brown hair and he has red hair. That's all (Before?) They were running from each other (To?) Good.

Although the following story, told by the same child as above, reflects an associative process, a more serious problem is indicated because the content is gruesome and the emotions are inappropriate. The narrator is pulled in by the emotional provocations of the stimulus and cannot keep his associations within bounds of socially acceptable content.

Card 8BM: They get mad. Then these two guys got a knife and are cutting a guy in half to get his bones out. And he's bleeding real bad . . . (Think?) They're thinking he's gonna die. (Feel?) They feel good. (To?) He just dies.

Three stories told by a second-grade boy demonstrate various aspects of the associative thought process. The story below proceeds through a series of associations to the stimulus and previous story content.

Card 1: One day a boy was looking at a violin that was on the table. Then he got real bored and real tired and he was thinking. The violin bow's on a white sheet. Then the boy had to go to a concert. He was looking at the violin strings.

Attention to minor stimulus detail (e.g., "rows in a garden") as well as the fabrication of irrelevant detail (e.g., "kitty cat running through the field") are evident in the following story, which evolves through the associative juxtaposition of elements rather than organized around a central concept.

Card 2: Here is a man making rows in a garden. A woman's standing by a rock. A girl—a teenage girl—is holding some books in front in the picture. When the man's doing the vegetables, the vegetables grow and it's hot. And the lady's looking by the view by the rock because it's a nice day. And the girl's looking at a little kitty cat running through the field. (Before?) Before that they were sitting in the house doing nothing so they came out. (End?) They all go back inside and have some of the vegetables and the kitty's inside and the lady keeps looking at the view. (Feel?) Happy. (Q) All of them are happy. (Think?) The cat's thinking, "Why's that lady looking at the view?" The man's thinking, "Why am I doing this?" And the lady's just thinking of the view. She's thinking of the cat.

The following story is built around each character's reaction to previous provocation without integration of feelings and motives around a central idea.

Card 3BM: One day a boy was crying on his bench because his mom said, "No, you can't have ice cream." The boy says, "Why not?" And the mom said, "It's close to lunch or dinner." The boy goes "Why?" And the mom yells at him to get down here. And he stays in his room because he's mad at her. He comes out in a year.

Level Two

There is some attempt to relate an organized story; however, there is a tendency to include content on the basis of associative thinking process such as reaction to previous story detail, stimulus, or personal association. Stories scored at this level are characterized by the following:

1. Parts of the story are not constructed according to a plan, but based on reaction to previous events or stimulus rather than contributing to the central theme.
2. The story seems to evolve as it goes along or it contains too many details and elaborations, but there is evidence of attempting to organize around a central theme.

The following story told by an 11-year-old boy with average intelligence unfolds through details triggered by the previous idea, although a central theme does emerge.

Card 1: Once upon a time there's this boy whose mother made him play the violin and he didn't really want to play the violin; he wanted to play the drums like his friends in the band. But his mom made him take solo practices, umm, with a teacher by himself. And, every time he played, when his instructor would leave, he'd go up to his room and always go to bed because he didn't like playing the instrument. And, the next day, his friends were all teasing him because he played the violin and they'd always call him a sissy. . . . And later on in the day when he'd stay at school and practice, they'd always say, "Do you like that instrument?" And he'd say, "No, but my mom made me play it." They said, "Well, why don't you tell her you don't want to play it?" He said, "Because my mom wouldn't let me give it up." And he asked his mom every night if he didn't have to play it and his mom would say, "Yes, just keep it up, you'll like it." But he never liked it. (Feel?) He's kinda upset. I guess he really doesn't like his mom making him play it, so he's angry at his mom.

The following two stories told by a kindergarten girl have no overall plan, as the narrator seems to be making up the details as she goes along. However, the story teller monitors these details so that the story endings incorporate all of the events and are not simply associations to the last detail or to the picture.

Card 1: I don't know what this is. (What do you think?) This little boy was playing with his toy. His toy water train. Cause it looks like water. He was feeling sad cause he didn't have directions how to do it. So he sat there and sat there. Then his friends came over, and they had the directions and the boy said, "Hey, you want to play with my choo-choo train?" And they said, "Yes," so it was time for them to go home and they forgot they had homework to do. So their teacher was mad because they forgot to do their homework. So the teacher sent them up to the principal. And the little boy was feeling sad cause he did it, and the teacher was mad cause he asked them. So, um, the little boy was in big trouble with his parents cause he had to do homework also. (To?) And then the boy asked them, "Do you want to play with my choo-choo train?" And the boy said, "No, we don't want to get in trouble again."

Card 3BM: Um, a boy was sick and he was driving his car and he hit a truck. So he, the uh, um, lessee—the ambul—whatever, I can't say it. And they took him to the hospital, and they put him on a bed, and they didn't know that the boy tried to get out of the hospital. And he dressed up like a doctor. And the boy got caught because the nurse said, "I never saw you before." And they took off the clothes and they found out it was the boy. And the boy felt sorry for himself since he tried to get out of the hospital. And the boy tried to think of another plan. He thinked and he thinked and he thinked and then suddenly he thought of a plan. He said to himself, "When nighttime comes and there's only a few people here, I'll sneak out." And then he tried to sneak out of the hospital. And then he remembered something that his mother said: "Never, never, never try to sneak out of somewhere."

The above stories evolve detail by detail as the narrator goes along, shifting action and circumstances that are not anticipated. The stories differ in content (their moral, realism) but the same associative, linear thinking is evident in both, along with an attempt to pull the story together at the end. The content reveals the child's subjective experiences of forgetting and difficulty with planning and anticipation. In the narrative told to Card 3BM, the boy ends up recalling a parental rule only after a series of unsuccessful actions.

Level Three

The story teller has the ability to maintain the focus of the narrative despite some obvious detours and distractions. Overelaboration of one element or going off on a tangent is mild, and the respondent easily returns to the story line (with or without prompting). The story has coherence but may be dominated by detail.

In the following story told by a sixth-grade boy, the respondent initially reacts to the stimulus (the gun) but then proceeds with the story in which there are overelaborations stemming from an associative process (e.g., "They lost her keys. She's missing her key. It fell off or something").

Card 3BM: What's this, a gun? Maybe before this picture, they were at this house and there's no one in the house. And they lost her keys. She's missing her key. It fell off or something, and now she's sitting on the steps, all tired, waiting for someone to come and help her. She's trying to get in. I think someone finds the key she lost and returns it to her and she gets into her house. (Think?) Don't know.

Level Four

The story is tightly organized around a central theme. The details are related to the main ideas and there is coherence among thoughts, feelings, actions, and outcomes, suggesting that the narrator was responding according to a plan and was organizing and monitoring the story content.

The following story told by a second-grade girl is focused around a central theme. Actions are consistent with the stated desire to learn to play music, and the seeming departure to learn a different instrument is reconciled by emphasizing the interpersonal benefits of playing the flute rather than the violin.

Card 1: Once upon a time, there was a boy who just started school and he wanted to play music and he didn't know how to play the violin. Then he felt sad that the other kids next to him knew how to do it. Then he starts studying how to play it. Then he starts playing the flute, and he learned how to play that because his father taught him. He said he liked to play the flute better. That made his father happy that he liked the flute better and now they can play music together.

In the above story, there are no loose ends, and the girl's style of articulation and the repetition of "then he" should not detract from the apparent organization and focus in the progression of ideas.

Summary

The regulation of attention is relative to characteristics of tasks, situations, and persons. The following aspects of attentional styles of persons are reviewed: (1) distractibility, (2) active versus passive attention, (3) continuous or sustained attention, and (4) emotion as director of attention. The impact of attentional processes on the production of projective stories is seen in (1) the use of stimulus properties, (2) planning and monitoring of the narrator and of the characters, (3) degree of reflection, and (4) production of ideas. Associative thinking, which emphasizes the manner in which ideas are produced in narrating the story, is scaled into four levels.

CHAPTER 9

Attention Deficits

The common features of an attention deficit hyperactivity disorder have remained essentially the same despite a series of changes of name. The three major defining elements are inattention, overactivity, and impulsivity. This phenomenon has been called Minimal Brain Dysfunction (MBD) (Clements, 1966), then designated Hyperkinetic Reaction of Childhood (APA, DSM-II, 1968), again renamed Attention Deficit Disorder (ADD) (APA, DSM-III, 1980), and subsequently, Attention Deficit Hyperactivity Disorder (ADHD) (APA, DSM III-R, 1987). The redefinition of *hyperactivity* as an attention deficit disorder reflects a shift in emphasis away from activity per se to the attentional components. However, reintroducing the term *hyperactivity* by renaming the disorder as ADHD indicates that the two, in most cases, go together into a syndrome. The change in name and diagnostic criteria within a seven-year time span was seen by some authors as premature (see Schaughency & Rothlind, 1991), and the term is likely to undergo further reconceptualization (see Barkley, 1990).

The DSM III (APA, 1980) specified two subtypes of attention deficit disorder to indicate that it can occur with or without hyperactivity. It may be fruitful to differentiate these two groups. Children displaying attentional deficits with hyperactivity are more likely to exhibit aggressive or overt antisocial behaviors than those who manifest attentional deficits without hyperactivity (Lahey et al., 1984; Lahey et al., 1987).

Regardless of what the entity is called, the essence of the problem is the failure to modulate cognitive processing and activity to engage in self-directed behavior that meets academic and social demands. Children exhibiting this syndrome manifest difficulty in organizing and completing work and make poor academic progress. Additionally, such children encounter a variety of associated interpersonal problems, ranging from disruptive behavior in classes to disturbed interpersonal relations including aggressive behavior. This syndrome is associated with poor ability to concentrate, behavioral immaturity, motivational deficits, insufficient goal-directed effort, deficient regulation of behavior by rules and consequences, difficulty making or keeping friends, antisocial behavior, and poor school performance (Barkley, 1990).

Children diagnosed with ADHD present a heterogeneous group with different problems that have a certain degree of situational specificity. Many of these children are able to maintain attention and withstand distraction in situations that rivet their interest. Strong motivational components of high interest and compelling stimuli help to sustain attention. Such children have most difficulty maintaining attention and inhibiting responses in situations that require focused, directed, and organized effort. The more complicated the task, the greater the probability that the performance of ADHD children will be lower than that of typical peers (Douglas, 1983; Luk, 1985). These characteristics have also been used to describe learning-disabled (LD) children in general. Indeed, there are many similarities among hyperactive and learning-disabled children with respect to attention (e.g., Ackerman, Oglesby, & Dykman, 1981; Dykman, Ackerman, & Oglesby, 1979). Furthermore, deficits in sustained attention are not unique to the hyperactive groups (Schachar et al., 1988; Werry, Reeves, & Elkind, 1987).

Behaviors characterizing children with attentional disorders may range from normal to handicapping levels. Most children manifest behaviors such as daydreaming, not finishing tasks, or not waiting their turn, which are listed in the DSM III-R but are not quantified. Associated features, including mood lability, low frustration tolerance, and academic underachievement, also exist in varying degrees. A clearer definition of the attentional components of this disorder such as distractibility, focus and shift of attention, and a delineation of the degree to which activity is unmodulated, uncontrollable, or purposeless would not only specify their presence but also indicate their severity under varying task and environmental conditions.

The diagnosis of ADHD, like other psychiatric syndromes, is based on behavioral criteria. However, it would be important to identify information-processing deficits that account for the difficulties of children with ADHD so that interventions can be designed to ameliorate these deficits (Landau & Moore, 1991). Failure to delineate these causal mechanisms will lead to interventions that address only the behavioral correlates of these processes.

Carey (1990) indicates that the traits of high activity, high distractibility, and low persistence (or low attention span) are temperamental characteristics that have been demonstrated to exist in the general population and are found in children with no demonstrated problems in school adjustment. Yet, there is an overlap between these temperamental attributes and ADHD, which leads to the question of how the clinical entity is differentiated from temperament. The issue relates to whether attentional deficits are extremes of a normal continuum or whether there is a fundamental difference between temperament and a clinical disorder. If attentional deficits or other clinical syndromes represent the extreme form of one temperament dimension, then it would be helpful to view them on a continuum. However, more likely, the clinical syndromes that have temperamental underpinnings are the result of a convergence of various configurations rather than single-trait dimensions. The heterogeneity of this diagnostic grouping may be due to variations in the underlying dimensions that contribute to the cognitive, emotional, and behavioral manifestations of this entity.

Associated Problem Areas

Children with attentional disorders manifest problems with peer relationships, aggression, and impulsivity.

Peer Relationships

Children diagnosed with attentional deficits are characterized by poor peer relationships (see reviews by Landau & Moore, 1991; Wallender & Hubert, 1987; Whalen & Henker, 1985), which have been viewed as central and pervasive features of this disorder (Ross & Ross, 1982). In distinguishing hyperactive from nonhyperactive children, peer interaction items on questionnaires were found to be as effective as items focusing on the three core symptoms of attention deficit disorder with hyperactivity: inattention, impulsivity, and hyperactivity (Pelham & Bender, 1982). Negative peer relationships of children are predictive of serious problems during adolescence and adulthood that not only involve interpersonal functioning but also include academic and occupational difficulty, arrest records, and psychiatric disturbance (see Asher & Coie, 1990).

Youngsters with attentional difficulties do not modulate their social behaviors in response to changing cues for appropriate behavior (King & Young, 1981; Whalen et al., 1979). Therefore, such children tend to be intrusive, boisterous, and generally aversive to others. Even when adolescents with this syndrome have the requisite social knowledge, they cannot apply them (Hechtman, Weiss, & Perlman, 1980; Waddell, 1984). Some have concluded that rather than suffering from a *social-skills* deficit, youngsters with ADHD have a *performance* deficit (see Loney & Milich, 1982). Accordingly, social problems of youngsters with ADHD stem from their inability to apply their social knowledge. They can choose the correct response if they are presented with the alternatives but cannot spontaneously generate them (Whalen & Henker, 1985).

Aggression

Children diagnosed with ADHD are heterogeneous with respect to aggressive behavior. Some have serious difficulties inhibiting aggression, whereas others only seem to have difficulty inhibiting social behaviors that are inept or intrusive. Some children are unable to calibrate behavior to subtle cues but can behave appropriately in structured interpersonal situations.

Loney and Milich (1982) reported that 65 percent of the children who met the criteria for hyperactivity also exhibited aggression. Other studies also found that two-thirds of the hyperactive group were diagnosed as having an aggressive conduct disorder, while three out of four of those with an aggressive conduct disorder were also hyperactive (Stewart et al., 1981; Satterfield, Hoppe, & Schell, 1982).

The substantial overlap between attention deficits and aggressive behaviors has prompted some to consider the idea that the two are not distinct disorders but overlapping variants of a single, global, externalizing disorder (Lahey, Green, & Forehand, 1980; Milich, Loney, & Landau, 1982; Quay, 1979; Sandburg, Rutter, & Taylor, 1978; Shapiro & Garfinkel, 1986; Trites & LaPrade, 1983). However, it should be noted that these disorders have somewhat different correlates and outcomes (e.g., Hinshaw, 1987; Werry, 1988).

Since childhood aggression is a stable behavior pattern and a prime predictor of later aggression and antisocial behavior as well as of adult psychopathology (Eron & Huesmann, 1984; Loeber & Dishion, 1983; Robins, 1979), it is important to distinguish between ADHD with and without aggression. Aggressive boys differ from their nonaggressive counterparts in their interpretation of social situations (reviewed by Whalen & Henker, 1985) in that they are more likely to attribute hostile intent to the behavior of their peers.

Impulsivity

Impulsive behaviors have been associated with many clinical disorders, including both ADHD and conduct disorders (see Chapter 22). As indicated above, impulsive behavior can range from being defiant or disobedient to becoming delinquent or aggressive. Such behavior can stem from being excitable, restless, short sighted, acting before thinking, acting on only part of the information, making quick decisions, frequent activity shifts, or difficulty with organizing ideas or behavior. Individuals who do not delay their responses to consider all of the information are prone to inaccurate conclusions and inappropriate behavior.

Impulsive cognitive style has been described as rapid responding with little systematic evaluation of alternatives (Kagan et al., 1964). Children with ADHD show a more impulsive cognitive problem-solving style than typical peers and display less critical evaluation of alternatives in problem-solving situations such as Matching Familiar Figures Test (Campbell, Douglas, & Morgenstern, 1971).

Attentional Difficulties and Projective Stories

The manifestation of attentional difficulties in projective stories is not synonymous with the diagnosis of ADHD, which should be based on the DSM criteria. However, analysis of stories, particularly in the context of a comprehensive assessment, can clarify the extent and nature of the attentional difficulties. Stories reveal the narrator's ability to monitor and integrate the sequence of ideas according to task demands as well as the extent to which behaviors are governed by socially accepted rules, long-term considerations, or inner conviction.

Constantino and colleagues (1991) used the TEMAS, a set of highly structured picture stimuli, to differentiate referred children who met the DSM III-R diagnostic criteria for ADHD from a normal comparison group. They found that examiners were three times more likely to prompt the ADHD children to include various story elements than the normal group members. Despite this extra "help," the ADHD children were more likely to omit details about the stimuli than normal children. However, the specific elements that were omitted differed according to ethnic group (Hispanic, black, white). The prospect of using picture stimuli to gauge attention to the perceptual details as well as monitoring and calibrating responses to the cues provided is intriguing and warrants investigation.

Below is a comparison of stories told by two children, Brian (age 5–7) and Cathy (age 6–0), with IQ (Stanford Binet) scores in the superior range at the 96th and 97th percentiles, respectively. Brian was referred due to concern about social and academic adjustment in kindergarten. His teacher described him as inattentive and unfocused on the tasks. Cathy was evaluated because her parents wanted to know if she was "gifted."

Cathy

C.A.T. Card 2: Three bears are playing tug-of-war, and one bear wants to win so bad but he doesn't think he's going to win. (Feeling?) Feeling OK, he's thinking, "Can I win? Am I strong enough to pull it so I can break it?" (To) Turns out they all win. The end.

Brian

C.A.T. Card 2: Three bears pull a rope, and they can't break it. And then they're going to fall on their bottom. (To?) The three bears eat porridge. (Thinking? Feeling?) Eat the rope.

Cathy sets a context by describing the three bears as playing tug-of-war instead of pulling a rope with no apparent purpose. She also coordinates one individual's desire to win with the cohesiveness of the group. Brian doesn't differentiate individuals from one another, and neither the individual nor the group has a mission, goal, or plan for actions. They simply fall on their bottom. The response to the inquiry regarding how things turned out reflects associative thinking to the story of the three bears ("eat porridge"). This is followed by a silly and tangential response to a query. They "eat the rope" is a further association to the theme of eating and suggests loss of focus related to the attentional problem.

Cathy

C.A.T. Card 7: The monkey is very scared because he knows if he doesn't move fast, he will be eaten. He feels he is not very safe in the jungle. So he feels that he is going to go out to the city to find a home. The tiger thinks he is going to be so fast he is going to eat the monkey. The end. (To?) Turns out that the tiger was wrong, and the monkey got safe and decided not to go out to the city after all. The end.

Again, Cathy's story has a balance among thoughts, feelings, and actions. The monkey and tiger are well differentiated in actions and intentions. The story's details are coherent and contribute to the main themes.

Brian

C.A.T. Card 7: The tiger is going to catch the monkey, and the monkey is going to be dead. The tiger eats the monkey. Eating . . . teeth, yeah, yeah. (Thinking? Feeling?) What a yummy breakfast. (Made monkey noises.)

Unlike Cathy's story, inner states and intentions are not elaborated. The story progresses in a linear, associative fashion. Catch the monkey, kill the monkey, eat the monkey. The story is not integrative, and the viewpoint of the monkey is ignored.

Cathy

C.A.T. Card 8: Mother monkey is telling her baby to be good. The monkey feels that he won't be good. The other monkey whispers to the other monkey, "I think he's going to be bad." The little monkey feels that he's going to be OK. How it turns out is that he thinks he's going to be OK, and he was good. The end.

The story involves the integration of inner feelings, outward expectations, and actual behaviors from different perspectives. The narrator attended to all the relevant aspects of stimulus and story instructions.

Brian

C.A.T. Card 8: The monkey goes to the doctor. They're drinking some tea. Then she came to take his temperature. He got up and started walking past the lady and jumped out the window. (Thinking? Feeling?) I don't want to get a shot.

The story details don't fit with the context. The transitions between ideas (e.g., drinking tea, she came to take his temperature) are not logical. Actions are impulsive responses to a whim (jumping out the window to avoid getting a shot). It is noteworthy that Cathy finishes the story herself. She does not need to be prompted more than twice to give an ending. Thematically, her concerns relate to the coordination of inner direction and external approval. Brian's concern is with what will happen to a character from the outside. Also, Brian does not exert as much control over the logic and coherence of his story.

Below are two stories told by Jason, Age 7–0 (IQ = 126), who was referred for evaluation because of hyperactivity and inattentiveness in school.

> Card 1: This boy is thinking how to use a violin cause he cannot figure out how to play it. He tries. He wants to ask his mom but his mom is not home. And is daddy is home, but he doesn't know how to play a violin either. So, he (boy) goes to the music store and asks the man how to play it. And he played it. (Feel?) Happy.

This story proceeds in a series of unlikely actions produced in an associative way. The child thinks of various alternatives but none of them entail a realistic approach to the dilemma.

> Card 2: Don't know about this one. I got it. A girl is on her farm. Her daddy is plowing the fields. Her mother is just standing there. The girl has some books that I think she's going to read. The end. (Feel?) Happy. No, sad. (Feel sad?) Yeah, because they don't look too happy. See! See! (What are they sad about?) Don't know.

The responses are little more than associations to the stimulus features as attention wanders from one stimulus element to another.

The following two stories were told by Richard, aged 9–5, who has average intelligence and displays attentional difficulties.

> Card 1: One day there was a little boy named Ralph. And he was sad 'cause he couldn't play the violin. Are these drawings or pictures? (What do they look like to you?) [no response] (Tell me what happened before) Well, before he couldn't play 'cause he lost his stick, and he was sad 'cause he couldn't play in the band. He couldn't go to the concert and play 'cause he doesn't have a stick. And all the people would boo. Then he couldn't make any money, and they'd have to tear the place down.

Rather than focusing on resolving the problem, the narrator's thoughts are a series of inevitable consequences triggered by the negative emotions generated by the card.

> Card 2: This is a story about . . . this is hard. One day there was a girl who lived on a farm with her mom and dad. Her dad liked to fix the crops with the horse, and her mom liked sewing things. And she (the girl) liked to

read lots of books. Well, the first thing . . . they try to make money by selling crops so she can buy books. And the mother is pregnant, and the mom needs the money for the hospital and for the baby. (What are they thinking and feeling?) That they want to have enough money or the mom couldn't have the baby and she couldn't go to school. (How does it all turn out?) They would have to sell their house, and the mom couldn't have the baby. They are worried about running out of money.

The story details are triggered as the narrator perceives card details (e.g., need money because the mother is pregnant and the girl needs books). Again, negative feelings lead to further unhappy thoughts and an unhappy ending rather than to problem resolution.

The stories below were told by Tommy, aged 9–1, who received a very superior IQ score on the WISC-R (135; 99th percentile). The three lowest subtests, (scored in the low-average range) were those that are adversely affected by distractibility—namely, arithmetic, digit span, and coding. The youngster is described by teachers as a poor reader and as exhibiting poor social interactions as well as poor organizational skills.

Card 1: What happened before? (Yes) All right. Michael didn't want a violin for Christmas but got one anyway. Then he wouldn't play it. His mother gave it to his older brother who needed it because he was in a band at school—the school band. The end. (Feel?) Like why did mom ever bother getting it.

The child is trying to structure the story according to the directions. The content suggests that he has difficulty processing intentions behind actions. The boy can't understand why his mom would get him the violin when he doesn't want to play. Subsequently, the violin is given to the brother, who plays it in the school band. Tommy's inactive processing style may be related to boredom and lack of interest. The boy does not want a violin and refuses to play it. Likewise, the mother is depicted as not being invested in who the recipient is (gives it to the brother).

Card 2: This one is going to be hard. (long pause) All right. Mary wanted to go to church. Her parents didn't want her to. Middle. After they went to sleep, she snuck off. What is she thinking? When will I ever be able to go to church? She gets to go to church. The lady looks ceramic like Chinese dolls.

The story's message that parents misunderstand their children echoes the one in the first story. But this time, the parents don't allow a girl to do something virtuous (go to church). The last comment shows the narrator's attention to be drawn to an irrelevant aspect of the stimulus. It is also important to note that the story teller continues to use the directions as an organizational crutch.

> Card 7GF: (long pause) Can we skip this one? (No, try it) (long pause) I think I got one. Jo wanted her mother to read her a story. Mother picked a story she hated the most. Then Jo dozed off. What is she thinking? When will this story end?

Again, the narrator uses the instructions inflexibly to structure his approach to the story. The content of the story shows his boredom and difficulty attending and reinforces the attribution of hostile intentions to authorities hinted at by the previous two stories. He is developing oppositional attitudes, expecting to be misunderstood and imposed on.

Summary

Despite a series of name changes, the conceptualization of attention disorder continues to emphasize inattention, impulsivity, and overactivity. A variety of difficulties coexist with attentional disorders that engender problems with peer relationships, motivation, learning, task persistence, and modulation of behavior to task demands and social expectations. These manifestations of attentional deficits in projective stories are illustrated.

CHAPTER 10

Integration

The stream of life events is multifaceted. Many day-to-day activities involve inferential judgments about complex situations requiring simultaneous processing of information on multiple dimensions. Accurate perception of a person's actions requires awareness of the history and context for behaviors, the current situational provocation, and inner qualities such as feelings, thoughts, and motives. Available information must be weighed and integrated with knowledge based on accumulated experiences. Thought processes aimed at organizing and integrating experiences make it possible to anticipate events, plan actions, and exercise control over daily life. These processes permit the individual to draw conclusions based on patterns of events rather than on the provocation of the moment and to comprehend the "flow" of conversation, including verbal and nonverbal elements. Discerning the intent behind the words also requires integrative capacities. Full reality testing is diminished to the extent that any of the components of the integrative process is deficient.

Elements of cognitive style contribute to individual differences in the manner of perceiving and integrating ongoing life experiences. The following three dimensions of cognitive complexity-simplicity (Bieri, 1971) taken together comprise the relevant facets of this construct (Messick & Kogan, 1966; Schroder, Driver, & Streufert, 1986): (1) number of concepts, categories, or dimensions utilized in perception and judgment; (2) degree of subtlety in differentiation (conceptual discrimination or articulation) among stimuli; and (3) conceptual integration or the multiplicity of connections among concepts including hierarchic relationships. A person with a complex cognitive style perceives fine distinctions and considers many linkages among concepts, whereas those with less complex and more concrete cognitive styles make vague or gross distinctions and few connections among concepts.

Messick (1987) cautions against formulating strictly cognitive theories of perceiving, remembering, and thinking. Lack of interest and negative affect are associated with less differentiation of stimuli. Negative emotion such as anxiety tends to initiate dedifferentiation of cognitive structures. For example, under pressure there is a tendency to become rigid in one's thinking, to be more polarized and dogmatic in one's opinions, and to simplify the integrative operations by using fewer dimensions in conceptualization and judgment (Messick, 1965; Schroder, Driver, & Streufert, 1986). Moreover, shallow processing (focus on discrete facts and information learned by rote) is more likely when a person has little interest in the material or has a heightened level of anxiety (Fransson, 1977). On the other hand, there appears to be a relationship between positive affect and more efficient organization of cognitive material. Positive affect is associated with access to a larger number of cognitive constructs, which in turn are more likely to be interrelated (Isen, Daubman, & Gorgoglione, 1987).

Integration falls into three broad categories:

1. The ability to synthesize, organize, combine, and restructure information. This capacity is needed to reconcile conflicting information and develop a time frame and context for ongoing events.
2. The ability to coordinate and integrate various levels of information that require inferences or attention to implicit facts. The coordination of different levels of information requires the capacity to "read" between the lines, infer emotions, and make judgments, which take into account the presence as well as the absence of information. This capacity is needed to grasp the unspoken demands of tasks and relationships.
3. The ability to coordinate inner and outer elements of experience such as insight or judgment with planful action. An individual may "know" what to do but be unable to apply it spontaneously due to a variety of reasons such as being "caught" up in the moment, lack of interest, or difficulty with timing or modulation.

The story telling task is highly integrative, and the manner in which the story evolves, its form and content, reveals the narrator's integrative process. Emphasis on the perceptual features of the stimulus cards, getting bogged down in story details, and an inability to set a context or time frame for feelings, actions, and outcomes suggest difficulty with this process. A study by Zimring and Balcombe (1974) with 21 subjects ranging in age from 18 to 40 found that a measure of cognitive integrative performance (memory for sentences after an intervening task) was correlated with the degree to which feelings were attributed to characters in T.A.T. stories. The authors concluded that the ability to formulate a "theme" that includes emotions (i.e., the ability to handle emotionally relevant material) shares a common process with cognitive integration.

In the Rorschach, the goodness-of-fit or perceptual match between the blot contours and the object reported constitutes the basic element of "reality testing." The response to the Rorschach task involves the matching of ambiguous stimuli with a memory trace (Exner, 1986). In the story telling task, the ambiguity lies with discerning the thoughts, feelings, and motives of characters depicted. The task demands not simply a perceptual matching but "experiential" matching. The response to the T.A.T. must integrate the stimulus with past experiences to breathe life into static human characters and to provide an interpretation of a character's inner reality (feelings, thoughts, and motives) as a basis for actions and outcomes. This is consistent with Bellak's (1986) notion of "apperceptive distortion," where past experience is assumed to be superimposed on current perception.

The story telling directions indicate that thoughts and feelings be included. Furthermore, directions call for a time dimension by asking the respondent to tell what's happening in the picture, what happened before, and how things turn out. The directions do not explicitly ask for a description of what people do to produce outcomes, so it is up to the story teller to include actions as explanations for outcomes. When telling a projective story, respondents superimpose their style of organizing experiences with human beings to the scene portrayed in the stimulus.

The complexity of thought process can be gauged by examining aspects of content such as time perspective and quality of insight. Tomkins (1947) indicated that the story teller's level of self-awareness can be gleaned from the insight attributed to the T.A.T. characters. The essence of the integration concept is the synthesis of various facets of experiences through the coordination of: (1) Perceptual and Conceptual Processes; (2) Details and Context; (3) Present, Past, and Future Time Frames; and (4) Inner and Outer Elements of Experience. These integrative processes are evident in the story telling task as described below.

Integration of Perceptual and Conceptual Process

Integration of perceptual and conceptual process requires an individual to organize facts that are present and absent, to make inferences beyond what is immediately apparent, to recognize implicit and explicit facts, to relate details to concepts, to relate a specific event with its context, and to reconcile discrepancies among facts or events.

The concept of perceptual integration (discussed in Chapter 7) refers to the use of the stimulus in meeting the task demands given in the directions. A high level of perceptual integration requires that the story reflects the complexity of the stimulus by: (1) inclusion of all characters depicted, (2) focusing on most relevant aspects of the stimulus, and (3) depiction of relationships and affects consistently with the stimulus. A key ingredient in the integration of perceptual and conceptual process is the ability to grasp the connections among the perceptual elements of a situation or stimulus.

The initial level of reality testing with regard to projective stories pertains to the use of the stimulus and relates to the story teller's ability to incorporate stimulus properties with the story events. For example, Card 4 of the T.A.T.

depicts a man looking away from a woman who is holding him. A description of these characters as two people in love fails to make distinctions between the characters demanded by the stimulus. It is possible that the story teller can only focus on one aspect of a stimulus configuration or cannot integrate the characters' physical proximity with their facial expressions due to difficulty reconciling discrepant sources of information. It is also possible that the narrator prefers not to deal with conflict or negative emotion.

The following story told by a young man with borderline IQ (age 19–3, completed grade 10) demonstrates exclusive reliance on the perceptual processes. The narrator is unable to move the story beyond the perceptual cues provided. The story begins and ends in reference to the stimulus properties. The character expresses interest in playing the violin, but ends up looking sad, as portrayed in the picture.

> Card 1: The little boy with a violin. He seems like he's thinking how to use it. I don't know the other part. (Feeling?) Looks sad. Looks interested in violin—want to learn how to play. (End?) He picks it up and looks like in picture. He's kind of sad.

Another indication of poor integration of perceptual and conceptual processes is when the story teller shifts from one part of the stimulus to another without positing a relationship among the characters portrayed. The process of telling the story below was to jump from one isolated piece of the stimulus to another, thus relying on purely perceptual processes without conceptual integration. The story was told by the same individual as above.

> Card 2: The man is working on a farm with two ladies. One lady is carrying books—like she's ready to go to school or go to read. One lady on tree looking toward something. (What's happening?) The man looks like he's just working on a farm, on a farm. Other lady by the tree is thinking about I don't know. You can't picture myself thinking, well in their position, I just can't picture it. I don't know how they would think. (Feeling?) The man is feeling strong. The other lady wants to read books. The other lady is looking at the sky, holding her stomach. (End?) I don't know.

In the above story, the inner states of individuals are described in the present time frame without enduring purpose and with minimal departure from the stimulus. "Carrying books like she's ready to go to school or go read" is an association to the stimulus. A more conceptual approach would be to relate longer-term aspirations or to link "books" with a specific purpose within the context of the rural scene portrayed in the background.

The same individual's story told to Card 3BM is also devoid of inner purpose, meaning, or context beyond the moment portrayed in the stimulus and reflects the inability to judge inner states.

Card 3BM: Laying on the floor crying. Look like it to me. (What happened?) Something must have happened, must have caused it at her or something. Something she didn't like made her upset so she is crying. (Thinking?) I can't tell what she is thinking. (End?) She sad 'cuz she still ain't got up.

Coherence of Details and Context

Provided that a story has been told, various facets contributing to the coherence of plot details can be identified: (1) clarity and differentiation of concepts, (2) process of reasoning, (3) coherence of story structure, and (4) coherence of story events.

Clarity and Differentiation of Concepts

Conceptual clarity refers to the relationship of details to concepts. Details of the story may fail to support the story's premise for three types of reasons:

1. The story is mired in detail so one can't see the forest for the trees, and additional details do not introduce new concepts.
2. Concepts are vague due to lack of supporting detail (e.g., "something bad happened. They will try to solve the problem."). Such haziness may represent vagueness in thought processes, concrete thinking, or an evasive response. Stereotypic description of characters and interactions may also be reflective of vagueness, evasion, or concreteness. Those who lack a genuine understanding of relationships may resort to vague or stereotypic descriptions because they cannot draw on their own experiences.
3. The story is replete with grossly incompatible details and errors in language (e.g., contradictions, perseverations, irrelevant comments, or bizarre language). Maintaining the logical coherence of the story requires self-monitoring to keep track of and organize story details and to screen out socially inappropriate content or contradictions in the logic among details and concepts.

The following story told by a 7-year-old boy (low average IQ) illustrates incompatability among story details. The boy escapes through a window despite the previous statement that there were no windows.

Card 14: Boy in this house—one door and none windows. It's spooky in there. The boy didn't like it. The door almost closed on him. There was one way to get out—by breaking the window. (To?) He climbed out of the window and he broke it. Nothing else.

Conceptual clarity requires differentiation and sensitivity to detail and nuance as well as their organization. Differentiation requires distinction of inner and outer experience, fantasy from reality, likely from unlikely events, wishes from realistic probability, and cause from effect. The narrator may attend to only one conceptual level and may, for example, describe only actions or feelings without incorporating context. The story teller may have a poor understanding of relation of cause-effect (e.g., effort-outcome; action-reaction) and describe characters who have no clear idea of why things happen (e.g., "Done something wrong and got punished").

Stories may represent genuine attempts to comply with task instructions but may be glib in the sense that they're not based on meaningful concerns. Stereotyped stories are frequently told on the level of words without reflection to inner experience. The ability to learn from experience is a function of integration and organization of past events. Therefore, evidence of such integration is important to note in projective stories. These include (1) coherence within characters and coordination of perspective among characters; attribution of feelings, purposes, motives, and inner life to characters in ways that are integrated rather than discrete or fragmented; (2) coordination between fact and interpretation or inference; and (3) sequence of events is guided by realistic thinking as opposed to idealized, naive, stereotyped, wishful, or magical thinking. Events described are likely rather than outlandish, incorporate realistic time frames, and are logically consistent and conceptually clear.

In the story below told by a 16-year-old girl of average intelligence, the daughter's intention is noble but her purpose lacks clarity as she has only vague ideas of how to help her family. She expresses high aspirations without describing realistic means toward their attainment.

> Card 2: Hmmm. Once upon a time, there was a family in England that was very poor in the early 1700s. And the family only had one small farm that they needed to till and plant. Sarah, the oldest daughter of the family, was more interested in books and school than planting. She wanted to be a teacher. She knew that she would help her people if she studied hard and helped to pass acts through Parliament. So she went off to Oxford, to be a school teacher, and that's it.

The following story was told by a 12-year-old boy who, despite a high IQ (VIQ = 133; PIQ = 126), received grades of C and D. The story is mired in details that are added associatively rather than conceptually. The narrator is not able to make decisions about the length and quality of the story and does not set priorities on facts. On the verbal parts of the WISC-R, he gave as much detail as he could rather than getting to the point in a concise manner. It is also noteworthy that he scored lowest on verbal subtests that required freedom from distractibility.

Card 1: Um. OK . . . This boy is a bit sad and is frustrated because his father is a musician of some sort and a violinist in particular and his father naturally wants him to be and he's a young child, and he's . . . he can't grasp or comprehend the skills it takes to play the violin and beneath the violin is the music he's trying to play and he's just staring at the violin asking how do I make you work? You know? And he's saying . . . um . . . he doesn't particularly want to quit . . . um . . . but he's frustrated, he's not boiling with . . . he's not angry . . . he's not dismayed in himself, he's just sitting there quietly thinking how can I . . . how do you . . . how can I get you to work violin? What do I have to do? Am I doing something wrong? He's just questioning himself . . . and he's going to pick it up and he's gonna . . . and he's gonna . . . he's gonna try his best, whether he gets it or not. He's going to still . . . if he gets it he's gonna feel the same way, he won't feel worse, but sooner or later it's just going to click and he's going to get it, reminiscent of my piano lessons. And he's going to become not a violinist like Pearlman, but he . . . and he isn't going to drop out and forget it in 20 years, he's just gonna . . . you know . . . it's just gonna be something he can do and when he comes home sometimes and he has nothing else to do he'll just pick up that old violin and start fiddling away and remember when he couldn't do it . . . and he's going to feel the same way later when he has something much harder and he looks at his old music and says oh that is so easy why didn't I get that . . . that is so easy . . . look at that, that is so easy . . . now this is hard. And he'll eventually say that about that piece again and . . . so he's not going to become an expert violinist and he's not gonna forget all about it, he'll just remember.

In the above story, the boy does not communicate with the father nor does the story communicate to the listener (reader). One index of the clarity of the story is in how well it conveys the main idea. The boy is stuck inside his associative thought processes that cannot be translated into appropriate action. Likewise, the story teller loses track of the format and scope of the story and is not in charge of the task.

Process of Reasoning

The analysis of the process by which projective stories are constructed can give clues about the integration difficulty. The process of reasoning is revealed by an examination of how the story evolves, which, of course, is evident in the structure of the story.

The reasoning process of the narrator can be examined by asking the following questions:

1. Does the story teller have a plan for approaching the task and for organizing the story?
2. Does the narrator monitor the progression of the story to focus on the most relevant ideas and keep from getting lost in the irrelevancies, to avoid repetitions and inconsistencies, to censor unacceptable thoughts, and to decide when to stop and start?
3. How are the ideas in the story evoked and how are they related to one another? Does the story teller reason by associating to the stimulus? Do ideas flow from emotion provoked by the stimulus? Does the story progress from detail to detail or from wishful thinking?
4. How does the story teller respond to inquiry or redirection of examiner?
5. What elements of the stimulus command attention? Is the focus on the most relevant aspects of the stimulus situation (e.g., foreground, emotions of characters)? Does the story teller center on part of the picture, excluding others? Does the narrator focus on one part of the picture, then another in a successive, linear, rather than integrative approach? Does the story teller get lost in the details of the stimulus?
6. What distinctions are made and how are they organized? What attributes of characters or situation are emphasized?

The story telling process is reflected in the structure and content of the narrative. The story teller's capacities for planning, organizing, and monitoring are evident in content depicting characters as planful or as being drawn from their purposes by unexpected events or as becoming aware of consequences after it's too late. Formal indices of the story teller's failure to monitor the story are overelaborations, repetitions, gross inconsistencies, gaps, and assumptions that are not shared with the listener.

Coherence of Story Structure

The story teller, who is in command of the story telling process, can plan and organize the story and make decisions about length, complexity, and type of story. On the other hand, the narrator can flounder through the process without an organizational plan or even without monitoring the content of the story as it unfolds. This process is reflected in the flow and logical coherence of the story. Disruptions and incoherencies in the story structure result from:

1. Shifting focus, inability to maintain a consistent point of view
2. Lack of planning of story content as evidenced by rambling, reacting to the stimulus, associating to feelings or previous story elements, getting lost in detail, or intrusion of personal thoughts

3. Indecision about stimulus or characters
4. Poor monitoring of story events, tenses, language, details, internal logic as indicated by incomplete sentences, perseverations, or by major contradictions within the story line.

The story below told by a boy, age 8–10 (VIQ = 105, PIQ = 100), illustrates the relationship of the story telling process and story structure.

> Card 1: What's that in front of him? I don't know what it is . . . Well, this boy's trying to put something together but messed up so he's thinking how to do it and thinking and thinking and then he got it. And then it was . . . um . . . he was . . . I'm thinking. OK, so he was going to try to put it together again and make something new out of it. So he took it apart and put it together again in a different way. And he made a sling shot. And he needed a sling shot because he was going deer hunting. But he didn't need it because his dad was going to shoot it with a gun. So he found . . . some squirrel. The end. Do you want to know his name? (If you'd like to give him a name) I don't know.

The above story was told without a plan or organizational strategy and little regard for responding to the stimulus. The story rambles through an associative thought process, which is reflected in lack of structural cohesion in the narrative and in the actions of the character. By the end, the boy was hunting squirrel, an activity that is far removed from the initial focus of the story and from the stimulus.

Coherence of Story Events

Conceptual oganization and integration of events within the story is indicated when:

1. The details support the main tenets, and the sequence of events and story details are compatible with a unified theme.
2. The story teller displays an understanding of cause and effect relationship such as the link between successful outcome and constructive effort.
3. There is congruence among feelings, thoughts, actions, and outcomes; the details of the story jive with intentions so that actions do not contradict thoughts or feelings (e.g., "he was bored but . . . practiced the violin for hours").
4. Sequence of events is likely, rather than highly improbable.

The coherence of story events is, of course, enhanced by characteristics of story structure, such as clarity of previous references, logical sequence of events, minimal indecision or vacillation, and overall plan in the evolution of the story.

Four general areas contribute to logical coherence of story events:

1. *Plot details*—logic and organization in the sequence of events.
2. *Cause-effect*—actions jive with intentions and consequences, efforts with outcomes, and possibility (wishes) with probability (reality).
3. *Intrapersonal cohesion*—characters attach meaning to experience, link events with appropriate feelings, balance insight and action, draw inferences and connections rather than respond to superficial elements, surface cues, or stereotypes. Inner cohesion is indicated when characters' activities are related to a purpose and organized around a clearly defined problem or dilemma where inner motives, outward actions, and consequences converge.
4. *Coordination of multiple perspectives*—accounting for the needs and viewpoints of all relevant characters with appropriate communication among them.

The story below, told by an incarcerated male, age 20–9, illustrates a lack of coherence of story events. It is about a boy whose mother brings him a violin, which is experienced by the boy as pressure to perform. Support comes indirectly from the friend and not from the mother. All this seems inconsistent with mom being so proud of him and so happy. There is a sense that the story is not based on real experiences but reflects an *idealized* fantasy.

> Card 1: His mother just bought him a violin. He is sad because he doesn't know how to play, but he doesn't want to disappoint his mom so he's trying to figure out how to play. He goes to a friend and he tells him about a lady who teaches violin. He goes to see her and she teaches him and then after that he learns to play. He plays for his mother and she's proud of him and he's happy. She's happy too.

Schroth (1977) attempted to adapt an integration scale for the T.A.T. originally devised by Slemon and colleagues (1976) for use with children on the C.A.T. The intent was to measure how well the stories were integrated in terms of coherence of plot details and appropriateness of story details to the stimulus.

Schroth's (1977, pp. 31–32) integration scale measured the degree to which a child successfully integrates themes into a coherent story on six points, ranging from 0 to 5 as follows:

0 = No theme or description.

1 = A meager story, primarily descriptive.

2 = Grossly incompatible themes in same story without attempting to integrate them and/or story which is completely unrelated to the picture. The subject may lose sight of the central theme of the story or the constraints of the stimulus. The result is a story which rambles.

3 = Somewhat incompatible themes in the same story with little or no attempt to integrate them and/or a story somewhat unrelated to the picture.

4 = Story integrated around one central or unified theme with perhaps some irrelevant details introduced.

5 = A complete, integrated story without irrelevancies.

The interrater correlations ranged from .80 to .84, and there was no correlation of the integration scale with IQ (r = .03). There were some age differences in integration in children between ages 6 and 10. Schroth's approach condenses a very complex area to a six-point scale that merges compatibility of story with stimulus, logical coherence of themes and basic ability to tell a story beyond mere description. There is no mention of other elements of integration such as coordination of character's needs, viewpoints, time perspective, or effort-outcome connection.

Integration of Time Perspective

The instructions require an historical context for ongoing events that integrates past, present, and future time frames (what's going on, what happened before, how it turns out). The narrator's conceptual integration of time is reflected by the realistic incorporation of time perspective with the other story elements. Thus, problem resolution or goal attainment occurs within a reasonable time frame, and actions are not just based on the moment but incorporate past, present, and future perspectives.

The following indicate faulty time integration:

1. *Immediate time*—The story teller only deals with the present time frame as depicted in the stimulus; the span of the story involves momentary changes in time such as "waiting to see if it stops raining"; the story deals only with immediate concerns, wishes, or preoccupations that are often trivial.

2. *Unrealistic use of time frame*—The basic question is whether resolutions or sequences of events are based on an appropriate time frame. Time is not meaningfully integrated when the sequence of events is dominated by passage of time rather than meaningful experiences or when the jumps are too great, and the intervening events seem to be "missing."

The following two stories told by a third-grade boy, age 8–10, in a self-contained class for emotionally disturbed children, illustrate these points. The progression of the narrative is driven by the passage of time without connection to meaningful experiences.

Card 13B: There was this one kid and his father bought a dog house and he sat on the porch with his feet outside. It didn't have a door. Then the kid grew up and the wooden house was all broken down. So he took the logs from the house and went and built his own and the end. (Thinking and feeling?) OK, OK.

Card 7GF: Can't think of a story for this one . . . This lady had a house and she adopted the kid and . . . I'm thinking . . . Uh, uh (sings) OK . . . and now I remember all the squiggly lines I had to do. (Bender) They moved and moved and kept on moving from house to house. Stayed in every house a month and then moved. Then moved in one house that they really liked and stayed there for 25 months. And then lived there and lived there and the older lady died and the little girl grew up and then she died. The end.

In all four stories that follow, told by a boy, age 6–7, there are no inner states or motives that guide the actions. The time element is not directly stated but implied. Each story proceeds by progression to the next "scene" in a linear manner. In Card 1, after you look at the violin, you play, then you set it down. In Card 2, after church, you eat supper. In Card 3, first, the girl's asleep, then shot, then dead, then people try to find the murderer. In Card 5, a mother talks on the phone, reads, and cleans the kitchen. There is no curiosity, purpose, or depth to the characters portrayed. These stories are not concrete in the sense that they don't depart from the stimulus. However, the story progresses by describing events associated with momentary changes in time rather than integrating meaning or inner life with actions.

Card 1: He's playing . . . a violin. He's looking at it, and he's gonna play and he's setting it down again. (Looked like a bat when you first turned it around).

Card 2: They're going to church. The old man is taking care of the garden for his mother, and his mother is on the thing. (What thing?) Tree. And when she gets back from going to church, she'll help and then they'll go for supper.

Card 3BM: The girl's asleep and she's going to stay asleep. The girl's shot, see the gun? And she's dead. When people get there and find the girl dead, they'll try to find the murderer.

Card 5: The mother comes in to get the phone, and she's talking and then goes back to reading a book and she'll clean the kitchen after she reads her book.

Coordination of Inner and Outer Elements of Experience to Establish Coherence within Individuals

Inner and outer elements of experience need to be differentiated and integrated as follows: (1) coordination of inner life with external expression; (2) attachment of meaning to experience by appropriately linking actions or external occurrences with emotions or intentions; (3) distinction of fantasy from reality, and wishful thinking from realistic appraisal (fantasy defined as internal processes not related to the situation at hand); and (4) relating efforts with outcomes and actions to consequences.

Inner representations, such as strivings, goals, and feelings of conviction or commitment, give meaning and coherence to external reality and allow individuals to step back, to delay action, to deliberate, and finally to act with purpose and direction. Children who tell stories only on the level of words, with no reflection to inner states, are not coordinating the inner and outer elements of experience. They are not looking beneath the surface and typically relate highly trivial or stereotyped content.

The directions for projective stories call for the inclusion of actions, thoughts, feelings, and outcomes that require the integration of inner and outer elements of experience. The coordination of inner and outer perspectives is evident when there is congruence in the relationships among thoughts, feelings, actions, and outcomes. Accordingly, actions of story characters are guided by inner motives, goals, purposes, or principles rather than emanating from external provocation. These actions, in turn, are coordinated with outcomes. Success or happiness results from realistic effort rather than unlikely or magical resolutions. Characters suffer the internal and external consequences of their inadequacies so that remorse, guilt, and shame as well as external punishment follow hurtful action. There is a context for perceived events, and characters act on the basis of their realistic insights and perceptions. Furthermore, the story content is free of contradictions or dysfluencies, which give the impression of an inability to monitor ongoing behavior.

Aspects of stories that indicate difficulty with integration of inner and outer elements of experience are discussed next.

Attaching Meaning to Experience

Words are detached from personal meaning and story content is shallow, superficial, or highly stereotyped. There is a glib quality to the story, which is told to comply with task demands. The content is not anchored to real experience or conviction. Actions and themes may emanate directly from the stimulus rather than from inner states.

The following story told by a fifth-grade boy illustrates these ideas:

> Card 5: The mother was inside the kitchen making dinner. She opened the door and yelled out, "Kids, it's time for dinner; set the table please." The children came out, set the table, then they all sat down and ate their dinner. (Feel?) After the dinner, the children said to the mother, "Thank you for the great meal." The mother said, "Clear the table and can you please do the dishes." And the children happily accepted the duty, then ran off to do their homework.

The story teller never addressed the examiner's query about feelings but continued with the glib dialogue. The message of the story is as follows: Children have no feelings; they do as they're told, act politely, and happily do chores.

Separation of Wishes from a Realistic Appraisal

The story teller may be preoccupied with wishes rather than realistic probability. Story content may include unlikely sequences of actions, magical or unrealistic resolutions, or grandiose exaggeration of a character's talents or power. In the following story told by a first-grade girl, the story teller escapes the negative scene depicted in the stimulus by describing a boy who does not deal with the situation at hand but gets caught up in thinking about a more exciting activity (festival).

> Card 3: A boy is sad. He dropped the scissors. And he is sitting down. He thinks about going to a festival. When he gets to the festival, he will have lots of tickets to go on rides.

Separation of Negative Emotions from Reality

Reality testing of emotions requires that one's feelings be evaluated separately from the target of the feeling. The story telling procedure may elicit anxiety either because of the stimulus features or the ambiguous nature of the task. The story teller may focus on threatening components of stimuli and react to these provocative aspects. Excessive preoccupation with worrisome thoughts or feelings intrude on the story telling process.

The following story told by a 9-year-old boy in a self-contained class for children diagnosed as emotionally disturbed shows the intrusion of anxiety-provoking thoughts (monster).

> Card 13: Kid was in his house. Then he went to the step and he has barefeet and he's sucking his thumb and a monster's coming up beside him . . . (Before?) I already told you. (To?) Good, bad, he dies. Can I stop?

Denial or Inability to Size Up Situations

The story teller cannot tell what's going on in the picture and cannot fathom the feelings of the people depicted. The story fails to acknowledge the tensions or conflicts inherent in the stimuli. Characters are unable to understand internal states and cannot anticipate reactions of others so that actions are judged only according to their external consequences, while inner states are ignored, misinterpreted, or caused directly by events.

The following story told by a boy, age 10–3, describes a child who cannot anticipate others' behaviors and misreads their intentions.

> Card 13B: I got one. (brightens up) There was a little boy who lived with his family but one day he woke up and they were gone. So he sat in the shed for two to three hours and he called the police. But they said they were nowhere to be found. But he said he wanted to stay in the house one more night. Three hours later, mommy and dad came back and said they only went to the grocery store. They did not think he would be up that long. The police came back and looked in the window and didn't bother the family.

Separation of Fantasy from Reality

The story teller is merging fantasy with reality when he or she is unable to read the most blatant external stimuli or to separate inner and outer reality. Stories reflecting preoccupation with fictional characters and events that are ineptly superimposed to fit the stimuli also suggest a merging of inner and outer reality, which is particularly problematic in the context of gross stimulus distortion and associative thought process. Some children do superimpose a canned or fictional story to compensate for difficulty making up a story. This does not reflect an integration deficit if they are fully aware that they are utilizing a strategy, and if they accurately interpret the stimulus and comply with task directions.

The following story illustrates a merging of fantasy and reality. It was narrated by a third-grade boy with a tendency to tell numerous "tall tales" about his everyday experiences.

Card 6BM: This guy was standing by a statue and looking at it and saw that it was diamonds in the neck of it. And he tried to get it out and he scratched the neck. The neck of the statue fell off. He tried to do that to the whole statue and threw it on the floor. And he picked up all the diamonds and took them and got lots of money and bought lots of things including another statue like that of him. And it was made out of diamonds too and whenever he touched the diamonds on that one he turned into a diamond statue.

Merging fantasy and reality is suggested by describing the guy and the diamond statue as one and the same along with complete disregard of the external realities of the stimulus.

Coordinating Self-Presentation with Social Convention

Self-presentation violates social convention when the story teller is unable to keep story content within bounds of conventionality and relates bizarre (gruesome, hostile, sadistic) or highly unusual events due to inability to monitor thought processing. This is illustrated by the following story told by a 10-year-old with above-average intelligence in a self-contained classroom for emotionally disturbed children.

Card 8BM: One day a kid named (9 seconds elapse) Rick that liked to watch movies. His mother went to the store and gave him money to see a movie called . . . (40 seconds elapse; examiner prompts him to go on) He saw "Doctor's Office." They show about a man killed, killed big people and fishes and then the doctor said, "Gonna kill you man" and cut open his stomach and tore out his guts . . . and then Rick left the theater and thought the movie was nasty and told his mother about it and then went home and had dinner and then watched a show called . . . (10 seconds elaspe) "The Price is Right" and then went to bed. And then his father got home from the bar and he went to bed and made a whole bunch of noise and woke everybody up and heard a knock downstairs, went down, took out a knife, and stabbed Rick's mother. And Rick took his . . . took his . . . sword and took it and chopped off his dad's arms and legs and head and called the police and . . . the police came over and said that Rick's father had seen the movie that Rick seen and tried to do it because he's drunk. And Rick went to a foster home and seen the same movie again . . . (10 seconds elapse) and Rick ran away to see his aunt and uncle. (Feel?) Happy. (Throughout the whole time?) Scared before.

Other examples of failure to coordinate self-presentation with social convention are irrelevant conversation, immature, unacceptable, or unusual behavior during test sessions. For example, one child said, "If the card falls forward, I'll tell the story. If it falls backwards, it means I can't." Another child threw the blank card of the T.A.T. across the room, yelling, "There's nothing on it. I don't need it." Such children cannot coordinate general behavior during testing with socially acceptable standards of conduct.

Coordinating Motives or Intentions with Actions and Outcomes

Lack of coordination of motives and intentions is suggested when the impetus for a character's action is external provocation or when there is no purposeful action. There may be an absence of goals, aims, or interests where actions are based on whim or are externally provoked. Motives and feelings may be inconsistent with actions or outcomes, as when a character is bored with the violin but ends up as a famous performer.

The inability of characters to resolve the tension or conflict depicted, to attain goals, or to meet expectations through actions that are appropriate to the task or dilemma indicates that the story teller did not integrate effort and outcome. The character may exhibit helplessness and inability to act or may take unrealistic and inappropriate action to cope with the dilemma posed. Favorable outcomes may come about by wishing rather than constructive action, suggesting that the causal relationship between action and outcome has not been realistically integrated.

The character in the following story told by a kindergarten girl is not engaged in any purposeful activity.

Card 3BM: A boy is crying because he fell down. He was running and he tripped. He tells his mother. (End?) Don't know.

The following story told by a kindergarten boy describes a character who is helpless to react or to understand the cause of events and, finally, copes with the unpleasant incident by forgetting about it rather than by taking constructive action.

Card 3BM: She's sitting down. (Feel?) Bad because somebody hit her. She forgets about it. (Think?) That someone hit her. (Q?) A girl hit her and she was being nice.

Coordination of Perspectives of Different Individuals

Another facet of integrating inner and outer perspectives is the ability to account for the needs and viewpoints of other people that incorporate their inner state and external circumstance. Such integration is suggested when viewpoints, needs, motives, and desires of different individuals are coordinated, and the impact of one character's actions upon another is understood. Even cards portraying one character (1, 3BM) have potential to reveal qualities of interpersonal relationships because they often elicit stories about the expectations and support of others.

How the story teller coordinates concerns of different characters is a key to understanding how the perspectives of self and others are integrated. The coordination of perspectives is indicated when:

1. All relevant characters depicted in the stimulus are included in the story rather than centering on only one character.
2. Character's thoughts and feelings as portrayed in the picture are recognized, and discrepant stimulus cues are reconciled (e.g., Cards 2, 4, 7GF).
3. Ages and roles of characters are appropriate to the stimulus and story content.
4. Characters are meaningfully related to one another rather than isolated, each with separate insights or concerns that are not communicated.
5. Story maintains a consistent point of view so that there is coherence around one perspective rather than arbitrary shifts.
6. Characters have independent aims or interests but relate in ways that are mutually enhancing. They are aware of each other's motives and intentions; they share ideas and feelings; they influence or support one another; and they find appropriate resolutions if they disappoint one another.
7. The relationship of characters is well defined rather than vague.

Stories that fail to coordinate more than one perspective focus on one aspect of experience at a time, as reflected by: (1) themes indicating superior-inferior relationships where one person seeks glory while the plight of another is not addressed; (2) emphasis on the needs or concerns of one character in a one-sided depiction of relationships; (3) actions that emanate from emotions or provocations rather than from purpose or insight; and (4) themes emphasizing the impact of one character's actions on another without incorporating intent.

The following story told by an incarcerated male, age 20–9, demonstrates the unrealistic coordination of the needs of the characters.

> Card 2: This girl has just come home from school and she's thinking whether she wants to stay on the farm or go off and make a lot of money and then come back to help them. She knows it'll never happen unless she gets a job because her mother is pregnant and her father is struggling with the farm and they barely have enough money to take care of them all. So one day the principal tells her that because of her grades she won a scholarship. She goes to college and becomes a famous doctor and gets alot

of money and comes back home to help her father and mother take care of the farm. Everyone is doing OK. Her father is out of debt and everyone is happy and she goes back to work.

The family appears to be in immediate need, but the girl decides to become rich and famous before offering help. While she is away, the family's plight back at the farm is irrelevant. They remain a helpless foil for the return of the heroine. The moral of the story is: If your family is struggling, you take your time to become rich and famous before you can help. Neither the needs of the characters nor time perspective are coordinated.

The following story was told by an 18-year-old incarcerated male to Card 10, which depicts two people. At first the focus is entirely on one character. Later, when the perspective changes to include both characters, there is a lack of differentiation between the two people who experience the same pervasive feeling of "loneliness inside them."

Card 10: He's sad. He could be saying that words can't describe how he's feeling. He looks real sad. Why, I don't know. (Happened before?) He could have walked up to the police or they were sitting there talking or maybe they feel the loneliness inside of them. (To?) Feels real sad.

Levels of Integration

The facets of integration described in this chapter are scaled below according to increasing levels of reality testing and organization applied to information processing. Tarvin (1989) reported 92 percent interrater agreement with this scale. Coefficient alpha, a measure of internal consistency across cards, was .84. Furthermore, the integration levels effectively differentiated between emotionally disturbed boys and a normal comparison group.

1 = Impaired Integration
Impaired integration is indicated by:

1. Depiction of *highly* unlikely sequences of events reflecting extremely poor judgment and clearly distorted understanding of cause-effect relationships (e.g., Card 8BM—cutting this man up to see what's inside). Themes stand out as unusual, highly unrealistic, or bizarre, indicating confusion and inability to monitor the content of the story.
2. Gross contradictions, logical inconsistencies, perseverations, or arbitrarily shifting perspectives. The individual is baffled by the task and/or cannot monitor the flow of ideas. The story outcome is grossly incompatible with actions, thoughts, or feelings of characters.

3. Emphasis on discrete details that remain unconnected or contradict one another. The respondent may be so taken with the stimulus pull that he or she cannot go beyond a narrow focus or reaction to a relatively isolated aspect of the stimulus.
4. Gross imbalance between perceptual and conceptual processes, as well as confusion between inner and outer states resulting in difficulty separating fantasy from reality.
5. Difficulty reconciling discrepancies in the stimulus coupled with extreme difficulty reading people's motives or intentions or with coordinating outward behavior with inner states. Emotions and relationships described are grossly incongruent with the stimulus.
6. Inability to maintain personal distance from the stimulus so the narrator is overly reactive or frightened by the picture.
7. Extreme helplessness where one character is entirely at the mercy of the capriciousness of others or of frightening external forces.

The story teller may display inappropriate reactions to the testing situation, particularly when encountering difficulty with the task (e.g., throwing the cards, hostility toward the examiner, repeated derogation of the cards or testing process, producing fantasy content or other aimless verbalizations). Such unusual behaviors suggest that the individual is unable to monitor self-presentation. Likewise, bizarre content or the inclusion of intense hostility, cruelty, and sadism suggests an inability to monitor self-presentation to accommodate socially acceptable standards. Stories that are well organized in terms of their structure, but contain highly unlikely or inappropriate content reflecting extreme helplessness or poor judgment, are indicative of integration failure.

Formal aspects of thematic *content* that reflect impaired conceptual integration may include overspecific statements, overgeneralizations, strained logic, personalized statements, lack of transitions, or highly unrealistic cause-effect relationships. The scoring criteria for emotional disturbance in Chapter 14 are compatible with disorganized thinking suggested at this level.

Impaired integration is illustrated by the following story told by a 10-year-old boy of above-average intelligence who is in a self-contained class for emotionally handicapped youngsters.

Card 13B: The boy went back into the woods one day and he got lost and he saw a cabin so he came and asked if he could come in. And the boy, he stayed there overnight. And, that morning he got up and he was looking out the window thinking, "I wonder if I will ever get back to my own house." He's thinking of his nice soft bed. Then he hears some voices calling and he gets up, runs to the door and it was his mother and father and he gets up and he runs to them. And, umm, then the boy, umm, goes to, goes to lunch and then goes home and says, "Whew, now I'm in my own bed."

This story reveals very poor judgment on the part of the story teller. The boy in the narrative is trapped in one perspective, focusing on a highly trivial concern ("own bed") and cannot coordinate the viewpoints of various characters. The sequence of events is highly unlikely: Parents don't call authorities, the child stays overnight with strangers who don't contact the parents or authorities; the child worries only about his "soft bed"; and the parents magically appear the next day and resume their normal routine so that the child simply gets lunch and bed. The emotions are inappropriate to the situation. The story teller cannot fathom the reactions of others to the boy's being lost. Others are viewed only in relation to the boy's comfort and not as separate from his immediate needs and wants.

The following story told by a 9-year-old boy of average intelligence, also in a self-contained class for emotionally disturbed youngsters, represents an unsuccessful struggle to accomplish the task. The story teller seems unable to screen out fearful thoughts, which impairs his ability to continue with the task. The boy's death ends the story.

> Card 13B: Kid was in the house. Then he went to the step, and he has bare feet, and he's sucking his thumb and a monster's coming up beside him . . . (Before?) I already told you. (To?) Good, bad, he dies. Can I stop? (Examiner says if he would like to and the child turns off the tape recorder.)

Another example of impaired integration is the following story told by a 21-year-old woman with below-average intelligence incarcerated for drug possession and prostitution.

> Card 8BM: They cutting a man open. They cutting a man and they in the hospital and that's a gun ain't that a gun? They cutting a man open and it look like they gonna kill him. (End?) I don't know. Tragedy. (Feel?) I can't see. I don't know how they feel. He look like he a lawyer or something.

2 = Superficial Integration

This level of integration difficulty is indicated by evidence of naive, stereotyped, or wishful thinking. The events depicted are somewhat unlikely. The story may be vague (e.g., "something bad happened," "It turned out good") or may express naive or stereotyped themes. Story details don't seem to "add up" but are not blatantly incompatible. The main point may be lost in the details and process of telling the story. The story teller may have difficulty making a decision. In fact, the entire story could be a decision about the stimulus, or may include two or more parallel stories or consist of separate vignettes for each character.

The primary integration failures are as follows:

1. Short- and long-range perspectives are at odds or not balanced.
2. Interpersonal relationships are not coordinated, as shown by disparity among characters or by emphasis on needs of one character.
3. Difficulty with attaching *meaning* to experience as shown by characters' deficits in commitment or investment in long-term endeavors or by accenting superficial aspects of characters who have no depth, inner life, motive, or purpose. For instance, feelings are based purely on the acquisition of material possessions, or the opportunity to engage in exciting, fun-oriented activities. The story teller displays efforts to tell socially desirable stories and may adapt stereotyped content from movies or books. However, thematic content or dialogue seems artificial, with emphasis on external appearances or conformity to superficial roles ("Then they thanked the mother for the wonderful dinner").
4. Actions and outcomes reflect wishful thinking (but not merging of fantasy and reality) and absence of genuine purposes or goals.
5. Characters react to immediate provocation; they do not actively plan, anticipate, or follow through on a strategy. Means and ends (effort and outcome) are therefore not well coordinated. Likewise, the story proceeds without an overall plan on the part of the story teller.
6. Lack of conceptual clarity is reflected in vagueness or fuzziness in the relationships among the story details.
7. Imbalance among feelings, actions, and thoughts is evident when the story deals with only one element of experience, as when only actions are described without integrating thoughts and feelings or when characters have insight but do not communicate or act.

The following three stories illustrating this level of integration were told by a 20-year-old male with low-average intelligence incarcerated for distributing cocaine. The first story depicts a man concerned about his masculine role. Relationships with female characters do not entail an understanding of inner experience or aspiration, but deal only with attributes that relate to the man's perception of his role as provider of basic necessities.

Card 2: Before, that when the guy was probably a farmer even since he was small. Now he has a family and still farming while his wife is a housewife. Knows that he has to work to keep his family well taken care of. (long pause) (Feel?) That since he's the man of the house, he knows he has to work. Just can't give up to take care of family—feeling strong about it. (To?) Family has food on table every night and family is well cared for.

The story below describes a man who has to "give in" to keep a relationship so that only one character at a time derives satisfaction from interpersonal interactions.

Card 4: Story here begins that woman . . . she's in love with this man and has feelings for him that are real strong. Wants to be with him. He seems not to want to have nothing to do with her. Trying to turn away from her. End is that he starts to pay attention to her. Being together. He ends up giving into her . . . listening to her . . . being together.

The following story depicts problems, relationships, and actions in vague terms.

Card 6BM: Seems like something happens in family and guy talks to mother about what happened. Feelings like he doesn't know what to do, upset, he's hurt. Mother's giving him some advice about what to do . . . (Before?) Had argument . . . probably with wife or something. Ends up that mother gives him some advice of what to do. Goes back to talk to wife and they work out some kind of agreement.

3 = Moderate Integration

At this level, stories generally depict a likely sequence of events and include inner motives that are appropriate to the stimulus. There are subtle integration difficulties in coordinating perspectives of different characters or in establishing consistency between inner motives and actions particularly in regard to short- versus long-term goals. The story below told by a fourth-grade boy is about a child who disobeys his parents and runs away. Yet, he leaves a note to express his feelings to his parents and while he's away he misses his parents and has some insight into his behavior. The child is happy to come home when the parents find him. The boy assumes that the punishment was fair given his behavior, and he no longer wants to disobey.

Card 5: Well, this is a boy's mother and the boy didn't, like, mind very much. He disobeyed his parents a lot and they punished him a whole bunch. And he ended up running away; but now his mother is checking in his room and he's not there. She finds a note that says he ran away and that when you're not nice to me I'll run away. Then they find him in the forest; so he came home and he didn't want to disobey them anymore. While the boy was away, he thought about home and how he didn't mind much and how it was much better at home than in the forest. When he got home he felt happy.

4 = Good Integration

The highest level of integration is indicated when the story flows smoothly and depicts likely events in a clear, specific, and realistic manner. Feelings, thoughts, actions, and outcomes are well coordinated within and between characters. Story details cohere around central concepts and are consistent with the people and emotions depicted in the stimulus (though objects may be left out or misidentified, especially by young children). Actions and concerns of characters reflect long-range goals, consideration of others, and well-integrated time frames. Events are placed in a clear context, which integrate multiple dimensions and perspectives.

Good integration is illustrated by the following story told by a fourth-grade boy with high-average intelligence.

> Card 1: The boy, well there's a lot of people in his school who play in his school band. He couldn't play the violin very well. So he starts to practice on the violin but he just couldn't do it. But his grandfather was really good at playing the violin, so he asked his mother if he could go over his grandfather's house to get a lesson from him. So his grandfather started out easy and first he showed him notes so he would know how to play it. Then he handed him a violin so he (boy) played it. At first, he was bad at it, but then after two weeks of practicing with his grandfather he became good enough to join the school band. He feels very happy then. He ended up being one of the best violin players in the class. In the beginning he was sad.

The elements in the above story reflecting high integration are as follows: The boy sets goals consistent with interpersonal and task-related interests, seeks appropriate help, and puts forth appropriate effort. The perspectives of the characters are well coordinated: The boy asks mother's permission, the grandfather paces teaching to the child, and the boy joins the band and becomes "one of the best," not the only virtuoso player. Inner states such as interests and goals are integrated with effort and outcome so there is a coherence within the character of the boy. Time perspective and stimulus elements are well incorporated.

Summary

Concepts relating to integration are described and ordered into four levels representing increased organization applied to processing experience. Integration is the synthesis of the various dimensions of experience, which are necessary for full reality testing such as: (1) perceptual and conceptual processes; (2) details and context; (3) present, past, and future time frames; (4) inner and outer elements of experience; (5) perspectives of self and other; and (6) viewpoints of various individuals. An individual's ongoing integration of experience is applied to the interpretation of the scene portrayed in the picture and to the composition of the story.

CHAPTER 11

Emotion

Emotions are embedded in a matrix of interconnected elements of experience such as physiological reactions, cognitions, as well as expressive and instrumental behaviors (Lazarus, 1991; Schwartz & Shaver, 1987). Any one of the components within the network triggers the other parts to which it is associatively linked. For instance, negative affect tends to evoke physiological reactions, ideas, memories, and expressive motor reactions associated with that emotion as well as elicit other negative feelings (Berkowitz, 1990). An emotion can be characterized in terms of each of its elements. For example, anxiety is associated with the subjective experience of dread and awareness of aversive physiological reactions; it has an impact on attention and cognition, learning, and performance.

Lang (1987) proposed that anxiety disorders may be distributed along a continuum that is defined by the degree to which the negative affective responses are prompted by many stimuli and the fluidity with which their evocation transfers to a variety of memory structures. General anxiety states represent maximum fluidity in the association of stimuli and affect involving multiple affective response structures.

Berkowitz (1990) assumes a time sequence between the initial reaction to and final appraisal of an event. The initial impression of an incident as unpleasant evokes the feelings without complex thought processes. Subsequently, higher-order thought processes begin to modify and refine the initial reaction as thought is given to what happened, why it happened, and what the possible consequence may be. Cognitions such as causal attributions can intensify, diminish, or reframe the initial reaction. The conception of emotion as being embedded in a complex network sidesteps the debate about which is primary: emotion or cognition. However, emotional states that exist without cognitive processing (Izard, 1984; Zajonc, 1980) have been differentiated from true emotions that are products of cognitive appraisal (Lazarus, 1991). The higher-order processing of the primary emotions is what gives meaning and context to the experience of emotion (Shaver et al., 1987). Individuals vary in the degree to

165

which they engage in cognitive processing of emotionally laden events. For instance, some individuals experiencing aversive emotions may quickly blame others without thinking over the event. Sometimes, these individuals can be stimulated to engage in such processing.

Affect and cognition are not viewed as separate but as opposite sides of the same coin, each contributing to the larger process of development (Piaget, 1981). The associative network is cumulative and develops as the product of individual differences in the emotional reaction to and cognitive processing of life's experiences. Projective stories provide clues for how the story teller links emotions with cognitions and events.

The following components of emotions are briefly reviewed with reference to three clinically relevant emotions of arousal, anxiety, and depression: (1) biological bases; (2) subjective awareness and cognitive interpretation of inner states and situational cues; (3) impact on general information processing, learning, and performance; and (4) emotion management.

Biological Bases

The biological basis for emotion has been well documented and, in all likelihood, further refinements in technology will lead to more precise delineation of the physiological processes involved in specific emotions (see Leventhal & Tomarken, 1986; Oatley & Jenkins, 1992, for reviews). There is evidence that different physiological reactions are associated with different emotions. Leventhal and Tomarken (1986) discuss neuropsychological models of anxiety and describe evidence suggesting that the perceptual processing of emotional stimuli (that is, the ability to judge non-verbal affective cues associated with spoken language), emotional expression, and positive and negative emotional states are differentially controlled by the right and left hemispheres of the brain. On the basis of their studies with infants, as well as other research evidence, Fox and Davidson (1984) proposed that the left and right frontal regions of the brain are the anatomical substrates of "approach" and "avoidance" tendencies, which are assumed to be associated with positive and negative emotions respectively.

Temperament theorists (e.g., Buss & Plomin, 1984) have emphasized the role of emotions for understanding personality, as well as the biological roots of temperament. According to Goldsmith and Campos (1986), the primary emotions that are biologically determined and that constitute temperament combine with learning and experience to produce the more complex emotions such as shame and pride, which have cognitive components. These complex emotions are considered units of personality.

Individual Differences in the Biological Components of Affect

Since the components of emotion are interrelated in an associative network, a change in any one of the components activates changes in the others. Accordingly, individual variations in any one of the components of emotion influence the others. For instance, difficulty in grasping the nuances of interpersonal situations, a cognitive factor, may lead to tension and discomfort during social interactions as well as to anticipatory anxiety and avoidance behavior which, of course, further undermines the development of social skills. Conversely, cognitive difficulties may be triggered by intense emotions.

The components of emotions that are biologically based can be broadly subdivided into the two categories of reactivity and self-regulation, such as proposed by some temperament theorists (Rothbart & Derryberry, 1981; Strelau, 1983). *Reactivity* refers to the mechanisms of arousal such as sensitivity thresholds, response latency, and intensity of reactions. *Self-regulation* includes attentional, behavioral, and emotional processes aimed at modulating arousal. Thus, reactivity refers to the characteristics of the emotions, whereas self-regulatory mechanisms consist of activities that serve to normalize stimulation accompanying emotions.

Reactivity

Individual differences in characteristics of emotional reactivity are viewed by temperament theorists as being constitutionally based and influenced over time by heredity, maturation, and experience (Rothbart & Derryberry, 1981). These differences are in frequency, intensity, and duration of positive or negative emotions as well as sensitivity thresholds:

> *Quality of mood* refers to the relative frequency of experiencing positive and negative emotions (Thomas & Chess, 1977; Goldsmith & Campos, 1986). It has been suggested that differences in arousal patterns may predispose individuals toward certain forms of affect (Derryberry & Rothbart, 1988) and that susceptibility to positive and negative emotion is related to cortical arousability (Eysenck, 1967).

> *Intensity of emotions* has been defined as the intensity with which individuals experience both positive and negative emotions (see Larsen & Diener, 1987). On the low end of the affect intensity continuum are those who experience emotions mildly with little fluctuation. Those at the other extreme are highly reactive, experience emotions strongly, and are subject to variable emotions.

Threshold of sensitivity to stimulation is defined as the increment of change required to provoke a reaction. More work needs to be done on this concept because individuals may exhibit different thresholds according to type of stimulation (e.g., physical, interpersonal threat). Highly reactive individuals are characterized by high sensitivity to stimulation and low endurance, whereas low reactives have low sensitivity but high endurance (Strelau, 1983).

Duration refers to the length of time to get back to baseline after being emotionally upset (Buss & Plomin, 1984), and may be related to adaptability subsequent to intial reaction (Thomas & Chess, 1977).

Arousal refers to the level of alertness ranging from drowsiness to extreme excitement or agitation. Emotional experience has an arousal (intensity activation, energy) component that is nonspecific and a qualitative component that determines the nature of the emotional experience. Excessive arousal is related to difficulties with attention, concentration, and disruption in information processing, whereas low arousal is associated with boredom, apathy, or drowsiness. Arousal level is the result of internal and external stimulation. High levels of stimulation (intense sensory input, risk, time pressure, novel, or complex stimuli) lead to increases in arousal. Level of arousal is related to positive and negative emotions (Eysenck, 1981). Unexplained arousal precipitates negative affect (Rogers & Deckner, 1975; Marshall & Zimbardo, 1979; Maslach, 1979). Anxiety and other emotions have been viewed as being related to generalized autonomic arousal (Mandler, 1990). Nevertheless, both positive and negative emotions can be experienced at various levels of intensity or arousal (see Larsen & Diener, 1987).

Self-regulatory capacity refers to the individual's ability to control arousal and emotional responses (see Strelau, 1987). Such control can be exercised by actively approaching or avoiding stimuli or by the selective attention or inattention to potentially arousing stimuli (Rothbart & Derryberry, 1981).

Self-Regulation

Individual differences in self-regulation refer to the capacity to maintain optimum arousal and comfortable emotional states. According to the regulative theory (Strelau, 1983), reactivity is the primary dimension of individual difference and has a biological basis. Activity which serves as a source and regulation of stimulation to assure optimal arousal can take many different forms, depending on the social environment and other individual characteristics. Various disorders and behavior disturbances may result from the inability to regulate arousal by matching activity with reactivity. Since emotional states and arousal are associated with efficiency of cognitions, all of these are being regulated at the same time. Self regulation is viewed as a capacity and requires control of information processing, attention, arousal, emotion, as well as behavior. Individual differences in the management of arousal and emotions are due to biologically based variation in the capacity for self regulation (Rothbart & Derryberry, 1981).

Approach/Avoidance

Selection of activities and information regulate emotion and arousal. Approach/withdrawal behaviors have been viewed as basic to temperament (Thomas, Chess, & Birch, 1968) and as being based on positive and negative emotions (Fox & Davidson, 1984). Individuals differ in their reactivity to stimulation so that a stimulus that evokes a positive reaction in one individual may be aversive to another. Therefore, individuals engage in behavior with different stimulating value according to their reactivity to stimulation (see Strelau, 1983). People seem to experience more positive (or less negative) emotions in situations that they select than in those that are imposed (Emmons & Diener, 1986). However, some highly reactive individuals choose behaviors that increase stimulation to uncomfortable levels and lead to stress. Furthermore, various disorders and behavioral disturbance may result from the inability to regulate arousal by matching activity and reactivity. Sociopaths, for example, exhibit very high needs for stimulation (Orris, 1969; Quay, 1965, 1977).

Regulation of Attentional Processes

Thomas and Chess (1977) consider attentional factors such as distractibility and attention span (persistence) as basic temperamental attributes evident from infancy. If attentional processes are not under deliberate control, the individual's activities are vulnerable to disruption according to the external input. Extreme difficulty regulating cognitive, attentional, and emotional processes interfere with regulation of behavior under normal circumstances.

Coping Skills

Application of emotion management techniques and use of problem solving or metacognitive skills to put emotions into context enhances self-regulatory capacity. Information-processing style such as conceptual complexity (Harris, 1981) has been related to coping with stress. Mechanisms to cope with feelings can exist at varying levels of abstraction. An individual can react to anger by focusing on the preservation of an ongoing relationship or simply attempting to boost a wounded self-esteem (Lazarus, 1991). Optimal arousal assures the availability of sufficient energy for the acquisition and utilization of the skills needed to respond adaptively. If the arousal system is responsive to the situation (e.g., adaptability), there is no need for extreme efforts to regulate arousal.

The following two approaches deal with emotions (Lazarus, 1991): (1) problem-focused coping is directed at changing the self or the environment to alter the actual person-environment relationship, and (2) emotion-focused coping changes the cognitions in one of two ways, either by selective attention or inattention or by changing the interpretation of the event. Both ways of coping alter the meaning of an event, and when meaning changes, the emotion also changes.

Cognitive Appraisal and Subjective Awareness of the Feeling

Cognitive appraisals of potentially stressful events determine the emotional response (Beck, 1967; Ellis, 1962; Mischel, 1973) and serve self-regulatory functions. These appraisals are embedded in beliefs, attitudes, expectations, and perceived competence to cope with events.

Anxiety has been viewed as a reaction to the perception that the self is being threatened, and has been described as a state of helplessness (Mandler & Watson, 1966; Seligman, 1975). Individuals prone to anxiety tend to believe that they cannot control their own actions to meet challenges. They are aware of a feeling of worry, apprehension, fear, or dread, and might see innocuous events as threatening. In addition, they may experience a variety of physiological stress reactions, as well as the sense of adverse impact on cognitive processing. Such individuals may be oversensitive to cues of threat or to the possibility of failure and to the ensuing consequence. Anxious individuals may be preoccupied with apprehension and self-doubt. The state of being overly anxious leads to an attention shift toward self-preoccupation, and this self-focused attention further increases arousal, leading to a narrowing of focus on the ever-increasing awareness of potential danger and sensitivity to signals of threat (Gray, 1981, 1982). For instance, high-anxious subjects more readily direct their attention to a negative stimulus than do extroverts (Derryberry, 1987) and nonanxious subjects (MacLeod, Mathews, & Tata, 1986). Thus, anxious individuals exhibit attentional biases (Mathews et al., 1990), which foster an awareness of uncomfortable physiological reactions, self-doubt, and apprehension.

The subjective experience of depression is characterized by sadness, giving up, hopelessness, despair, and by physiological symptoms of depression, which are accompanied by fatigue, sleeplessness, apathy, and inability to function as expected. Depression has been viewed (Beck, 1976; Seligman, 1975) as a byproduct of a person's interpretation that events are beyond control. Cognitive distortion among depressed individuals about the self, the world, and the future are common (Beck, 1967). For example, depressed patients tend to recall incidents of loss or failure which they attribute to their own shortcomings (Brewin, 1988). The main features of these distortions are cognitions that are characterized by pessimism, sensitivity, overgeneralization, and self-derogation.

Information Processing, Learning, and Task Performance

Affect is inextricably embedded in information processing (Fiske & Pavelchak, 1986). Emotional states can lead to selective attention and learning of information (Bower & Cohen, 1982). A change in an individual's affective state can cause alterations in the interpretation of an event, just as a change in interpretation can cause an affective shift (Hoffman, 1986). Negative affects such as fear, anxiety, and overarousal lead to disruption of learning and attention. The result is the formation of distinctions that are less organized, less differentiated, and less integrated (Eysenck, 1981, 1982; Sarason, 1975). Also, such states lead to greater emphasis on negative aspects of situations that are mood congruent. Finally, defense mechanisms against such negative emotions may lead to distortions in cognitive processing.

In general, negative or depressed mood impairs cognitive processing, whereas positive mood facilitates processing (e.g., Isen & Means, 1983). States of depression are associated with impaired learning and memory (e.g., Cohen-Sandler, Berman, & King, 1982; Leight & Ellis, 1981; Masters, Barden, & Fard, 1979). Motivational deficits, which may or may not be related to these cognitive deficits, are also associated with depression, which appears to limit the allocation of resources toward effortful processing of information (Cohen-Sandler, Berman, & King, 1982).

Affect intensity also influences cognitive processing of emotional stimuli (see Larsen & Diener, 1987). Individuals high on affect intensity focus on the most emotionally provocative aspects of the slides presented, tend to personalize events, and overgeneralize from the events depicted in the slides (Larsen & Diener, 1984) (regardless of whether the affect depicted is positive or negative).

The impact of anxiety and arousal on task performance appears to be similar. Performance on some types of tasks involving short-term information transfer measured by tasks such as reaction time, vigilance, simple arithmetic, and letter cancellation are facilitated by arousal, whereas tasks involving processes of short-term memory are weakened by arousal (Humphries & Revelle, 1984). Likewise, anxiety has a curvilinear relationship to task performance; high levels facilitate learning of a simple task but interfere with performance of more complex tasks (Sarason, 1980).

The three most common features of overarousal are similar to those of anxiety: (1) subjective state—awareness of feelings of discomfort, apprehension, fear, or dread; (2) presence of physiological stress reactions; and (3) adverse impact on cognitive processing of complex information.

Self-Management of Emotion

Individuals engage in behaviors to self-regulate their mood (Morris & Reilly, 1987) and utilize emotion management techniques to change subjectively unpleasant or unacceptable feelings (Thoits, 1984). It is normal for individuals to engage in some self-deception to enhance mood, and failure to acquire any self-enhancing biases has been associated with depression (Lewinsohn et al., 1980). However, self-deceptive strategies that are too discrepant from reality leave the individual vulnerable to deflation by feedback and force the person to engage in avoidance of reality information—a process that promotes vicious cycles in self-regulation. The issue is not whether or not someone engages in self-deception but the efficacy of regulatory efforts over time. Strategies that promote a momentary sense of well-being may be detrimental in the long run. Depressed affect is associated with preference for immediate gratification rather than delayed but more substantial rewards (Rehm & Plakosh, 1975; Schwartz & Pollack, 1977; Wertheim & Schwartz, 1983).

Individual differences in stimulus seeking is a prominent personality and motivational variable. Arousal theories assume that an individual is motivated to attain an optimal level of arousal and that individuals differ in their arousability and in their sensitivity to signals of positive and negative stimuli (Gray, 1981, 1982). Individuals who are low in arousability need strong stimuli to attain or maintain optimum arousal. Those who are highly arousable (reactive) experience optimal arousal with lower levels of stimulation.

For each individual, the optimal level of arousal (Hebb, 1955) is associated with (1) maximum efficiency of cognitive processing, (2) minimum physiological stress reactions, and (3) positive emotions. The work of Strelau and colleagues (Strelau, 1983) focuses, in large part, on the role of temperament in self-regulation. An individual who selects activities or situations that deviate from the optimal stimulative value incurs psychophysiological costs (e.g., stress) that depend on the level of reactivity (since both high and low levels of activation coincide with negative emotions).

Stimulus seeking can take the form of engaging in behavior to increase contact with novel, varied, intense, and complex stimuli to increase arousal, whereas more extreme forms of stimulus seeking involve high-risk activities (Zuckerman, 1979). Emotionally arousing behaviors that are common daily activities (e.g., going out on a date, attending a sports event) are distinct from sensation-seeking behaviors that involve risky, thrill-seeking activities that depart from the usual (e.g., skydiving) (Larsen, Diener, & Emmons, 1986). Anxious individuals display more caution, more reflection, and more avoidance of activities or information that increase arousal. Individuals with high-affect intensity engage in day-to-day activities that are more emotionally provoking than individuals low on affect intensity. However, these are distinguished from sensation-seeking behaviors (see Larsen & Diener, 1987).

Some individuals might be more motivated by self-regulative needs, whereas for others, such considerations are less central. Those who are low or high on the temperament continuum of reactivity may be preoccupied with maintaining equilibrium in many situations.

Differences in cortical arousability may predispose individuals toward certain forms of affect (Derryberry & Rothbart, 1988), which are subject to self-regulation through processes such as attention and characteristic patterns of approach/avoidance that function to regulate the individual's biologically based reactions to changes in the environment. Thus, a key aspect of emotion seems to be arousal, which in turn plays a central role in processing information and shaping preference for behavior to promote optimal arousal (engaging in activity consistent with preferred levels of arousal).

In the context of motivation, emotions are viewed as prompting or directing behavior (Tomkins, 1962). The experience of emotion energizes the individual, motivates search for selective information, leads the person to approach or avoid situations, and stimulates the acquisition of skills, knowledge, and attitudes.

Environmental Contributions to Emotion Management

Assistance with emotion management can be provided by others such as parents, friends, teachers, and other professionals when self-regulatory mechanisms are not sufficient. Carey (1985) indicated that providing parents with information about their child's temperament can help enhance parent-child relationships in at least three ways: (1) general discussions educate parents and increase understanding and awareness of normal individual differences in behavior; (2) identification of the temperamental profile of a given child provides parents with an organized framework from which to view their child's behavioral style; and (3) parents are encouraged to consider alternative methods of child management when dissonance between the child's characteristics and environmental demands result in reactive symptoms and undue stress.

Social support can play an important role in emotion management by (see Thoits, 1984): (1) intervention to alter demands or circumstances such as changes in classroom or school, modified expectations, increased structure, or tutorial support; (2) assistance with information processing such as encouraging alternate interpretations of events; (3) promoting normalization of feelings by expressing empathy or acceptance rather than judgment; and (4) teaching improved self-regulatory strategies such as problem solving by providing advice about how to change the circumstance or deal with expectations.

A variety of behaviors can be viewed as serving self-regulatory functions. If the social milieu has been responsive, an individual may have acquired strategies for eliciting needed social support. The following are some reasons why individuals may seek to rely on the environment for support:

1. *Limited Experience*   Need for remedial assistance to overcome deficits due to previous environmental drawbacks that preclude opportunities for mastery.

2. *Cognitive or Metacognitive Limitations*   Need for structure because of cognitive or metacognitive resources that are insufficient for organizing efforts and establishing priorities or standards. Such a need for external guidance is exemplified by a third-grader who kept checking her work against the work of others. She was referred for behavior problems when she actually wanted to make sure that she was on the right track in carrying out her assignments.

3. *Intense Emotions*   Need for approval or feedback stemming from self-doubt and lack of trust in one's judgment triggered by anxiety or other negative emotions. The impact of intense emotions or sensitivities on cognitive processing may result in a need to obtain feedback on perceptions. Furthermore, the anxious individual may desire reassurance to feel understood or secure.

4. *Rigid Information Processing*   Need for help to promote more effective information processing or to become aware of alternatives. The individual may be locked into one mode of thinking and may exhibit a tendency to jump to conclusions or to misinterpret events.

5. *Motivational Deficits*   Need for incentives such as rewards or pressure to overcome apathy, inertia, and disinterest, and to provide external sources of motivation for effort.

Stories that express need for help, support, or structure should be evaluated in terms of the underlying processes that contribute to the dependency.

Development

In Piaget's (1981) view, affect does not show a developmental progression because it has no inherent structure. What does develop is the cognitive context of the affect. *Emotion* relates to the intensity and valence of experience (magnitude of investment in moving toward or away), whereas *cognition* refers to the specific content of experience and to its underlying structure (Cowan, 1982). These internalized structures are generally described in cognitive terms (e.g., Concrete Operations) but incorporate both cognition and affect in progressively more adaptive organizations. Cognitive and emotional changes occur in tandem, but neither is viewed as causal for the other. More complex emotions such as shame and pride have cognitive components and develop from the interactions of the primary emotions (which are assumed to be biologically based) and learning history (Goldsmith & Campos, 1986).

The basic features of emotions that are biologically based are relatively independent of development and provide "an invariant core of affective continuity" (Campos & Barrett, 1984). What does change developmentally are: (1) *coping responses*—growth in cognitive and self-regulatory skills allows broader context and framework for understanding emotions and leads to increased perspective and acceptance of stress and frustration; (2) *bases for evaluating events*—if events are viewed as more manageable through experience, they are no longer evaluated as threatening, and the individual is less susceptible to stress and conflict; and (3) *the nature of the demands*—as individuals get older, behavioral and task expectations change, and more choices are available for selecting activities or environments to manage emotions.

The developing sense of competence is a result of growth in self-regulatory processes, including the control of emotion. A child who overreacts is at a disadvantage socially and may be afraid of new situations due to anticipation of overwhelming emotions that disrupt cognitive processing of interpersonal information.

Development and Individual Difference

The neo-Piagetian view is that cognition and affect are not separable because they are aspects of a common process where neither leads to or governs the other (Kegan, Noam, & Rogers, 1982; Piaget, 1981). Piaget's work suggests that the activity of development is the context that gives rise to both cognition and affect through the process of equilibration, which consists of a series of reorganizations in the capacity to integrate experiences at increasingly mature levels.

The individual's dispositions set the basic themes and processes for the fundamental activity of organizing life experiences that begins during infancy. These characteristics are expressed and responded to in the same environment (family). The neo-Piagetian perspective, as expressed by Kegan, Noam, and Rogers (1982) is that "the distinctive features of infancy are to be understood in the context of the same activity which is the person's fate throughout life. The recurrence of these distinctive features in new forms later on in development are not understood as later manifestations of infancy issues, but as contemporary manifestations of meaning making" (p. 117). Thus, basic processes and themes are established early, and these can be traced throughout the life span. Furthermore, development recycles for each new experience so it cannot be tied to specific ages.

Emotions have been viewed as organizers of experience through their influence on the cognitive processes, motivation, and behavior. Theorists generally assume that affect functions as part of a system that regulates energy for action. In Piaget's (1981) terms, emotional schemes direct interest and action toward and/or away from objects and cognitive operations. Affective characteristics such as fear or empathy direct interest toward certain aspects of the environment, and strong affect pulls thoughts and behaviors (see Larsen & Diener, 1987). Furthermore, subjective interpretation of events has been associated with the relative frequency of positive and negative affect in conjunction with high- and low-affect intensity. The emotion of fear leads to greater avoidance of new experiences in favor of the familiar and to limited interest in exploration, which in turn slows the rate of intellectual development. Thus, development proceeds in a coherent pattern with affect providing an organizational framework.

Kellerman (1980) theorized that certain personality types develop as a consequence of defensive styles employed for the purpose of modulating specific emotions. Meaningful relationships have been reported between various personality dimensions and specific emotions such as the tendency of extroverts to report feeling more joy (Emmons & Diener, 1985, 1986). Emmons and Diener (1986) conclude that certain feelings are associated with specific personality types, and that "it is clear that any viable theory of personality must recognize the role of emotional functioning within individuals" (p. 383).

Summary

The emotional, cognitive, physiological, and behavioral components of experience are embedded in a complex interconnected network so that each has a reciprocal influence on the others. Emotion in conjunction with cognition lends coherence to construing life events (1) as a focuser or director of attention, energy and action toward or away from objects, information, people, or ideas (Cowan, 1982); (2) as an organizer of experience. Emotional states connect various components of experience such as appraisal of situations, concerns, and behavioral tendencies in a functionally meaningful way (Schwartz & Shaver, 1987); and (3) as an organizer of memory that coheres around emotional states (see Leventhal & Tomarken, 1986).

CHAPTER 12

Emotional Maturity

The characteristics of thinking about emotionally laden events constitute the defining elements of affect maturity (Thompson, 1986). The distinction between emotional states such as distress, excitement, or arousal and true emotions such as anger or anxiety is based on the cognitive activity accompanying them (Lazarus, 1991). Emotional states are automatic, relatively rigid reactions to external stimuli akin to reflexes that are rooted in physiological processes. In contrast, emotions are based on the reaction to the meaning of an event, thereby requiring judgment and the capacity to learn from past experience. Accordingly, pain and pleasure become emotions when the individual discerns their implications and appraises their significance.

Lazarus (1991) notes that meaning is generated in many different ways, ranging from automatic, nonvolitional processes to deliberate, rational thought. Emotions such as *resonances* are not clearly articulated but represent a global sense of compatibility or incompatibility between the individual's personal identity and the outside world (Shepard, 1984). Evidence (e.g., Stenberg & Campos, 1990; Bahrick & Watson, 1985) points to the likelihood that babies evaluate events according to a rudimentary sense of their own identity and of goal relevance. In Lazarus's (1991) view, cognitive activity is necessary to emotion; the development of an emotion depends on how the infant or young child derives meaning through the appraisal of events.

Thompson (1986) posits that mature affect has two essential components: (1) the affect is specific to a situation, person, or event rather than globally experienced (e.g., an affect state is more global when the individual is distressed by entering the school environment than when only a specific class is distressing); and (2) the affect is embedded in a cognitive network that becomes increasingly organized and structured with the development of cognitive capacities along Piagetian lines. Thompson discussed the implications of Piaget's stages of cognitive development for the organization of affective states and experience of relationships. In her view, less mature affect in later development is due to regression, which occurs when the elements in the affect system are released from their hierarchical context and thereby become unsystematized.

If an individual's thoughts about affect states are not integrated into organized, hierarchical systems but are loosely connected to or independent of each other, the following would hold (Thompson, 1986): (1) emotions would have meaning for the individual only in connection with a specific event; (2) it would not be possible to have mixed feelings but the individual would experience a series of successive affect states where one feeling is substituted to replace the existing one without reconciling them; and (3) other people and experiences would be evaluated simplistically as good or bad, depending on the emotions generated at the moment.

Hoffman (1986) presents a continuum of increasingly complex information processing of events relative to the way affect is generated: (1) direct affective response to the physical or sensory aspects of the stimulus; (2) affective response to the match between the physical or sensory qualities of a stimulus and an internal representation or schema; and (3) affective response to the meaning of the stimulus beyond its immediate impact such as its causes, consequences, or implications for the self or comparison with a standard.

Affect states that are experienced in relation to events that are external to the individual are not amenable to reconceptualization. Without a cognitive context for the experience of affect, an individual is unable to regulate affect states internally because the affect and the sense of self would change only with changes in external events. A change in circumstances results in total disappearance of the original affect state, which is replaced by a different one. Furthermore, the experience of affect as "global" leads to the feeling of being totally enmeshed in the feeling state connected with an event so that cognitive representations of self, reality, and other people are changed only when the event changes.

When emotions are generated by an internally organized frame of reference, there is a recognition that the emotion experienced now can change and that objects of emotions can be evaluated independently of the affects experienced. The capacity to distinguish between "how the individual feels" about the object and "how that object really is" allows for the beginnings of reality testing of the emotions themselves (Thompson, 1986). For instance, emotions can be judged as appropriate or inappropriate, as justified by the real characteristics of objects or not. The internal coordination and integration of affect states allow for mixed feelings toward the same objects and for the separation of intent from impact. Negative affects that are related to the self in a meaningful way allow the individual to recover from self-doubt or failure by putting emotions into a proper context. Likewise, positive emotions may be related to an enduring sense of the self or may consist of fleeting reactions elicited by the immediate event (e.g., glee).

Without an internally organized frame of reference, others are not appreciated according to their individual characteristics. People are not evaluated according to an understanding of who they are but on the basis of internal need states of the perceiver. Therefore, a person is devalued if he or she makes the perceiver feel uncomfortable. Rather than experiencing mixed or ambivalent feelings about others, the individual vacillates between opposites (substitutes bad feelings for good or vice versa). If an individual cannot separate affect from the situation that evokes it, then the feeling and a particular sense of self have reality for the individual only while experiencing the affect-laden event. The inability to separate affect from a specific event implies that affect and self-esteem are not regulated internally. That one's sense of well-being is tied to external events reinforces the tendency to view other people in terms of what they can provide in the moment.

Development

The development of affect maturation evolves as a child's ability to put events into context grows. As the cognitive system becomes more complex, the interpretation of events and accompanying affect states become more organized. As development proceeds, a particular sense of self increasingly integrates past, present, and future rather than existing only while experiencing a specific event. Other people can also be evaluated from a longer-term perspective rather than on the basis of their immediate affective impact. In this way, feelings and concepts of self and others assume reality for the individual beyond the immediate experience. Furthermore, the individual can look at situations from various perspectives and develop increased alternatives for constructive action.

According to Thompson's purely cognitive view, emotions cannot be reality tested until the child has reached the stage of concrete operations (age 6 through early adolescence) and can evaluate the target of an affect separately from the affect itself. The development of the operation of reversibility allows the evaluation of emotion as separate from its object and, therefore, permits the experiencing of mixed or contradictory feelings toward the same object. Finally, self is differentiated from the affect to form the beginning of the understanding of affects as internal psychological states that the individual may choose to express, inhibit, or feign. With "decentration," a more complex evaluation of objective features of affective situations becomes possible. During adolescence, the development of formal operations permits the incorporation of a broader perspective into the conceptualization of affect so that the individual becomes aware of the relationships among affects, situations, self, and other people over time.

Strictly cognitive interpretations are not sufficient to explain affect maturity. Individual differences along many lines lend coherence to development in ways that are unique to the individual. Differences in temperament (i.e., intensity and type of affect) and in cognitive processing style override a purely cognitive developmental time table. *Affect maturity* refers to the manner in which meaning is attributed to events. The prior integration of cognitive and affective components of experience provides the context for the appraisal of a current occurrence but is not strictly age related. A 3-year-old may readily accept the postponement of a promised trip to the amusement park due to illness of a parent. In contrast, a much older child may focus on the missed opportunity and may immediately demand to know when the trip will be rescheduled. The former child evaluates the event (or in this case, the nonevent) in a context that includes an empathic response to the parent and an appreciation of the intention of having planned the trip in the first place. The latter child evaluates the situation on the basis of its immediate relevance. The frustration and disappointment of this child is felt keenly because intent and impact are not differentiated. This capacity for affect maturity is a joint function of cognition and affect. In the example just cited, the affect of empathy, together with cognitive integration, provide the coherence to the child's relationship with parents. If this empathy is reciprocated, there will be further development in reciprocity and in understanding the internal framework of the other. It is evident from the stories of empathic children (see Chapter 13) that as early as kindergarten such youngsters operate from an inner framework and are inclined to notice the intentions of other persons.

The maturity of affect is not judged by the intensity of the feeling or loudness of its expression (e.g., tantrum) but by the nature of the provocation and the control over the place and timing of its expression. Affect that is directly provoked by an external circumstance is less mature than affect that is evoked by the meaning of the event as conceptualized through the organization of an internal framework. Individuals who can grasp the complexities of an event (e.g., present versus future, impact versus intent) would experience more mature affective reactions. Feelings and thoughts cohere in the process of continuing development so that increasing cognitive capacities are selectively applied according to the emotional or motivational relevance of the information.

Affect maturity, then, is conceptualized broadly as information processing of affect-laden experiences, which is the basis for self and interpersonal perception. An individual's processing of affective states and experiences may differ according to a specific type of affective information. The differential sensitivity to nuances or details of experiences may be fine-tuned for some types of information and not for others. The following questions are relevant to assessing affect maturity with projective stories: First, what are the distinctions made in processing affective information? What characteristics of situations, the self, and other people are viewed as relevant? Second, how directly are affects elicited from the situations? Do affects emanate from immediate provocation, from expectations about consequences, or from the meaning of the event? Third, what is the manner in which various sources of affect-laden information are integrated? Are perceptions of different aspects of a situation synthesized or does the response consist of successive reactions to different isolated aspects? This nonintegrative approach may be due to a variety of factors not necessarily related to development (extreme concreteness, the temporarily disorganizing impact of intense affect, or difficulty with attentional processes).

Hallmarks of Emotional Maturity in Projective Stories

Three dimensions of emotional maturity relating to the preceding discussion are described and illustrated with projective stories:

1. Internal frame of reference for understanding the *origin* and *resolution* of negative affect states
2. Reality testing and modulation of emotions in relation to the stimulus and story context
3. Specificity and articulation in relating emotions to their context

Internal Frame of Reference

The development of an internal frame of reference is essential to affect maturity. Individuals who react only to momentary variations in the circumstance can easily lose their bearings or become trapped by the pressures of the moment. Those with an external frame of reference may need more outside structure, support, or approval to perform tasks or direct their behavior. On the other hand, those whose responses are more internally organized can be more autonomous. Indeed, an internal frame of reference is necessary for cognitive restructuring and performance on cognitive tasks (Widiger, Knudson, & Rorer, 1980). Conversely, the development of an internal frame is facilitated by actively organizing information and reflecting on life experiences. Restructuring information implies that some meaning beyond the literal is understood and is therefore tied to the ability to draw inferences and conclusions. Thus, an individual with an internal frame of reference can derive satisfaction from self-appraisal, not just from external sources such as approval or material rewards.

Projective Stories and Internal Frame

The story teller's frame of reference can be inferred from the manner in which affects are generated and from the resolution of negative emotions or conflicts. The key issue pertains to whether affects are directly provoked by external elicitors (e.g., consequences, pictures, preceding story elements, inquiry) or emanate from an internal frame of reference (e.g., purpose, standards).

If feelings reside in the individual, then persons are seen as regulators or organizers of their own emotional reactions, and therefore participate in the resolution of emotional tensions. If not, then persons look to external events, remaining helpless or vacillating between opposite emotions. Thus, the manner in which the initial negative affects are resolved is directly tied to the origin of the feeling. Emotions may remain unresolved or modified by arbitrary changes in circumstances or be dealt with by constructive, purposeful actions to relieve tensions or to ameliorate problems or adverse circumstances.

Mature affects are related to inner states such as enduring motives, values, genuine concern for the welfare of others, and pride in accomplishment rather than only to external events, consequences, or outcomes. The presence of an internal frame allows for self-monitoring and lends some stability to behavior as opposed to raw, impulsive, direct, unmodulated reaction to the stimulus or provoking situation. An internal frame allows for cohesion among experiences and balance between inner and outer preoccupation. If the individual simply reacts without reflection to inner states, then the emotion is not differentiated from the experience and the intent of an action cannot be distinguished from its impact. Reality testing of emotions requires the separation of objective attributes of the target person or situation from the emotional reaction of the perceiver.

Stories that reflect a balance between inner and outer concerns depict characters who are aware of and assume responsibility for feelings and actions. They display insight and view inner motives or emotions as spurs for actions rather than being provoked by external demands or the stimulus ("He got hurt because he was cutting with scissors!"). Characters direct their actions purposefully rather than just reacting to the sequence of events and seem lifelike rather than superficial or stereotyped. At one extreme, the narrator may exhibit excessive reliance on external cues and feedback either because of minimal awareness of inner life or as an attempt to bolster a fragile internal framework. At the other extreme, it is possible to be so preoccupied with inner life that the individual is detached from the external world.

At mature levels, story resolutions incorporate all characters who are potentially affected by coordinating their concerns while maintaining their integrity as separate but related individuals. The resolution reflects an awareness of the connections among experiences and an ability to extract the meaning of external events.

The following Form and Content features relating to the manner in which meaning is tied to feelings are relevant for determining the level of affect maturity.

Form

1. *The Relationship of the Affect to the Stimulus*   Affect is an internal attribute of the character rather than directly evoked by the stimulus.

2. *The Relationship of the Affect to the Story Context* Affect is embedded in an appropriate context rather than directly provoked by preceding story detail or tacked on as an afterthought in response to task demands or inquiry.

3. *The Relationship of Affect to Thoughts and Actions* Inner states (feelings and thoughts) guide actions or goals rather than external impetus.

Content

1. Affect is related to characters' long-term interests rather than to immediate needs or provocations. Characters react to the "meaning" (e.g., values) of events rather than to external pressures or consequences.
2. Feelings of characters are coordinated rather than each being entrenched in a solipsistic view.
3. Characters display goals, motives, or inner states that drive actions rather than merely react to external events.

Level of Maturity of the Internal Frame of Reference

Increasing maturity of the internal frame of reference is differentiated into four levels, as follows:

Level One No inner states, motives, or purposes are attributed to characters. Emotions do not reflect inner attributes but are specific descriptions of the stimulus, direct reaction to the feeling state in the stimulus, or raw, inappropriate emotion.

The following story was told by a kindergarten girl.

Card 5: A lady is opening the door. She sees some flowers. She's looking in the door. (Think?) She thinks they're pretty. (End?) She smiles.

In the following story told by a first-grade girl, the initial source of affect is in relation to the physical qualities of the stimulus and then to the mother's forgetting.

Card 7: The girl is looking at her doll. She doesn't like it cuz it's not nice like the other girls' dolls. It doesn't have much hair—see? (points) Her mother said she'd get her another doll and she forgets. She thinks her mother is mean. (To?) She thinks about being in another family.

The following story told by a fifth-grade boy, age 10, in a self-contained class for emotionally handicapped youngsters also illustrates the source of affects as tied in a fragmented way to external events rather than being internally organized.

Card 3BM: He's crying by the bed. He was cutting something because the scissors was by his bed. He had to go to his room (?) Don't know, he got into trouble. He gets grounded.

The following story told by a 12-year-old boy also in a self-contained class for the emotionally handicapped centers on one person's basic safety. The character is helpless and experiences a global affect state, which is associated to the stimulus. Things just happen without integration of motive, purpose, or consequences to the wrongdoer.

Card 3BM: I think the lady's on a subway. She was stabbed (child laughs). (Pause). She's thinking right now how much pain (laughs) she's going through . . . and she's going to go to the hospital and be all right, I guess. (Feeling?) A lot of pain. She's scared.

Level Two   Emotions are reactions to isolated events or to immediate need rather than the incorporation of a larger context (e.g., a series of events, a longer-term view, or separation of intent from impact). These feelings either remain unresolved or change because of purely external circumstances. Characters' emotions may be superficial, phony, overly justified in relation to the stimulus or to immediate external events, or greatly vacillating.

In the following story, feelings stem directly from immediate gratification of materialistic wishes. Changes in affect are provoked by the preceding event rather than by the entire context.

Card 7GF: Maybe this girl's mad about her mother . . . because her mother gave her a yucky food. And maybe her mother said, "Today I'll buy you new shoes," and maybe she said, "Mother, you are telling a lie." And she said, "Do you know these are new shoes I bought you yesterday?" (What is your story about?) She (girl) sits in her room and she is very mad and she breaks the door and she breaks the lamp and her mother said, "I will go outside shopping." And when she came back, she says, "Mother, you bought me new shoes, hooray!" She said, "That's the end."

Level Three   Feelings are internal to the characters, but the locus of self-evaluation is external. In the following story told by a kindergarten girl, the feelings and actions are within the person but are elicited by external feedback.

Card 1: The boy lost his bow to the violin and his mother came in and said, "Why aren't you fiddling?" "Because I lost the bow to my violin." She said, "You look for it and if you don't find it you'll be in big trouble." Then the end. He found it and his mother said, "Good, before you finish fiddling I'm going to give you a treat." (Feel? Think?) In the beginning he's thinking, "Boy, I lost my bow, wait til my mom finds out." He's sad. At the end, he's thinking, "Oh goodie, I'm getting a treat." End.

Level Four Inner states such as emotions, motives, or convictions guide deliberate, purposeful actions. The following story told by a girl in kindergarten illustrates a balance between external and internal frames of reference. The perspectives of parent and child are integrated; characters communicate and act constructively on their feelings.

Card 1: A boy is looking at his violin. He's going to play. He doesn't like it. His mother told him to play it. He tells her he doesn't want to play. She says he can play it later. He puts it away. He plays it after dinner. Then he likes it. His mother likes it.

The following story told by a sixth-grade girl relates the identical theme in a more sophisticated manner expected of an older child. Both stories depict a character who takes internal responsibility for feelings and actions.

Card 1: This is a boy who really wishes he was out playing baseball but his mother said he had to learn to play the violin. He's bored and he's sitting there trying to figure if he's going to sit there all afternoon. He decides the sooner he gets finished, the sooner he'll get to go out and play. So he finishes up quickly and feels relieved when he's finished.

Level of Maturity in the Resolution of Feelings

The view of feelings as being embedded in an internal frame would dictate that shifts in affect result from inner-directed actions or reconceptualizations. Therefore, the maturity of the inner frame is reflected by the manner of resolution or change in affective state. Thus, affect resolution is a broader concept that incorporates the origin of the feelings.

Levels of affect resolution are listed below according to increasing degree of maturity.

Level One: No Conflict; Inappropriate or No Resolution Resolutions are grossly inappropriate to the story context, or the story does not recognize inner states to be resolved. Content is incoherent, bizarre, or gruesome; resolutions reflect extreme helplessness, fear, or hostility, or involve clearly antisocial actions or poor judgment. The affect gets worse as the situation keeps deteriorating or the resolution is highly maladaptive, implausible, or inappropriate. Characters remain in an extreme state of deprivation and abandonment with no resolution.

In the following story told by a first-grade boy, there is a state of tension but no resolution.

Card 3BM: Somebody won't play with him when he wanted. And he was playing with a friend and they were mean and pushed him away. (Feel?) Sad. He's crying in his bed (To?) Sad.

The following story told by a 10-year-old boy in a self-contained class for the emotionally handicapped illustrates emotions and resolutions that are not appropriate to the story context.

Card 13B: The boy went back into the woods one day and he got lost and he saw a cabin so he came and asked if he could come in and the boy, he stayed there overnight. And, that morning he got up and he was looking out the window, thinking, "I wonder if I will ever get back to my own house." He's thinking of his nice soft bed. Then he hears some voices calling and he gets up, runs to the door, and it was his mother and father and he gets up and runs to them. And, umm, then the boy, umm, goes to, goes to lunch and then goes home and says, "Whew, now I'm in my own bed."

Level Two: Inadequate Explanation for Affect Shifts   The explanation provided for changes in emotional states is not sufficient, as illustrated by the following: (1) a change in affect is the outcome; (2) affect is ignored or the problem just disappears; (3) the feeling state may swing to its opposite without adequate explanation; and (4) shifts in events without a reasonable process, such as a capricious change of mind or passage of time (where action is appropriate) or improbable (but not bizarre or impossible) sequence of events, lead to affect change.
    Sequence of events and resolutions are unlikely when:

1. Feelings, events, or actions are incompatible.
2. Time perspective is ignored.
3. The resolution entails the wish that things will improve or dreams of success.
4. Goals, events, actions, thoughts, or feelings are not realistic. There is a naivete or inability to predict the likely reactions of other characters. Characters are grandiose or exaggerate their importance.
5. Resolution addresses only part of the problem.
6. Acceptance or rationalization of wrongdoing.
7. Overgeneralized resolution where a specific outcome such as immediate gain leads to a general state of happiness or satisfaction.

The story below told by a kindergarten boy describes feelings as being resolved by the passage of time rather than constructive action.

Card 5: A lady's looking inside someone's room. She wanted to see if her kids were in there. They went outside when she was in the room. (Feel?) Sad because the kids aren't there. She didn't see them anywhere so she goes up in her room and watches TV and feels sad. (End?) They come home and say, "Hi, mom." Then she feels happy cause they're home.

The following story told by a sixth-grade boy illustrates an overgeneralized resolution where the bad girl becomes good to get a share of the lottery winnings.

Card 7GF: There are two sisters. The one with the doll is a very good girl. The one with the book is a very bad girl. And, so the mother had just called and this girl paid no attention to her. So when the mother told them that something very good happened, the girl still didn't know it. See, what happened was they won the lotto and the mother was saying that they'd divide it among the family. This girl didn't even know that and this girl did. And so this girl didn't get any money. When she realized what not paying attention to her mother did, from then on she was very good.

The resolution of the following story told by a kindergarten boy does not address the tension depicted in the stimulus.

Card 4: The man's staring at something—another lady. She's probably looking at the man. The man feels worried. She feels happy. (Q?) Don't know (End?) They watch TV.

The following story told by a 10-year-boy is an example of a resolution that addresses only part of the problem. The connection between affects and events fails to integrate the multiple aspects of experience. At the end of the story, the character is happy that he can play with the other children despite the fact that these children had previously made fun of him.

Card 3BM: The boy was in the room playing with some guys and he was, he was sitting in his room, sitting there and he asked his friend, you know, to come outside and they wouldn't come outside and play with him. Well, they were making fun of him and acted like a girl and stuff, and so he went back inside and crying and then he fell asleep while he was crying and he was feeling real bad because he, umm, because everybody was laughing at him and stuff. So, when he got up, he went over and he started and then asked him again to play football or something like that. And he said yeah and that made him happy.

Level Three: Change in Affect Realistically Tied to External Change in Circumstance   The rationale for change of affect is a realistic change in the external circumstance. Characters' feelings and reactions are clearly delineated. However, they do not initiate constructive action when such action is possible; instead, they rely on others or are resigned to their circumstances rather than finding solutions or alternatives. Without external change, the character would be trapped in the original negative feeling, but not in an extremely deprived state.

The following story told by a girl, age 15, describes a youngster who is upset but waits for someone else to act and, thereby, change the circumstance.

> Card 3BM: OK. This girl got a phone call from her boyfriend. He wanted her to go and meet him at the movies. This is someone she's never been out with before. So she gets ready and gets in her car. She drives down there and she waits and waits and waits. And then she comes home and she throws down the keys by her bed and she starts to cry and the phone rings. She was very upset, sad and mad, too. And the phone rings and it's the guy and he apologizes and he's very sorry and his sister hurt her leg when he was watching her and he took her to the hospital and when she was fine, he called her from the hospital and asked her if she wanted to meet him later. And she said yes and she met him and he brought her a rose because he was very sorry. And everything was fine and dandy.

The affect is appropriate to the stimulus and the story. The narrator operates from an internal frame because the character recognizes others' motives and separates intent from impact. However, the negative feelings change when the boy apologizes and compensates for his previous action even though it was not intentional.

Level Four: Affective Shifts Associated with Adaptive Coping   Characters take responsibility for their feelings and engage in realistic, planful, active problem-solving effort (where possible) to resolve negative feelings. When no action is possible, an appropriate philosophical resolution is generated. Affect changes because a character comes to feel differently about an event for any of the following reasons: (1) gets used to an inevitable situation, (2) accepts reasonable influence of a loved one, and (3) puts initial affect into perspective or reconciles feelings with needs of others. Affect resolution reflects integrative processes when: (1) thought, affect, action, and outcome are coordinated; (2) wrongdoing brings internal and external consequences as well as efforts at restitution; and (3) when affects of all relevant characters are coordinated.

There are adequate explanations for change in affect with well-elaborated transitions in the following story told by a 12-year-old girl.

Card 13B: It's Saturday morning, and his parents went to market and older sisters and brothers are milking cows and collecting eggs for breakfast because they live on a farm. He's trying to think of a way to let his parents know that he's responsible enough to have a job too. So when his parents come home, he tells them he thinks he's responsible enough to work also. So they let him watch his brothers and sisters milk the cows and collect the eggs. So two months later, he's collecting the eggs and he feels happy.

In the above story, feeling is tied to the boy's wish to be treated more responsibly. The boy does not demand respect but takes responsibility for changing the situation, which alters his feeling. Events are realistic, integrate time frame, and coordinate the viewpoints of the various characters.

Reality Testing of Emotions

Adequate reality testing of emotions is a prerequisite for modulation and adaptive expression. Reality testing of emotions includes various components, which will be discussed next.

Identification of Affective States

Emotions are consistent with the picture stimulus and with the unfolding events in the story. Apparent contradictions in the stimulus are reconciled, and the feelings of all the characters in the relationship are coordinated rather than narrowly focusing on one at a time. A common example of difficulty in reconciling a seeming discrepancy in the stimulus is when characters in Card 4 of the T.A.T. are viewed as being "in love" by those who respond to the physical proximity of the characters and yet disregard their facial expressions and body language. When presented with discrepancies between verbal and nonverbal messages, emotionally disturbed children are unable to deal with the ambiguity and focus only on the more obvious verbal message (Reilly & Muzekari, 1986).

The inability to identify emotions in relation to the stimulus and story context is illustrated by two stories told by two different kindergarten boys. The first is compatible with the stimulus but depicts a character (and, by inference, the story teller) who doesn't understand why others act in a particular way.

Card 3: She's sitting down (Feel?) Bad because somebody hit her. She forgets about it. (Think?) That someone hit her. (Q?) A girl hit her and she was being nice.

The second story is an association to the narrator's image of what a married couple does without reconciling the emotions portrayed in the picture.

Card 4: They're hungry, they love each other and are happy. (Before?) They were walking around and buying stuff at the store. (Think?) They think about their car—something's wrong with it. They walk around and hold hands and buy stuff to take home. (End?) They make a garden together and get lots of plants.

Meaning and Coherence of Emotions

Emotions are meaningful when they reflect durability of inner motives and convictions rather than reactions to the moment. Meaningfulness is evident when the story teller can back away from the stimulus or situation to describe characters who act from conviction and not provocation. In resolving conflict, characters take a long-term view and separate an action's intent from its impact. They are not driven by trivial or momentary concerns but by a cohesive, durable sense of convictions. Thus, they are not spurred by immediate gratification nor do they resort to face-saving maneuvers that are aimed at bolstering self-esteem in the moment by emphasizing appearances rather than reality. There is recognition of coherence among thoughts, feelings, and actions; emotions have a reality of their own and influence deliberate, constructive actions. Initial emotional reactions, though distressing or intense, acquire meaning when they are reframed or put into perspective.

Lack of meaning and coherence is suggested when actions and outcomes are grossly inconsistent with feelings, as illustrated by the following story told by a 10-year-old, fifth-grade boy with an average IQ, in a class for emotionally disturbed children.

Card 1: He's sad because he has to practice and he don't know how to play and he's bored cause he thinks it's boring. His mother and father made him practice and he's sad because he can't watch TV or go outside or ride his bike (End?) He'll practice real hard and when he grows up he'll be on stage.

The following story also told by a 10-year-old boy in a self-contained class for the emotionally handicapped illustrates reality testing of emotions from outside, as the character needs external bolstering and approval to determine the appropriateness of his actions. The character does not experience a sense of meaning and coherence without external confirmation.

Card 4: Umm . . . This lady, one day, she, umm, her and her husband want to get her a ring; and her ring was fake, he gave it to her fake, cause he didn't have enough money for a real one. So he gave it to her and it was gonna leave, he was gonna leave and he couldn't give it and he felt ashamed and she came back and said, "I don't care that you did that, I'll just, I'll just get married with this one." And then they lived happily ever after.

Integration and Coordination of Emotions

Full reality testing of emotions requires integrative capacities to put emotions into a broader context that incorporates various levels of reality as indicated by (1) coordinating feelings of several individuals and (2) separating internal and external reality such as the objective qualities of the target person or situation from the emotional reaction of the perceiver.

Emotions cannot be adequately reality tested when they are based on fragments of experience that are out of context. Poor reality testing is suggested when characters are unable to "read" emotions or anticipate consequences or emotional reactions of others. Resolutions or changes in affect that follow from an unlikely sequence of events indicate misunderstanding of causes and their effects. Reality testing is distorted if emotions drive perceptions and actions so that judgments are made purely on the basis of feelings (e.g., characters get what they want by simply wishing it). Formal elements of stories reflecting cognitive or attentional difficulties such as loss of focus or rambling also suggest the possibility of impoverished reality testing.

In the following two stories, the narrator, a fifth-grade boy, aged 10, with average IQ in a self-contained class for emotionally disturbed children, cannot coordinate different levels of reality or keep a consistent perspective. The narrative indicates that the story teller is unable to separate internal and external reality, appearances from the way things really are or intent from impact.

Card 4: It looks like a dummy in a story window. He's in a beauty parlor. She's going to fix him up. She's looking to see how he looks; if anything is wrong with him. She's a nurse. (Beauty parlor?) It looks like it. (Happen?) Don't know, he's going to go for a check up cause he looks pink.

Card 8BM: He's at the doctor's office having an operation on his stomach. He might have cancer or something. They are trying to get something out of his stomach. He looks like he's crying even though he's asleep. That's it. (Crying?) He's having an operation.

The story below told by a kindergarten boy illustrates how wishful thinking distorts perception.

Card 1: He's thinking about maybe this Sunday is his birthday and his father will get him a new car and I know how to spell car: C-A-R. Maybe he's feeling like when should his father let him have a party because his father doesn't let him have a party. He's feeling like he's very sad and he said, "When will my daddy give me a new racing car?" (To?) He keeps thinking it.

The story is based on wishful thinking, where actions, feelings, and outcomes are not meaningfully related to each other or to the stimulus.

Clarity and Specificity of Emotion

Another element of affect maturity is clarity or specificity of emotions in relation to thoughts and events versus description of vague or global emotional states. Mature emotions are characterized by the following:

1. Clear identification of events (e.g., something bad happened versus a specific context) and their relationship to a character's feelings.
2. Identification of characters in specific terms and in their proper roles (e.g., playing with a friend versus doing something with someone). Giving names to characters does not indicate clarity nor does it contribute to delineating the nature of the relationships among characters.
3. Clear distinction of different characters' feelings (e.g., "They both feel something").
4. Clarity in differentiating between inner states and external provocation (e.g., "wants to commit suicide because there's a gun").

In the following story told by a first-grade boy, there is a vague relationship between affect and context. Affect is not clearly tied to events but is vague and global.

> Card 6BM: Those two had a fight . . . and the mother is standing at the window and she's thinking, ah, how bad she was and, ah, he's thinking about how mean she was and he's feeling angry and she's feeling angry. And it turns out they're going to not hate each other.

Summary

Emotional maturity is the assignment of meaning to emotions through an internal frame of reference. When emotions are viewed as inner psychological states rather than inevitable characteristics of external reality, several things follow: (1) individuals regulate affective states internally, are capable of ambivalence, insight, and of reframing their feelings rather than being trapped in global affect states associated with an event; and (2) emotions can be reality tested because the target of the emotion is separate from the feelings of the perceiver. Concepts pertaining to emotional maturity are applied to the interpretation of projective stories.

CHAPTER 13

Empathy as the Interplay of Affect and Cognition

The defining characteristics of empathy focus on affective responding as well as cognitive indices such as social perspective taking, which entails the cognitive understanding of feelings and motives of others. Bryant (1987) differentiated between the affective and cognitive components of empathy. She considered the feeling of connectedness to others as the essence of empathy and regarded social perspective taking as an instrumental skill. She found that empathy, but not social perspective taking, was related to indices of mental health. Furthermore, social perspective taking was not related to age. Empirical studies (Bryant, 1982, 1987) suggest that the development of empathy appears to entail a change in the nature of the stimuli to which a child responds, rather than an increase in the number of stimuli that elicit empathy.

Hoffman's (1982) definition of empathy as "a vicarious affective response more appropriate to someone else's situation than to one's own" (p. 93) provides a conceptual distinction between the affective and cognitive components. Individuals may care about one another's plight without really understanding their state. They may even lose sight of the other person and superimpose their own empathic interpretation. On the other hand, a person may be quite perceptive about another's state but feel a limited connection. Indeed, such a person may have an exploitative interest and use the knowledge for manipulation. *Empathy*, then, is the confluence of affective connection and concern, coupled with the cognitive understanding of another's state as differentiated from one's own. Finally, the expression of empathy requires the translation of these affective and cognitive components into behaviors that are perceived by the recipient as helpful.

Lazarus (1991) considers empathy as meeting the defining characteristics of an emotion. However, since empathy is viewed as "sharing another's feelings, then it cannot be a single emotion because its response characteristics depend on the emotion manifested by the other person" (p. 821). Therefore, Lazarus prefers to regard empathy as a capacity or process rather than an emotional state. He substitutes the concept of compassion as an emotion experienced when an individual comprehends another's distress and desires to ameliorate this condition.

The affect of empathy is said to influence moral behavior. Hoffman (1982) emphasizes the role of affect on moral action and moral thought. He considers moral judgment without appropriate affect as being an empty exercise of reasoning that is not likely to influence action. Empathy is the impetus for action, whereas moral reasoning provides the means.

For Hoffman (1982), the answer to what it means to be moral is: "a moral person has an internal motive to consider others and . . . this motive can be elicited when the welfare of others appears to be contingent on his or her actions" (p. 84). According to this view, empathy has far-reaching implications and provides a motive for selective information processing: "If children are motivated to consider others, they should be selective in their observational learning and more apt to pick up ways of acting morally than immorally" (Hoffman, 1982, p. 99). Empathic children are more likely to focus attention on other's affect than their less empathic counterparts (Barnett et al., 1982). The following story illustrates the impact of empathic connection on problem solving (*Readers Digest*, May 1982, p. 79. Quoted from Jim Whitehead, quoted by Seymour Rosenberg in Spartanburg, SC *Herald*):

Two hikers were walking through the woods when they suddenly confronted a giant bear. Immediately, one of the men took off his boots, pulled out a pair of track shoes and began putting them on. "What are you doing?" cried his companion. "We can't outrun that bear, even with jogging shoes."

"Who cares about the bear?" the first hiker replied. "All I have to worry about is outrunning you."

One of the hikers quickly and effectively sized up aspects of the situation that were pertinent to his most immediate personal interests. The other hiker may have been unable to come up with that solution because he was thinking in terms of *we* rather then *me*. These are automatic tendencies that reflect individual differences in affective and cognitive underpinnings of processing information and solving problems.

Johnson, Cheek, and Smither (1983) reported numerous correlations between empathy factors and other personality variables. They noted that components of empathy such as Social Self-Confidence and Even Temperedness are similar to temperamental dispositions (Sociability and Emotionality) reported to have significant heritability (Buss & Plomin, 1975, 1984). In addition, empathic individuals are generally well adjusted, not self-absorbed or anxious (Deardoff et al., 1977; Hogan, 1969; Spielberger, Gorsuch, & Lushene, 1970).

Coherence in personality refers to the interaction of individual aspects of personality to form larger, coherent patterns (Allport, 1961). The expression of empathic behavior requires the coherent interplay of affective and cognitive factors that are separate but interdependent components of empathy. Seemingly empathic behavior could actually be self-serving, and genuine concern can be expressed in a clumsy manner. Projective stories are well suited to assess the integration of these elements because the respondent incorporates the character's thoughts, feelings, and actions with outcomes. The manner in which the narrator integrates the three major components of empathy—cognitive, affective, and behavioral—is evident in the thoughts, feelings, actions, and outcomes of the characters.

Development of Empathy

The four stages in the development of empathy described by Hoffman (1982) that were derived from empathic affect and a cognitive sense of the other are presented in Table 13–1, along with other information. The essence of empathy is the affect or the interpersonal connection that is evident from the outset. However, empathy becomes more mature as the self and other are more accurately differentiated to promote increased understanding in the way affect is attributed to self and other. At the highest levels of maturity of empathy, the vicarious affective response is not based merely on immediate cues but stems from a knowledge of the other's condition beyond the situation at hand. Empathy gives coherence to actions and behaviors, providing the interest, energy, and motivation for the cognitive understanding of others and for prosocial behaviors.

Empathy has components that are age related and some that are tied to basic individual differences. Their respective roles have not been clearly delineated. However, it seems fair to say that there is variation in developmental sequences among children, depending on their affective connection and organizational capacity to understand interpersonal transactions. At extreme levels of distractibility or in the face of emotional or cognitive disorganization, the individual difference component may outweigh the general developmental sequence shown in Table 13–1. Distractibility, for example, has an inverse relationship with empathy (Bryant, 1987).

In terms of development, a young child can "feel" with another, but may not be as complex or as precise in the understanding of the other's state. Furthermore, the child may not have the instrumental skills to translate the feelings into effective expression. The degree of self-other differentiation when empathizing has been studied developmentally (e.g., Feshbach, 1978; Kohut, 1978). The essential connection is evident from an early age. There is, however, age-related growth in awareness, sense of autonomy, and self-other differentia-

TABLE 13–1 • Affective and Cognitive Components in the Development of Empathy

View of Others/Empathy	View of Self	Cognition	Affect
First Stage: Hereditary Organizations		Reflexes and reaction patterns (instincts) present at birth	Inborn affective reactions
Second Stage: The first acquired feelings Self-other fusion; empathic response to another's distress is present but no clear distinction as to who is in distress, self or other. Hoffman refers to this as "global empathy."		Hereditary capabilities and schemas are differentiated as a function of experience. Progressive differentiation of perceptions of objects and situations (e.g., stops crying upon hearing footsteps). Perceptions of size and distance become more precise.	Perceptual affects—feelings that have become attached to perceptions through experience. Differentiation of needs and interests tied to feelings of contentment/disappointment. True emotions occur when the infant is aware of a transaction with the surroundings. The subjective experience depends on the event and structures within the infant such as expectations (see Sroufe, 1979).
Third Stage: Affects regulating intentional behavior Exchange relationships replace symbiotic relationships when self is differentiated from the other. Object is viewed as permanent and independent of immediate perceptual experience. People are separate individuals and have feelings. Person permanence and awareness that another, not the self, is in distress, but the other's inner state is not known or assumed to be identical to one's own. Hoffman refers to this as "egocentric empathy."		Cognitive differentiation of means from goals. Coordination of means to achieve a goal (e.g., pull blanket so object on it can be reached).	Feelings are directed toward other people to the extent that the baby can distinguish between self-other. Affective-decentration manifests as interest in sources of gratification which are recognized as distinct from the self.

Fourth Stage: Intuitive affects and the beginning of interpersonal feelings. Begins at about 2 years (2–6: pre-operational thought) Interpersonal and moral feelings are possible and can be progressively organized. Beginnings of schemas for interpersonal relationships. Rudimentary awareness that others have internal states and feelings independent of one's own (by 2–3 years). With development, empathy becomes an increasingly accurate reflection of others' experience. Hoffman refers to this as "empathy for another's feelings."	Beginning of estimation and evaluation of self which lasts beyond the immediate circumstance. Beginnings of schemas for self-evaluation. However, symbolic representations of the self like other objects are fluctuating and unidimensional. Little need for self-consistency and little carryover for positive or negative self-evaluation from day to day (Cowan, 1982).	Emergence of representational thought and language. General tendency toward centration or focus on one attribute of a situation at a time.	Because affects can be internally represented and past events can be evoked, affects endure beyond the immediate stimulus. Semi-normative feelings (e.g., non-generalized, situation-specific norms—it is wrong to lie to parents but not to friends). Although morality is internalized, it is viewed as external to the individual. Accordingly, actions are judged by outcomes rather than intent. Fluctuating emotional states due to centration. In the absence of long-term schemas, have fluctuating, dichotomous feelings (Cowan, 1982).
Fifth Stage: Normative affects. Begins at about age 7/8. Child's ability to coordinate his/her point of view with perspectives of others leads to awareness that others have their own identity and history of experience beyond the immediate situation. The observer responds to a coordinated network of information rather than to immediate stimulus value. The observer can consider the other's general situation and condition, not just his/her immediate feelings or actions. Hoffman calls this "empathy for another's experience beyond the immediate situation." The development of enduring sentiments about people; more lasting and meaningful friendships.	Feelings of autonomy and will relate to decentering. Through the operation of "will," the child bases decisions on values and, given a conflict, will manifest a sense of duty. Can settle conflict between short- and long-term consequences. Can delay and prioritize actions (Cowan, 1982).	Internalized system of cognitive operations which are reversible. These are referred to as concrete operations because the child can reason abstractly about real experiences but not imagined ones. The new logic structure allows concepts of hierarchies, classes, and their relations. Conservation of values. Rules can be modified by mutual consent. Actions judged by intentions (Piaget, 1981).	Normative affects are defined by 3 criteria: (1) moral norm is applicable to all analogous situations, not just to identical ones; (2) moral norm endures beyond the immediate situation; (3) moral norm is linked to a feeling of autonomy. The ability to exercise decentration permits the mastery of the present situation by relating it to a broader context (past/present/future). This makes possible a change of perspective permitting the development of a will which is the exercise of deliberate, volitional control over two conflicting tendencies. The will is defined as the "affective analog of intellectual decentration." (Piaget, 1981, p. 64)

TABLE 13–1 • *(Continued)*

View of Others/Empathy	View of Self	Cognition	Affect
Sixth Stage: Idealistic feelings. Begins about age 11/12.	The self can "hear" negative feedback and even seek information which leads to adopting new perspectives and behaviors (Hoffman, 1982; 1987).	Logical (hypothetical-deductive) reasoning can be applied to possible as well as to real experiences. This makes introspection and self-reflection possible. According to Cowan (1982), these advances in cognitive structures are necessary but not sufficient for the highest internal standards or moral judgment as described by Kohlberg (1976).	Idealistic feelings—feelings directed at ideas.

Note: The first three columns were adapted from Piaget, 1981; the fourth column was adapted from Hoffman, 1982, 1987 tion. Hoffman (1982) does not think that cognitive processing such as self-other differentiation is necessary for primitive, empathic responding to another's distress. He suggests that a young child may connect (be reminded of) another's emotional state with his or her past experience of a similar emotion through an associative process that requires limited cognitive mediation.

Cognitive skills of role taking (Feshbach, 1978; Hoffman, 1982) require the ability to (1) discern and label other's affective state and (2) assume the perspective of another person. Nevertheless, it is probable that individuals are often aware of the other's emotional state and react accordingly without labeling that emotion or taking the other's perspective (Dunn, 1988). Thus, role taking is not necessary for prosocial behavior, just as knowledge of grammar rules is not a prerequisite for talking. A 4-year-old may use the pronouns *I* and *me* appropriately but be unable to explain the rule. Similarly, through an associative process, a child may be reminded of relevant information that enables him or her to resonate to the feelings of another without necessarily knowing why.

On the basis of close observation of interaction within the family, Dunn (1988) concludes that young children have a practical social understanding. She cites numerous studies documenting the coherence in children's understanding of interpersonal relationships, intentions, as well as the relations between actions and consequences. The fundamental social understanding displayed by young children as observed in a family setting is not consistent with research conducted in the Piagetian tradition. Dunn (1988) states that research on egocentrism tells "little about the nature of children's capabilities in the setting of their daily family life or about how these change with development" (p. 3). She indicated that conclusions about children's social development reflect the way the topic has been studied rather than the way children's capacity develops.

In her observations of young children interacting in their family setting, Dunn described remarkable cooperation among siblings, including unsolicited cooperative actions, compliance with requests, role reversal, and joint pretend play involving the sharing of the other's framework. By age 18 months, 30 of the 40 children she observed acted cooperatively when requested to do so by a sibling, and many were observed to give unsolicited help consistent with sibling intentions and goals. The findings that the proportion of children's cooperative exchanges with siblings did not increase further between 24 and 36 months warranted the conclusion that "even though the children's skills of cooperating grew over the third year, it seems that their motivation to do so did not increase" (Dunn, 1988, p. 114).

It is a given that cognitive development influences a child's ability to reflect on others and on the social world. But the growth of this understanding involves more than the unfolding of cognitive abilities (Dunn, 1988; Piaget, 1981).

Piaget (1981) viewed affect as pertinent to his theorizing about stages of cognitive development. Affect was conceptualized as guiding the expenditure of energy and investment in intellectual activity. Accordingly, empathy would lead to increased processing of information regarding the welfare of others. For Piaget (1981), judgments about moral issues always involve affective considerations. The usual practice of presenting children with stories or dilemmas to assess systematic changes in moral reasoning (Kohlberg, 1976) requires that children make moral judgments about dilemmas that are hypothetical and remote from their affective experience.

In Piaget's view, affect per se does not follow a developmental progression. Rather, the developmental stages (preoperational, concrete operational) incorporate both cognition and emotion in ways that are more differentiated, integrated, and adaptively organized. Neither is a direct consequence of the other, but both are components of the broader process of development. Affect plays an important role in regulating energy, directing interest toward or away from cognitive operations or stimuli. Sroufe (1979) suggests that measures of emotions during infancy are more useful than cognitive measures as predictors of later cognitive performance. Lines of development, as they relate to the organization of interpersonal relationships and moral behavior, are based on the joint contribution of affect and cognition.

Development does not occur in the emotional response of empathy if empathy is viewed as an affective state that stems from and is congruent with the apprehension of another's condition or state. However, given the affective underpinnings, a child's or adolescent's awareness of inner experiences of others may increase with development. Piaget's stages are not unitary but are learned in separate domains. Therefore, a gradual extension of the application of formal operational thinking is likely to occur throughout the life span as individuals face various issues (Levinson, 1978). Some adult experiences, such as parenthood, may provide the emotional spur for further development of schemes in the social/emotional domain (Cowan, 1982).

By the age of 4, children have developed a remarkable capacity to understand their social world. They show an impressive breadth of interest in and a coherent grasp of the bases of human actions and can separate the intent of an action from its impact.

Empathy and Projective Stories

Locraft (1988) asked teachers of elementary-school children, from kindergarten to sixth grade, to rate children's level of empathy. Ratings were obtained toward the end of the academic year to assure teachers' familiarity with the children. It was assumed that teacher ratings reflected empathy that was behaviorally expressed and therefore capable of being observed. The T.A.T. scoring was effective in differentiating between three empathy groups designated as low, medium, and high. The protocols were scored on the following dimensions of empathy, each of which was highly related to teacher ratings: (1) realistic expression and comfort with feeling; (2) flexibility/durability of feeling; (3) source of positive feeling; (4) source of negative feeling; (5) view of people; and (6) coherence among outcome, thoughts, feelings, and behaviors.

Group differences as well as age differences emerged. Older children received higher total empathy scores than did younger children. However, the differences between older and younger children were minor compared to those among empathy groupings. Age interacted with only one of the T.A.T. pictures used (1, 2, 3BM, 4, 5, 7GF, and 8BM). The data indicated an age-by-card interaction for Card 2, which is the most complex and which young children found most difficult to integrate (e.g., foreground with the setting and relationships of characters). Furthermore, projective empathy scores were unrelated to gender or intelligence and correlated negatively with teacher ratings of ineffective interpersonal functioning.

Examples of stories told to T.A.T. Card 4 by children who were rated as high and low in empathy illustrate the essential features distinguishing the groups. Stories of kindergarten, fourth-, and sixth-grade children (all of at least average intelligence) were randomly selected to illustrate developmental trends. (The author would like to thank Dr. Constance Locraft for sharing these data.)

The following stories were told by kindergarten children rated *high* in empathy:

Kindergarten Boy

He wants to cut down a tree cuz bees keep getting in it. She doesn't want him to cut the tree, she likes it. She says, "Don't cut the tree down." And he says, "We have to get those bees out of here!" The wife gets a can of bug spray, and they spray the tree and the bees go away. They're happy and they go have a picnic in the yard.

Kindergarten Girl

A girl, a man. The girl's trying to see what's the matter. He's angry. (Before?) Somebody started a fight with him. (Think?) Should he fight them back? He keeps feeling angry. (To?) She says don't fight back. He doesn't. They go away.

Kindergarten Boy

A man and a woman. She's looking at the man and the man's not paying attention. She wants him to cook and he wants to mow the grass. The lady helps him cook and he helps her cut the grass. (Feel?) The man is sad 'cause he wants to cut the grass and he's mad at her. In the end, he feels good. (Q?) 'Cause they helped each other.

In all three of these stories, the central tension between the characters is stated as a disagreement about a specific issue. In the first story there is a disagreement about how best to get rid of the bees; the second story involves a disagreement about whether the man should fight someone else; and the third story involves a dispute about dividing up household chores. In each of these stories, the characters communicate and resolve the disagreement to their mutual satisfaction by compromising or by constructively influencing each other. In doing so, the characters respect each other's feelings and retain a sense of autonomy. There is a broader context for the disagreement that relates to a previous event or current situation, not just an immediate provocation. In each of the stories, the "problem" or disagreement between the characters relates to a sense of autonomy of characters. In each case, the man and woman have an active role. Each has a different perspective or is actively thinking about the problem. Therefore, each is capable of compromise and of changing perspective in an autonomous manner. The inner life of the characters is evident. Their feelings stem from their thoughts and actions in relation to an issue rather than from external provocation.

In contrast, the following four stories were told by children in kindergarten rated as *low* in empathy:

Kindergarten Girl

The dad is looking this way. She's looking this way. This lady's sitting on the couch here. The man is seeing something. The woman sees the man. He sees something. (Q) The man won't tell what it is. (Feel?) He feels sad because the woman won't let go of him to get the thing he sees. He doesn't go see it.

Kindergarten Boy

The man's staring at something—another lady. She's probably looking at the man. The man feels worried. She feels happy. (Q?) Don't know. (End?) They watch TV.

Kindergarten Girl

A man and a lady. The lady is hugging the man. (Feel?) She's happy. (Q?) Don't know. (End?) They eat.

Kindergarten Boy

A mother and father. They're hugging. They're happy. (Thinking?) I don't know. (To?) Don't know.

In the stories of kindergarten children rated low in empathy, the definitions of the problem are vague, or the tension depicted is not recognized. The central disagreement is ill defined or formulated in a way that is not conducive to being resolved. In the first two stories, characters are looking in different directions or have different feelings, but the reasons for the feelings are not well articulated (i.e., someone's looking at something or feeling something). In the third and fourth stories, the disparity in the emotions depicted in the stimulus is not recognized. The third story focuses only on the lady's feelings, whereas the fourth makes no distinctions. There is a lack of coherence among characters' thoughts, feelings, and actions in relation to story outcomes. In the first story, the man is mad because the women won't let go of him to get what he wants. Why the woman won't let go and what the man wants remain unclear. Since the problem or tension pertains to only one character who doesn't tell what it is, the two characters cannot act as autonomous, independent individuals to resolve the tensions. The problem is not "owned" by both characters, and the resolution is not mutually satisfying (e.g., compliance with another character).

In the second story, the man and woman are described as having different feelings, but they don't relate to any characteristics that are internal nor are they evoked by an external event beyond the stimulus. The resolution does not address the differences in their feelings. They simply go about their business (e.g., watch TV) without communicating about their feelings. In the third and fourth stories, the characters are not even differentiated in terms of the disparate emotions so clearly displayed in the stimulus.

Thus, the high- and low-empathy groups in kindergarten can be distinguished in terms of definition of the central problem as relating to a mutual concern of autonomous characters; differentiation in characters' viewpoints and feelings in ways that are consistent with the stimulus and evolving story; communication of characters around the problem; compromise that is either mutually satisfactory or allows each of the characters dignity and autonomy; feelings that represent inner characteristics rather than external appearances or unmodulated reaction to external provocation; and coherence among thoughts, actions, and feelings in relation to story outcomes. Though stories of older children are longer and more complex, the same essential features can be abstracted. These are illustrated by stories of fourth- and sixth-graders.

The following stories were told by two fourth-grade boys who were rated *high* in empathy.

Fourth-Grade Boy

He feels mad because someone ran into his car. He looks at the smashed side of his car and he gets even madder. His wife is trying to comfort him but he's too mad to hear what she's saying. She stays there with him and when he cools down a little, he tells her he has an important business meeting in the morning and now he can't get to it because his car is so banged up, it won't run. She tells him not to worry because she can drive him to the meeting. He starts to feel some relief and he's glad she's there with him. His car gets towed to the repair shop. In the morning, she drives him to work.

Notice that the problem is defined in specific terms. The man puts his initial reaction in perspective, communicates with his wife, and the problem is resolved. The autonomy of the characters is noteworthy. The husband is concerned about meeting work obligations; the wife offers help on her own, not as a response to a demand.

Fourth-Grade Boy

The man has to go away to war and the lady doesn't want him to go. He doesn't want to go but he has to. At the end he leaves and she accepts that. (Think?) That they both don't want him to go.

This situation has no resolution other than acceptance of an undesirable reality. The problem is clear, and characters understand each other's feelings and actions.

The following stories were told by fourth-grade boys who were rated *low* on empathy:

Fourth-Grade Boy

The man feels that he should go do something. (Q?) Work—do a job. So he goes and he works all day and comes back. (Feel?) That he should get a job.

The central problem is defined only in terms of the man's concerns and ignores the relationship. In addition, there is no context for the man's concerns.

Fourth-Grade Boy

A man wants to have a divorce with his wife because she went out with another man. He feels so mad that he went out and beat up the man. She began crying and yelling at her husband for what he had done. (End?) They leave each other.

Characters react with anger to each other's provocations (e.g., a preceding action) without communication or understanding of the other's internal states such as feelings or intentions. The reactions are extreme and fail to consider the possible context for the events.

Fourth-Grade Boy

He probably has to go out and have a bullfight. His wife doesn't want him to because he might get killed. He pushes her back because he has to go to the bullfight. She keeps on holding him so he won't go. Then he gets angry and pushes her harder and starts to run. He takes this red sheet and fights the bullfight. His wife was still trying to stop him and she ran into the bull field. Then he was real angry. The bull started chasing after her. He didn't do anything to save her; he stood there and let the bull chase her. Another man started chasing after the bull. They snatched her out of the field. While her husband was looking at something else, the bull came after him. He had turned back just in time and he ran before the bull reached him. He ran out. (Think?) He was thinking while he was standing there that instead of saving his wife someone else would probably save her.

The husband wants to be in a bullfight and the wife is set on stopping him. There is no possibility of compromise because the characters do not respect each other's point of view. Each character reacts to the escalating provocation of the other. The husband reacts with rage to the perceived intrusiveness of the wife, and the wife continues to exert her will on the husband.

The following stories were told by three sixth-graders who were rated *high* in empathy:

Sixth-Grade Boy

This man has just been insulted by another person he works with. He is angry and wants to get revenge and his wife is trying to stop him. She is trying to tell him how it will make matters worse. She is coaching him not to talk to him and to walk away. He is deciding whether he should deal with the man in his own terms or to do what his wife says as she is urging him to stay home and not worry about it. The next day when he goes to work he does what his wife says and avoids this man. He still has some anger but he is trying to do the right thing.

In this story, the wife is trying to influence the husband not to fight. Rather than seeing this as an intrusion, he thinks about it and comes to his own autonomous decision.

Sixth-Grade Girl

She wants him to stay and he wants to go. She likes him and he doesn't like her and wants to go back to his house. (Before?) They were talking. She was telling him how much she liked him. He tells her he likes somebody else. So he leaves. In the end, she meets someone else and they like each other and they get married.

Again, the two characters want different things. This time the disagreement is about the continuation of the relationship. Since the feelings are not mutual, it seems reasonable to end the relationship. It is noteworthy that both characters retain their dignity and autonomy.

Sixth-Grade Boy

The woman looks like she's trying to stop the man from going somewhere and doing something risky like skydiving. She's upset because he could get hurt. I think the man has his mind set on what he wants to do and she's trying to change his mind. Her mind is working on getting him to stop. He thinks about whether he should go or stay. He stays because she wanted him to and he thinks she's right that it's too risky. She feels relieved and he feels good that she cares.

The woman's efforts to stop the man from skydiving are not considered as intrusive. The man does not merely comply but decides for himself that she is right and even comes to appreciate her concern for his safety.

The following stories were told by four sixth-graders who were rated *low* in empathy.

Sixth-Grade Boy

I can't think of anything for this one. It doesn't look real. I guess they could be actors. OK. They are actors and they're practicing their parts. There's a chorus girl in the back there. The actors are rehearsing a scene, trying to get it right, trying to be real convincing. They get it right and it gets filmed. (Feel?) Good. (Q?) Because they finished the scene. (Think?) Maybe she's thinking the part she has isn't very good.

The description of the characters as acting in a film takes the focus away from a relationship, and no interpersonal dilemma is formulated.

Sixth-Grade Girl

A woman is holding a man back. He pulls away and walks out into the next room. (Feel?) She needs to talk to him. (Q?) I don't know what about. (Think?) She's thinking she wants to talk to him. He'd rather be somewhere else, anywhere else besides there. (To?) She goes into the next room and says, "Don't run away from me, we have to talk." (And?) I don't know.

Here again we see the vagueness and absence of context in the definition of the problem and in delineating feelings or intentions. We do not know why the woman wants to talk to the man or why the man wants to get away from her. There is an obvious absence of mutual respect with one character making demands that are resented. Finally, the story teller is unable to formulate a resolution.

Sixth-Grade Boy

This man is, umm, a cowboy. He wants to go camping in the desert catching cows. This is his wife and she doesn't want him to go. So his wife threatens to kill him; then he threatened back. Then they decide that she can go to the desert with him. From now on they live happily ever after in the desert catching cows.

The characters threaten each other to get what they want; then when they get their way, there is a generalized happy ending, which is based on an unrealistic compromise that does not address the source of the dispute. The resolution is reminiscent of the one told by a low-empathy youngster in kindergarten where the couple watches TV while ignoring their discord.

Sixth-Grade Girl

It looks like he's being called to do something or go somewhere with friends but she wants him to stay with her. It turns out that she's very hurt that he did not stay with her and he's feeling guilty that he did not stay. (To?) He feels guilty and she's hurt.

Characters make demands on each other that they can't sustain and both end up feeling bad.

Summary

The stories of children designated by their teacher as being high or low in empathy illustrate the general conclusion that the essential features that characterize empathy groups are similar from kindergarten through sixth grade, despite the fact that stories of older children tend to be longer and more complex. The interpretation of these stories can be based on meaningful units that have relevance across all ages regardless of sophistication of language.

CHAPTER 14

Emotional Disturbance

Defining characteristics of emotional disturbance are viewed within the overall framework described previously that incorporates emotions, cognitions, and behaviors as interconnected systems of functioning. Indices of emotional disturbance in projective stories that were useful in differentiating disturbed and comparison groups are described.

Disturbance versus Temperament

The normal continuum encompasses a wide range of individual variation in emotional states and in emotional management behaviors. Nevertheless, research has demonstrated a relationship between particular temperament constellations in children and increased incidence of emotional and behavioral problems (Barron & Earls, 1984; Bates, Maslin, & Frankel, 1985; Cameron, 1977). Some of the symptoms relating to classifications of child psychiatric disorders such as attention deficit hyperactivity disorder are conceptually related to the temperament dimensions of activity, distractibility, and nonpersistence (Carey, 1990).

This overlap between disturbance and temperamental extremes leads to the question of whether a disturbance is an extreme in the normal variation of temperament or something qualitatively different. When is an emotion or, in fact, any trait such as activity level or distractibility a source of disturbance rather than an extreme in temperamental predisposition? Where is the line between being normally active or overactive, between being emotionally sensitive or labile? Generally, the answer is that extremes of temperament traits per se do not constitute a disorder (Maziade et al., 1990; Rutter, 1987). Furthermore, some traits are better conceptualized as being qualitatively different rather than as being on a continuum (Magnusson, 1987), just as Downs Syndrome is clearly distinct from a low score on the IQ continuum (Kagan, 1989).

A basic question arises as to which traits are temperamental. Buss and Plomin (1984), in the tradition of Allport (1937), assert that *temperament* refers to those personality traits that emerge early in life and that show high heritability.

However, some traits require particular environments to be manifest and behavioral indices of temperament change with age (Rutter, 1987). Thomas and Chess (1977) argue that temperament represents the *how* of behavior—that is, the style is distinct from the *why* or motivational component and the *what* or content of behavior. In accordance with the above definition, Rutter (1987) excludes from temperament those behaviors that are defined in terms of content, motivation, or cognitive components, emphasizing simple stylistic, nonmotivational, noncognitive features rather than complex behavioral tendencies. Accordingly, emotional reactivity is temperamental, but a specific fear is not; negative mood is included but helplessness or depression is not. Activity level is, but the ways activity is controlled or the purposes that it serves are not.

Rutter (1987) does include within the temperament rubric the composites or constellations of simple temperamental traits such as the "difficult" child. Therefore, children who are "difficult" due to these temperamental configurations can be viewed as being within the normal range.

A behavioral pattern may be attributed to a single temperament dimension or to some configuration of temperamental characteristics. Aggression, for instance, fits the temperamental definition because it is very stable over time (Olweus, 1979) and shows substantial heritability (Rushton et al., 1986). However, is aggressivity a temperament trait in its own right or is it a combination of temperamental traits? Buss and Plomin (1975) argue that aggressiveness can be explained in terms of a combination of three temperamental features: activity, emotionality, and impulsivity. Thus, behavior can be the expression of a simple temperament, of constellations of simple temperaments, of more complex trait interactions (e.g., cognition plus temperament), or of the interplay of any of these with past experience and the current situation.

Temperament is the tendency to respond in particular ways to specific circumstances. A temperamental trait (or cluster) can be a source of disturbance when the range of circumstances in which the individual can function adaptively is so narrow as to preclude the possibility of finding a niche within the available environment. If so, the predictability, acceptance, and support of the environment play a key role in adjustment. Millon (1981) refers to the adjustment of a vulnerable individual to a benign environment as "illusory" because when the supports are withdrawn, functioning is likely to deteriorate.

Disturbance and Self-Regulation

Disturbance is not a simple function of temperament but results when an individual cannot self-regulate emotions, information processing, or behavior to engage in reality testing, maintain relationships, master learning tasks, and display socially appropriate behaviors. Two children, for example, may avoid participating in class due to shyness and inhibition (temperamental traits). One child is attending and learning, while the other is too overwhelmed to process the information or tunes out altogether. The former child's self-regulatory attempts are functional, but those of the latter are not sufficient to allow learning.

Attempts at self-regulation (approach/avoidance) that lead to behavior that is self-defeating or injurious to others are not functional. School refusal is an example of avoidance behavior that disrupts development. Frequent absences from school are most often attributed to one of two types of reasons: (1) extreme anxiety, fear, depression, and uneasiness in social situations; or (2) extreme boredom and disinterest in relation to academic learning tasks. Most children with high absenteeism exhibit the latter (conduct disorders) rather than school anxiety. However, they both represent difficulties in self-regulation in the school setting that makes school aversive.

Self-regulation of emotions is enhanced by the development of metacognitions of emotions that permit the individual to monitor reactions to failure, rejection, or frustration and formulate strategies for constructively coping with these feelings. The following is an example of the use of metacognition in self-regulation in a 4-year-old boy attending a birthday party held at a bowling alley. The child was immediately uncomfortable in the unfamiliar, noisy, and bustling atmosphere. He decided that he would not put on bowling shoes or throw the ball. Nevertheless, he had by then learned an appropriate strategy for dealing with his reaction to new situations. Upon arrival, he told his mother, "I'll just watch, I don't want to do it." He remained to socialize with his preschool classmates, to observe others, and learn vicariously. On the way home, he said, "If you take me bowling once and show me how to throw the ball, the next time I can do it at a party." The child was able to identify the reason for his emotional discomfort and avoidance as well as the remedy. He did not become disorganized nor did he wish to leave the party.

Emotions and cognitions are intertwined in the functional units of behavior such as social interaction or problem solving (Piaget, 1981). An individual who cannot organize thought processes and who does not connect experiences may, as a result of faulty cognitions, feel emotionally overwhelmed. Thus, fragmentation in cognitive processing has an impact on self-regulation of emotions. The reciprocal influences of affect and cognition are difficult to tease apart. The literature on identification of emotional disturbance through projective stories suggests that formal elements of narratives reflecting cognitive disorganization are most effective (see McGrew & Teglasi, 1990) in differentiating disturbed and comparison groups.

Classifications of Disturbance

Gresham (1985) reviewed two basic approaches to the classification of childhood psychopathology. The first is clinically derived classification systems, as exemplified by the Diagnostic and Statistical Manual of Mental Disorders. These systems are founded on the observations of professionals and are consensually validated and formalized into a classification system. The second is empirically derived classification systems that rely on the use of multivariate statistical techniques such as factor or cluster analyses to delineate patterns or dimensions of behavior. The data are typically obtained from behavioral rating scales usually containing a large number of items. These behaviors are then grouped into factors indicating that several items correlate and tap the same underlying construct. Gresham (1985) claims that what is needed is a classification system that would not only adequately describe behavioral problems but also provide for a functional analysis of conditions maintaining those behaviors.

Educational classification systems for Emotional or Behavioral Disorder are mandated by law and tied to the availability of programs and financial reimbursement of the school district. These definitions emphasize the impact of the "disturbance" on the educational process and focus on matters such as "discrepancy" between ability and achievement. If the disorder does not affect performance to a marked degree, then it is not serious enough to warrant classification that makes a child eligible to receive services. Therefore, educational definitions remain broad and do not attempt to discriminate among specific types of emotional-behavioral disturbances, whereas subcategories of clinical classifications do attempt such distinctions.

The educational system excludes Social Maladjustment, which seems similar to Conduct Disorder in the DSM-III-R. The intent of the legal definition is to exclude from eligibility, not to negate the fact that such a diagnosis represents a disturbance. School psychologists are aware of the impact of this condition on the educational process and of the difficulty posed by not having programs in place for such children. However, to comply with the spirit of the legal classification, states have adopted guidelines to define social maladjustment and clarify emotional-behavioral disorder.

Generally, disorders are distinguished along the three dimensions of functioning: (1) *cognitive*—impaired functioning in reality testing or thought organization (e.g., schizophrenia, obsessions, paranoia); (2) *emotional*—impaired affect modulation (e.g., anxiety, depression); and (3) *behavioral*—impaired regulation of actions according to social expectations (e.g., conduct disorder) (APA, 1987). Some syndromes like Attention Deficit Hyperactivity Disorder have elements of all three, although they are not clearly differentiated in the diagnostic criteria. The personality disorders represented on Axis II (Millon, 1981) tend to integrate the cognitive, emotional, and behavioral domains of functioning.

Millon (1981) addresses the relationship between manifestations of clinical symptoms and personality disorders. Individuals with certain personality organizations are more likely to break down under stress and exhibit specific clinical symptoms of disturbance. Shapiro (1965) indicates that defenses and symptoms are consistent with established styles of functioning and cognitive processing. Object relations theory also classifies disorders according to the structure of personality as reflected by affective and cognitive modes of experiencing interpersonal relatedness.

Elements of Emotional Disturbance

Affect

An emotion is disturbing when it is subjectively experienced as aversive, nonacceptable, normatively inappropriate, and/or interferes with the ability to process information to meet expectations for social conduct and task performance. Emotional disorders encompass subjective states such as upset, nervousness, anxiety, depression, alienation, emptiness, and physical reactions such as insomnia. Negative feelings are acceptable in response to adverse circumstances, but the normative expectation is one of affective neutrality or positive affect. Furthermore, prolonged negative feelings or high levels of arousal are stressful. Another indication of affective disturbance is the inability to modulate feelings according to the situation (e.g., to feel sad when hearing about a tragic event). The DSM III-R diagnostic criteria for disturbance include adjectives describing emotions such as "unusual," "bizarre," "inappropriate," or "excessive," which clearly refer to deviations from the norm.

Cognitive Organization

Emotional disturbance is associated with poor judgment, poor reality testing, and sometimes bizarre ideation. The individual may feel easily threatened, be unable to concentrate, be constantly vigilant, or fail to process all of the information. Furthermore, there may be disruptions in the biological systems of sleeping and eating that exacerbate the above difficulties. The cognitive disorganization of severely disturbed individuals (e.g., psychotic) is reflected in more extreme self-other confusion and fragmentation within the self than those with less serious disturbances (Adler, 1980; Gedo, 1988; Kernberg, 1970; Rinsley, 1980).

Traditional indicators of thought disorder best discriminate between emotionally disturbed and comparison groups (McGrew & Teglasi, 1990). The following signs of thought disorder were found among 30 schizophrenics: odd phrasing, tangentiality, bizarre fantasy content, and vague or diffuse thinking. In addition, perseveration and poor impulse control appeared to be associated with impairment in recent memory, concentration, abstraction, and judgment (Hamilton & Allsbrook, 1986).

Negative emotions are generated when situational demands require cognitive processing or behavioral skills that exceed the individual's capacity. An individual who experiences difficulty in processing interpersonal or emotionally laden information would feel overwhelmed under normal circumstances. Conversely, extreme emotional states such as high arousal or anxiety may disrupt cognitive processing of information, leading to difficulty in concentration, selective attention, and thought organization. The interpretation of complex or discrepant information may be most affected. Distortion may be most pronounced in the interpersonal realm, whereas other aspects of cognition relating to performance of specific tasks remain intact. It is important to note the types of situations in which the cognitive processes are dysfunctional.

Reality testing is limited by distortion of experience as a result of cognitive processing style. The paranoid individual is capable of active, intense, and searching attention but incapable of anything else (Shapiro, 1965). A person who focuses on detail and misses the point is vulnerable to misinterpretation and to a loss of a sense of proportion so that trivial "facts" preoccupy the mind. If this cognitive tendency of taking clues out of context is coupled with feelings of anger and suspiciousness, then a paranoid thinking style of interpreting facts within a biased framework may develop.

Cognitive distortions may also be due to rigidity characterized by being inattentive to information that disconfirms the initial premise. Baron's (1985) definition of *cognitive rigidity* (dogmatism) is inattention to new facts. Such individuals are not influenceable because they cannot grasp the other's framework. Judgments may be made on accurate perceptions that are incorrectly interpreted according to rigid preconceptions or expectations.

Another way of being cognitively rigid is through concrete thinking manifested by being extremely stimulus bound or literal. The emphasis is on detail so that the holistic flavor of the situation is lost. This is exemplified by the child whose father praised her essay but made a mildly critical remark about the handwriting. She concluded that the father had a negative view of the entire essay.

Difficulty with volitional control of attention is also a source of cognitive-processing deficits. Attention may be captured by one aspect of the situation or task rather than shifting deliberately. An individual who is unable to maintain focus on the most relevant aspect will display poor judgment.

Self-Regulation

Adverse subjective states not attributable to external circumstances such as distress, discomfort, anxiety, or terror disrupt functioning. Mechanisms to reduce anxiety or to promote equilibrium are ineffective; emotions are not regulated by choice of situation or activities, by cognitive interpretation, or by supportive relationships. Some youngsters cannot exercise options for self-regulation because the social and academic requirements of the family and/or educational system are too difficult. Their efforts may be ineffective and cause vicious cycles. Attempts at self-regulation are evident in the use of defenses such as denial, avoidance, externalization, splitting, or projection.

Behavior

Behavior that falls short of expectations or that is disturbing to self and/or to others is considered dysfunctional. The individual is considered disturbed to the extent that emotional, cognitive, and behavioral processes interfere with functioning in socially accepted ways. A problem is noted when there are disruptions in interpersonal relationships, socialization, learning, and task (or job) performance.

Extreme emotion, anxiety, or arousal may result in impulsive, inappropriate, or unmodulated behavior, as well as unacceptable verbal expression. Distorted cognitive interpretations can lead to the inability to judge the impact of one's behavior on others. An individual may be aware of societal expectations or of proper behavior in a particular circumstance but be unable to apply that knowledge spontaneously because of difficulty with timing, control, or modulation.

Biological Indicator

The search for biological indicators places emphasis on finding physiological markers associated with a set of symptoms. Some forms of emotional disturbance are caused by physiological or neurological processes that produce cognitive deficits as well as affective disturbance. Sometimes, cognitive deficits lead to errors in judgment and maladaptive behaviors, which are viewed by others as emotional disturbance. A child who is unable to organize experiences may become extremely emotionally upset when demands exceed cognitive capacities.

Diagnostic Issues and Projective Stories

The ambiguous task of projective story telling requires self-direction and organization that reflect aspects of functioning needed in similarly unstructured circumstances. One 10-year-old boy earnestly described his anguish about making and keeping friends. However, when he was observed in a structured play group, he seemed quite comfortable. The child was capable of functioning much better with guidance and support when he was not responsible for the regulation of his own behavior. Similarly, his difficulties were not obvious on the more structured tasks in the battery but were evident from his responses to the T.A.T. cards.

Although it is possible to discern strong emotional reactions to picture stimuli such as the T.A.T., to focus on emotional reactions alone would be too simplistic. The projective story is the product of the individual's integration of cognitive and emotional attributes and of learned coping components acquired through experience and maturation. The specific emotions such as fear, worry, sadness, anger, boredom, or curiosity are illuminating. However, the meaning of the emotion is derived from the organization of affect and cognition into the network of the individual's subjective experience. The interpretation needs to consider the role of emotion in the story process and content, including the relationship of affect to the stimulus and unfolding events, as well as the intensity of its expression.

Continuity in subjective experience tends to be perpetuated by continuities in cognitive, affective, and attentional processes that promote similar interactional patterns and interpretations. These continuities are bolstered by those in the family, neighborhood, and school environment. A particular subjective experience reflected in projective stories could be produced by different person and environment interaction patterns. For instance, a child's view of parents as critical and punitive may be a product of one or more of the following: (1) a history of discipline in response to disorganized, impulsive behavior; (2) the child's tendency to be oversensitive and react strongly to mild criticism; (3) parental overreactivity, perfectionism, or intolerance of normal, age-appropriate child behavior (in such cases, the child hopefully will encounter or seek others who are more supportive); and (4) the child's inability to organize experiences and failure to develop a basic trust of the self and others in certain situations. The examiner interprets stories in the context of data from various sources in an attempt to construct the subjective world of the story teller and the factors contributing to its maintenance.

The diagnosis of depression and anxiety should utilize the DSM III criteria. Characters in projective stories can be unhappy because the narrator cannot overcome the negative stimulus pull, and therefore does not describe individuals with resources to overcome adverse circumstances. Scores for anxiety and depression have been derived from projective stories (e.g., McArthur & Roberts, 1982). However, information gleaned from projective stories may be more relevant to Axis II, where the basic, enduring emotions are related to personality organization rather than to specific, clinical symptoms.

The classification or diagnostic function differs from use of the data to describe personality organization. Diagnostic criteria typically include extreme deviations from normative expectations. These can be further refined by establishing differential expectations according to classification groups. Therefore, for diagnostic purposes, indices that characterize stories of disturbed children must depart from expectancies of normal or less disturbed individuals. Accordingly, the focus must be on identifying aspects of projective stories that can be easily quantified and therefore conducive to normative comparisons.

Studies that successfully differentiate between emotionally disturbed children and a comparison group with projective stories are summarized in Table 14–1. These studies have relatively small numbers of subjects. Furthermore, there are variations in the stimuli, in the comparison groups, and in the methods of administration of picture stimuli. Yet, there are several areas of consensus.

TABLE 14-1 • Summary of Studies Differentiating Maladjusted Children from a Comparison Group

Author	Age of SS	Subjects	Measure	Authors' Conclusions
Gurevitz & Klapper (1951)	5–12	10 schizophrenic and 18 cerebral palsy	C.A.T.	Greater tendency among the schizophrenic children toward bizarreness, perseveration, associative confabulation, evaluating stimuli (e.g., "This is funny"), affect-laden responses (e.g., react to the cards presented, "Oh wow"), card criticism, helplessness, and hostility and authoritarianism in description of interpersonal relationships. Perseveration, bizarreness, and associative confabulations express the child's difficulty maintaining control over thoughts and emotional processes.
Cox & Sargent (1950)	Seventh grade (mean age of disturbed group was 13-1; stable group was 12-6)	15 stable and 15 disturbed boys rated by teachers and staff and receiving psychological/psychiatric referral	T.A.T. pictures projected on 3 × 5 screen	Greater constriction in stories of disturbed boys indicated by shorter length, greater frequency of stories that contained no expression of feelings, needs, threats, actions, or outcomes. Normal boys expressed more threats of disaster, death, and domination. Thus, they dealt with the conflicts and threats introduced by the stimuli.

(Continued)

TABLE 14-1 • (Continued)

Author	Age of SS	Subjects	Measure	Authors' Conclusions
Leitch & Schafer (1947)	5–17 (mean age of 11)	15 psychotic and 15 maladjusted nonpsychotic	T.A.T. cards	The aspects of thought organization and perceptual and emotional functioning that were more characteristic of the psychotic group were: incoherence; contradictions (mutually incompatible ideas—"one sunny night"); odd verbal expressions; introduction of the examiner into the story; poor logic (overgeneralization, symbolism, strained reasoning); themes unrelated to the picture; and unmodulated expression of affect (motifs of violence and death).
Bachtold (1975)	Boys, 13–16	Students in self-contained public school classroom for emotionally disturbed learners (all of normal and above average IQ but underachieving in school subjects [N = 20])	Based on Whitely's (1966) scoring for adaptive functioning which emphasizes the subject's ability to deal with the task of story telling and the character's anticipating and evaluating the consequences of an action	Relatively few of the boys told complete stories that went beyond card description. The stories indicated an inability to conceptualize or to express the anticipation and evaluation of the consequences of an action. A large majority expressed extreme anger, hostility, and coercion. Only 15% of the stories viewed the hero as trying to accomplish something, and 30% of stories saw the hero as avoiding restraints or obligations.

| McGrew & Teglasi (1990) | Boys, 6–12 (average = 9.2 years) | Students in self-contained classrooms for emotionally disturbed learners (N = 40) and a comparison group (N = 40) matched for age and ability | T.A.T. | Characteristics that distinguished stories of disturbed boys from the comparison group were: poor organization and flaws of internal logic; difficulty overcoming the negative pull of the stimulus to produce realistic positive actions or outcomes; poor judgment and failure to understand cause-effect relationship with respect to actions and outcomes, including magical thinking where success is achieved by wishing or dreaming; difficulty modulating affective expression and story content (extremely violent or morbid) to stay within the bounds of conventionality; inappropriate verbal expressions such as irrelevant, bizarre, or unrelated comments; and references to being inadequate or unable to complete the task. |

Generally, the findings with respect to emotional disturbance have borne out the conclusion of Leitch and Schafer (1947): "For the purpose of diagnosing, the analysis of the formal structure of the stories and the formal characteristics of their content is more useful than the analysis of ideational content" (pp. 337–338).

Leitch and Schafer (1947) focused on characteristics of thought organization and perceptual and emotional functioning. The following formal characteristics of stories were decisive in diagnosing psychotic conditions: (1) *ideation*—incoherencies, contradictions, odd verbalizations, strained (autistic) logic, and themes unrelated to the picture; (2) *affect*—particularly vivid descriptions of violence and death; and (3) *perceptual functioning*—omitting important details of the card, distortion of details, and perceptual uncertainties that remain unresolved.

One of the chief components of emotional disturbance as well as of disturbed behavior is the absence of competency to interpret and organize experiences. According to Leitch and Schafer (1947): "The relatively unstructured nature of the test material [T.A.T.] calls upon the subject to organize the material presented, to derive its meaning and build around it a story consisting of relevant thoughts and affects. The subject produces material in which his mode of psychological functioning is reflected and its pathology revealed" (p. 337).

Whitely's (1966) scoring method to determine adaptive functioning in T.A.T. stories emphasized the protagonist's approach for handling conflict: accepting responsibility for behavior and its consequences, and control of impulses and modulation of behavior to environmental demands. Dymond (1954) developed a method of scoring T.A.T. protocols to assess mental health. These included the ability of the hero to solve the problem set by the story teller through self-reliance rather than dependence on others or magical solutions, and the characters' ability to engage in constructive interpersonal relationships. Dana (1959) indicated that his system was able to tap three concommitants of mental illness: diminished awareness of reality, difficulty or inability to organize experience, and diminished desire or capacity to give a socially acceptable account of oneself.

Indices of Emotional Disturbance in the T.A.T.

McGrew and Teglasi (1990) adapted scoring categories for the T.A.T. that were previously reported to be effective in distinguishing between disturbed and normal groups. The scoring criteria, which are discribed below, were effective in differentiating between disturbed elementary school children (kindergarten through sixth grade) and a matched normal comparison group.

I. Verbalizations Unrelated to the Story

Each category is scored once per story (adapted from perceptual personalization [Dana, 1959; Nawas, 1965]).

Picture Criticism These are negative comments about the cards or the scenes portrayed (e.g., "This card is too old fashioned," "This boy doesn't belong here," "This picture is stupid").

Expression of Frustration or Disinterest These are noncritical comments or questions about the cards, the story telling, or the testing situation that express frustration or disinterest. These comments/questions must occur following presentation of the first card after instructions were given and initial questions answered (e.g., "How many more?"). Picture criticism or expression of inadequacy is not scored in this category.

Irrelevant Comments These are other irrelevant comments or questions unrelated to the story, the task, or the cards. These remarks are generally attempts to converse with the examiner after the task has been introduced (e.g., "Do you have children?")

Expression of Inadequacy Such expressions may be either general or specific to the story telling task. One and two points per story are assigned respectively for minor and major expressions of inadequacy.

Minor Expression: These include spontaneous comments as well as responses to inquiry that indicate minor or indirect references to the child's lack of ability, dissatisfaction, frustration, or lack of confidence (e.g., "This is hard," "I can't tell what this is," "I've never done this before," "I can't think of anything else [after having told a nearly complete story], "Am I doing OK?" I don't know if I can do this too well.") Minor expressions reflect difficulty with the task, being unsure what an object is, or concern with meeting standards. The child is seeking reassurance rather than being unable or unwilling to accomplish the task.

Major Expression: These include direct and clear reference to the child's lack of ability, strong frustration, dissatisfaction with performance, or unwillingness to attempt to complete the task (e.g., "This is too hard," "I can't do it," "This is the best I can do," "I don't have a story for this one," "I'm all done" [when story is substantially incomplete]). This category is scored when no story is told; direct and strong expressions of inadequacy reflect very poorly on the child's self-evaluation; and more than two minor expressions are voiced to one story. Such statements of inadequacy are not scored as personal reference (in the next category).

II. Disruptions to the Internal Logic of the Story
(adapted from Neman, Brown, & Sells, 1973)

Contradictions within the Story   This category is scored when nonsequiturs such as uncorrected statements of incompatible ideas, meanings, or actions are expressed without apparent awareness on the part of the story teller (e.g., "He was trapped in a room with no doors and no windows . . . he finally escaped through the window"). Included also are illogical use of language (e.g., "They didn't have water to eat") and irrelevant or contradictory responses to the examiner's inquiry. Mild confusion such as incorrect pronoun reference or interchanging a response to thinking or feeling queries is not scored. A concrete response to the question, "What is he feeling?" (answered, "The table") is also not scored.

Perseveration of Story Content   This category includes plots that are essentially repetitious of the previous story (e.g., identical action, identical outcome); the clear continuation of prior story content or characters to a subsequent card (assuming that the characters are different, as in the T.A.T.); and verbatim and purposeless repetition of sentences or major parts of sentences within a story. This category also includes reiteration of previous story content in response to inquiry. If a child repeats a clause or sentence to expand on or clarify part of the story, then perseveration is not scored.

Personal Reference   This is the inclusion of personal information (not "I think" or "It looks like to me") that is somehow related to the characters or action of the story (e.g., "We have a dog too," "That happened to me once," "You'd feel that way too, wouldn't you?").

III. Judgment and Reality Testing (influenced by studies
in Table 14-1)

Inappropriate or Bizarre Actions or Verbal Expressions that Occur During the Testing Session   These include very inappropriate comments, gestures, weird noises, animal sounds, nonsense words, inappropriate laughter, throwing test material, or hostility toward the examiner.

Inappropriate, Bizarre, or Highly Unlikely Story Content   These include clearly regressive content (e.g., characters playing with their food, magic, baby talk); gross misperception of stimuli (e.g., fields in Card 2 is a cemetery); supernatural or highly unlikely events; extremely morbid, gruesome, or violent references; and explicit sexual content. The story teller seems unaware or does not care that these are not socially acceptable responses and cannot keep up a veneer of normalcy. Actions and reactions of people in the story are grossly out of keeping with expectations. The maximum score is one per story.

IV. Actions and Outcomes (adapted from Arnold, 1962)

Difficulty with understanding basic cause-effect relationships can be inferred from the structural elements of story content relating to actions and outcomes. *Action* refers to activity of the characters in response to adversity, in attempting to solve a problem or in pursuit of goals. Each story may be scored for both positive and negative actions if they apply.

Positive Action (1) action that is deliberate, planned, constructive, socially acceptable, and realistic (passivity where action is possible as well as magical or highly unrealistic actions are scored as negative); (2) formulating a plan or approach toward a problem or a conflict that the character seems intent to carry out; (3) positive attitude that permits the character to make the best of a bad situation or to deal with threats in an adaptive and constructive manner.

Negative Action (1) actions or plans by any of the characters that are destructive, asocial, malicious, manipulative, socially unacceptable, or that indicate alienation, self-reproach, confusion, failures, or inadequacy; (2) evasive, distancing, magical, unrealistic, forgetful, impulsive, vague, wishful actions or plans; (3) character displays a negative, unremorseful, rationalizing, intellectualizing, or very unrealistic attitude; (4) deals maladaptively with problems, threats, or misfortune; (5) character fails to act positively when constructive action is warranted.

No Action Action does not fit any of the above categories. (1) only card description is provided; (2) no clear opportunity for action or for expression of positive attitude is indicated in the plot; (3) mundane action not intended to accomplish anything in a story that depicts no conflict, need, or goal (e.g., "They played, ate, and went to bed").

Outcome *Outcome* is the final state of events, the way things turn out at the end, with consideration of the intervening thoughts, feelings, actions, and circumstances. Each story can receive a score from one to five.

Five
A socially acceptable goal, need, or purpose for action must be stated (such as achievement goal, overcoming adverse situations; resolving tension) and accomplished through realistic positive action without detrimental impact on

anyone. The character's feelings, actions, thoughts, and outcomes are balanced and realistically conceptualized (e.g., character has a positive attitude toward achieving a goal, works hard and succeeds in attaining it). If the protagonist is bored or dislikes work, it would be unlikely/unrealistic to expect that character to exert great effort and achieve success.

1. Disagreements or tensions between close friends or loved ones are realistically resolved. Noncriminal wrongdoing is followed by remorse and genuine attempts at restitution.
2. A goal is stated that a character cannot achieve in the present, but a greater goal (long term) is accomplished with no negative side effects.
3. Appropriate values, attitudes, and constructive principles are learned. These cannot be superficial or phony.
4. People are viewed as helpful, providing good advice, and setting a positive example in a way that helps others to make their own decisions, to accomplish goals, or to maintain an autonomous course of action.

Four
A socially acceptable goal, need, or purpose for action is stated. However:

1. Success is difficult to achieve or involves stress, sacrifice, or some unhappiness, failure, or disappointment (e.g., success but being too tired or overwhelmed to enjoy it until later).
2. Reliance is placed on the realistic goodwill of others rather than one's initiative. Character takes no action, but people behave positively ("He was lucky that someone returned his keys").
3. Initial failure (clearly stated) is overcome by special help (e.g., tutoring, counseling, parental intervention); second chance (e.g., make-up test, another operation, new friends); learning from past mistakes (e.g., resolve to do things differently next time; modifying means or goals realistically); and better luck that is realistic rather than reflecting magical thinking (e.g., "the drought ends and the crops survive").
4. Noncriminal wrongdoing is reasonably and justifiably punished, with logical consequences. Punishment is accepted as appropriate and necessary for bad deeds. Inaction or unrealistic action leads to failure.

Three
Outcomes are given but there is no need to be met, no conflict to be resolved, no threats to be overcome, and no goals to reach. Consequently, outcomes do not accomplish anything. Neither success nor failure is evident, but action is positive or appropriate (e.g., "They were plowing the fields like they should").

Two

There are either no outcomes, or there are modified failures, moderately negative endings, or unrealistically positive resolutions.

1. Usually, there is either no outcome or the story just ends on a feeling. If there is an outcome, it seems to be tacked on to comply with directions or in response to examiner inquiry without appropriate transition.
2. A positive action has an unhappy context, negative side effect, or is not very helpful (e.g., "Father tried to help but his advice backfired").
3. Partial success has a mildly negative impact on other people (e.g., "Others think you're snobbish").
4. Characters try to accomplish something with no assurance of success nor any indication that a resolution to a problem is forthcoming. Despite positive action, the resolution is unhappy (e.g., "Keeps practicing, but will play the wrong notes during the performance," "He will try to communicate better").
5. The character can't decide about the outcome or doesn't know what to do in the end (e.g., "He couldn't make up his mind," "He was afraid because he knew he would get into trouble").
6. Unrealistically positive endings are not based on appropriate instrumental action (e.g., success is gained only because of one's status; through a passive, unwarranted dependence on others; as a result of the passage of time; or simply by wishing for it).
7. Success is desired only for self-centered motives that are, however, not immoral, unethical, or antisocial (e.g., "They read the will and handed out his possessions").
8. Success is achieved despite the character's lack of interest, absence of sufficient effort, or failure to modify means when necessary.
9. Success or active effort is defensively viewed as undesirable or not worth it in the end, so it's a rationale for inaction. (e.g., character really doesn't care).

One

The endings are either very negative or completely unrealistic and highly improbable:

1. Characters fail to achieve needs or goals with no positive side effect (e.g., major tragedy, things don't work out as planned, helpless to give positive ending).
2. Protagonists or others die or are lost through violence; there are permanent separations based on anger or impulse.

3. Punishment is too harsh, inappropriate, or has negative consequences. Punishment doesn't fit the crime, is viewed as unfair, damages the child, or indicates lack of empathy of authorities.

4. Story ends either with negative feelings or with generally negative statements, attitudes, or outlooks (e.g., story turns out "sad," "mad," "terrible," or "bad,"; future looks bleak; general pessimism; character just cries in the end).

5. Story ends with negative action.

6. Very bad relations among friends or family remain at the end of story, such as abusive relatives; there is discord and characters run away.

7. Characters fail to act as a result of sheer passivity. They sleep rather than resolve the problem, or rely on others for rescue.

8. Stories are magical, bizarre, or unbelievable (e.g., the outcome totally contradicts action; dead person comes back to life).

9. Success is pursued for unethical, immoral, criminal, or antisocial purposes. Wrongdoing is not punished or leads to success so that bad influence prevails and characters get away with criminal, antisocial actions.

Summary

Characteristics of disturbed affect, cognition, or behavior can be distinguished from the wide variation in the "normal" range of functioning. Indices of emotional disturbance in projective stories relate to quality of judgment, reality testing, and problem solving based on the organization of thought and regulation of emotion in relation to the integration of life experiences.

CHAPTER 15

Object Relations

Object relations is the terminology for person relations. However, the term *object relation* does not pertain to an observable relationship between two people; rather, object relations theories deal with the manner in which actual interactions become subjectively represented within the individual in the process of development (Fairbairn, 1952; Klein, 1948; Winnicott, 1965). Subjective representations or internal images of both self and others are referred to as *objects*. The inner experience, the manner in which the interaction is experienced inwardly, is referred to as *object relations,* whereas *object relatedness* refers to actual, observable transactions between people (Meissner, 1971, 1972). The subjective experience of relatedness is based on how the individual perceives the self and others, including the manner in which the person draws distinctions among individuals or differentiates the various attributes of a single individual.

The object-relations model of Fairbairn (1954), later elaborated by others (Guntrip, 1968, 1974; Kohut, 1977), attempts to correct some of the deficiencies of classical psychoanalytic theory by emphasizing interpersonal relatedness in understanding development and behavior. Thus, object relations is the elaboration of the interpersonal aspect of classical Freudian drive theory (Guntrip, 1974), giving it wider scope by integrating noninstinctive motivational factors along with basic Freudian principles (Kernberg, 1976; Winnicott, 1965).

The importance of object relations lies in the contention that individuals relate to other people according to the internal patterning of self-other experiences that become the template for all future relationships. Object relations represent the organization of accumulated experiences and provide the schema for how the individual relates to the interpersonal world. If a child has limited ability to organize interpersonal experiences, the development of inner representations will reflect these limitations.

Object representations are complex schemata that have both affective and cognitive components and serve to organize an individual's conception of self and other people. The concept of internal objects, first postulated by Melanie Klein (1932), assumes that actual relationships become intraspsychic structures

(Guntrip, 1968), so that even when one is isolated from other people, it is possible to feel connection to internal objects. Through development, these schemata become increasingly less diffuse, less grounded in the immediate situation, more symbolic or conceptual, and more consistent. These object representations organize an individual's understanding of self and of others and determine the subjective experience of relatedness.

Internalization

The process by which early interpersonal experiences are reflected in personality organization is conceptualized as internalization (Meissner, 1981). According to object-relations formulations, the child's ongoing interactions with caregivers are internalized to form object and self-representations (Fairbairn, 1952; Jacobson, 1964; Klein, 1932; Winnicott, 1965). Object representation is a theoretical construct pertaining to cognitive and affective schemata resulting from perceptions of past relationships that organize current interpersonal perceptions and actions.

According to Meissner (1981), internalization and object relations have a reciprocal relationship. That is, the nature and quality of the object relations influence and shape the level and type of organization and integration that characterize the internalization. The quality of the internalizations themselves is reflected in and influences reciprocally the quality of object relations.

The concept of internalization is fundamental to object-relations theory. Schafer (1968) defined internalization as "all those processes by which the subject transforms real or imagined regulatory interactions with his environment into inner regulations and characteristics" (p. 9). Hartmann (1939) borrowed the term from biology to describe the evolution of an organism from greater to lesser dependency on the external world. Through an inner world of memory and thought, humans filter their response and perception of the external world to organize new experience. The more developed this inner world, the less directly one responds to immediate events, and the more one emphasizes the meaning attributed to those events. The representation allows an increased capacity for delay and for tolerating separation from the object (Mahler, 1968).

Object relations as internal structure perform the self-regulatory functions previously provided by caregivers. This inner structure enhances capacity for internal regulation in the sense of providing inner resource for organizing experiences in the absence of external support or guidance. The object relations also contribute to the motivational system. The internalized psychic structures as they increase in complexity gradually motivate the individual in ways that external objects did previously.

Internalization Process and Inner Structure

As inner structure builds, the need for externally imposed structure to direct an individual's activities diminishes. If such functions of external objects as support and guidance have not been internalized, then the presence of a real object is required. An adolescent said, "Others have people inside of them, holding them up so they walk upright. I'm walking around hunched over and cannot walk straight without someone to lean on. Because I am empty inside, I'm always looking around for other people to boost me up."

The internalized object feels like an inner presence that influences the person's inner state and behavior in lieu of external guidance. These internal representations are organized and determine how the individual experiences the self and object in a relationship. Sometimes these internalizations are organized as polarities whereby people are categorized in a dichotomous fashion as aggressor or victim, superior or inferior (Meissner, 1981). A reciprocal relationship is inherent in these polarities. For example, an aggressor implies the presence of a victim so an individual has internalized both. However, at any given time and circumstance, an individual can be either one or the other. A person who feels the self to be a victim of other's aggression may justify being the aggressor at another time. Similarly, feelings of worthlessness imply that others are special or privileged. Those with low self-esteem may feel entitled to the trappings that they associate with feeling special or gratified.

Through the process of internalization, an "internal world" is created, an inner sense of "true self" develops rather than a superficial "false" inauthentic self that is oriented to external appearances (e.g., Guntrip, 1968; Kernberg, 1976; Kohut, 1977; Winnicott, 1965). Autonomy relates to the degree of self-direction and resistance to responding to immediate provocation. For a teenager, autonomy is not the ability to drive a car but the inner conviction to decide when, how, and where to drive.

What is internalized reflects both the circumstances of the environment as well as the sensitivities and organizing capacities of the individual. The combination of these determine how the person experiences the behaviors of parents, siblings, and significant others. A very sensitive person may perceive more criticism and internalize objects that are more judgmental. At the same time, individual differences in various characteristics elicit different behaviors from others. For example, a child who is easily distracted or does not persist on tasks is likely to elicit more control and structure from parents, teachers, and other authorities.

Shapiro (1965) indicates that the organization of experience in memory is related to the style of the original cognitive process that determined the nature of the experience in the first place. The hysterical personality, for example, engages in cognitions that are diffuse, global, and impressionistic. Therefore, such individuals tend to notice and recollect what is striking, flashy, or obvious. If an individual's style is characterized by the general absence of focused attention, then not bringing to sharp focus facts that are uncomfortable seems more related to this style of thinking than to defense mechanisms of repression or denial.

Self-Regulation and Internalization

Internalization is a process by which external relationships and external sources of self-regulation become part of the inner psychic structure, which is subjectively experienced as the regulatory functions (Meissner, 1981; Hartmann, 1939). For Schafer (1968), internalization is a matter of degree, reflecting the extent to which external regulations have been taken over by the individual. Both emotional and cognitive limitations detract from the development of inner self-regulatory structures. The domination of awareness by that which is immediately striking, concrete, and personally relevant is the chief cognitive limitation that is not compatible with the development of long-range interests, values, or aims. The primary affective hindrance to the development of internalized values is impairment in the capacity to sustain emotional involvement in interests that are relatively remote from immediate personal needs (Shapiro, 1965).

The concept of ego and superego within the psychoanalytic framework implies the existence of internal structures that regulate behavior. Hartmann (1939) viewed the primary function of the ego as one of internal regulation. The superego possesses prohibitions and directives, but also a positive vision for the future, thereby providing guiding and motivating functions that are internalized. After the formation of a conscience, an individual can assume some self-regulatory functions (Kohut, 1971), though still rely on the external world.

Although both the ego and superego have self-regulatory functions, it is not necessary to adopt the psychoanalytic framework to assume that internalized structures play a self-regulatory role. The regulatory functions of cognitive schema are widely accepted. In fact, any storehouse of experience, knowledge, or ideals against which to measure immediate experiences plays a role in self-regulation where an individual's understanding guides behavior rather than momentary provocation.

Development

Through developmental learning there is increasing stabilization and delineation of object representations. Distinctions within the self are prerequisite to the differentiation of self from other (Meissner, 1981). Individuals cannot make subtle differentiations among others without possessing insight to the nuances and distinctions within the self. Thus, the general developmental course of object representation is paralleled by an increasing differentiation of the self-representation reflecting the emergence of structural differentiation in the self. Refinement of object representations gradually moves toward the emergence of a concept of individuals as separate, independent, and enduring in time and space.

As stated previously, the development of object representation is a function of the actual relationships plus the nature of the child. The manner in which a child integrates interpersonal experience is a product of complex processes involving emotion, cognition, and memory. Mahler's (1968) notion of libidinal object constancy goes beyond the purely cognitive notion of object permanence because it implies not only that others exist as enduring entities but that a person can sustain the feelings of attachment in the absence of others in a manner that is free of need states.

Sandler and Rosenblatt (1962) differentiated between the *inner* world, which consists of cognitions and representations, and the *internal* world of intrapsychic structure. Raynor and McFarlin's (1986) description of the behavioral and self-systems bears a striking resemblance to the inner and internal worlds, respectively. Meissner (1974) made a similar distinction between two processes: (1) the process of learning cognitive representations that are functional and that enlarge the child's repertoire of adaptive skills; and (2) the development of the internal world leading to the organization of psychic structure and enhancement of certain ego functions. The development of the internal world is subject to laws that differ from those that apply to other learning processes. The reinforcement of behavioral responses furthers the development and organization of functional structure that contributes to the child's adaptive skills. However, the development of increasingly complex and differentiated self and object representations takes place at a level of organization that is different from that of acquiring behavioral patterns through reinforcement.

Indeed, the continuing growth of internal structure depends not so much on obtaining reinforcements but on the stability and continuity of the relationship and affective involvement with another person (object). What develops is the capacity to tolerate separation from the object and to shift from a focus on object-derived reinforcement to an emphasis on sustaining interest without extrinsic reinforcement. The availability of an inner object makes that shift possible. For Meissner, the learning paradigm in terms of specific reinforcements is absorbed into a larger framework of the object relation. Internalization as a form of experiential learning requires synthesis of experience and a capacity for representational organization. Not all people synthesize and integrate life experiences, nor seek consistency in perception of self or other (Raynor & McFarlin, 1986).

Hartmann (1956) pointed out that the child is prepared at birth for primary autonomy through the availability of processes such as perception or memory, which provides the means, though in rudimentary form, for dealing with reality. Development of the mechanisms for secondary autonomy hinges on maturation and experience. Beebe and Lachmann (1988) review empirical evidence to support the emerging view that such infant capacities as memory and cross-modal perception constitute an early representational system (in the first year) prior to the development of symbolic functioning and language. This "pre-symbolic" representation is the foundation for later symbolic representation and provides the continuity in conceptualizing the growth in self-object representation from birth.

The ego psychologists as represented by Hartmann define the ego in terms of its functions. Ego functions such as perception, memory, capacity for abstraction, and symbolism are fundamental building blocks for the development of mental representations. The *synthetic* functions are clearly related to the competency of the individual to assimilate, organize, and integrate life experiences. These factors operate from the beginning of life, and impairment in the neonate's ability to process and integrate environmental stimuli will have an impact on the development of internal representations. Only what is perceived can be represented.

Internalization is viewed as an active, continuous process stemming from within the child. The outcome of this process depends on the child's endowment and the nature of early relationships. Mahler, Pine, and Bergman (1975) describe the interplay between the child's natural endowment and the environment in terms of the match between the child's attributes and the responsiveness of the caregivers during the neonatal period. An infant is well matched with the environment if the child is able to elicit a response from the environment and can extract and organize cues from the surroundings in any of the following ways:

1. The child elicits a response and caregivers are responsive.
2. A child with diminished capacity to extract responses and information from the environment whose caregivers extend themselves.
3. A child with high capacity to extract from the environment who elicits appropriate responses from otherwise less responsive caregivers.

An infant would be poorly matched with the environment if:

1. A child with adequate capacity to extract from the environment is matched with caregivers who are incapable of responding.
2. A child cannot "connect" with the caregiver no matter what pains are taken.

The separation-individuation process (Mahler, 1966; Mahler, Pine, & Bergman, 1975) essentially describes the cognitive-affective mechanism relating to the mental representations of self and object. This process refers to the child's psychological growth as the internal representations of the self and others increase in complexity, subtlety, and individuality. Mahler, Pine, and Bergman

(1975) delineated four subphases of the separation-individuation phase, ending with the attainment of object constancy at about 36 months when representations of self-other become stable and enduring despite frustration or separation. As development proceeds, global or diffuse mental representations of self and other become increasingly more differentiated, more integrated, and more articulated.

While the separation-individuation phase roughly covers the age from 6 to 36 months (Mahler, 1966, 1971), the issues surrounding separation-individuation continue to be recycled as cognitive development proceeds. Furthermore, the role of affective experiences in lending coherence and continuity to the line of development cannot be overemphasized. Besides the developmental considerations, there are important individual differences in the ways the issues of individuation and separation are "played out" (Speers et al., 1971). Gardner (1983) recognized these individual differences in interpersonal functioning by designating the capacity for insight and self-awareness as a separate aspect of intelligence.

According to Meissner (1974), "The primary and basic accomplishment in the development of the child's personality is the establishment of the rudiments of the self and the gradual differentiation of inner representations of the self and the inner representations of objects. This accomplishment is a major task of the earliest months of life and an extremely important one, since the rest of the structure of the personality must be built on this foundation" (pp. 183–184).

Kernberg (1976) postulates three major sequential processes of internalization in the development of the self: introjection, identification, and ego identity. The internalized images of self and object develop together, and there is progression from perceiving fragments of objects or global diffuse objects to greater differentiation and more organized stable identity formation, resulting in coherent and consistent representation of self and others. At the highest developmental stage, past experience has been consolidated into a system of values and abstract principles of conduct, which may transcend the specific objects that have been internally represented.

The quality of the relation to the object depends on the level and nature of internal organization with which the individual approaches the relationship. Failure of self-object differentiation and lack of self-cohesion create a situation in which the characteristics of the object cannot be appreciated apart from the needs of the perceiver. A person who is terror stricken and experiences a loss of self-cohesion cannot organize the internal or external world. Hence, relationships are laden with confusion, fears of engulfment, or panic upon separation.

The mechanism of splitting where all experiences are dichotomously classified as either all good or all bad reduces ambiguity and therefore anxiety. However, without integration of various facets of experience, the individual is confined to live in the present and to appreciate only what others provide in the moment. Intense emotions can be overwhelming and make immediate comfort provided most salient. Likewise, the inability to integrate experience due to cognitive limitations leaves the individual trapped in the one-dimensional, immediacy of experience without the capacity to coordinate self with other or now with later.

The phases of separation-individuation have been completed by age 3, when the child is equipped with a sense of an individual self. Increased structuring of self and object representation proceed as well as further elaboration of ego identity, ego ideals, and superego prohibitions (Kernberg, 1976; Mahler, 1968). The basic elements of mutuality, reciprocity, acceptance, and expression of a broad range of emotions without undue disparagement of self or other have been laid down by the time a child can tell a projective story. Beyond that, there is no strict time table apart from a general development toward greater refinement in and synthesis of the distinctions made, as well as increasing capacity to be interested in another person and to feel connected despite temporary frustration. Not all adult pathological states can be traced back to a normal stage of child development to which an individual has regressed or at which the person has become fixated. We cannot look at a projective story produced by a disturbed adolescent and say this is normal for a particular age. Individual differences and developmental considerations are separate but interwoven concepts.

Relationship to Pathology

The capacity to represent interpersonal (object) relations is considered by many psychoanalytic investigators to be related to severity and type of psychopathology (Blatt & Lerner, 1983; Procidano & Guinta, 1989; Spear & Lapidus, 1981).

Mahler observed that the breakdown of basic ego functioning in psychotic children is associated with an inability to create an adequate internal representation of a loved object and attain separation-individuation. Difficulty organizing experience limits the capacity to engage in the complex integrative task of internalization. Three pathological modes of relating have been described within the psychoanalytic framework (e.g., Horney, 1950; Kernberg, 1975, 1976; Kohut, 1971): (1) relating to others as "self-objects," (2) relating to others as "transitional objects," and (3) relating to others as "part-objects." All three modes are appropriate during specific developmental moments but are pathological if they persist (Klein, 1948; Mahler, Pine, & Bergman, 1975; Winnicott, 1971).

Self-object relations refer to viewing others in terms of how the individual wishes or needs them to be. The functions or attributes of the other that do not pertain to the self are not valued or perhaps not even noticed. Such a solipsistic view has a distorting influence on the perception of the other and precludes the possibility of granting that individual autonomous status. At the most primitive level, the lack of self-cohesion and absence of self-object differentiation is associated with delusional distortion, fragmentation, or loss of cohesion of the self.

Normally, the symbiotic phase where self and object (infant-mother) remain undifferentiated, and mother is experienced as part of the self occurs between 2 and 5 months of life (Kernberg, 1976; Mahler, 1968). During the stage of symbiosis (Mahler, 1968), the ego and object (self and mother) are not differentiated sufficiently to experience a distinction between self and other. Kohut (1971) refers to Mahler's developmental phase of symbiosis as being maintained by the fact that the infant is at the mercy of the mother's organization. If the caregiver cannot maintain meaningful ties to the infant, then he or she feels disintegration because of the inability to separate the self. Eventually, the self-object becomes internally organized, and internal and external authority are differentiated. At this point, the concept of internal structure becomes relevant. When self and object discrimination has been solidified, a variety of defensive and/or dependency motivations may modify self and object representations.

The term *transitional object relations* was introduced by Winnicott (1971) who described "transitional phenomena" to refer to objects that are intermediate between an actual person and the internal representation of that person. He alluded to the anxiety-reducing function of a transitional object such as a teddy bear at bedtime when loneliness or insecurity threaten the child. The transitional object provides comfort that still comes from outside the self but not directly from another human being. As the child matures, self-soothing and self-regulation of mood proceeds internally.

Winnicott (1971) applied this model to distorted relationships. Accordingly, object relations in which there is an interplay of introjective/projective mechanisms are transitional object relations. Rather than assuming the self-regulating and self-soothing functions through internal means, persons use other individuals the way a normal child uses transitional objects. In other words, they place the regulation of their mood, self-esteem, or actions on others. A child who will do homework or practice a skill only when a parent or other external source of motivation is present is relying on support and approval rather than on the internal structures. Such individuals externalize responsibility from the self onto others, which detracts from stability in both self and object representations.

Part-object relations is a component of object-relations theory that was originally advanced by Klein (1948), expanded by Sullivan (1953), and further refined by Mahler, Pine, and Bergmen (1975) and Kernberg (1976). Part-object relations refers to relating to others only on the level of the function they provide. Accordingly, characteristics of individuals that are not related to carrying out specific functions are not noticed, and a particular individual is evaluated only in terms of how these specific functions are carried out. This type of interpersonal orientation could be due to fearful avoidance, inability to make the distinctions, or simply lack of interest. Participants of a car pool may limit their prime concern to whether other drivers arrive on time and play out their function regardless of their life circumstances. Sullivan's (1953) conceptualization of parataxic distortion and "personifications" (where others are seen in terms of social and personal stereotypes) is similar to the ideas of part-object relations.

Summary

A brief overview of object-relations theory was presented to distill the concepts that provide the bases for delineating relevant characteristics of relationships expressed in projective stories described in the subsequent chapter.

CHAPTER 16

Measurement of Object Relations

Five levels of object relations and based on the concepts of differentiation, integration, and mutuality of autonomy are described in relation to the analysis of projective stories. An assessment of object relations "involves learning not so much *what* the individual's ideas and feelings about people are, but rather *how* the individual experiences and organizes these feelings" (Urist, 1980, p. 828). Westen and colleagues (1990) scaled into five levels each of the following four dimensions of object relations: complexity of representations of people, affective tone of relationships, capacity for emotional investment in relationships, and understanding of social causality. Each of these four dimensions, when coded from responses to the Thematic Apperception Test, distinguished borderline personality disorder from major depression and normal functioning.

Urist (1980) proposed three dimensions of object relations as the basis for variation in the experience of interpersonal relatedness. He scaled each of these according to levels of increasing maturity but without a developmental time table: (1) the richness and complexity dimension focuses on the degree to which individuals are able to grasp subtlety and complexity in others and the self; (2) the differentiation and individuation dimension describes the affective component of the richness and complexity facet and represents the extent to which the individual values and appreciates another's uniqueness and individuality; and (3) mutuality of autonomy refers to the capacity to see the self and others as they really are rather than how the perceiver expects or wants them to be. These three dimensions overlap. Indeed, the full development of the capacity to value others as they are entails the differentiation as well as appreciation of individuals' attributes. Therefore, the scale presented in this chapter incorporates all three dimensions into five multidimensional levels of object relations. It should be noted that individuals do not always operate up to their capacity for three primary reasons: (1) the situation may compel a relationship where the primary interest is not on the interaction but on the skills relevant to the task or job; (2) an individual may be temporarily overwhelmed by stress or intense feelings resulting in a narrow or solipsistic preoccupation; and (3) emotions such as anxiety, envy, jealousy, or prejudice distort specific relationships and result in misreading of what others may think or feel.

Autonomy and Mutuality of Autonomy

Autonomy is the subjective experience associated with a sense of initiative, conviction, and the deliberate, purposeful pursuit of goal-directed activities. *Autonomy* in projective stories refers to the narrator's ability to manage the task requirements as well as the competency of characters to solve problems and to pursue goals in keeping with their interests and convictions.

Mutuality of autonomy refers to the relative autonomy of the interacting individuals. An autonomously functioning person does not require external bolstering at another's expense and is, therefore, capable of evaluating others separately from needs, wishes, or prevailing mood states. With respect to projective stories, the competency of any one of the characters is not the issue. If the protagonist saves others who are helpless, the relationship is not mutual in terms of the relative autonomy of the individuals. On the contrary, the heroism of one character is made possible by ineptness on the part of others.

Mutuality of autonomy is possible when attributes of self and others are not distorted by the perceiver's need states or cognitive limitations. Such mutuality is enhanced with development in the capacity to grasp the complexities of individuals, including inconsistencies and ambiguities, particularly when coupled with the affective component of genuine caring, appreciation, and enjoyment of others' unique qualities. Subtle distinctions among persons for the purpose of using the nuances of their reactions to manipulate them obviously do not foster mutuality of autonomy.

Emotional states influence perception of self and others primarily in ways that make judgments congruent with affective experience (see review by Clark & Reis, 1988). Thus, transitions, stresses, and preoccupations may temporarily disrupt a higher level of relatedness. Furthermore, anxiety or other intense emotions associated with specific types of relationships (e.g., authority figures) may result in distortions that only apply to those interactions.

Differentiation and Integration

Differentiation refers to the type and variety of attributes or dimensions used in processing information about a person. These qualities constitute the distinctions that are of interest or that the individual is capable of discerning. *Integration* refers to the manner in which these attributes are coordinated in distinguishing among individuals or in understanding a particular individual. Together, *differentiation and integration* refer to the quality of awareness and insight regarding human characteristics and motives and, thereby, provide the foundations for interpersonal perception.

Differentiation

It is assumed that attributes that are distinguished within a person provide the basis for differentiation among individuals. An individual who possesses a richly elaborated inner life is capable of attributing such a quality to another person. Likewise, an individual must experience a sense of autonomy to appreciate the autonomy of others. Thus, full mutuality of autonomy requires the interaction of individuals with their own goals, motives, styles, and capabilities who recognize and value their own and each other's attributes. That is, they are able to perceive and differentiate attributes without distortion or threat to personal integrity and to value these attributes as interesting and relevant. Anything that detracts from a sense of autonomy also detracts from mutuality of autonomy. Feeling limited, helpless, or easily threatened, individuals may look to characteristics of others that enhance their own sense of competence or comfort. Impaired capacity for cognitive integration limits autonomy but also detracts from the capacity to coordinate perspectives of self and other, resulting in an imbalance of mutuality.

In terms of projective stories, *differentiation* refers to the demarcation of the characters, whereas *integration* relates to the manner in which the distinctions are reconciled. The following questions are relevant:

1. How are distinctions related to the stimulus?
2. What are the bases for differentiating people in the story? Are distinctions among characters based on inner motives; on superficial characteristics such as status, looks, or power; or on the stimulus cues? Are inner attributes vivid, unique, or stereotyped? Are people differentiated apart from the preoccupations, needs, or desires of the other characters? Is there focus on a single aspect of personality?
3. How clearly are characters' viewpoints and attributes delineated? Do descriptions of characters reflect dichotomous thinking, which is indicated when persons are either all good or all bad? Are there global idealizations or dwellings on minor flaws?

Impoverished differentiation can be based on a combination of limited experience with a certain class of relationships or situations, inability to grasp inner qualities of people, and/or intense emotions that constrict thought content. Difficulty distinguishing inner attributes of persons is expressed by dwelling on superficial qualities or resorting to stereotypes in the depiction of characters rather than reflecting on real experiences. When story characters simply respond to external provocation, it is likely that the narrator's behavior is not directed by an inner framework or conviction.

Integration

Integration is the synthesis of experience that hinges on the coherent organization of the distinctions that are perceived. Such capacity is evident in projective stories when

1. Negative feelings, tensions, and conflicts are integrated into a meaningful context rather than inferred directly from the stimulus or generalized from a narrow clue to the whole personality.
2. Positive and negative facets of people are noted and reconciled rather than focusing on isolated attributes or momentary events without a sense of continuity to inner life.
3. The perspectives and needs of all characters are balanced so that past, present, and future interests of the self and community are coordinated.
4. Insight and awareness are communicated to others and translated into actions that are motivated by purpose, principles, and understanding.

An individual who has difficulty making inferences or responding to implications beneath the surface might choose a level of adaptation where subtle information is neglected in favor of a simplified processing framework. A judgmental attitude of relating through a filter of right and wrong actions or expectations means less ambiguity and less information to process. Cognitively, complex persons usually engage in more extensive information seeking than cognitively simple individuals (Stein & Stone, 1978; Streufert & Streufert, 1978), and persons with less complex conceptualizations may have lower toler-ance for ambiguity or absence of structure than those with more abstract con-ceptual structures.

At first glance, it would appear that a young child would not be capable of functioning at a high level of differentiation and integration. However, young children seem to read cues and emotions accurately and be capable of differenti-ating others apart from their own needs. Yet, they may not have the level of understanding and cognitive differentiation to fully comprehend the other's concerns. These capacities increase with experience and further cognitive de-velopment. If allowance is made for the fact that cognitive distinctions may be less well articulated, the rudiments of autonomy and mutuality in relatedness are evident at an early age.

The following aspects of projective stories relevant to internal representation of relatedness are evident in some children by kindergarten:

1. Differentiation among story characters is consistent with the stimulus, is appropriate for age and role, and includes shades of gray rather than being dichotomously good or bad.
2. There is simultaneous expression of two feelings or of ambivalent emotions rather than consecutive feelings; emotions are realistically resolved rather than suddenly turned into their opposite.
3. Good interactions are mutually beneficial, and the characters are balanced in their relationships; one is not a hero while another is totally helpless. People are depicted as supportive and cooperative but can disagree or compromise.
4. Bad interactions are realistically resolved; abuse is not tolerated, and people recover after a loss of relationship.
5. Reaction to threat, anxiety, or adverse situations is realistic; characters are capable of coping rather than panicking, thinking magically or acting impulsively.
6. There is evidence of good reality testing; the sequence of events is not improbable but conveys a grasp of the relationships among causes and their effects. Descriptions refer to entire persons rather than parts.
7. Empathy, concern, and awareness are mutual, not solipsistic or focused on one character.

The internal representation of the world provides the lens through which experiences are perceived and the template for how the perceptions are organized. Self and object images develop in tandem so that the degree of differentiation within the self corresponds to the subtlety of the nuances with which others are distinguished. An individual cannot be perceptive about others without awareness of inner motives, feelings, and patterns of behavior. The assumption that an individual cannot attribute to others an awareness that is not possessed (Tomkins, 1947) allows for inferences about object relations even if only one character is described in a projective story.

Levels of Object Relations

Level One: Disorganized Experience of Relatedness

Distinctions within the self and between self and nonself are very primitive (global, undifferentiated, fragmented) due to a basic disturbance in the ability to organize intra- and interpersonal experiences. Inner life is either highly disorganized or globally diffuse, and individuality among others is not perceived.

The individual experiences feelings of disintegration, fragmentation, detachment, or loss of cohesion of the self, which may be accompanied by delusional distortion. In the face of such disorganization or because of the inability to screen out anxiety-provoking thoughts, relationships may be experienced as fragmented, parasitic, sadistic, or otherwise gruesome. Detachment from relationships may be so extreme that humans are experienced as blurry, impersonal entities.

Perceptions of human relationships in projective stories are disorganized and distorted by serious integration failures associated with poor reality testing. The story teller may be unable to keep characters' perspectives straight or to separate self and nonself, or fantasy from reality. Relationships seem so highly unlikely as to suggest extreme disorganization, fragmentation, and impaired thought process. Distinctions between people are blurry and characters have no individuality (e.g., can "read" each other's mind) and may be described as violent, malevolent, coercive, intrusive, manipulative, extremely vulnerable, helpless, or deprived. The basic safety and integrity of characters are threatened, and people are viewed either as totally helpless or as all powerful.

In addition to story content, this level is scored if the narrator exhibits any behavior during testing that is highly inappropriate.

Two stories told by an 11-year-old boy in a self-contained class for emotionally handicapped children illustrate the following characteristics of this level: (1) blurry distinctions drawn between and within characters, (2) complete absence of autonomy or purpose for action, (3) arbitrary changes in perspective, and (4) disorganized thought process.

Card 13B: I see this boy, this ugly house he's got, and he got no family, no family got, he's poor, he got no money and he doesn't have any friends or money. He's sitting outside on the porch, and . . . he's . . . doesn't do anything. (turns card over and sees number) So 13B (What happens to him?) I don't want . . . walks back in the house (turns card upside down) now he's upside down, upside down, upside down, die, die, die, die. He got back inside and tell his family, "Some people are coming, mom and dad, mommy." "Oh, good hooray." They got some money. (begins singing ta da da da to de dee dee) They got some money. Hooray, hooray. (How does it end?) Then they live in . . . they need some clothes . . . now, ummmm, somebody . . . live ever after, ever after. The end.

Card 8BM: I see this picture over here killing some people and this boy wanting to walk on the way from his father and the doctor. They get a knife, killing his body. He's killing him and the boy walks away. He went back to the house. No one knows whatever happened, ever after. The end. (What is he thinking?) He's thinking that, "What is man killing this man over here, why's he killing him?" . . . Maybe he thought he has a gun.

Let's see, then he got shot and hurt, then over with a knife, then his father says, "Stop! Now stop you two, stop." "I can't." "Now shut up you little brat." He punches him in the face, Boom. Then, um, he's telling his father, "Take the knife." He said, "Are you OK?" He said, "I'm fine" and they live happy ever after. And he said, "Get some water for me. Get some water for me!" (yells) (How is he feeling?) Umm, sad . . . so that's all. (Note that throughout the stories the child changes voices with the characters.)

These stories appear disorganized; the respondent has difficulty monitoring the progression of ideas and can't keep a consistent train of thought. Relationships are intrusive, confusing, and demanding. People kill without purpose. Events just happen without reason, and content is directly provoked by the stimulus.

The following story was told by a 14-year-old girl, also diagnosed as being emotionally disturbed and placed in a residential facility. The structure of the story is intact, but the characters act and react without a sense of interpersonal relatedness. They are brutally intrusive, violent, or helpless. When a father discovers his daughter's scheme, he retains no connection with her but is driven by his outrage to kill her.

Card 6GF: She looked at her father, astonished that he knew her whole scheme. Yes, she had been a maid for five years and yes she was stealing a lot of their jewelry and also yes, she was going to turn it in for a lot of money and yes, she had planned to kill their, the family's husband. How could her father have known and how, if he wasn't sure could she have possibly avoided all these accusations. Thoughts are running through her head as she thought quickly of a way to deny it. Nothing could come. Her father slowly pulled out a pistol. She got really scared and afraid and ran for the door, but he was too quick. He grabbed her by the arm, knocking all the jewelry out of her pockets. Scared, she started trembling and crying down on her knees. "Please don't shoot me, please, I'll give it all back. I'm sorry." But her father didn't listen. He just sat there, cold, ice in his heart, knowing that his own daughter had betrayed him and his family and one of the families he was closest to. Without thinking and without further hesitation, he put the gun to her head. Bang. That was the last sound she heard.

Level Two: Momentary Experience of Relatedness

Personality is not experienced as a continuous, cohesive whole. In the absence of an enduring sense of self, which organizes perceptions of the self or others, the experience of self-cohesion exists in the moment and is, therefore, subject to disruption. Given this vulnerability, characteristics of others as they pertain to immediate need states are noticed. Furthermore, contradictions in one's behavior are not bothersome because consistency in self-presentation and self-evaluation is not taken into consideration.

Short-sighted, narcissistic activities are used to promote momentary self-perceptions or maintain good feelings. Relationships are experienced as isolated islands of connection without historical context. People and their specific function are interchangeable. If the gratification desired fails to materialize from one person, another will do just as well. Immediate external provocations, wishes, feelings of entitlement, anger, feared consequences, or anxiety color the individual's perceptions of others and have a distorting influence on processing interpersonal information.

Others are devalued unless they contribute to a momentary sense of well-being. The perceiver may have the cognitive capacity to evaluate the other person objectively but is so wrapped up in his or her own needs that those distinctions are irrelevant. The perceiver may be unable to depart from the feelings that are elicited by another person and may reason from the emotion generated without reality testing. Feelings of deprivation or entitlement rather than concepts of mutual benefit distort reciprocity and interfere with recognizing the right of others to remain autonomous. The individual may become intensely close in a needy way but becomes angry, demanding, or sullen when the other is not available. Feelings of vulnerability in the face of threat or ambiguity lead to relationships being handled according to a self-protective formula and rigid defensiveness to maintain the stability of one's thoughts and feelings.

Since personality is not seen as organized or continuous, perceptions about self and others shift according to circumstances, personal threat, or whim of the moment. There is little or no capacity for reflection, and others are evaluated in terms of vacillating emotions of the perceiver. Seemingly close ties may be based on momentary benefits. Lack of autonomous motives reflects the inability to experience the self as organizer of emotions and actions. Thus, inner attributes of others are ill defined or stereotyped, and actions are not guided by constructive insight or clarity of purpose. Distinctions are superficial so that outward appearances and dichotomous attributes such as weak-strong are emphasized.

The emotional roots or mutuality imbalance may be embedded in (1) extreme emotional vulnerability such as fear of rejection or (2) the absence of empathic interpersonal connection. The "connection" with others can be absent or not seen as enduring because feelings of relatedness to others come and go depending on the current exigencies. Without an empathic connection, there is no basic motive to consider the feelings and needs of others apart from practical implications. Likewise, to avoid becoming overwhelmed by emotions, a person may restrict interpersonal relationships or processing of interpersonal information to the most superficial or simplified level.

The cognitive basis of mutuality imbalance is the disruption of processing interpersonal information resulting in (1) failure to coordinate one's needs with those of others, (2) focus on a narrow part of the individual which fails to comprehend the entire person; and (3) lack of coordination of individuals' perspectives. Blatant lack of concern or disregard of the property of others may not necessarily be due to ill intentions per se, but may result from failure to reflect on the impact of an action on others. Individuals may find themselves at odds with family, peers, or teachers, not because they want to be contrary but because their poor judgment, inaccurate perceptions, or difficulty with timing their response has adverse consequences that they are unable to anticipate or avert.

In sum, this level of interpersonal relatedness reflects a tendency to organize relationships around the moment and to make distinctions that are relevant to the immediate circumstance. An enduring sense of self-other has not developed, and relationships are easily broken or replaced. Inner life is nonexistent or appears phony, vague, or streotyped. Others are seen in terms of what they can do now. People are viewed as interchangeable because the gratification is more important than the person who provides it. There is a noticeable absence of reciprocity or mutuality.

1. Projective stories depict characters who are highly disparate in mutuality of autonomy. Narratives emphasize one perspective, as when characters engage in heroics to accomplish singlehandedly what usually takes cooperative effort (e.g., characters are too powerful, too independent, or grandiose).

2. Characters are differentiated on the basis of momentary need, immediate gain, or as obstacles to immediate gratification without the sense that they are whole persons.

3. People with negative impact on each other are portrayed (e.g., one gains at the other's expense; characters harbor malice and derive satisfaction from seeing others downtrodden).

4. Characters are displayed with a basic absence of interpersonal connection (e.g., marked absence of nurturance or valuing material possessions over human life).

5. Interpersonal relationships are extremely superficial or stereotyped. The narrator may have difficulty attributing thoughts or feelings to characters and may have little experiential basis for distinguishing inner attributes. The story teller may be trying to present a good image or struggling to be socially conventional by describing highly stereotyped relationships.

6. There is a failure to account for differences in characters portrayed in the picture (e.g., all characters are assumed to feel the same way in spite of disparate facial expressions or circumstances). There may be poor differentiation of internal states of people or inappropriate role distinctions.

7. There is excessive dependence on stimuli to read emotions.

The following story told by a first-grade girl to Card 1 demonstrates a lack of connection or concern with the feelings, rights, or property of others. In the absence of genuine interest in others, human attributes are not well differentiated. Immediate concerns or provocations drive actions or perceptions of people. A sense of glibness pervades the story where words or actions are detached from the truth, from meaningful emotional experience, and from an enduring sense of self or other.

> Card 1: What is that? (Whatever you want it to be) I don't know what it is. I think the boy is looking at something. He doesn't know what it is. He thinks it looks dumb. He puts it in the trash. His mother comes in and she says, "Did you see my thing? I left it on the table." He says, "No, I didn't see nothing." (To?) He goes out and plays. (Feel?) Happy cuz it's a nice day and he can play with his toys.

The following story told by a kindergarten girl depicts the character's desire to gain satisfaction by taking from others, which is restrained only by external influence.

> Card 5: There's a woman opening the door because she heard a noise. Someone was knocking on the door and the books fell down when someone knocked. A woman was knocking. She wanted to steal a magic book. She doesn't steal it because the woman came. (Feel?) Sad. Because she thinks they stealed the magic book.

The following story told by a kindergarten boy depicts the disconnection between what someone sees and the actions taken. There is a remarkable absence of a sense of autonomy and of relatedness.

> Card 5: The girl is looking out the door. She sees a kid—someone's kid hitting somebody. (Feel?) Bad. (Who feels bad?) The kid, because somebody's hitting him. (To)? The lady sits down and watches TV.

The following story told to Card 8 by a fourth-grade boy is about money compensating for loss of life, suggesting that people and their function are interchangeable.

> Card 8: Well, he's sad because his dad's getting operated on. And they have to cut him open and he's really sad and worried that he might die. He was shot, and they're trying to get the bullet out. And what happens in the end is that they get the bullet out and he lives. But latter on he dies because the bullet rusted and some of the rust pieces got in his blood and killed him. (Think?) That the doctors didn't do a good job and they sued them. And then they got lots of money—the kid and the mother.

Level Three: Functional Experience of Relatedness

Characteristics of people are differentiated and organized around a rudimentary sense of self-other, which is based on a more continuous awareness of the general functions or need satisfactions they provide. There is a crude effort to combine the needs of self and others through a *quid pro quo* reciprocity where individuals give to others to earn the right to expect favors in return. Thus, one person benefits at a time as individuals engage in mutual "self-sacrifice," taking turns rather than being equals together at the same time. The focus of a given interaction is on aspects of personality that are relevant for the functional give and take, whereas other aspects are unimportant or devalued. The emphasis is on obligation, duty, and compliance with expectations, not on individual autonomy. Differentiation across people has developed to the point that they have distinct personalities, but qualities are distinguished on the basis of what characters want from or do for each other. People are valued for their function rather than for who they are; their personality beyond their general function is dimly understood.

People fall into categories and are evaluated according to their conformity to these expectations. For example, a friend is judged according to ideas about friendship, which are based on predefined notions of how people in various roles and at various ages should be, rather than on awareness of personal characteristics. Individuality is lost either because there is no genuine curiosity, joy, or interest in the other's uniqueness, or such qualities are not discerned. There is the ability to cooperate on mutual tasks and goals, but the focus in on the function of the other with limited appreciation of their attributes or of their circumstances.

Nonnormative feelings, or perceived difficulty in meeting others' expectations that are pervasive, interfere with mutuality and autonomy due to efforts to normalize the self in ways that interfere with accuracy of person perceptions. Self-cohesion and self-definition in relation to meeting others' expectations are chief issues, and difficulty managing them may lead to short-sighted thinking or rationalizations.

The underlying emotions of connection are limited (e.g., parents are self-righteous and judgmental with children) with emphasis on meeting expected societal roles and standards of cooperation or give and take. Individuals are restricted in autonomy and initiative so that inner conviction, purpose, or effort are not well coordinated. Inner life remains relatively poorly elaborated, and distinctions among others incorporate few shades of gray.

1. Projective stories depict characters who are distinguished primarily on the basis of external attributes. Portrayal of superficial and shallow interactions reveals the narrator's naivete. Characters are unidimensional, with emphasis on function served by the person rather than the human connection. They comply with others' requests so that their own needs will be met (rigid *quid pro quo*).

2. Individuals are not fully autonomous, and people attempt to get by rather than formulate long-term goals or standards.
3. Inner states and intentions may be described, but these are not coordinated with actions and inner states of other people.
4. In the struggle to meet others' expectations, the characters accept responsibility, though they are unable to communicate effectively or to forge a mutually satisfactory compromise. Punishment for wrongdoing is accepted and even expected.

The following story told by a boy in kindergarten illustrates acceptance of appropriate punishment but provides only a vague description of inner life of characters. The impact of the punishment is the primary consideration.

> Card 7GF: She's feeling sad. She's thinking about maybe she can go out and play after her punishment. She feels sad. When her punishment is over, she feels happy. (Before?) She was punished and feeled a little bit sad and a little happy. (To?) I already told you!

In the following story told by a fifth-grade boy, relationships are set aside temporarily for adventure, though they endure. The feelings of the characters are differentiated but not coordinated or reconciled.

> Card 4: One day a man goes out and gets the mail. While he's looking through the letters, he finds a note from the armed forces. Before he even opens it, he know that he's been drafted. He hesitates to tell his wife but then the day comes he had to. Then he tells her he wants to go and the lady doesn't want him to go. The man feels grateful to be drafted. (Q?) Because not all people get drafted. And the lady feels scared that he might not come back from the war. The man is thinking of what adventures he might have. The girl is thinking of what problems he might have. (Q?) Like getting shot or breaking a leg. (To?) He comes back from the war happy to be home and happy because they won the war.

In the following story told by a sixth-grade boy, the character struggles to do what is expected and to be like his peers. However, the sense of autonomy and mutuality are limited. There is no indication of intrinsic interest or pride in the activity; the boy is unable to succeed in his goal and does not attempt to enlist assistance.

> Card 1: I think the kid in the picture got real angry with himself because he couldn't play something. And he's supposed to play. He feels really gloomy and everything because he thinks he's going to be left out from the people who can do this, and I think he's trying to practice on it so he can be like everyone else, because that's what he really wants to be.

The following story told by a fifth-grade boy describes a child who is severely punished by his mother for stealing cookies. He accepts his punishment without alienation from the relationship. There is an attempt to reconcile perspectives, but there is also a rigid *quid pro quo* interaction where a child apologizes before being permitted to eat dinner.

> Card 3BM: One day a boy stole some cookies from the cookie jar and was whipped severely by his mother. She told him to go to his room and stay there for the rest of the day. While he's in there, he's wondering why his mother had to whip him so severely, and after a while he stops crying. His mother comes in and told him not to steal anymore cookies, and he says he's sorry. He's allowed from his room and he has dinner. And he feels better after that. The mom felt bad because she had to whip him. (Q?) The boy was thinking about not stealing any more cookies.

Level Four: Fair Play

Individuals experience continuity and consistency in relations with others and within the self. Relationships are recognized as mutually beneficial, and concepts of fair play extend beyond the immediate situation or personalities so that expectations for reciprocity do not have the demanding *quid pro quo* quality of the previous level. The emphasis is on conventional ethics, which are internalized and can be more flexibly applied than the demand to conform to rigid expectations characterizing the previous level. More enduring attributes of individuals come into play, giving the interaction more allowance for reciprocity over time. Distinctions drawn within and between individuals are more complex, emphasizing more elaborated self-issues relating to identity or conformity with internalized conventional ethics.

1. Projective stories have characters that are clearly differentiated in terms of motives and inner states and are aware of purposes and reasons for actions. The emphasis is on attributes of people as these contribute to each other's sense of autonomy. Accordingly, people can disagree and have different feelings and personalities. Relationships are durable and disagreements are accepted, though not necessarily resolved.
2. Autonomy is mutual in that characters support each other's self-determined activities, give good advice, and are reliable, responsive, and helpful. Parents support children and help them attain their goals. Additionally, autonomous characters may be engaged in separate pursuits.
3. Characters follow rules and behave consistently with their roles; they comply with requests because of internal acceptance of legitimate authority or rules of conduct. Actions are constrained by both internal and external

considerations. Characters not only experience the consequences of their harmful actions but feel bad and make serious attempts at restitution. The perspectives of the victim as well as of the wrongdoer are incorporated and, if people misunderstand and hurt one another, they patch things up so neither is subservient.

Although characters are well differentiated, pursue their activities in an autonomous manner, and display mutual respect, they are not described in ways that indicate full appreciation of uniqueness, subtlety, depth, or complexity as required to score at the highest level. Although characters can reach an appropriate compromise, they may struggle to bring their perspective to each other's awareness. At the highest levels, characters have a natural inclination to anticipate or respond to each other's viewpoints.

The following story told by a third-grade boy illustrates the characters' taking responsibility for having unintentionally produced a negative impact on others.

Card 3: He was playing baseball with his friends and broke a guy's window. The guy got very angry with him. He went home and didn't want to talk to anyone. He feels very bad for what he's done and he says he'll do anything to repay the man. Then the man forgave him and he paid for the broken window.

The following story told by a fourth-grade boy shows the acceptance of different viewpoints and durability of the relationship, though with some irritation.

Card 7: Looks like she just got a doll and her friends want to see it. She's ignoring her friends because she wants to see it. She's afraid she might hurt it. She—the friend—doesn't ask her anymore and they go play something else. Then it's time to eat and her friend leaves and she plays with her doll. (Feel?) She feels that I might lose my friend but she doesn't let her see it. She feels, oh boy, what a friend, she won't even let me see her new doll.

In the following story told by a fourth-grade boy, the child demonstrates appropriate autonomy but there is no interpersonal context, support, or appreciation for his efforts. However, the constructiveness of his autonomous activities suggests that he would be capable of attributing similar autonomy to others.

Card 1: He's thinking of playing the violin. He's looking at it to see how it's made and how it works. He tries to play it and reads the instructions in a book. He feels like he wants to play it. He learns how to play it.

The following story told by a fifth-grade girl incorporates the perspectives of both mother and child in arriving at an appropriate compromise. However, this story would not be scored at the highest level because the mother must be prompted to realize that the daughter is "mad and bored," and the girl has to muster the courage to convey her feelings. These elements detract from the impression that the characters are in tune with one another and genuinely appreciate each other's uniqueness.

> Card 7GF: She looks like she's mad and bored. She wishes she was someplace else. She sees kids outside playing, and she doesn't want to hear the story. She wants to ask her mom if she could go outside and play but she can't find the courage because she's taking the time to read the story to her. It ends that she finally gets the courage to ask her mother and she says yes.

Level Five: Mutuality of Autonomy

Individuals experience genuine concern for and appreciation of others as they are, apart from any self-serving element. Persons are viewed with an awareness of their current situation, historical context, as well as their internal motives, needs, shortcomings, strengths, and aspirations. The interests of self and other are balanced according to general principles of justice and awareness of individual complexity beyond the dictates of fair play. Integration and organization of interpersonal experiences reflect the narrator's capacity for insight and awareness of nuances. The story teller has the cognitive capacity to make subtle distinctions and the emotional qualities to appreciate those distinctions. This level is characterized by appreciation of diversity and uniqueness of others, as well as by acceptance of strengths and shortcomings of the self.

1. In projective stories, perspectives of all characters are distinguished and integrated. Viewpoints of characters are delineated in a clear, coherent, and precise manner without distortion. The demarcation of characters is fully consistent with the emotions portrayed in the stimulus and with the context of the story. The narrator deals in a forthright way with the negative emotions depicted in the stimuli.
2. Inner life and thoughts are well elaborated, and conflict resolutions are based on genuine appreciation, caring, insight, and appropriate communication. There is a sense that people operate on the basis of inner conviction rather than be directed by outside influence. They display genuine interest and self-directed action to attain goals even if initially set by another.

3. Characters communicate in ways that imply mutual respect and recognize the legitimacy and value of the other.
4. Help is offered or sought in ways that are timely and in tune with the needs and viewpoints of other individuals.
5. The characters have compatible aims so that mutuality of autonomy is not disrupted by helping or cooperating.
6. Both positive and negative qualities are accepted, and relationships are permitted to end when they are not mutually productive.

The stories scored at this level demonstrate a good grasp of subtle interpersonal nuance, appreciation of various facets of personalities, and tolerance for ambiguity or ambivalence. Descriptions of people are not overly narrow, yet not global or diffuse. Time perspective, viewpoints of characters, inner life, and external constraints are fully integrated, with appropriate balance between achievement and interpersonal concerns.

These elements of interpersonal relatedness are illustrated by the following story told by a kindergarten girl in which the initially conflicting desires of parent and child are differentiated and reconciled to their mutual satisfaction.

Card 1: A boy is looking at his violin. He's going to play. He doesn't like it. His mother told him to play it. He tells her he doesn't want to play. She says he can play it later. He puts it away. He plays it after dinner. Then he likes it. His mother likes it.

The following story told by a kindergarten boy illustrates mutuality of autonomy. The mother doesn't react to the noise and mess produced by the children but appreciates their good-natured fun. The children, in turn, are responsive to the mother's concerns.

Card 5: The mother heard a lot of noise and laughing in the living room. She looks in to see what's happening. She's surprised. Her children made forts with sheets and blankets all over the room. They put sheets over chairs and furniture. The sister said, "We'll clean up and put everything away when we finish; please can we play some more?" The mother says, "OK" cuz she saw they were having fun. And they play and play. Then they put everything away.

Three stories told by a sixth-grade boy illustrate these same characteristics in an older child. In the first story, the child exhibits autonomy by his desire to play the instrument, by purchasing a lesson book, by seeking help, and finally by practicing.

Card 1: The kid decided he needed something to do so he decided to play an instrument. He picked the violin, thinking it would be easy to learn. He buys a lesson book and tries to teach himself. He decides he needs some help. He looks discouraged and feels he can't do it. So he goes for help to a music teacher. With help and practice and telling himself he can do it, he finds that he can.

In the second story, the needs of the family conflict with legitimate desires of the girl. A compromise is reached that accommodates everyone. Communication is clear, and characters maintain their autonomy through this process.

Card 2: This girl lives in the midwest and she wants to go to school but for some reason her mother wants her to stay home and help with chores. Looks like in this picture she is going despite her mother saying no. She leaves her mother and father doing daily chores while she goes to school. She feels good that she did what's right for her but she also feels sad for her parents because they have so much to do and have no one to help them. She feels that she has a right to go to school and learn things so she can get ahead, but she doesn't want to desert her mother and father. In the end, she decides her parents really do need her at the farm. She decides to put off school for a year or two until her little sister can help with the chores. She talks to her parents about this and they agree with her decision.

The third story reflects tolerance of ambivalent feelings, the durability of relationships, and commitment to family members. Despite the negative content, people are viewed as capable of changing their condition. Furthermore, characters can appreciate what an individual could become if given proper help.

Card 3: This boy has an alcoholic father and his father got home drunk that night and the kid didn't clean up the house to his liking. So he beat him that night. In this picture, the kid is crying, he's hurt. He wishes his father could change. He does love him but he doesn't want his father to be so violent. In the end, he and his mother go to one of those programs and try to get father enrolled in it so he will stop getting drunk every night. They get him to go and he gets helped. The father appreciated the help he got and he's a happier person now.

The five levels described here represent general tendencies or capacities to experience relatedness. However, individuals may operate at various levels in different types of interactions. For example, a person may appreciate the unique qualities of peers or family members but have difficulty perceiving the personal qualities of authority figures apart from their role function (e.g., teacher, supervisor). Specific areas of vulnerability of self-esteem or limitations of autonomy may, in some instance, have a distorting effect on the perception of self in relation to others. Self-evaluation maintenance theory (Tesser, 1987) has relevance for understanding situation-specific distortions to interpersonal relatedness in individuals who are otherwise capable of higher levels. Tesser (1987) proposed that people are motivated to maintain favorable self-evaluations by comparison of their own performance with that of others who are close. Self-evaluation suffers when "comparison" favors the other on a task that is relevant to self-definition. However, on tasks that are not central to self-definition, the relative success of the other is seen as a source of pride and enhances self-evaluation through the process of "reflection." If an individual's self-evaluation is tied to comparative performance in many situations or tasks, then such a person would be likely to feel more threatened by the accomplishments of the other than pride. The capacity to appreciate the other is limited by the areas in which self-comparison is seen as less favorable.

Summary

Five levels of interpersonal relatedness are described and illustrated with projective stories along the lines of object-relations theory. The inner representations of self and others reflect empathy and interpersonal interest, along with insight and complexity of information processing applied to experience. The capacity of individuals to relate to one another as whole persons rather than as need gratifiers and the capacity to enjoy the nuances of others' personality separately from one's own needs, desires, wishes, or expectations entail the following:

1. Sense of personal autonomy and investment in relationships with acceptance of strengths and weaknesses in oneself and in others
2. Relative freedom from threat to one's sense of autonomy and self-esteem, which insulates the individual from feeling that relationships are controlling or intrusive (during times of stress or uncertainty, an individual may focus more narrowly on attributes that are personally relevant or specific to a limited interaction)
3. Reality testing and ability to make organized cognitive distinctions among individuals and within the self
4. The emotional qualities to appreciate these distinctions
5. Flexible frame of reference that allows the individual to view the self and others from different perspectives with awareness of inner motives, current external circumstances, and historical context.

CHAPTER 17

Motivation

Motives and goals function to direct information processing and to energize and select behavior (McClelland, 1987). They (1) determine the amount of effort, persistence, and energy mobilized toward the pursuit of purposeful activities; (2) influence preference or choice of tasks and activities; and (3) lead to selective attention to and selective processing of information (Kuhl, 1986; Srull & Wyer, 1986). Thus, motivation is woven into the fabric of personality and has behavioral, cognitive, and emotional manifestations.

The complex interplay among motivation, affect, and cognition is increasingly recognized (Farr, 1987; Fiske & Pavelchak, 1986; Hidi, 1990; Sorrentino & Higgins, 1986). Affective underpinnings of motivation are interest, absorption, and joy, which direct persistent and organized activity (Messick, 1987). Positive emotions such as interest or curiosity lead to initiation and maintenance of attention and promote the integration and differentiation of cognitive structure. Anderson and colleagues (1987) reported that the interest of children's reading material, which they define as its capacity to elicit an emotional response, enhances both recall and comprehension. It seems likely that disinterest, boredom, apathy, or frustration may result in a failure to make distinctions and/or to use active learning strategies. The converse may also be argued. Namely, the inability to make relevant distinctions precedes the experience of boredom or apathy.

Srull and Wyer (1986) reviewed research that demonstrated that an individual's goals and intentions play a key role in the encoding, organization and recall of interpersonal information. Goals influence what people attend to, how they perceive objects and events, how they utilize reasoning process to make causal inferences, and how events are organized and represented in memory. Thus, goals and intentions influence the cognitive system in ways that relate to motivation. Srull and Wyer (1986) define the concept of *category accessibility* as the tendency of individuals to be prepared to pick up some things in the environment while simultaneously ignoring many others. Information most likely to be perceived, processed, and recalled relate to an individual's goals, concerns, and values.

Intrinsic versus Extrinsic Motivation

A definition of *intrinsic motivation* is a desire to engage in an activity for its own sake rather than to attain a goal, receive some external reward, or avoid a negative consequence. An individual is considered extrinsically motivated if the factors drawing him or her to an activity are extrinsic to the task such as recognition, competition, or desire to cooperate or to attain a certain outcome. It should be noted that factors extrinsic to the task can have intrinsic value. A person may engage in an activity because the activity itself is interesting or rewarding or because other aspects of the task or activity provide satisfaction.

Thus, a task or activity can capture the individual's interest for intrinsic or extrinsic reasons as follows (Malone & Lepper, 1987): (1) the most direct intrinsic motivation is when the learning material or activity is emotionally appealing or intellectually relevant in that it fits with previous knowledge; (2) the desire to maintain or to increase competency in a valued area motivates learning; and (3) the social context—a common external motivator—spurs the individual who is not otherwise interested in the activity or learning material.

Basic explanations of intrinsic motivation for a task or activity are briefly reviewed under the following five rubrics: optimal arousal, interest/challenge, affect regulation, perceived competence, and self-assessment.

Arousal Theories of Motivation

Individuals differ in their basal level of arousal, and any particular individual will vary in degree of arousal depending on the situation or time of day. The relationship between arousal and performance is curvilinear (Hebb, 1955; Yerkes & Dodson, 1908), particularly for complex tasks. Each individual has a preference for an optimum level of arousal that is related to subjective comfort and cognitive efficiency. Individuals choose tasks and situations in accordance with their attempts to regulate their level of arousal (Strelau, 1983).

An activity is intrinsically motivating when it generates optimal arousal and stimulation (Berlyne, 1966; Hunt, 1965; Piaget, 1952). Some individuals pursue novelty, variety, and stimulation (Zuckerman, 1974), while others seek order or routine. Risk-preference theories of achievement motivation (Atkinson, 1957, 1964, 1974) are no doubt related to arousal regulation (hence, the similarity between anxiety and arousal-based theories of cognitive efficiency and risk preference). Individuals who are anxious or who have a high basal level of arousal are at greater risk of overstimulation and subsequent loss of cognitive efficiency, which increases the possibility of failure. Sensitivity to failure or preoccupation with negative outcomes promotes feelings of helplessness and motivational deficit.

Interest

Interests are important contributors to intrinsic motivation because they serve to direct attention selectively, lead to increases in energy and alertness, and promote activity to seek relevant information or situations (Tomkins, 1962; Getzels, 1966; Rust, 1977). They function to maintain self-determined activity and continued cognitive processing in the absence of external reinforcement and to promote persistence in the face of failure or obstacles.

Interest has been defined as positive affect accompanying activities (Anderson et al., 1987). Positive affect in general has been associated with access to a larger number of cognitive constructs and more efficient organization of these constructs (see Isen, Daubman, & Gorgoglione, 1987). It is therefore not surprising that interest is closely related with knowledge and developed abilities.

Hidi (1990) reviewed research demonstrating that interest has a profound effect on attentional processes, cognitive functioning, and persistence. Interest is central to the selection of the type of information to be processed, in the persistence of the processing, and in the amount of effort to integrate information. Interest appears to elicit spontaneous rather than deliberate selective allocation of attention.

One of the factors contributing to interest and curiosity relates to the concept of optimal challenge. Curiosity is keenest when there is an optimum level of informational complexity (Berlyne, 1960; 1965) or an optimal level of discrepancy or incongruity of the information from current knowledge or expectation (Hunt, 1961; 1965; Piaget, 1952). Accordingly, a task will be intrinsically interesting if it is not too easy and not too difficult (Deci, 1975; Harter, 1978; Weiner, 1980; White, 1959). Challenge models of motivation suggest that interest is enhanced when the probability of achieving a goal is uncertain (McClelland et al., 1953)—that is, when tasks are at an intermediate level of difficulty. It should be noted that such tasks also provide the maximum information about an individual's ability. Therefore, persons who are seeking to avoid self-assessment would not be motivated to seek challenge or uncertainty.

Affect Regulation

Affect regulates behaviors and exerts a powerful influence on learning and performance. Positive affect facilitates learning and performance, whereas negative affect has a debilitating influence. Therefore, attempts to regulate affect have an impact on learning and performance. Affect can be regulated in one of two ways: approaching activities that increase positive affect states or avoiding activities or situations that are associated with negative affect states. Individual differences in the general tendency to approach or avoid new situations (e.g., Thomas & Chess, 1977) are, in part, associated with efforts to regulate affect.

In some areas a person may be motivated by positive goals, whereas fear and avoidance predominates in others (Cantor et al., 1986). Fear of failure or protection of self-esteem may be paramount in influencing effort, choice, and persistence. It should be noted, however, that avoidance of negative feelings about the self may lead individuals to approach positive endeavors.

Raynor and McFarlin (1986) maintain that striving for positive and removal of negative emotional states do not predict behavior in similar ways in regard to achievement motivation. They cite the example of the reactions of three college students to getting a bad grade on a test. One seeks relief from bad feelings by getting drunk, thereby removing negative value without attempting to produce positive value. Another student drops the course in anticipation that the poor test performance will have a significant impact on the final grade. The third student decides to change study strategies and to redouble efforts. Of the three students, only the latter can be described as working to produce anticipated positive value rather than to avoid negative value.

More work needs to be done on avoidance motives (McClelland, 1987). Anxieties and fears are powerful motivators to avoid situations that increase these negative emotions. There is substantial literature indicating that highly anxious individuals (high scores on manifest anxiety) display the following three essential features of being motivated (McClelland, 1987): (1) being activated or energized, (2) being selective in sensitivity to information, and (3) being quicker to learn motive related information.

Anxiety is one of the most commonly accepted causes of motivationally induced deficits in learning and performance. However, the impact of anxiety on cognitive performance varies with characteristics of tasks and situations (Humphries & Revelle, 1984). Anxious individuals spend more time worrying and being distracted by off-task thoughts than less anxious individuals (Leon & Revelle, 1985; Sarason, 1975). Anxiety is related to greater sensitivity to failure (Atkinson, 1974) and to punishment or nonreward (Gray, 1981). Thus, anxious individuals would be characterized by fear of failure, which may lead to task avoidance, conservative task selection, careful approach to the task, or excessive concern with making errors. Generally, anxious individuals will prefer a lower level of risk or challenge.

Atkinson (1957) proposed an expectancy x value model of achievement motivation where choice of a task or tendency to achieve on a task is a function of the motive to achieve, expectancy of success, and the incentive value of success. The value of success is proportional to the difficulty of its attainment. Thus, moderately difficult tasks have the greatest incentive value unless the person is fearful of failure, which would predispose that individual to avoid tasks that risk failure (Atkinson, 1958).

Competence

According to a competence view of motivation, tasks are intrinsically motivating if they enhance competence and provide challenge (Harter, 1978; White, 1959) in ways that contribute to a sense of control and self-determination (Deci, 1975, 1981). Attribution theory (Heider, 1958) views every human as a naive scientist, attempting to find causes for events to achieve greater control. Tasks that are beyond an individual's capacities undermine the sense of control or competence as well as motivation (e.g., Dweck & Goetz, 1978). If a child doesn't attribute success and failure to a controllable factor, such as the level of effort, the child is unlikely to persist in strategic problem-solving activities (Borkowski, Carr, & Pressley, 1987).

Self-Assessment versus Self-Enhancement

The manner in which an individual seeks to assess and enhance the self relates to the way that person seeks and evaluates competence. Cantor and colleagues (1986) suggest that an understanding of motivation entails a knowledge of the representation of goals and motives within the self-concept. Self-concept has been viewed both as process and as cognitive structure (Markus, 1980; Markus, & Sentis, 1982). Accordingly, the self-concept is a system of knowledge structures about the self or self-schemata that both structure the individual's experience and guide the processing of self-relevant information. The self-schemata are assumed to be based on past experience, but they also contain images of future or possible selves (Cantor et al., 1986). Possible selves are aspects of the self-concept that reflect the individual's perceived potential to develop (ideals, hopes) and to deteriorate (self as a failure or as homeless).

Self-knowledge is viewed as a regulator of behavior. New information about the self is integrated into existing knowledge structures. Some individuals seek consistency within their system of values. Rokeach (1973) demonstrated that pointing out inconsistencies in values to undergraduates was a powerful motivator for students to alter their value rankings. However, as Raynor and McFarlin (1986) point out, not everyone is concerned with maintaining consistency in their values, in their self-presentation, or in their inner convictions. They assert that "People do not *require* or *need* to have a self-system to function in society. Rather, the self-system is something that may or may not emerge as a phenomenal means of self-identity" (p. 320). These authors posit two systems in relation to motivation—a behavioral system and a self-system. In the behavioral system, information has value in terms of the affective consequences of the outcomes of action. Both informational and affective value of feedback is experienced in relation to the outcome without relevance to subjective evaluation of the self. Motivation in the self-system requires subjective awareness of self-image and definition of personal attributes such as ability. Information is affectively valued in the self-system if it relates to feeling good or bad about the self; the emphasis is on finding out about the self by clarifying perceived abilities, attributes, or self-images.

Trope (1986) elaborates on two approaches to understand the individual preferences for type of feedback information—one based on the premise that self-assessment is the primary goal, and the other based on the assumption that self-enhancement is of paramount importance. In the latter, information is being sought for its affective value (feeling good or avoiding bad feelings), whereas in the former, it is appreciated for its informational value (finding out).

The orientation to seek information about competence in relation to self-conceptions or in relationship to consequences and outcomes has implications for the types of goals pursued. Learning and performance goals have been differentiated as follows (Dweck, 1986):

1. *Learning Goal*   Those who seek to increase competence by understanding or learning something new set learning goals. Such individuals desire realistic feedback to aid self-assessment and feel free to seek challenges to foster learning.
2. *Performance Goal*   Those who wish to enhance their sense of competence by seeking the favorable judgment of others or by avoiding negative feedback about their competence set performance goals. Such individuals focus on the outcome rather than being invested in the task. Therefore, they may choose to protect their ability from negative evaluation.

The ideas of learning and performance goals are related to the concepts of intrinsic or extrinsic rewards. If satisfaction is gained through mastery, rather than through external evaluation, then the individual is intrinsically motivated to learn. Intrinsic motivational factors may not be salient in a performance goal. In fact, performance goals may undermine intrinsic interest (Deci & Ryan, 1980).

Learning style has been related to the type of goal and type of feedback desired. Three styles of learning, labeled *meaning, reproducing,* and *achievement,* have been identified which entail, respectively, a search for personal understanding, memorization, and whatever it takes to get good grades (Entwistle, Hanley, & Hounsell, 1979). Three similar styles, labeled *internalizing, utilizing,* and *achieving,* involve identical processes (Biggs, 1979). The internalizing learner is intrinsically motivated and stresses the meaning of information; the utilizing learner emphasizes memorization and is extrinsically motivated by fear of failure; and the achieving learner stresses the organizational and study skills required to achieve a specific outcome and would be motivated by hope for success.

Self-Efficacy

Perceived competence is an important component of motivation. The ability to envision outcomes and set goals regulates human motivation. Persons will strive to attain valued outcomes provided they believe or expect that such outcomes are within their reach. According to Bandura (1989), goals create motivational involvement by setting conditions for positive self-evaluations. People set goals and work toward them partly because of perceived efficacy to accomplish them (Bandura, 1986). Goals and standards are reevaluated and readjusted depending on their attainment (Campione & Lord, 1982).

The independent impact of self-perceptions and actual ability in math has been demonstrated (Parsons, 1982; Phillips, 1984). Children's self-concepts were more influential determinants of future course selections and expectations than were previous grades, a seemingly more objective indicator of math ability. Children are hampered in their achievement efforts independently of their actual level of competence by the following patterns: (1) giving up easily in the face of failure feedback, (2) interpreting mistakes as evidence of incompetence, and (3) anticipating failure (e.g., Dweck & Licht, 1980; Garber & Seligman, 1980; Parsons, 1981).

As early as the age of 3, children relate success and failure outcomes to the notion of the self as competent or incompetent (Heckhausen, 1967). Veroff (1969) suggests that self-evaluation of performance, an important part of achievement motivation, occurs even earlier, somewhere between 1½ and 2 years of age. However, the concept of achievement in comparison to what other children can do develops later. Furthermore, the meaning of the performance to the child becomes more complex with development (Raynor, 1982).

Motivation and Volition

Heckhausen and Gollwitzer (1987) differentiate between motivational and volitional states of mind. A motivational state of mind exists when an individual is faced with a decision of choosing alternative courses of action. Then, the typical motivational constructs such as expectancies, values, goals, choices, risk taking, preferences, interests, wishes and consideration of likely consequences of endeavors are relevant. However, once a decision has been made, the individual's concerns shift to instrumental actions or plans to implement the decisions. This volitional state of mind occurs regardless of having made one's own decision or having been assigned a course of action. Thus, a complete unit of motivated behavior has two halves—motivation plus volition. The *motivational* part is the wish or intention to do something that can be distinguished from action-control, which is the ability to carry out the intention (Kuhl, 1984). This concept of *volitional* control bears a striking similarity to other constructs such as a sense of internal control (DeCharms, 1976), self-efficacy (Bandura, 1982; Heider, 1958;

Weiner, 1980), or will (Rangell, 1986). Shapiro (1965) described maladjustive styles of personality as being grounded in deficits in the subjective sense of deliberate volitional control.

Understanding achievement-oriented behavior requires the integration of two facets of motivation beyond the individual's intentions, wishes, and goals (Kuhl, 1984):

1. *Action control* refers to the persistence of the intentions in the face of competing motivational tendencies and the distracting effect of external or internal forces that promote alternative actions (e.g., distractibility, frustration, absence of intrinsic interest, or desire for immediate gratification). Many factors contribute to the durability of intentions and these need to be more comprehensively studied.
2. *Performance control* refers to the competencies required to carry out the intended action in pursuit of the goal.

Performance control, or the ability to implement problem-solving strategies to carry out the tasks or accomplish goals, is an important part of the motivational system. Self-efficacy, which is a person's sense of mastery, relates to three elements of motivation: (1) a sense of conviction and desire to pursue a goal or direction, (2) action control, and (3) performance control. Individuals who have a realistic basis for confidence in their problem-solving abilities can maintain efficiency in thinking in complex decision-making situations, whereas those who are troubled by self-doubt are erratic in their analytical thinking (Bandura & Wood, 1989). The stronger the belief in one's competence, the more persistently one exerts effort (Bandura, 1988). On the other hand, individuals plagued by self-doubt about their capabilities give up in the face of challenge. A positive sense of well-being requires an optimistic sense of personal efficacy (Bandura, 1986), allowing the individual to deal with failures, setbacks, frustrations, and inequities.

Expectancy × value theories of achievement motivation implicitly include self-efficacy. The perceived probability of success depends on the individual's self-evaluation in relation to a task or goal (Heckhausen & Krug, 1982).

Performance control requires two qualitatively different categories of competencies: (1) specific skill and knowledge that can be brought to bear on the problem at hand and (2) tactical resources or metacognitions for applying specific skills such as self-monitoring. Three types of knowledge are relevant to the development of metacognitive strategies (Paris, Lipson, & Wixson, 1983): (1) recognition that they are needed, (2) knowing how to apply them, and (3) realizing when to deploy them. An alternate strategy will not be used if the individual does not perceive that the current one is ineffective (e.g., if the person does not recognize that the solution to a math problem is out of line with a reasonable estimate).

Ineffective learners are frequently unaware that they have failed to comprehend or master the information and, hence, do nothing to correct the problem. The least successful students in a regular classroom show little awareness of the difficulty of reading passages and, therefore, are less able to alter their approaches by modifying their pace or concentration. This results in poorer recall of the stories compared to more successful students (Owings et al., 1980). Effective learners use different strategies for achieving different learning goals (e.g., Bransford & Stein, 1984; Brown et al., 1983). However, less successful learners are less likely to size up accurately the difficulty of a learning task and, therefore, cannot adjust their study time or strategy to meet the task demands (e.g., Bransford et al., 1982; Owings et al., 1980).

Competencies are specific to tasks and environments so that one of the vital functions of metacognitions is to evaluate the self in relation to task demands. Realistic choices and a sense of control are possible when the individual is able to engage in task analysis and is aware of how he or she functions in different circumstances. Some people utilize their knowledge about the impact of the environment on their functioning, while others do not make use of strategies to alter their situation.

Active Involvement in Tasks and Problem Solving

Some have argued that the ability to use what one knows is among the hallmarks of intelligence (e.g., Brown & Campione, 1981; Flavell, 1979; Scardamalia & Bereiter, 1985; Sternberg, 1984). Effective problem solving requires more than knowledge of appropriate strategies; those who have knowledge of general strategies may not use them spontaneously. For instance, children who were taught strategies to improve recall, such as organizing lists of words or pictures into common categories and then rehearsing category names, often failed to use such strategies on their own. However, when explicitly cued to do so, their memory performance improved (Brown et al., 1983; Brown, Campione, & Day, 1981). Thus, an important component of solving a problem is actively organizing and restructuring information. Volitional or motivated behavior is assumed when an individual engages in organized, active, deliberate, and focused effort to set and implement goals. Individuals who fail to exert such strategic organizing effort appear unmotivated.

The process of volitional action breaks down for a variety of reasons, which have implications for learning and motivation.

Failure to Use Active Strategies
Torgesen (1977) introduced the concept of the *inactive learner* to describe learning-disabled students who exhibit a learning style characterized by minimal planning and limited use of strategies to make the learning task more manage-

able. Learning requires active strategies to organize and recall information such as rehearsal or breaking down the task. Poor readers do not exert as much cognitive efforts to make sense of difficult passages (Myers & Paris, 1978) or to remember them (Brown, 1980). They rarely use active strategies such as giving priority to important ideas over less relevant details; skimming for main points; or monitoring their comprehension. They do not adjust the pace of their reading for the purpose (e.g., "fun" or skim for particular facts). With respect to mathematics, less capable performers do not estimate the solution nor do they know when to recheck their work. They are inaccurate in gauging the difficulty level of a task so they cannot adjust study effort or seek assistance. Many students with learning disabilities do not develop the metacognitive strategies necessary to accomplish the task at hand (Feagans, 1983; Torgesen, 1980) and may, therefore, feel helpless when faced with tasks requiring such skills.

Difficulty with Organization

The issue relates to how incoming information is processed. Basically, is the information attended to as is, or is it actively organized and restructured? A manifestation of the inactive style is the tendency to respond to a passing thought or initial impression without further processing (Shapiro, 1965). Some children accept the flow of information as it comes in rather than actively reorganize it. In such a passive cognitive mode, the implications and potential drawbacks of actions are not considered.

The seeming attentional deficits of learning-disabled children may actually reflect problems with organization (Keogh & Margolis, 1976; Kistner, 1985). Their initially poorer performance on laboratory measures may be due to inefficient strategies and problems with organization rather than to actual deficits in their ability to attend. Likewise, the relatively poor memory performance of learning-disabled children is related to inefficient strategies in the organization of the material to be recalled.

Reading involves both decoding and comprehension. A good reader uses a complex set of skills that requires active monitoring and organizing of information. The reader must check comprehension against the end goal, recognize when comprehension has failed, or realize that a change of strategy is needed (e.g., Forrest-Pressley & Waller, 1984). When children do not conceptually organize the story in a manner that distinguishes the most important bits of information, they are less likely to comprehend and recall important story elements (Feagans, 1983).

Experience with a particular domain guides attention to the relevant components of the situation. So, background knowledge aids reading comprehension. Previous knowledge about a topic can provide a context that helps the reader organize the information in the text, to ascertain what information is important, and draw inferences about information that is not explicit (Pearson, Hansen, & Gordon, 1979). Lack of relevant background information against which to structure and organize information or concepts can be rooted in the absence of opportunity or in the cumulative impact of prior failure to integrate the available information. Active integration of knowledge forms the basis for future information processing. To understand something, the individual must integrate current information with already existing knowledge. New information must be related to what the individual already knows and that requires active, constructive integration.

Interest, Active Investment, and Task Orientation

Sustaining attention and organizing effort require some investment and interest; absence of active, effortful, strategic processing may be related to low investment or lack of energy. Children who have little interest in academics can usually apply strategies for short durations with a great deal of external incentives but will not sustain such activity independently. Their focus wanders, and they have difficulty gathering and organizing their efforts. If left on their own, they will fail to apply sufficient and strategic effort to information processing. Some children appear to be actively struggling with inefficient strategies and eventually tune out because they cannot master the material. Nevertheless, investment in the material makes the organizing effort less tedious. Learning-disabled students are not as actively involved in learning tasks behaviorally, and not as invested emotionally (Bender, 1986; Torgesen, 1977). Classroom studies find such children to be off task more frequently and to be more easily distracted than children who are not learning disabled.

It is not uncommon for an individual to be able to exert more active energy and effort in one area and not others. An example is that of a third-grade girl who at similar levels of difficulty could comprehend interpersonal passages but not factual ones. Adults may be experts in one field and take a very inactive stance toward other domains. Individuals may selectively tune out information due to lack of interest or difficulty meeting the processing demands. Some individuals may manifest their inactive learning style in a few subjects, while for others it is pervasive. The active, searching, organizing efforts are not only necessary for learning and task performance but are also essential for processing of cues in the social environment.

Story Telling and the Inactive Learner

The inactive learner finds the story telling task difficult because it requires active organizational effort. The individual may or may not be aware of having difficulty in producing an adequate story. Below are examples of youngsters with average intelligence who were referred for testing because of apparent motivational problems or failure to use active organizational strategy to facilitate learning.

Example 1

Melanie, age 8–3 (third grade, FSIQ=107) was referred for underachievement. The Digit Span scaled score of 15 indicated well above average short-term auditory memory. However, a substantial discrepancy between her ability to repeat digits forward and backward showed that her performance was better on tasks that did not require as much concentrated effort to restructure the material. Prior to evaluation, Melanie received tutoring, which reportedly had been helpful. Nevertheless, independent standardized tests and school performance are below expectation; reading and listening comprehension were in the 26th and 20th percentiles, respectively. Classroom observations indicated that she daydreams but perks up when there is a social event. During testing, she kept track of the number on the back of the T.A.T. cards to make sure she didn't have to do too many.

Both parents are professionals and restrict Melanie's TV watching. They hired a tutor and also work with her on homework, but she simply cannot get invested in academics.

A few responses to the Children's Sentence Completion Test highlight her preoccupations:

"The thing I want to do most of all—is watch TV."

"The thing I like to do best is—watch TV."

"What I want to happen most—watch TV."

Several of Melanie's stories to T.A.T. cards illustrate her inactive style.

Card 1: Um . . . What's this? (pointing to violin) (Tell me what you think it looks like) He's in class . . . can't say anything about this story. (Start with what's happening in the picture) I don't know. He's staring at something, that's what's happening . . . and . . . um . . . thinking about something and staring at something. It helps him think better . . . Thinking about what's going to happen tomorrow at school because it's his first day. He wonders if the kids will be bad or nice and it turns out that some of them are bad and most of them are nice. (OK, you did fine.)

Melanie has difficulty getting started and requires structure and support. However, her story basically ignores the task demand implied by the violin and describes the child's social concerns. Neither the narrator nor the character exhibits an active organizing effort to deal with the violin or task demand.

Card 2: That person looks like Dorothy and her aunt in the Wizard of Oz, and that looks like the horse the other old man had. She lives on a farm. (child points to a tree) Looks like face (pointing) . . . eye, nose, and mouth. She's going to school and she walked by a farm near her and she always wanted a horse and she saw the prettiest one. And at school she's daydreaming and she didn't really see the horse because the farm was just an old one. (Story was interrupted by someone coming in room and asking a question) Really she was daydreaming about a horse that wasn't really there. (End?) She gets a horse at the end but that was her only birthday present. And she makes the farm very pretty and keeps the horse there every night.

The initial response to the card is an association to the Wizard of Oz. Then the narrator is distracted by the features of the tree, which "looks like a face." The story finally begins with "she's going to school . . ." where she dreams of a horse. At the end, the daydream becomes reality.

Card 3BM: She fell and she's on the steps of her house and she couldn't walk up the steps. She kept on calling for her mom, but no one came because they weren't home. And her brother came home from school. He was younger than her and helped her up to the house and got her ice and then her mother came home and settled everything.

In the above story, a person fell, couldn't walk up the steps, and received help from family members. It is noteworthy that the protagonist was not engaged in any purposeful activity prior to falling (no context) and did not exhibit resourcefulness after falling. She doesn't even know that her mother is not home and simply calls for help until her younger brother arrives.

Card 5: There was a girl and her mother wouldn't let her go to this party and her mother wouldn't let her go to any party so she snuck out of her window and when her mother went up to say good night, because she sent her up to her bed because she was being crabby. (She was being what?) Very crabby and crabby, and really under her other clothes she had a pretty dress on and she went out to the party. Then her mother found her there and she decided to let her stay and the boyfriend drove her home.

The story describes a girl at odds with her mother (family). When restricted to her room, she sneaks out. In the entire set of stories, this is the only one where active energy or effort was invested. However, the effort was directed at avoiding consequences of behavior.

Example 2
Another child, Michael, a 13-year-old male seventh-grader, has a history of difficulty putting forth the active organizing effort required to perform in school. On the WISC-R, he obtained a Full Scale score of 102. Verbal and

performance scores were 112 and 92, respectively. His scaled scores on subtests indicating freedom from distractibility (Arithmetic = 8, Digit Span = 7, and Coding = 6) were significantly lower than his mean. During testing he complained, sighed, sat back, but complied. He daydreamed and looked away between subtests.

> Card 1: OK, this story is about a kid who plays the violin and he doesn't like it very much so his mom tells him to go to practice the violin but he actually sneaks in a tape recorder and plays some symphony or whatever . . . um . . . and he just sits there staring at the violin. So one night, his mom signs him up for a concert, and he's in the concert and he has to go to the concert and he's in the concert. He's sitting there and everybody's saying for him to play stuff. It's his cue. So when he tries to play, it sounds really awful and the kid's humiliated and he finally he learns to play the violin. The end.

The above story is about a boy who cleverly avoids parental demand to practice but is publicly humiliated by his lack of preparation. It is the humiliation that leads to learning, and not the engagement with the task. It is noteworthy that the boy in the story doesn't foresee the humiliation and allows events to overtake him without effort to intervene.

Example 3

The following stories were told by a 12-year-old sixth-grader, Frank, who had been retained in the second grade (December birthday). He was described by his teachers as conscientious but disorganized. Presenting concerns included difficulty completing written assignments and need for more lengthy processing time. At the time of testing, report cards indicated on-grade level performance with occasional difficulty with completion of independent work. Frank was highly aware of his deficits and was concerned about academic problems and disorganization. Scores on the WISC-R were as follows: Verbal IQ = 118, Performance = 96, Full Scale = 109. Significantly lower than his verbal mean were Arithmetic and Digit Span. Coding and Object assembly were significantly lower than the other performance scores (7s). The lack of active organization can be seen in his long and detailed stories that suggest that school and work are burdensome.

> Card 1: Billy always wanted to be a musician. Then that final day came when he finally got his violin. He sat there and looked at it, tried to figure out what the little yellow block inside was. What the bow was made of, what the strings were made of, how it sounded. He loved the violin, but he didn't know how to play it. Then he got a card. He opened it and read,

didn't bother to read it, so what it said inside was, this entitles you to five free lessons of the violin. He was so happy. That day came when he came to his first lesson and he brought everything with him and teacher said, "Now rosin your bow." He said, "What's rosin?" That was the little block inside. So he takes out the block and starts rubbing it onto his bow. Then after he had rubbed about 50 times, they started to play, First she taught him basic notes A, G, B, D, and C. Then she gave him a little piece of music to play. Time rolled on and after about two years, he was ready for his first concert. A couple of music critics were there and heard him play. They thought it was wonderful. So they brought him back where they, to Los Angeles. He played for their boss and he was accepted into the orchestra. After some time, he became very famous and made lots of money. He still has his old violin and his old bow and he uses them both. Except now, he has a new rosin stick.

The above story describes a child who wants to learn but focuses on too many irrelevant details. In addition, he relies on unlikely means rather than organized effort to achieve (e.g., five free lessons; being discovered at his first concert).

Card 2: Does it have to be a story? I was thinking about a poem or something. As Mary walked to school, she saw the men working in the fields. She wondered, "Why do I have to go to school? It's not fair. They don't just get to stay outside all day. They get to ride their horses, plow the fields, plant the corn, pick the corn, take afternoon breaks. What do I get? I get an hour of lunch. There are too many books to carry, too much to do, and mama, she does her work. Dad, he just plows the fields. School teacher, man, she's a witch. Life would be a whole lot better if we lived in Oz." She went on with that thought for the rest of her life. Then one day, she got into a plane and flew around the world and came to China. She liked it so much there that she stayed there and raised a family.

The above story tells of a girl's escape from the burden and tedium of school.

Card 3BM: John told Mary she shouldn't have gone out with the guys and gone drinking . . . just too much for her, dropped the car keys and fell on the stairs. Luckily John was home. When she woke up, she couldn't remember what happened and was just babbling so John called the doctor. The doctor said, "No more monkeys jumping on the bed" (smiles and laughs) and he came over and looked at Mary and said that she had a minor concussion and she might have to come back to the hospital. When she got back . . . when they got to the hospital they found out it was more than just a minor confussion . . . that she would have to . . . she would probably be alive for about another 15 hours and she was in a very deep coma. So 15 hours went by and she died.

The above story describes grave consequences to an individual who acts in a self-indulgent manner. Again, there is distraction by associative thinking ("no more monkeys . . .").

Card 7GF: Sarah really wasn't interested in what her mom was reading. She just kind of stared off into space, half listening so that if her mom asked her any questions she would probably be able to answer them. She really wasn't that interested. She much rather would be outside playing in the rain with her dolly. But oh no, she just had to stay inside and listen to mom. Then mom started to get tired, so she told Sarah she would continue reading tomorrow. Poor Sarah, she was crushed. After her mother went to bed to take her nap, she took her dolly outside and started splashing around in the puddles. She got back inside, she saw that her mother was still asleep so she invited a couple of friends over and they had a little party. When her mother woke up, she asked what was going on and Sarah said, "Well we just decided to celebrate since it is the first rain we've had in so long."

In the above story, a girl feigns interest when her mother reads to her and waits until the mother is asleep to do what she really wants. Despite perceived good intentions of a parent, a child who is unable to meet expectations feels burdened by the parent as conveyor of these demands. The child in the story is in conflict between trying to maintain the relationship with her mother and avoiding the tedium associated with fulfilling her expectations.

Summary

Motivation, affect, and cognition operate as interactive parts of a functional entity that determine what dominates a person's awareness and what instrumental actions are taken. A variety of approaches to the study of motivation are reviewed under two major rubrics: intrinsic versus extrinsic motivation, and volitional aspects of motivation. For the analysis of story telling, it is useful to identify two major components of motivation: the individual's aims and the instrumental behaviors to accomplish them. The aims of motivation would consider the individual's interests, preferences, goals, or wishes. The volitional aspects of motivation involve the deliberateness and organization of strategies or actions in pursuit of aims.

CHAPTER 18

Measurement of Achievement Motivation with Projective Stories

Motivationally relevant concepts can be applied in specific terms or viewed as general characteristics. A specific view might focus on willingness to exert energy and effort toward the organized use of strategies for efficient performance of a particular task or activity. A task such as the Digit Symbol, a subtest on the Wechsler Scales, taps a very specific instance of motivated behavior under highly structured conditions but says nothing about general initiative or tendency to persist in efforts. A more general approach might examine (1) how individuals choose to spend time, (2) what captures interest, (3) the aims of an individual's actions, and (4) the manner in which actions are evaluated (e.g., emphasis on the immediate consequences, future implications, or the intent).

Vocabulary is one of the best single measures of general intelligence because it is acquired through experiences and reflects a person's tendency to learn through reading and other sources of information (Sternberg, 1985). The fact that vocabulary assesses acquired knowledge rather than problem solving adds a general motivational dimension that is pertinent to real-life functioning, much of which is self-directed. Studying, for instance, is done independently, often in the absence of immediate feedback (Nolen, 1988).

A certain measure of motivation may apply only to the specific task and operate only in a specific setting. Motivation toward short-term compliance is evident in responses to structured tasks and reaction to external contingencies and can be gauged by a child's willingness to do homework with or without external pressure. Projective stories assess the general rather than the specific functions of motivation which

1. Determine what is of interest or what the individual will extract from the environment. Sensitivity to specific types of information in the environment influences what dominates awareness.

2. Determine what the individual seeks in terms of choices of tasks, activities, goals, and risks.

3. Compel the direction and organization of effort and energy on chosen or on imposed tasks.

4. Determine what the individual values about accomplishment (e.g., outcomes, process, standards). To some extent, values are shaped by culture and previous choices, which have a cumulative influence.

Projective stories represent the product of the accumulated selective perceptions, self-regulatory mechanisms, and problem-solving capacities. Their analysis can bring to light dysfunctions that are not evident on more structured tasks that require respondents to do something specific rather than to apply previous knowledge or set their own goals or standards.

The story teller is required to set a performance goal and to compose an integrated story that takes account of the important elements in the picture and complies with the instructions. The respondent's ability to direct efforts toward the accomplishment of the story telling task can be gleaned from the form and content of the stories. The key aspects of content relate to what the characters want (aims and goals) and how they regulate actions (efforts) to accomplish their intention. Formal elements of stories provide clues about the respondent's capacity to attend, conceptualize, and integrate information.

The suggestion to measure motivation by category accessibility (Srull & Wyer, 1986) is compelling because what captures a person's attention or interest is basic to the motivational system. Motives direct attention so that motive-relevant information is more readily perceived and, therefore, becomes more accessible in memory. These predominant concerns are reflected in thoughts and behaviors, as well as in the content of projective stories. An individual will not set realistic long-term goals if preoccupied with immediate gratification. If the person's thoughts are drawn more toward the outcome of success rather than the process of working on the task, then ambitions may not be compatible with actual interests or abilities. The individual may set high aspirations without realistically estimating capacity to carry out the requisite activities. The discrepancy between aspiration and genuine interest would be reflected by projective stories that fail to incorporate appropriate effort toward outcomes because task involvement was not a readily accessible construct.

Motives and goals influence perception in everyday life where individuals select what to focus on from among numerous possibilities. A young man imprisoned for armed robbery commented on the symbol for a Rolex watch (in fact, he knew the distinctions among all fine jewelry brands) but didn't know basic information items on the WAIS-R such as the direction in which the sun rises. Similarly, when driving to work, an individual might pay special attention to the pertinent aspects of the traffic report, especially if information is relevant to immediate decision to alter one's route. Individual differences in what captures attention and in what dominates awareness is perhaps the clearest index of motivation. Some individuals readily tune out information that is not relevant to their immediate goals because they have a narrow range of interests.

The information that is stored in memory reflects the individual's interests and forms the context for subsequent processing. Memory is conceptualized (see Gitomer & Glaser, 1987) as "consisting of an organized store of knowledge . . . an associative network, with highly related concepts closely linked within the network, [and having] multiple pathways through which they can be connected" (pp. 301–302). Thus, the manner in which memory is encoded and organized determines how it is accessed and reflects the cumulative impact of previous information processing. These stored memories represent not only the content but also the style of thinking, which are superimposed on the organization of projective stories.

McClelland, Atkinson, and their co-workers (McClelland & Atkinson, 1948; McClelland et al., 1953) assumed that if an individual were strongly oriented toward a particular state, then thoughts pertaining to that motive would dominate awareness. Accordingly, the use of projective story telling to measure motivation is ideal since the open-ended response format and the ambiguous situations presented by the picture stimuli would elicit the thoughts that most readily come to mind (Sorrentino & Higgins, 1986).

McClelland and colleagues (1953) coded stories told to picture stimuli in terms of achievement imagery, which they defined as content relating to setting a standard of excellence or involvement in a task. To get an overall score for achievement motivation, the presence or absence of various categories were assigned a score and totaled. These categories clearly relate to the achievement content, but not to the manner of integrating the elements involved in the achievement imagery.

Arnold (1962) defines a *motive* as "a want that leads to action" (p. 32). Accordingly, motivation has two central components: (1) emotion, want, or desired goal; and (2) action taken in pursuit of those desires. In her approach to coding projective stories, emotions or desired goals do not become motives unless a character acts on them in a realistic, planful, and constructive manner. Arnold indicates that "the difference between an emotion and a motive lies in the fact that an emotion may or may not lead to action, while a motive always does" (p. 33). Before an emotion can become a motive, there must be a deliberate decision that a particular course of action is desired. Once the decision is made, the means to accomplish the intention becomes paramount. The type of problem set and how it is resolved reveal the story teller's motives, which are blueprints for action.

Actions that are motivated by long-term purposes have different implications than those that are motivated by immediate gratification or provocation. Arnold's approach emphasizes the connections among goals, means, and ends. Emotion may be acted on without thought, deliberation, or appraisal of alternatives. Therefore, in a projective story, an individual's desire to pursue goals or to meet standards is not reflective of motivation without deliberate action to carry out the intention.

Motive-Related Aspects of Projective Stories

The following aspects of stories are relevant to motivation: (1) goal or problem formulation, (2) reaction to goal or problem, (3) goal-directed action, and (4) problem resolution or goal attainment.

Goal Formulation

With respect to projective stories, an important part of goal formulation is the definition of the central problem portrayed in the stimulus. An individual who is highly motivated describes tensions or conflicts in ways that permit deliberate action to attain a goal or resolve a dilemma. Thus, characters in projective stories are goal directed rather than reactive to immediate need, wish, or provocation and can delay action and formulate more complex rather than trivial goals. Those lacking the capacity to formulate goals are trapped in the moment where actions are provoked, rather than guided by purpose.

Formal Characteristics of Structure
1. Appropriate interpretation is made of central conflict or tension state portrayed in the stimulus.
2. Decision about who the characters are and about what they are doing is made without undue vacillation.
3. The story is coherent, logical, and to the point without rambling or getting lost in details.

Formal Characteristics of Content
1. Characters set a realistic, prosocial goal or describe a conflict or moral dilemma to be resolved rather than react to the provocations or desires of the moment.
2. Events are set in a context that clarifies the goal, thereby giving purpose and direction to subsequent action.
3. Characters display emotions of interest, curiosity, pride, concern, empathy, and commitment to standards or ideals that foster achievement or prosocial activity.

Characteristics of the Goal
Characteristics of the goal can be described along the following dimensions: presence–absence; internally set–imposed by others; clear–vague;

long term–short term; prosocial–antisocial; realisitic–unrealistic; process goal–outcome goal; attain positive–avert negative; interpersonal–task; substantial–trivial; and spiritual–material.

Reaction to the Goal

Provided that a goal has been set, what is the reaction of the characters? If the goal is externally imposed, does the character accept the goal and the effort involved or seek to avoid the goal? Are characters competent to attain the goal or solve the problem through likely means? Are there insurmountable obstacles or unforeseen events that would interfere with (prevent or delay) goal accomplishment or goal-directed actions? Lack of perceived competence and the anticipation of external barriers would undermine motivation and persistence. If the goal is unacceptable, are there alternative goals? Why is the goal unacceptable—Lack of interest? Boredom? Fatigue? Is the emphasis on avoiding the responsibility or necessity of working toward a legitimate demand? Is there any elaboration or modification of the original goal? Do characters seek help from parents, authorities, friends? Is there a clear idea of the goal and of what is needed for its accomplishment?

Does the story teller and, hence, the character evolve a conceptual framework that gives direction to goal-directed activity? Some individuals can formulate lofty goals but lose track of their intentions, and fail to generate plans, or if they do, the plans are unrealistic, insufficient for the task or goal, or incompatible with characters' thoughts or feelings.

Formal Characteristics of Structure

The narrator exhibits the ability to approach the story telling task in a planful and autonomous manner:

1. The story proceeds according to a plan rather than made up detail by detail.
2. The story teller is relatively autonomous rather than requiring a great deal of reassurance and questioning by the examiner to meet the story telling task demands.

Formal Characteristics of Content

Provided that a goal has been set, the reaction of the story characters indicate that:

1. They are competent to attain the goal. They do not anticipate failure nor are they preoccupied with internal barriers to achievement (e.g., problems with concentration, boredom, etc.).

2. They do not perceive external barriers as insurmountable or frustrating.
3. They display foresight and the ability to plan and anticipate reactions or consequences.
4. They desire to accomplish the goal versus seeking to avoid responsibility.
5. They perceive the goal as interesting, valuable, or legitimate versus boring, burdensome, intrusive.

Goal-Directed Activities

The translation of an intention or plan into productive action requires, at a minimum, the capacity to initiate, maintain, and modulate sequences of complex activities in an orderly manner. The breakdown in capacity to carry out purposive behavior is evident in a projective story telling task. At the formal level, story telling is disrupted by perseverations, logical fallacies, and lack of integration. In terms of content, goal attainment is not directed by appropriate instrumental actions or characters' intentions are thwarted.

Formal Characteristics of Structure
1. The story teller maintains interest in the task—does not express (verbally or nonverbally) boredom, frustration, or desire to stop.
2. The story is logical and revolves around a central theme without rambling, indicating that the individual can maintain self-directed behavior and follow through on intentions.
3. The narrator is aware of difficulties in generating or completing the story but is not overly self-critical.

Formal Characteristics of Content
1. Actions are prosocial, instrumental, and directed to a purpose rather than provoked.
2. Characters display self-determination and realistic confidence.
3. Actions are realistic and sufficient for the expected outcome.
4. Inner motives and external constraints are realistically balanced.

Characteristics of Actions
Instrumental actions in the pursuit of appropriate goals are indicative of motivation when such actions are realistic and consistent with feelings, thoughts, and anticipated outcomes. Actions can be characterized according to: presence–absence; planful–haphazard; realistic–unrealistic; self-reliance–external reliance; prosocial–antisocial; proactive–reactive; seeking–avoiding; and goal directed–aimless.

Outcome or Resolution

The story outcome is the most useful vantage point for inferring motivation (Arnold, 1962) because it incorporates all the elements described previously: goal, reaction to goal, and action. The goal or problem definition sets the parameters for possible resolutions, and the outcome is the product of thoughts, feelings, and efforts directed toward goals or dilemmas. If success is accomplished or goals are attained through wishful thinking alone, the outcome is not a result of volitional behavior. No matter how well defined or how high the aspirations or standards, outcomes that are not pursuant to realistic instrumental actions are not indicative of motivation. On the contrary, the higher the aspirations, the greater the effort and planning required.

Characteristics of Outcomes

Outcomes can be described according to the following dimensions: presence–absence (the original state prevails; tensions are unresolved); realistic–unrealistic (outcomes are clearly tied to a realistic process or likely sequence of actions and follow logically from the story context); and positive–negative (successful resolution or acceptance of inevitable versus remaining in a negative state or deterioration beyond the original situation).

The positive or negative nature of the outcome is not the issue but rather the convictions and motivating attitudes expressed through a reasonable connection among thoughts, feelings, actions, and outcomes. Thus, a successful outcome with no instrumental action or from antisocial or ill-intended action reflects a negative attitude. Conversely, failure that follows from minimal effort reflects a positive conviction.

Motivation as a General Set of Convictions

High achievers operate on the basis of a set of principles that are evident not only in relation to attitudes about achievement but also with respect to convictions about right and wrong actions, interpersonal relationships, and responses to adverse life situations. Accordingly, a story can be scored for achievement even if the thematic content has little to do with achievement per se. Arnold (1962) describes the convictions in relation to these four areas.

Achievement

High achievers exhibited the following convictions about achievement:

1. Success and happiness are contingent on actions based on good intentions, whereas failing to act on positive convictions results in failure or unhappiness.

2. Altruistic or ethical values are preferable as opposed to material or expedient values.
3. Success comes through active effort, including control over emotions, self-denial, and reasonable action, and failure results when these actions are omitted, from impulsive action, or personal inadequacy.
4. Positive orientation toward work (interest, intrinsic satisfaction) leads to success, whereas work done with reluctance and boredom leads to modest success.

In contrast, low achievers exhibited the following attitudes regarding achievement:

1. Goals are not articulated or they are shifting and uncertain.
2. Success is the result of ill-intentioned or selfish motives or can be attained without ethical or well-intentioned actions.
3. Success is doubtful, and failure is more likely.
4. If success is achieved, it is due to luck, fate, or fantasy rather than produced by active effort.
5. Success is defined as that which pleases others or simply as effort or intention.
6. Failure is blamed on the malice or ineptness of others or the circumstances.
7. Success can be achieved by unlikely, phony, or "heroic" means or by the use of force, dishonest, or devious methods.
8. Work is viewed as boring, frustrating, burdensome, harmful, and degrading.
9. Failure is overcome by illegitimate means or leads to despair unless fate comes to the rescue.

Right and Wrong Action

High achievers' attitudes toward right and wrong were as follows:

1. Right action depends on an individual's choice or will.
2. Wrongdoing should be admitted, appropriately punished, repented, and changed.
3. Individuals should work toward justice and resist temptations to do wrong. When injustice must be faced, the individual should not seek revenge but overcome resentment, bitterness, or other negative emotions.

Low achievers' attitudes toward right and wrong were as follows:

1. Wrongdoing may get a person in trouble but punishment can be avoided in the present or future (e.g., by admitting fault or apologizing).

2. Wrongdoing is forgiven by loved ones, especially when such actions bring success.
3. Wrongdoing is caused by external factors such as environment, upbringing, heredity, and others' deviousness.
4. Wrongdoing is justified when it suits self-interest or when the end is worthwhile.
5. Punishment is undesirable and ineffective; it leads to resentment or despair.
6. Clever people get away with wrongdoing, lack of scruples, or angry defiance.

Interpersonal Relationship

High achievers' attitudes toward human relationships were:

1. Legitimate pressure from those in authority is acknowledged, whereas illegitimate pressure is resisted.
2. Self-determined efforts overcome unfavorable environment or bad influence. Behaviors are not dictated by others, and reasonable actions are carried out despite objections and disagreements.
3. A balance is struck between accepting reasonable advice or influence and charting one's own course. Individuals act independently, yet seek help when needed.
4. People have a positive influence on each other. They cooperate, comfort, inspire, or persuade others to be reasonable.

Low achievers' attitudes toward human relationships were:

1. Lack of love or rejection (in childhood or later) leads to failure or unhappiness; rejection by others undermines confidence and leads to failure. Therefore, individuals should yield to the will of others for the sake of maintaining the relationship.
2. The individual can make no constructive efforts without help and support from others.
3. Love overcomes all difficulties.
4. There is rebellion against authorities.
5. Interpersonal obligations can be avoided if they conflict with self-interest.
6. Good relations are contingent on receiving care or gratification.11
7. People are seen as troublesome and self-seeking. They gloat or brag about success and do not listen to constructive advice.

Reaction to Adversity

Attitudes of high achievers toward overcoming adversity were:

1. Such circumstances can be overcome by positive, self-determined action or through the help and cooperation of others.

2. If adversity cannot be overcome (no action is possible), then a positive attitude is taken.

Attitudes of low achievers toward overcoming adversity were:

1. There is sheer passivity or unwillingness to make a constructive effort; positive effort is useless to overcome insurmountable obstacles, dangers, or difficulties.
2. Helpless dependence is placed on others who come to the rescue.
3. There is resignation to failure or escape through fantasy, wishful thinking, general pessimism, not expecting help but feeling doomed without it.
4. Other people cause adversity and are obligated to help.

Levels of Motivation

Formal elements of story content from the vantage point of the outcome are scaled into four levels of motivation based on the foregoing review that emphasized Arnold's (1962) work.

1 = Extremely Poor Motivation

Positive Outcome
Success, happiness, or overcoming failure occurs under the following conditions:

1. Negative motives or ill intentions.
2. Nonconstructive actions, absence of effort, or delay of necessary action. Fantasy substitutes for active effort, or means toward success are magical, highly unlikely, antisocial, or ineffective (e.g., use or threat of force, dishonesty, manipulation); success is predicted by external features ("He's wearing a suit").
3. Goals are unrealistic, not firmly pursued, trivial, abandoned when difficult, only dreamed about, unstated.
4. Character wonders what to do or what will happen; general pessimism about life and other unconstructive attitudes but everything turns out fine.
5. Boredom or obvious lack of interest.
6. Blind dependence on, rebellious defiance of, or humiliation by others.
7. Negative attitudes that belittle success or successful people (e.g., success comes to the unworthy, superior achievers are flawed, success serves antisocial or unethical purposes or is associated with feelings of inadequacy).

8. Adversity or failure is overcome by unlikely or harmful means (e.g., fluke, accident, providence, awakening from a bad dream, or finding that the adversity was unreal because of mistaken judgment).

Negative Outcome

Failure, unhappiness, despair, disappointment, giving up, or destruction occurs under the following conditions:

1. Is expected or just happens despite active effort and realistic goals; optimistic expectations, cooperation of others, good intentions, self-determined choices.
2. Negative attitudes where failure is blamed on others or fate. Positive efforts are misunderstood, professional help is useless, other's advice leads to failure, obeying legitimate commands leads to failure.
3. Adversity or failure is not overcome but leads to despair, ends in emotion (worry, tears, frustration); results in paralysis or inaction, pretense or deceit; leads to escape, fantasy, dream, or sleep.
4. Adversity, failure, or inaction has desirable consequences; the character gets to play, is rewarded, consoled, or comforted by others.
5. Positive action leads to harm.

Summary of Extremely Poor Motivation

Extremely poor motivation is scored when there are magical, unrealistic, wishful resolutions rather than realistic explanations for the outcome, such as when capricious changes in circumstance or an unlikely sequence of events leads to favorable outcomes. Antisocial goals or actions succeed, or an individual becomes highly successful despite boredom, frustration, or seemingly insurmountable barriers. The absence of a clearly defined problem and actions that are not directed at problem resolution also indicate extremely low motivation. Another indication of extremely low motivation is the depiction of characters who are helpless to resolve the dilemma posed or whose actions are aimless and provoked by the stimulus or immediate circumstance. Characters may possess insight or perceive mistakes but lack the ability to act on them (e.g., daydreams or fails to communicate). Also related to poor motivation are negative attitudes toward success, work, or achievement, such as viewing work or routine as undesirable, unimportant, boring, or frustrating. Extremely poor motivation is also scored when the narrator lacks sufficient resources to handle the task demands as evident in the formal characteristics of the story.

The following story told by a kindergarten boy illustrates the "pathological inertia" described by Lezak (1982). There is no connection between the character's perceptions and actions.

Card 5: The girl is looking out the door. She sees a kid—someone's kid hitting somebody. (Feel?) Bad. (Who feels bad?) The kid, because somebody's hitting him. (To?) The lady sits down and watches TV.

The story indicates no goals or constructive action. An adult sees a child being hit by another but simply ignores the situation and watches TV.

The two stories below told by a 19-year-old incarcerated female (low-average IQ) who had completed the eighth grade also illustrate extremely poor motivation. In the first story, the issue is whether the character will try to learn to play the violin or give up. There is no benefit or purpose to learning. In the second story, the woman is locked up, depressed, and crying. The goal of "getting herself together" is vague and no plans or actions are included. The stock ending may "sound good" but fails to resolve the issues presented through a realistic process. In both stories, the goal or dilemma is not set in a context but is a direct reaction to the stimulus demands. The outcomes refer to vague predictions about the future rather than brought about through constructive plans or actions.

Card 1: He's frustrated because he can't play the instrument. He's trying to learn how to play this but he can't play this. And he's thinking of giving up but he probably doesn't. (To?) He probably doesn't give up.

In the above story, a child is frustrated because he can't learn to play an instrument, he wants to give up but doesn't want to admit it.

Card 3BM: Woman locked up. She's depressed and crying. She's locked in a room. (H) She's probably crying. (To?) She'll probably get herself together later on.

The woman in the story is locked in a room, depressed, crying, and thinking that perhaps she'll get herself together eventually. However, there is no indication of any purposeful activity or plan. Furthermore, no reason is given for being locked up, which would provide a context for subsequent coping responses.

2 = Poor Motivation

Positive Outcome
Success, happiness, or overcoming failure occurs in the following conditions:

1. Less difficult or onerous goals are substituted, or despite failure to modify goals or means as necessary.

2. Actions are not directly pertinent to the task at hand; they are undertaken for approval, recognition, conformity, or self-centered motives.
3. Optimism is expressed without good reason or sufficient action; the character hopes for success or thinks about the problem.
4. Actions are taken without commitment or curiosity. Any action for its own sake (e.g., sleep), reluctant action where the character is resentful, refrains from negative action because others intervene, acts constructively when persuaded by others, or is passively dependent on help or advice.
5. Means to goals are vague or an adverse situation is overcome with less than the required effort.
6. Adversity or failure is not overcome but tolerated though action is possible. The character makes the best of it, hopes for better, quickly forgets, is consoled by having tried, is happy anyway, or disagrees with other's judgment.
7. Success is not satisfying but empty, meaningless, leads to failure, worry, or discord.

Negative Outcome
Failure or poor performance occurs under the following conditions:

1. Thinking and planning have occurred but no action is taken.
2. There are extraneous factors such as accident, fate, lack of ability, lack of help or support, or mistakes of others.

Summary of Poor Motivation
Poor motivation is suggested when problems are defined and a dilemma is posed, but efforts are vague or insufficient. For example, a character gets a violin teacher and succeeds after lessons but doesn't mention practicing. Internal or external barriers to constructive effort limit resolution of problems or attainment of goals. Fatigue, boredom, anxiety, or stress limit actions or success toward recognized goals. Others must provide incentive or motivation. There is overemphasis on the outcome, while the role of effort is minimized, though not completely ignored. Cost is attached to effort and success. There are positive but passive attitudes such as decisions or resolutions without action. Work is praised because it's a first effort or because of good intentions despite poor or mediocre performance. Success is attained despite lack of regard for others; characters pursue their goals despite harmful impact on others.

The following story told by a girl age 15–2 illustrates the emphasis on the outcome rather than effort. High aspirations are expressed, but the work itself is demanding and frustrating.

Card 1: Trying to figure out what that is. Oh, it's a violin. Before a while ago, he was in music class playing the violin and he has to write a piece of music for his recital. His teacher told him to and this is the sheet of paper and there's a pen right there and he took out his violin and tried to play it and he got frustrated and he put everything down. Now he's thinking about his recital and how he's going to write his piece and what it's going to be like. (How do I want to end it? Want me to go into the future?) Little boy sitting there thinking of something to write. Gets a whole bunch of words and writes it down. Has the lyrics and writes the melody to go with it. Then he has his recital and it's really good.

Despite being frustrated with trying to meet the teacher's difficult demands (write the music), the child is convinced that success and approval will come easily with some work.

3 = Mildly Positive Motivation

Positive Outcome
Success or happiness occurs under the following conditions:

1. Goals are modest, effort is expended but the outcome is uncertain.
2. Some failure or loss, which is a minor or temporary annoyance (missing out on some things), is associated with success.
3. Success is viewed as a possibility given resolution to achieve with recognition that deliberate planning and active effort are needed. Success follows from adequate planning rather than acting.
4. Success or goal attainment is conditional (e.g., when the time is right).
5. Success follows reasonable action with some dependence on others. Success is a result of getting adequate support from others or follows from positive action that is inspired by others. Advice or help is sought before doing everything possible, but the advice is judged on its merits, not blindly accepted. The character tries to think things out but then actively seeks help.
6. Active effort is expended despite lack of appreciation or negative attitude of others. Others' disapproval has temporary effect. The individual continues to act constructively despite being sad.
7. Self-determination but with some misgivings (e.g., special opportunity). Adversity or failure is overcome by active effort with the help of incidental factors, second chance, adopting a more realistic goal, learning from mistakes, with the help of others.

Negative Outcome
Failure or unhappiness occurs under the following conditions:

1. Lack of planning, mistakes, procrastination, negative attitudes, poor organization.

2. Excessive independence, refusal to heed good advice, or refusal to defer action to meet circumstances.
3. Results in punishment and increased work.

Summary of Mildly Positive Motivation

The goals are clear and realistic, but there are limitationss surrounding actions and outcomes. Work is done because it is valued, though it is difficult. Effort is appreciated despite failure, which is viewed as temporary. Negative actions are based on good intentions and have appropriate consequences.

Mildly positive motivation is shown by the story below told by a sixth-grade girl.

> Card 1: In this picture it looks like he just had a bad experience with his violin. He wanted to play the violin and didn't really understand how. And when he thought about playing, it seemed like fun but when he actually tried to play it, he failed. The notes didn't come out right when he tried to play. Right now he probably feels depressed because he tried to do something and he failed. In the end, he'll probably try again and succeeds.

In the above story, a boy wants to play the violin and thinks it would be fun but has trouble making it sound good; he feels bad but keeps trying until he succeeds.

The story below told by a kindergarten boy also demonstrates a similar conviction.

> Card 1: He's playing violin. He's sad; he can't make it move; he's looking at it. He's gonna get a stick and it will play when you move the stick up and down and it makes music. (Before?) He got the violin at the store. (Think?) He wants to play "Twinkle, Twinkle, Little Star." He plays it for his mom and dad.

Despite some initial difficulty, a boy figures out how to make the stick move to play "Twinkle, Twinkle, Little Star" on the violin.

4 = High Motivation

Positive Outcome

Success or happiness occurs under the following conditions:

1. Good intent, constructive actions, initiative, control of emotion, altruism, and sticking to principles.
2. Realistic goals that are adapted to circumstance.

3. Help or advice are actively sought when needed but only after the protagonist has done everything possible. Character's decisions and actions indicate self-determination but also acceptance of legitimate pressure.
4. Positive attitude toward work; it is interesting, done cheerfully, and allows individuals to go back to play.
5. Preference for values that are abstract, ethical, and altruistic rather than materialistic or expedient.

Negative Outcome
Failure or unhappiness occurs under the following conditions:

1. Ill intent, self-glorification ("be the best"); self-centered goals, unreasonable actions or no actions; blaming failure on others.
2. Boredom, disinterest, lack of active effort, neglect, inadequate means, or impulsive action.
3. Blind dependence or rebellious defiance, such as acting on another's advice without reflection or refusing to seek advice when the circumstance warrants or ignoring reasonable advice of legitimate authority.
4. Negative attitudes lead to harm, unhappiness, or punishment, even if accompanied by success (e.g., bragging is punished).

Summary of High Motivation
High motivation is indicated when realistic, purposeful, instrumental action leads to appropriate resolution of the central conflict or attainment of a well-defined goal. Even when characters require appropriate help and support of others, they recognize the value of their own self-determined efforts. There is a coherence among goals, actions, feelings, thoughts, and outcomes. Interest guides effort, and actions lead to appropriate consequences. The elements of the story are realistic and reflect understanding of cause-effect relationships. Positive prosocial actions result in favorable outcomes, whereas negative, antisocial actions result in punishment, failure, remorse, and restitution. Realistic barriers are recognized and antisocial goals are thwarted by legitimate authorities (person robs bank and goes to jail). New problems may be set through insight gained, and inevitable situations are faced with a positive attitude.

High motivation is demonstrated by the following two stories told by a 12-year-old girl.

Card 3BM: There's a family thinking about money and the house is too small, so they want a bigger one. The girl doesn't want to move; she's attached to the house. So the parents decide to move and they all go. She's thinking of all the things she could do in the old house, remembering and all, and she's feeling sad and angry at her parents for moving. It turns out that she doesn't really like the house but tries to get used to it. In the end, she gets more used to it.

The narrator sets a context for the "problem" conveyed in the stimulus. The problem (or goal) definition sets the parameters for subsequent actions. In the above story, a child's family decides to move to a bigger house. She is angry and sad but accepts the situation and eventually gets used to the new house. The character chose the most appropriate resolution, given the dilemma. The next story permits more constructive action to attain the child's wish.

Card 13B: It's Saturday morning and his parents went to market and older brothers and sisters are milking cows and collecting eggs for breakfast because they live on a farm. He's trying to think of a way to let his parents know that he's responsible enough to have a job too. So when his parents come home, he tells them he thinks he's responsible enough to work also. So they let him watch his brothers and sisters milk the cows and collect the eggs. So two months later, he's collecting the eggs and he feels happy.

The above story describes a child who thinks he's old enough to have more responsibility to help the family. The youngster persuades his parents through appropriate effort.

Summary

The following elements of motivation are incorporated in the delineation of a four-point scoring system:

1. *Goal or Problem Formulation*   Is there a clear goal or dilemma to be resolved, as opposed to an immediate need, wish, or provocation?
2. *Reaction to Goal or Problem*   Are goals acceptable, interesting, manageable, or relevant?
3. *Goal-Directed Action*   Are aims or intentions translated to planful, deliberate instrumental actions?
4. *Outcomes*   Are story resolutions appropriate given the problem definition, attitudes expressed, and actions taken?

Motivational levels are determined by examining story outcomes in relation to the individual's aims, wishes, and self-determined instrumental actions taken to pursue them.

CHAPTER 19

Self-Regulation

Virtually all conceptions of personality include strategies for self-regulation as a basic aspect of human functioning. Self-regulatory efforts can be proactive, planful, and deliberate, or reactive, haphazard, and nonvolitional. Self-regulation is intricately tied to capacity for reality testing, which takes place in the context of the subjective world, in accordance with the individual's interests and values. It should be noted that the coherence and organization of self-regulation can temporarily shift during stressful conditions or transitions.

Self-regulation is highly dependent on the degree of integration applied to the interpretation of reality. Full reality testing requires active processing of multiple sources of information to consider what is most relevant for the present and future and to balance self-interests with the perspectives of others. Reality testing in the moment may be adequate but devoid of the wisdom that grows through the cumulative integration of experience.

If the capacity to organize experience is limited to a small range of circumstances due to integration failure, the result is severe constriction in the flexibility of personality. The individual may be unable to maintain a sense of continuity of experience over time and may judge individuals on simplistic normative expectations or on the basis of the immediate circumstance. If the individual cannot integrate feelings and thoughts, then self-reflection is limited and reality testing can occur only in the context of shallow relationships. If the individual cannot reconcile discrepancies or deal with ambiguities, then the information-processing demands of many social interactions are overwhelming. Self-regulation is governed by the nature of the integration applied to experience, which sets limits on the range of environments in which the person can function.

Classes of Self-Regulation

Self-regulatory capacities encompass the regulation of internal processes such as attention, arousal, emotion, cognition, as well as overt actions. The manner in which the individual integrates the affective, cognitive, and behavioral self-regulatory systems influences the organization of experiences and shapes the individual's subjective world.

Self-regulatory processes fit into three general rubrics, which vary according to emphasis on: (1) *self-monitoring*—the maintenance of internal balance such as cognitive efficiency, attention, and optimum emotional arousal to calibrate behavior according to the demands of the immediate circumstance; (2) *self-direction*—the organization of resources to direct behavior beyond the pull of the immediate circumstance to meet goals or to respond to anticipated external demands; and (3) *self-determination*—the development of structures or guiding principles that allow the individual to balance external influences with inner values and ideals.

Self-Monitoring

Self-monitoring refers to the regulation of internal states such as affect and cognition, as well as behavioral responses within the immediate situational context. The key question concerns the individual's capacity to regulate emotions and cognitions and monitor behavior to meet the momentary situational demands. These processes involve the regulation of:

1. Arousal and emotion to maintain optimal efficiency in information processing
2. Cognitive processes such as focusing, sustaining, or shifting attention in response to immediate external stimulation
3. Behavior in response to the immediate situational demands of a social interaction or task

Self-monitoring generally requires modulation and calibration of responses to the immediate circumstance rather than continuous evaluation of the individual's activities over time. In the testing situation, some children have difficulty balancing interpersonal and task demands or cannot match their response to be in tune with the situation. For example, a child who maintains a steady chatter during testing without awareness of the examiner can generate a stream of responses but cannot calibrate it to clues in the environment. Some children can give a response if they initiate it, but they find the coordination of their response in give and take interchange problematic. They can seem controlling but their difficulty lies in spontaneous, reciprocal interaction. Such difficulties may characterize initial reactions to threatening, novel, or complex situations, or they may be more pervasive.

Self-monitoring in the immediate situation has two levels: First is the capacity for modulation and calibration of response to explicit, immediate external cues. The second involves the capacity to perceive implicit cues in the current situation. The latter is more difficult because it requires integration and active processing of patterns of cues. Children who are labeled as having emotional problems find this aspect of self-regulation particularly difficult and are, therefore, helped by increasing structure and by providing clear, predictable cues.

Within the context of administering projective story telling tasks, the following reflect a child's capacity for modulation and calibration of response to immediate external cues:

1. *Child's behavior with examiner*—The child modulates speed of telling the story with the examiner's writing pace. The child's conversation with the examiner is interactive and behavior is socially appropriate.
2. *Child's use of stimulus*—The child accounts for stimulus elements but is not too sensitive to irrelevant aspects or to minor details. The child is able to reconcile apparent discrepancies in the stimulus and does not overreact to nuances of the card. The child is able to grasp the "gist" of the entire card rather than respond to isolated elements.
3. *Story content*—The story is not a series of associative responses but reflects some organizational and integrative effort. Characters discern each other's reactions and feelings. They are not stymied by reactions of others nor do they act on a trial and error basis.
4. *Acceptability of story content and structure*—The story content and child's behavior reflect the ability to present the self in a socially acceptable manner. The respondent can deal with demands of the story telling task and monitors the story, so there's a freedom from gross contradictions and serious flaws in reality testing. The narrator refrains from content that is bizarre and clearly inappropriate.

Self-Direction

Self-direction refers to regulation of cognition, affect, and behavior to meet goals and long-term demands. Self-direction requires that the individual be able to extricate the self from the pull of the immediate situation to set priorities or goals and to direct behavior toward long-term adaptation consistent with socially accepted values.

The capacity for delay of gratification is a key to ego development in many personality theories (e.g., Mischel, 1986) and is necessary for self-direction, which requires sustaining and monitoring behavior over time to:

1. *Generate goals, plans, and actions*—The individual takes initiative based on investment in long-term endeavors.
2. *Accomplish tasks*—The individual generates strategies to carry out a complex sequence of behaviors.
3. *Keep commitments and responsibilities*—The individual meets long-term external demands, carries out intentions, and keeps commitments made to others rather than attending only to current presses.

In projective stories, a key question is whether characters direct actions toward larger purposes, deal with long-term goals or expectations beyond the pull of the stimulus or of the immediate circumstance described in the narrative. An emphasis on adaptation to immediate demands is indicated by content, which is restricted to reaction to the stimulus or to previous story events. Self-direction, however, involves the narrator's ability to set a context for actions and events that goes beyond the stimulus pull and overcomes the press of external circumstance or immediate provocation.

Self-Determination

Self-determination is the sense of autonomy, purpose, and conviction that lends meaning and continuity to life experiences. Self-determination requires that inner and outer elements of experience be reconciled, such as self-presentations with feelings, actions with values or internalized standards of self-evaluation, and short-term gain with long-term goals. The integration of these aspects of experience fosters a sense of continuity of experiences and coherence in the perceptions about self and other. Self-determination relies on the development of a cohesive internal frame of reference and involves complex functions of temperamental, perceptual, and conceptual processes as they bear on the integration of life experiences.

In projective stories, self-determination would be reflected by characters who evidence volitional, deliberate, purposeful, and organized action based on an integrated, well-elaborated inner life, and reliance on internal standards or motives beyond external reinforcers.

Elements of Self-Regulation

Self-Appraisal

Self-regulation has been related to self-evaluation (Breckler & Greenwald, 1986), and different facets of the self may be subject to different types of self-evaluation. The evaluation of the diffuse self relates to the attainment of positive affect; the public self is assessed by the approval of others; the private self is appraised through internal standards (inner representation of what others would think); and the collective self is measured on the basis of internalized goals of the reference group. Strategies for regulating behavior to enhance self-evaluation vary according to the facet of self that is salient at the time.

Self-esteem can shift with each external provocation or can be regulated according to more long-term considerations. When reactions of others contradict self-concept, some individuals attempt to maintain self-consistency by resorting to external blame, projection, or rationalization to "save face." In Kohut's (1977) self-psychology, the mind is continuously attempting to restore narcissistic equilibrium. To do so, some individuals engage in narcissistic activity, which is defined by Stolorow and Lachmann (1980) as follows: "Mental activity is narcissistic to the degree that its function is to maintain the structural cohesion, temporal stability, and positive affective coloring of the self-representation" (p. 10). Individuals who employ defenses, rationalizations, denials, and justifications that emphasize regulating self-esteem to the moment do not balance feedback from external sources with internal experiences.

There are multiple sources of information concerning an individual's capacities and typical modes of functioning across situations that can be processed, weighed, and integrated. The more self-reflection, the more internally systematic and consistent an individual's view of self-regulatory functions, the more the self-appraisal becomes internal and reassessed through internal processes. Self-appraisal that incorporates external feedback with inner standards promotes the recognition of the conditions under which self-regulation is optimal and permits the use of experience to build on strengths and compensate for limitations.

Time Perspective

A temporal framework is needed to place events in a context, to anticipate likely consequences of actions, and to plan for the future. Goals and plans focus the individual's efforts and, therefore, motivate and regulate behavior. The time frame for self-regulatory efforts is evident in projective stories. The key questions relate to the purposes of actions and definitions of problems. For example, are actions directed toward dealing with immediate provocation or to achieving long-term goals? Are problems defined in terms of immediate needs, provocations, or wishes, or are they viewed in a broader time frame? Do coping responses have a "trial and error" flavor, or do they reflect planning and foresight? Time perspective in projective stories can be characterized as focusing on (1) immediate stimulus; (2) immediate present; and (3) integration of past, present, and/or future.

Motivation

Bandura (1989) describes a motivational system of self-regulation that combines proactive and reactive elements. The capacity to let long-term goals and future consequences direct action rather than immediate pulls or short-term gain is necessary to exercise proactive control of behavior. Feedback control, which refers to modulation of efforts according to input from external sources, is also necessary because the execution of a skill or application of knowledge must be constantly varied according to changing cues and circumstances. However, self-regulation that relies only on external feedback is insufficient because internal controls must at times override current feedback, and immediate reward must be outweighed by other considerations.

External feedback is utilized differently depending on proactive or reactive regulation of behavior. An individual exercising proactive control will raise the level of aspiration and set higher standards of success following mastery of a previous standard. However, individuals whose motivational state is induced externally are inclined to reduce their efforts following success until the next demand spurs them.

Autonomy and Volitional Control

Autonomy is a subjective sense of self-direction, competence, and pride in accomplishment. Adequate integrative capacity, freedom from disorganizing emotions or tensions, and basic empathic connections, as well as positive emotions and interests promote the development of autonomy. An individual who cannot meet information-processing demands of interpersonal situations or who is prone to overreact or jump to conclusions may be unable to put events into perspective and, therefore, may develop a subjective sense of loss of volitional control in social situations.

A frail, rigid, or unstable sense of autonomy may entail resistance to authority or great concern, sensitivity, and awareness of being subject to the will of others or to the disorganizing influences of one's own feelings. Individuals may perceive a request as a demand and may defend their sense of autonomy from internal or external threat by expressing autonomy through a superior-inferior dichotomy with concerns around power, rank, and status.

With respect to projective stories, autonomy is reflected by the extent to which characters feel at the mercy of external events or experience a subjective sense of self-determination. Autonomy is low if behaviors of characters are (1) elicited by immediate stimuli or directly provoked by other characters (the restrictions on autonomy are not as great when the narrator shows awareness and ability to impose perspective subsequent to the initial reaction); and (2) considered according to immediate benefit for self or immediate consequence. Autonomy is high when the character's behaviors are (1) set in a reasonable context and evaluated according to possible consequences in the future; (2) judged according to their abstract, moral significance and impact on other people; and (3) planful, realistic, competent, purposeful, and effective in resolving the dilemma.

Internalization

The concept of internalization has been viewed as a general, evolutionary, biological principle that promotes growth in adaptive functioning so that the individual gains increased independence from environmental stimuli and processes (Hartmann, 1939). Internalization is a complex process by which external relationships and external sources of self-regulation become part of the inner psychic structure (Meissner, 1981), allowing the individual to gain greater capacity to master the environment, to endure stress, and to delay gratification of impulses. The subjectively experienced structure is a product of the individual's capacity to organize and synthesize life experiences (Sandler, 1960).

The concepts of ego and superego within the psychoanalytic framework imply the existence of internal structures that regulate behavior rather than strict reliance on external consequences. Freud (1923) took the view of the ego as an organizing problem-solving agency that performs the function of adaptation and self-initiated, self-monitored behavior. Hartmann (1939, 1950) viewed the primary function of the ego as one of internal regulation and expanded beyond the formulation of Freud by attributing autonomy and conflict-free activities to the ego in adapting to the environment. Rangell (1986) advocated that the ego functions of initiation be emphasized as much as the ego functions of adaptation. The more internal the regulation, the more proactive rather than reactive control over behavior.

It is not necessary to adopt the psychoanalytic framework to assume that internalized structures play a self-regulatory role. The regulatory functions of cognitive structures in general are widely recognized. A well-developed internal frame of reference functions like a scientific theory that guides observations and is modified by them. This storehouse of experience, knowledge, and conviction modulates perception and mitigates against being swayed by other's opinions or immediate presses. With respect to projective stories, the questions pertain to (1) standards, if any, for self-evaluation or conduct that are expressed or implied; (2) aims or organizational framework that gives coherence to the stream of events; and (3) sense of internal principles that govern behavior.

Levels of Self-Regulation

Self-regulatory processes can be characterized as operating at different levels of efficiency and complexity and can proceed from the very basic level of adjusting to incoming stimulation to directing efforts toward long-term goals or ideals. Furthermore, individuals may be struggling or may feel comfortable at each level.

Self-regulation occurs through the selection of environments and the interpretation of events. People tend to avoid information, tasks, and environments that are not compatible with (boring) or that exceed (anxiety provoking) their coping capacities. These decisions have a cumulative influence on development because each choice promotes certain opportunities for mastery and sets parameters for the range of subsequent choices (Bandura, 1986). Depending on the level of self-regulation, these selections can be made on a moment-to-moment basis or can incorporate multiple considerations. Additionally, choices can be made on a deliberate, volitional basis or by drifting from one temptation to another.

An individual's level of self-regulation can vary depending on the circumstances. An individual who functions well under some conditions (e.g., structured, low risk) may become indecisive and disorganized under the impact of threat. Individuals may lose their bearings during stress or transitions and function below customary levels. Thus, a person's capacity to operate at a higher level may be temporarily disrupted by emotional overload or stress. Each level represents a style of organization of experience that has early roots. What influences development is not the occurrence of particular events but the capacity to organize these experiences. These organizational capacities determine the consistencies in the pattern of personality development.

These levels of functioning are inextricably tied to the phenomenology of experience, which has two major components: (1) *Differentiation of thoughts and concerns*—Differentiation of thoughts and concerns refers to the distinctions that are made and the information that dominates awareness or draws attention; and (2) *Integration of thoughts and concerns*—The content of awareness can be meaningfully organized or may consist of fleeting reactions to immediate provocation. The organization of multiple facets of experience rather than responding to isolated bits of information is key to self-regulation. A grasp of reality that is dominated by islands of experience, each having little relationship to that which preceded it or to that which will follow, leaves the individual without enduring interests, convictions, or goals. Such a person is ill prepared to focus efforts in pursuit of long-range plans.

The five levels of self-regulation described below are sequenced so that higher levels are associated with the following:

1. Increased organization of inner life governs actions and standards for self-evaluation rather than reaction to external events or anticipation of external consequences. Such development is reflected in the description of characters with rich and complex inner states who can reflect on their actions, thoughts, and feelings and balance self-other interests with general principles of justice and social responsibility. They possess the perspective

and insight necessary to modulate short-term reactions or overreactions and to put events into an appropriate context.

2. Increased emphasis is placed on well-organized concerns or goals rather than being driven by trivial or momentary considerations. Actions serve long-term purposes or realistically overcome obstacles with due consideration to balancing the perspectives of all relevant characters.

3. Increased autonomy, planning, and deliberate action that convey a sense of initiative and transcend the immediate environmental pull or provocation. This is reflected in stories that demonstrate an increasing ability to (a) use strategies to anticipate, plan, and organize efforts; (b) gauge reactions of others and benefit from feedback; and (c) modulate reactions.

Level One: Disequilibrium

Form and content of stories reflect tenuous organization and fragmentation of life experience. The story teller cannot simultaneously process or integrate the relevant components of a situation and may focus on isolated aspects of an experience.

The individual is functioning largely without awareness of the implications of actions for others and for the self and cannot meaningfully integrate even the most pressing immediate concerns. The individual reacts to faulty perception, provoked by minute, irrelevant considerations, or is driven by raw emotions such as fear, panic, terror, anxiety, or extreme anger. In an effort to maintain cognitive or emotional equilibrium, the individual is compelled by momentary considerations, which are not effectively organized because of an inability to size up situations. Anxiety is not a signal for coping but results in panic and helplessness. Defenses are not functional and affects are so disorganizing that the sequence of story events is highly unlikely and content may include illogical or bizarre elements.

In telling stories, the respondent may focus narrowly on elements of the picture without capturing the meaning of the stimulus, or express global reactions to the stimulus as a whole. Differentiation of persons is so primitive that physical details (e.g., eyebrow) taken from the stimulus are unrelated to the entire person or story context. All of the characters may be locked into a particular feeling consistent with the mood evoked by the stimulus as a whole. However, the characters cannot fathom the reasons for the feeling and cannot react appropriately. For example, the entire scene portrayed in the picture may be described as spooky or scary, with the characters helpless to act constructively. A magical or unlikely turn of events could modify the situation or simply contradict previous content.

Another indication of this level of functioning is given when the child's behavior during testing is inappropriate or unmodulated (e.g., throwing the card). The following story told by a third-grade girl has these characteristics of this level: (1) people react to isolated events without continuity or context; (2) actions are based on misperceptions or on momentary provocation; (3) feelings shift with capricious change of circumstance; (4) actions are not guided by purpose; (5) confused time perspective; (6) faulty logic or gross contradictions; (7) highly unlikely or bizarre content; and (8) content is evoked by reaction to narrow aspects of the stimulus, which fails to capture its gist.

> Card 8: Chris's father had a heart attack. His mother (i.e., the father's mother) died of a gun. When he saw this gun in the hospital room, he had a heart attack. The people in the room were using a butcher knife. Chris thought that they shouldn't use it. He looked back and didn't look. The operation was over and his father was dead. The people looked mean. His friends told him, "Did you know those people weren't doctors?" Lots of times Chris went back to the hospital room to see his dad, and he was really sad and mad. His friends told him that those people weren't really doctors. Chris looked back one time and the skeletons were gone; he wondered why. He looked back and the people were gone. He looked back and his father was dead again. Then they asked, "How would you like it if one day those thieves were put in your room and the doctors are not really doctors?" Chris still had his mother because it was his father's mother that died. Chris and his mother lived happily ever after but were still mad and still sad.

Level Two: Immediacy

The individual makes distinctions and processes information on the basis of momentary relevance and deals with the immediate situation but without adequate reflection on consequences or on implications to others. Interpersonal information is distorted because such individuals see what they want or need to see and do not anticipate interpersonal consequences. Moreover, actions are based on what immediately dominates awareness without effort to organize or integrate salient aspects of the current situation with past or future. Self-presentation may pass muster in the moment, but over time the inconsistencies and lack of inner conviction become obvious to others. Long-term self-regulation is hampered because individuals cannot maintain interest in situations that do not contribute to their immediate well-being.

Behavior is not guided by an enduring sense of self but geared toward attaining emotional comfort to maintain or increase good feelings and decrease or avoid bad feelings in the moment. Thus, actions are aimed at seeking immediate gain, entertainment, or relief from aversive states such as boredom. However, low tolerance for emotions leads to short-sighted coping and to giving up long-term benefits for immediate relief. Ambivalent feelings are impossible because affects are not regulated internally but are evoked by immediate outside circumstances. The narrator may rely excessively on concrete external cues to read emotions because of an inability to draw inferences about internal states. Story characters judge one another on the basis of their momentary affective impact without considering their intentions or circumstances.

The story teller is not concerned with maintaining consistency in self-concept but engages in immediate "face-saving" maneuvers rather than being oriented toward effective problem solving. Affects, intentions, actions, and outcomes don't "add up" with respect to time perspective or intra- and interpersonal context but are not jarringly incompatible. Although content is not bizarre, affects are not based on real experience but are attributed to the characters based on stereotypes or the stimulus properties. There is lack of specificity in description of inner states, thoughts, feelings, and intentions (e.g., "They had a problem and then they did something about it. They learned to communicate better."). General vagueness of content or emphasis on superficial qualities can relate to (1) lack of experience base relative to the interaction portrayed in the scene; (2) poor cognitive integration, concreteness, or rigidity in processing, which interfere with organizing interpersonal information; (3) defensive information processing of threatening or emotional aspects of relationships or the stimulus; (4) preoccupation; and (5) disinterest in interpersonal relationships and lack of reflection or insight lead to difficulty grasping the inner characteristics of self and other people.

Specific reasons for self-regulation to the immediate demands of the situation that are not independent of one another are illustrated below.

Wishful Thinking

Awareness is dominated by the present, and actions are not restricted by anxiety about likely consequences. Information processing is determined by what the individual desires rather than by realistic considerations. In the following story told by a first-grade girl, the narrator ignores the stimulus features and fails to discern the different emotions of the characters. The story proceeds according to the wishes of the characters within the cultural stereotype.

> Card 4: She's gonna have a marriage and go on a honeymoon. After that she'll go home and have dinner. He is looking at something. (Feel?) Happy cuz they're gonna get married and go on a honeymoon. My uncle got married and went on a honeymoon. (To?) They live happily ever after.

Grounding in the Present

The story teller deals only with surface information and does not make inferences or apply standards in formulating judgments due to highly concrete thinking or inability to depart from cues that are immediately available. The following two stories, told by the same girl as above, illustrate the story teller's concrete thinking and preoccupation with the immediate aspects of the situation.

Card 5: She's coming into her room. She looks at the flower and the lamp. She's gonna lay down on her bed. (Before?) She just came in the room. She goes to sleep, wakes up, and then it's dinner time. Then she watches TV. (Think?) Can't think of anything. (Feel?) Happy cuz it's a nice day.

Card 7: The girl is looking at her doll. She doesn't like it cuz it's not nice like the other girls' dolls. It doesn't have much hair—see? (points) Her mother said she'd get her another doll and she forgets. She thinks her mother is mean. (To?) She thinks about being in another family.

It is understandable that someone who is concerned with the moment will think that socializing adults are mean, especially when they demand delay of gratification. It is also noteworthy that the story teller doesn't deal with motives or intentions for parental "forgetting."

Emotional Lability

Intense negative emotions lead to the use of avoidance or other defensive mechanisms for affect regulation, which emphasize short-term relief and avoidance of conflict. The emotions are generated by the stimulus or unexpected events or provocations that are not clearly or logically tied to a context. The affects at this level are not as raw or disorganizing as at the previous level. Thus, characters are not in a state of panic, terror, or blind rage. The story below was told by a first-grade boy who appeared upset by the provocative stimulus and wished to avoid the anxiety generated.

Card 8BM: I can't see behind the light. I don't even like the way this picture looks. It's scary. I had a dream like this picture last night but it was worse. This boy, and there was his brother and he got sick and they had to take him to the hospital and they had to do something about it. And the boy went home and said, "My brother is sick and he won't be coming home for a while." (Feel?) Sad. (To?) Bad. (Happened?) You don't want me to say it, do you? (Yes) You know what I mean, don't you? (Not really) Never mind. (Go ahead and say it) Never mind. I forgot.

Lack of Purpose

Characters simply act or react without a plan or context. They react to external demands or opportunities but don't set their own goals, plans, or purposes. In the following action-packed story told by a 9-year-old boy (IQ = 133), things just happen, and actions are performed without purpose or direction.

Card 3BM: I'm taking a walk and my shoe falls off and I find my shoe and go home. The dog bites me. I lay down on the couch. There's a tack on the couch when I lay down and I jumped off. Landed on a pin cushion and jumped. The dog bit me again. (To?) Then I went to bed. (Feel?) I was limping and felt sick.

Lack of Insight

The narrator does not integrate events with inner affective experience, and the story is marked by lack of insight and unawareness of inner motives. There's the sense that the stories have no meaning beneath the verbiage. In the story below told by a first-grade boy, a woman is extremely vigilant while the "kid's asleep." However, the reasons for the concern are obscure.

Card 5: She's looking in to see if the kid's asleep. She keeps an eye on him every four, five minutes. So he's asleep—if he wakes up, she can sing a song to him so he can go back to sleep. She loves him and she doesn't want him to get hurt. Somebody she didn't know could come in the window. It turns out to be OK; he doesn't get hurt overnight.

Organizational Deficits

The narrator doesn't spontaneously use resources to structure the story telling task but relates story elements without applying critical thinking skills to analyze the situation or to realistically sequence events. Such poor organization can be associated with attentional or other cognitive limitations, as well as with a passive orientation to tasks where the individual fails to exert active effort to be precise in the organization or structure of the story.

The following story was told by a 13-year-old, seventh-grade boy having difficulty in school due to poor organizational skills. The boy in the story acts independently to buy a violin and then, without even knowing what the strings are for, starts to play very well. He then becomes a famous musician (Beethoven) at which point he's happy and all his worries are over. The various components of the story do not "add up" in a conceptually meaningful way.

Card 1: This kid goes and buys a violin and brings it home. He wants to learn how to play. He takes it out of the box and sets it down. He's looking at it and wondering what the strings are for and then he starts to play and he's very good. And gets to be a professional and he becomes a real professional and becomes a real Beethoven. (To?) "Boy, do I want to be really good at this now that I am—no more worries." (Feel?) Happy, glad.

Problem-Solving Deficits

The resolution of tensions in the stories reflects ineffective problem solving or inaction. Characters rely on the passage of time or on being rescued by others. They may also ignore, unrealistically escape, or avoid the problem.

The following story told by a kindergarten girl begins with a description of each character that is closely anchored to the stimulus. The girl deals with a verbal provocation through physical aggression and then leaves the scene.

Card 2: A girl is going to school. And her brother is with the horse. It's a white horse. He's mowing the fields. The mom is by the tree. The brother is bringing the horse to the shed. She goes to school. She gets in a fight with someone and she gets real mad. (Before?) Someone called her names and she punched them. (Think?) She thinks everybody's mean. She goes home.

Extreme Readiness to Respond

The story reflects a tendency toward emotional overreactivity, especially with anger and external blame. The proclivity to react to isolated provocation rather than objectively sizing up the situation results in failure to learn from the experience. In the following story told by an incarcerated male, age 20 (with below-average IQ), the characters display an extreme readiness to respond to provocation.

Card 8BM: Once upon a time many years ago when I was a young boy around 15 or 16 (personal chatter), I used to go with my next door neighbor—she had a younger brother, Johnny, a good kid—always done what I said—that's why I liked him so much. When she got older I fell in love with her—I used to hang around with Johnny a lot. One day I had too much to drink. I saw his sister, was talking to her—her dad didn't like me—so he struck me—I hit him back. She said, "Stop! Don't do that ! It's my dad." I said that's OK. Later I heard a noise. It was Jimmy. I yelled, "Jimmy, what you doing here so late? I came to shoot you for hitting my dad. But we been friends for so long. No, I'm going to kill you. I don't want to hurt you. I guess you have no choice, we used to be the best friends until now. So do what you have to do cause I will too." In a split second got shot. "No Jimmy, I quit. I will put my gun on the ground and I will apologize to your dad and sister cause we are best of friends." So Jimmy agreed with me—put his gun down. I picked my gun up and shot Jimmy inside. I thought I had killed him but I didn't. I took him to the doctor three houses down. They put him on table—operated—found bullet deep in his abdomen. Said he might live—sixty/forty chance. So from that day on, Jimmy got well. So I moved away from there so I could start a new life. Seven years later I hear Jimmy got married and had three kids, two boys and one girl. His sister Betty got married, one son, and what I'm doing now is I own my own business and have a nice wife and home.

Absence of Internalized Connection

Experiences or activities are not tied to an enduring sense of self, nor to interest, empathy, or commitment to ideals. Without such connections, there is extreme need for external restraint since the individual's words and actions are detached from inner meaning and are tied only to the whim or contingency of the moment.

The following story told by a first-grade girl indicates no sense of inner restraint or matching action to provocation. Rather, the story teller simply reacts to the violent cues provided in the picture without context, distance, or reflection.

> Card 8: Those men are going to kill that man because he stole their money. I can't think of anything else. (Think?) . . . (Feel?) . . . (To?) He dies and they get their money back.

The following story told by a kindergarten girl illustrates a lack of commitment to an initial intention.

> Card 1: A boy with an airplane. He has a picture here. He's thinking to fix the airplane that's broken. (Before?) He was playing with it, and it just got broke. He leaves it there. (Feel?) Don't know.

Level Three: External Self-Maintenance

Behavior is guided by external standards rather than by the provocation or wish of the moment or by perceptual (stimulus) details. Various elements of the current situation and relationships are more realistically assessed than at previous levels. Exchanges with others are closely monitored because external reactions provide the clues to self-evaluation and for the operation of a crude notion of reciprocity. The individual relies on external sources to monitor and direct behavior, even when the tasks or goals are accepted as legitimate or self-imposed. The individual is able to anticipate the reactions of others and seems oriented to regulate behavior accordingly. However, self-esteem is vulnerable to fluctuation and, therefore, may be a central concern. Feelings about the self and others can shift dramatically, compelling the individual to regulate behavior to the immediate feedback or to seek acceptance or approval. The person cannot initiate or sustain autonomous behavior without external feedback or bolstering. The story content revolves around more long-term expectations, more general, less narrow, or trivial concerns such as conformity to more complex external demand (grades, social expectations) rather than momentary whim or avoidance of socially expected activity (e.g., going to school). The story is not unlikely but might be mildly unrealistic or naive.

Interpersonal reciprocity is quid pro quo, and the individual relies heavily on rules and expectations that are applied to the evaluation of people. Highly judgmental attitudes may be expressed by or about characters. There may be awareness of a sense of struggle to feel normal or to meet expectations in some situations. An example would be a moderately impulsive child who wants to be good and has some awareness of impulsiveness. Likewise, if stories are inadequate, the narrator has insight and appropriate discomfort.

Because the individual's perception of self and other is not well differentiated, there is a sense that emotions attributed to characters are somewhat simplistic or naive. Characters are capable of some insight, but such awareness does not always help them in modulating their behavior.

Emotional or cognitive impediments associated with self-regulation at this level are (1) The individual can size up situational demands and anticipate consequences of actions but there is some difficulty giving inner direction to efforts without external guidance. Emotional reactivity or difficulty organizing ideas may lead to reliance on external feedback and structure. (2) Self-esteem is vulnerable to upset because it is externally bolstered. Therefore, there is reluctance to take risks and limited initiative or resourcefulness of characters or of the narrator in dealing with the story telling task.

Behavior is socially appropriate, with awareness of interpersonal reciprocity and basic notion of right and wrong. However, the individual needs help in defining or solving problems and general bolstering. The child may perceive day-to-day expectations as legitimate but burdensome. Tolerance for frustration and persistence of independent action is boosted by external support.

Characteristics that necessitate reliance on external sources for self-regulation are illustrated below.

Limited Differentiation of Inner Motives

Reliance on external guidance or expectations is associated with limited distinctions of inner attributes and motives. Emphasis on external events rather than insight or inner direction is illustrated in the story below told by a kindergarten boy. The character responds to how others treat him without constructive insight or action. However, he is not trapped in the present (as in the previous level) but can envision feeling better and doing something else in the future.

> Card 3: He's crying right now. Doesn't feel good . . . sleepy. He's thinking when he isn't sleepy, he can go out places and do things. He's sad. (Before?) He was all happy and now he's tired. Sad cuz his friends don't want to play with him anymore. (To?) He's all happy and people will play with him.

The following story told by a kindergarten girl includes all of the characters in the picture but does not differentiate their feelings as depicted by the stimulus. Setting the family into a "picture" provides a context for a common activity, which offers a partial explanation for the unusual stance of the characters portrayed.

> Card 7GF: There's a girl and she's carrying a little baby. Her mother is looking at the baby. They're taking a picture. They play with the baby and they feel happy.

Reflection to External Demands Rather than Inner Direction

Perceived norms and consequences guide behavior rather than inner drive. Characters do the right thing due to external pressure, approval, duty, or reward. The following story told by a fourth-grade boy is about a girl who decides to go to school to gain the family's approval and to avoid being ignored. Otherwise, there is no genuine interest expressed in school or in the family.

Card 2: The mother sent her daughter to school and she doesn't want to go and she just stands there. So they ignore her so all she can do is go to school but she doesn't want to. So she thinks about whether she should stay or go to school. She decides to go and gets a good education and her mom likes her for doing that. Well, she . . . mom does like her but what I mean is, she approved of that.

The following story told by a sixth-grade boy has elements similar to the one above. The child's efforts are driven by parental pressure. Furthermore, his improved performance is unrealistic (no mention of studying or extra help but gets an A+). The narrator seems aware of external constraints but perceives them to be unfair, given his difficulty meeting these standards.

Card 3: It's a boy about 12½ years old. And he got invited to a big party. When he got home from school, he asked his parents if he could go. The boy had a D average in math, and his parents wouldn't let him go unless he passed his next test. A week later, he comes home with his test and he got a D on it. He went to his bedroom and didn't come out for a few hours. When his parents saw him, they felt sorry for him. They thought they were hard on him. So they gave him another chance. The party was still a week away and there was another math test the same week. The day after the test, he came home with an A+ and his parents let him go to the party. (Feel?) He's mad because his parents wouldn't let him go the party unless he gets a passing grade. (Think?) Thought it was unfair his parents wouldn't let him go.

Constructive Action Does Not Follow Insight

The following story told by a fifth-grade boy illustrates some insight about the feeling of the character. However, the story resolution does not indicate that the character can act constructively on the insight.

Card 3: She looks like she's crying. Something bad happened to her, like she got in trouble. She didn't do her housework. She's sitting on the floor, crying on her bed. That's all. (Think?) She's thinking she should have done her chores and she wouldn't have got in trouble.

Motivational Difficulty

The character has difficulty meeting legitimate external demands or attaining goals or aspirations without external incentive. The child may find tasks odious but desires successful performance.

The following story was told by a third-grade girl (age 8–3) referred for not completing school work (VIQ = 141, PIQ = 130, FSIQ = 140, low scores, Digit Span = 8, Coding = 6). The narrative is imprecise, given the child's intelligence, but seems consistent with the reported lack of motivation and concerted effort. The character is pressured to succeed despite obstacles and lack of interest and achieves a wistfully grandiose and fantastical success.

> Card 7GF: This little girl, she didn't want to practice her piano lessons and she didn't really want to become a pianist. Well, she had to because her mom forced her just by saying, "Susan," which was the little girl's name, "you go to class, your piano class, or else I'll take your ballet." So she says, "Alright, mother," and she goes to class and she becomes a major pianist and she wins an Academy Award for music and she becomes famous and they, and she lived happily ever after.

Affective Sensitivity

The narrator needs support because of a tendency to become easily upset and/or to experience frustration in response to external performance demands. The character is unable to move beyond the emotion to constructive coping effort but seems aware of falling short. Unlike the previous level, the emotion itself is not based on fragments of events but on the appraisal of the entire scene.

The following story was told by an eleventh-grade girl (age 16–9) referred for testing by parents due to academic difficulty (e.g., poor organization and problems finishing tests on time; VIQ = 117, PIQ = 108, FSIQ = 114).

> Card 4: Um . . . The man came home from work one day and his wife or girlfriend was not there and he was suspicious of her because she's usually home and when she finally did get home . . . um . . . they had a fight and he decided to leave, but she tried to stop him and explain to him where she had been, but he was so angry that he didn't bother listening, and he left.

In the above story, efforts to put events into perspective and take appropriate action do not succeed because of intense emotions.

Level Four: Normative Standards

At this level, behavior is guided by standards that are inner representations of the values of others and that the individual feels competent to attain. Since these are internalized, there's more initiative and a greater tolerance of frustration in resolving conflict and pursuing socially accepted life tasks or goals. Story resolutions are effective, and narratives include constructive action that may involve actively seeking appropriate use of external support.

At the previous level, a person could find a niche and enjoy a sense of adjustment, provided that the external environment gave adequate support or guidelines. At this level, the individual displays self-reliance in the pursuit of long-term interests and maintains relatively durable interpersonal connections. Interactions or undertakings are not usually fraught with threat to the integrity of the self-esteem system. Despite some specific blind spots, individuals can balance personal goals with concerns for family and friends and coordinate long- and short-term considerations. Reciprocity is expected but does not have the demanding flavor of the previous level.

Initiative and effort are exerted to attain desired ends, but emotional investment and genuine interest in the process are not fully described. Stories focus on meeting adaptive demands rather than investment in an activity or commitment to principles.

The story below told by a fourth-grade girl describes a boy who wants to be a good violin player and who realizes that effort is needed (getting lessons). However, the absence of genuine interest and practice is noteworthy, particularly in light of the boy's great ambition.

> Card 1: A boy's thinking about how to play the violin. And he thinks it's very hard because he never played it before. He asks his mother if he can take lessons. She takes him to the store and buys a violin and looks in the telephone book for a lady to teach him violin lessons. He plays in the orchestra and some people think he was very good in playing the violin and they want him to join a group called the "Violin Stars." He feels happy. He joins the group. After he grows up and some people heard of him and they asked, "So, you want to play music in the orchestra for opera stars?" He accepts the job and becomes a success.

In the following story told by a fourth-grade boy, the character seeks help and successfully overcomes a serious problem, enabling him to assume adult responsibility.

> Card 3BM: He feels sad because he lost his job or has a drinking problem. He's crying cause he's so sad and doesn't know what to do. He'll probably call for help to help him with his drinking problem which caused him to lose his job. He gets help and gets a pretty OK job.

The following story told by a 15-year-old girl describes a character who, with the help of her mother, is able to put an initially angry reaction into perspective. Her decision to act constructively is not driven by external provocation but by her reframing the event. She relies on her own conciusions rather than blindly following parental advice.

> Card 7GF: It's this little girl's birthday. Earlier that day she had a birthday party and her best girlfriend gave her a doll and at the party, umm, they got in a very big fight over a boy. She was very upset and crying and mad at the girl. After the party, she was going to throw away the doll. And her mom came in and saw she was very upset and she said, "Do you really want to throw away the doll?" and the little girl said, "No. This is the favorite present that I got but my best friend Cindy I don't like her anymore, she's being mean to me." And her mom tells her how good a friend they were and they shouldn't fight but make up. Girl said OK and calls Cindy on the phone and apologizes and then Cindy comes over and they play dolls. (The little girl felt she was wrong?) Yes, and her mother made her realize that and that's why she called her best friend. She wasn't mad at her.

Level Five: Autonomy

An individual functioning at this level is characterized by information processing that is not restricted by immediate feelings or needs, and that integrates multiple perspectives. The individual has the capacity to reflect on feelings (not in a ruminative sense) and evaluates the impact of actions as separate from the intent. The person is capable of experiencing the full range of affects, including mixed or contradictory feelings, and makes clear distinctions between the evaluation of the target of an emotion and of the emotion itself. Such persons are able to communicate, understand, and accept each other's framework, as well as to balance the needs of self and of others. They do not gloss over the negative emotions depicted in the stimuli and describe characters who display genuine interest in other people, tasks, or activities. Thoughts, feelings, actions, story events, and characters are well coordinated in relative emphasis, context, and time frame. Persons are viewed as well differentiated and autonomous.

The following story told by a fourth-grade girl illustrates the character's genuine interest in learning to play the violin, which is fostered by the family; the child's success brings satisfaction to the family as a whole.

> Card 1: A boy with a violin, and he's curious, wondering how do you play it, how do you get different sounds out of it. He thinks it might be an interesting instrument to learn to play. So he picks up the bow and pulls it across the strings and sees it does make sounds but he doesn't know how to make a song out of it. Since he was interested, he asks his parents for

lessons and they let him go every week. After about five years, he was playing longer symphonies. (Before?) The instrument was a gift from one of his relatives. Because he learned if you practice, you can do most anything. His parents were happy they let him take the lessons because he becomes quite good at it and he enjoys it.

In the following story told by a second-grade boy, the girl accepts responsibility for her chores despite initial frustration and later communicates her good feelings to her family.

Card 3: There was this girl named Kathy. She was down because she couldn't go to a party with her friends. She had to wash dishes and clean her room, so she was crying on her bed. And then when she was finished crying, she finished all her work and went to the party because she did all her work. Then she came back and told her mother and father about the fun she had and then she went to sleep.

Summary

Self-regulatory styles operate at various levels depending on the degree of organization applied to the processing of experience. These styles shape the content and structure of an individual's awareness as reflected in the person's preoccupations, aims, actions, and reactions. Individuals regulate cognitions, affects, and behaviors to (1) monitor their responses to changing clues in the current situation, (2) direct their attention and efforts beyond current demands to more distant concerns, and (3) determine the values and priorities that give coherence and meaning to their endeavors. Five self-regulatory levels are described and illustrated with projective stories.

CHAPTER 20

Impulsivity

Impulsive behavior reflects a failure of adaptive self-regulation. Emotional expressions and cognitive appraisals of the situation at hand are based on immediate reaction without processing other considerations. Impulsivity is commonly recognized as one or more of the following: lack of reflection to inner standards and long-term goals; lack of consideration of alternatives (or details) in tasks or problem-solving situations; insufficient self-monitoring of behavior to meet external social standards or to modulate behavior to changing cues or circumstances; focusing on immediate needs and wishes rather than planning; and failure to anticipate consequences of actions to self and other people.

Impulsivity is a multidimensional construct that can be studied in terms of cognitive aspects of judgment, emotional reactions, or impulsive action. Impulsiveness has been conceptualized as a personality trait, which includes three factors (Barrat, 1985): (1) motor impulsiveness—acting without thinking; (2) cognitive impulsiveness—making quick cognitive decisions; and (3) nonplanning impulsiveness—orientation to the present time and to immediate gratification. Impulsivity is associated with a number of diagnostic syndromes in the DSM III-R and with dysfunction in various domains, such as cognitive organization and judgment, interpersonal relatedness, and self-directed autonomous behavior.

Cognitive Organization and Judgment

Disorganization and looseness of association in thought and limited capacity for sustained thinking interfere with problem-solving and task performance as well as with forming and carrying out realistic, long-term plans. Difficulty distinguishing what one senses (outer reality) and what one makes up (inner reality) leads to poor reality testing due to distortion of awareness. Information processing that is limited by efforts aimed at protecting self-esteem or selectively tuning out unacceptable possibilities (Baron, 1985) also leads to distortion. Impulsive behavior results when the rationale for action is devoid of reflection, planning, and anticipation and when the individual attends only to parts of reality by focusing on what is immediately relevant rather than assuming a broader perspective.

Interpersonal Relatedness

Acting on the provocation of the moment rather than in the context of a durable sense of relatedness leads to difficulty in experiencing continuity in relationships and maintaining a stable internal representation of self and other. Emphasis may be on the immediately shared activity, with inner experience of the relationship being less compelling.

Self-Directed Autonomous Behavior

The capacity for modulation or self-monitoring is disrupted when the individual cannot calibrate behavior to the demands of the situation. The absence of internal sources of self-regulation of emotion, cognition, and behavior result in a need for external structure to compensate for difficulty with persistence, planning, and organization, as well as for motivational deficits and emotional sensitivities that interfere with self-directed behavior.

Impulsivity can vary in degree of severity and in the underlying processes contributing to the behavior. For instance, relatively mild impulsivity may be associated with a general readiness to respond without reflection. Such quick reactions may result in accidentally causing problems, engaging in actions that are careless (e.g., grabbing), or subtle difficulties with interpersonal interactions. A more extreme manifestation of impulsivity includes recurrent socially unacceptable behaviors that violate the rights and property of others (e.g., stealing; fighting; robbery; failure to display remorse, shame, and guilt).

The essential feature of impulsivity is the reaction to immediate provocation without perspective. A teenager who feels humiliated by a much younger child has not put the provocation into a context and has not evaluated the source or intent of the jibe. The more extreme types of impulsive behavior are based on an absence of emphathic concern and connection to others, along with the subjective experience of boredom and lack of reflection on inner standards or long-term interests.

Self-Regulatory Failure

Deficiencies in the following are reviewed in reference to impulsivity: regulation of affect/arousal, regulation of cognition and attention, and regulation of behavior.

Regulation of Affect/Arousal

Self-regulation of affect/arousal is subdivided according to whether the regulatory efforts are aimed at reducing arousal or negative emotion or at increasing arousal or positive emotion.

Stimulation Reducing

Individuals who are anxious, easily overstimulated, oversensitive, easily provoked, or have poor control over emotional expression are likely to engage in avoidance or defensive behaviors that reduce threat and limit stimulation. The impulsivity is based on the disorganizing impact of fear or anticipation of adverse events. Such an individual resembles what Shapiro (1965) called the "weak" impulsive who gives in to others due to being too overwhelmed to resist their request. Such individuals may stay within the bounds of conventionality because of fear and need for approval but may have limited self-awareness and inconsistent standards for self-evaluation. Because these individuals struggle to regulate emotional arousal to keep functioning from becoming disorganized, they are very quick to rationalize or blame others and will become very short-sighted especially when threatened. They are extremely self-aborbed and utilize a variety of maneuvers to keep their emotions from having a disorganizing impact. At times, defensive and stabilizing efforts, which are designed to "save face" in the moment, are contrary to long-term interests. Under increased threat, information processing is restricted to the most immediate concerns, and observers may detect inconsistencies in actions or verbalizations.

Stimulation Seeking

Individuals who exhibit oversensitivity to reward and insensitivity to punishment seek thrills or stimulation to avoid feelings of boredom or frustration. The thrill seekers need high levels of stimulation to function efficiently and may engage in risk taking or other behaviors that are directed toward short-term gain rather than long-term self and community interests. Generally, intellectual or aesthetic details are not viewed as stimulating, and these individuals engage in thrill seeking to avoid boredom rather than to pursue complex, varied, novel, or challenging activities.

Emotions or wishful thinking determine selective attention and lead to affective centration where strong emotions or wishes pull attention. Oversensitivity to rewards and insufficient processing of possibilities for adverse consequences may prevent the individual from awareness of potential complications of actions. The process of reflection or self-evaluation does not occur unless the individual has experienced the consequences of behavior.

The subjective experience underlying impulsive behavior are boredom and lack of investment in aims and values that have little immediate personal relevance (Shapiro, 1965). There is a lack of sustained plans for personal goals or aspirations, as well as an absence of more abstract goals and ideals. Lack of empathy may lead to problem solutions which fail to consider the welfare of others. In the absence of such an internal frame of reference, an individual does not search beyond what is relevant at the moment because interests and emotional involvements are limited to immediate gains and satisfaction.

In summary, impulsivity related to difficulty in regulating emotion or arousal can be due to (1) excessive need for stimulation or (2) being easily overstimulated and reactive to emotional provocation. Individuals who cannot regulate emotion/arousal may be irritable, aggressive, easily provoked, and tend to jump to premature conclusions. The anxious person may dwell unproductively on the possible negative fallout of every action without grasping the larger context and, failing to process the entire picture, may react impulsively to only part of the information.

Indices of Emotional Impulsivity

1. Oversensitivity to card stimuli in a global way; the story teller associates to the emotions evoked by the stimulus so that the story evolves from general emotional provocation of the stimulus.
2. Overreacting to part of the stimulus; selective attention is given to aspects of stimuli that are threatening or that provoke strong emotions.
3. Characters are provoked to action by emotional reactions to previous events that do not consider broader context, only the immediate reaction. Characters react to their own feelings, are easily provoked, and jump to premature conclusions or generalizations based on emotional reactions. Initial reaction guides behavior without consideration of other possibilities. Emotions are overplayed relative to other story parts. Emotion leads to misperception, threat, or thought disorganization.
4. Characters are thrill seeking.
5. Attention and awareness are dominated by wishful rather than realistic thinking—wanting something so much that the individual attends only to part of the information. Stories may include description of highly unlikely events based on wishful thinking or actions.
6. Specific intense emotions predominate. Characters cannot control angry or explosive outbursts; fear, helplessness, loss of control pervade story content (e.g., mountains in the background erupt). Avoidance is apparent— not wanting to deal directly with interpersonal conflict.
7. Characters are devoid of enduring interest in tasks, values, activities, or relationships. They feel bored and lack curiosity or investment in tasks.
8. Characters blame others for their fate or bad feelings.
9. Emotional reaction is given to the task—the story teller becomes fidgety and changes in activity level, facial expression, body language, and/or speech patterns are evidenced.

Regulation of Cognition and Attention

The judgment of impulsive individuals is clouded by failure to organize actively or integrate information. The hallmark of impulsive cognition is a focus on part of the information without considering realistic alternatives or long-term consequences. The initial impression, which may not be correct, is not checked out by weighing all the information. The poor judgment that accompanies impulsive action may be due to one or more of the following cognitive processes: (1) difficulty shifting and focusing attention on the most important elements of a complex stimulus, task, or situation; (2) distractibility or loss of attention when more compelling stimuli impinge; (3) failure to organize or restructure information actively; and (4) concrete thinking.

Realistic planning requires the capacity to process multiple facets of information based on objective realities of the situation. Active processing of information and some degree of abstract thinking as well as capacity to shift attentional focus are needed to weigh alternative possibilities, to account for multiple perspectives, and to coordinate past, present, and future considerations.

Impulsive thinking is basically concrete in the sense that concrete cognitions are inevitably dominated by the present, and the individual responds to immediate concerns or current provocation. Concrete cognitive functioning is associated with acceptance at face value of what is presented without delving beneath the surface or seeking additional information. From the social-cognitive problem-solving perspective, children's atypical behaviors may be the result of deficits in understanding, analyzing, and modulating reactions to interpersonal conflicts with peers and/or adults (Elias, Rothbaum, & Gara, 1986; Garmezy & Rutter, 1983; Meichenbaum & Asarnow, 1979). Failure to make critical distinctions, either through ignoring or overemphasizing detail, may lead an individual to overreact to irrelevant aspects of tasks or social situations. The person may display a tendency to focus exclusively on the immediate, reacting to the obvious but missing subtle cues, or may concentrate on detail but miss the larger picture.

A key manifestation of impulsive or concrete cognitive styles in projective stories is that the stimulus rather than the respondent's inner framework determines content directly (e.g., "This is a gun so there must have been a shooting"). Furthermore, characters respond to immediate provocation and display absence of planning or of reflection. The sequence of events does not fit a realistic time pattern and does not include logical consequences to actions. There may be overspecific details, overgeneralizations, personalized statements, lack of transitions, and difficulty incorporating realistic cause-effect relationships into the story line. Judgment and problem solving fail to display sufficient (1) reality testing, (2) planning, (3) cause-effect understanding, and (4) realistic action-outcome sequences.

Indices of Cognitive Impulsivity

1. An unplanned story is told. The narrative evolves haphazardly; events are not in logical framework but are directly pulled by the stimulus or by previous story elements.

2. There is evidence of poor planning on the part of characters. Story content reflects poor understanding of cause-effect relationships. There is a vagueness or lack of clarity in processing of long-range information so that it is unrealistic. Actions are inefficient or in the wrong temporal order. Characters do not anticipate consequences or reactions of others. Information processing is based on immediate preference or wishful thinking rather than on realistic assessment of long-term consequences (e.g., character attains success just by wishing it or is preoccupied with immediate needs and wants).

3. Response is given to only a limited part of the stimulus card or focuses on isolated elements of the stimulus card without integration. Important cues in the picture are ignored or some trivial aspect of the picture are overly emphasized.

4. There is difficulty in monitoring the flow of the story; overelaboration of certain feelings or details; seeming lack of awareness of problems with telling the story; difficulty pacing the delivery of the story to the examiner; taking back part of the story; giving a lot of alternatives or elaborations that are repetitious and do not add up conceptually; lack of distance from the stimulus or from the story telling tasks as indicated by using first-person pronouns or injecting irrelevant personal comments during the story; and perseverative overelaboration or overinvolvement in trivial detail.

5. There is vagueness of thoughts (e.g., something bad happened to someone). Characters react to appearances or act on the basis of stock formulas and stereotypic expectations rather than integrative thought process. Stories are extremely glib, shallow, superficial, stereotyped, and lack insight or reflection.

6. There is difficulty in monitoring self-presentation; ideas are bizarre or socially inappropriate.

Regulation of Behavior According to Rules or Purposes

One could argue that an impulsive person is lacking an internal context or elaborated cognitive schema that serves self-regulatory functions. Without the stabilizing context of an internal frame of reference, an individual's interests may shift according to the feelings or contingencies of the moment. It is difficult to tolerate frustration, postpone gratification, or endure stress because the individual's goals and values may shift according to external provocation. If interests are restricted to the immediate concerns, there is no impetus for prioritizing actions according to long-term objectives. Externalization of responsibilities is consistent with the absence of self-reflection and the fact that the impetus for action is indeed external. Impulsive children make moral judgments on the basis of consequences rather than intentions (Douglas, 1972).

Shapiro (1965) describes the essential process of the impulsive style of functioning as an inability to base actions according to long-term stable interests coupled with the absence of the normal feelings of deliberateness or intention that motivates action. Rather, an impulsive individual acts on a whim or on the basis of an initial impression without further evaluation. A vague inclination to do something or a whim is not integrated into a fabric of current aims or interests, and actions are not constrained by enduring values or long-term concerns. Impulsive behaviors that stem from difficulty in delaying or inhibiting a response because of a tendency to react too quickly or to accidentally blurt something out does not preclude subsequent efforts to put such reactions into perspective. This type of impulsivity can be distinguished from behaviors stemming from failure to develop a conscience or standards of moral behavior.

Limitations in cognitive operations such as concreteness or integration deficits inevitably lead to a world view that is fragmented and shifting according to the external circumstance. It is difficult to exercise restraint when the individual is overcome by the immediacy of a situation and cannot put an event in context. Children diagnosed with ADHD have difficulty with governing their behavior according to internalized rules or standards as well as external consequences (Barkley, 1990). An index of behavioral impulsivity in projective stories is the absence of internal or anticipated external controls over inappropriate action. There is a general absence of a durable context for action such as goal, purpose, mission, relationship, value, ideal, principle, or stable interest. Furthermore, there is insufficient anticipation of consequences; characters get away with hostile or socially unacceptable goals or actions.

Indices of Behavioral Impulsivity

1. Characters' behaviors are provoked rather than governed by inner restraint, stable interests, or external standards. Actions lack purpose beyond immediate satisfaction. Action occurs without inhibition or modulation to the circumstance. Characters are easily provoked to yelling, withdrawing, and hitting. Emphasis is placed on action without accounting for intent. External events control fate rather than deliberate, planned action.
2. There is failure to incorporate all relevant characters into the story. Characters act without regard for the welfare of other people. Relationships lack mutuality.
3. Characters seek excitement and stimulation through power, grandiosity, and risk-taking behaviors.
4. There is absence of internal constraints to behavior such as feelings of shame or remorse for socially unacceptable behavior. Characters display absence of moral restraint and disregard for the rights, feelings, or property of others. They get away with cruelty, selfishness, antisocial, hostile, aggressive, vengeful action or explosive affect.

5. Behavior is aimed at obtaining immediate reinforcement and short-term gain. Characters pursue trivial or materialistic goals.
6. There is absence of realistic external consequences for socially undesirable actions. Inappropriate behavior does not have appropriate consequences. External guides to behavior are spurned. Expectations of authorities are seen as intrusive, unreasonable, and to be avoided.
7. There is lack of self-control over behavior; things happen accidentally. Characters say or do things that are later regretted; they hurt or alienate others without meaning to; they are bewildered by consequences that were not anticipated, and repeat misbehavior after punishment.
8. There is an unrealistic relationship of effort and outcome. Efforts are inadequate to the task, or outcomes are grandiose, unlikely, or wishful.

Summary

Impulsivity is a multidimensional construct expressed in diverse ways and in varying degrees. It is assumed that self-regulation failures in the basic cognitive, affective, and integrative mechanisms underlie impulsive behavior. Indices of emotional cognitive and behavioral impulsivity are somewhat artificially divided. The defining elements of each are: (1) *Emotional*—actions and perceptions are restricted or compelled by immediate concerns connected to emotion, arousal, interests, or motives; (2) *Cognitive*—insufficient organizational strategies are applied to information processing; and (3) *Behavioral*—internalized values, goals, or enduring interests that ordinarily guide behavior are absent. Neither inner restraint nor external inhibition is sufficient to govern behavior according to inner standards or external rules.

CHAPTER 21

Projective Stories and Aggression

The studies of aggression demonstrate the complexity in predicting from T.A.T. themes to overt behavior. It is difficult to compare studies because their methodologies vary in (1) the stimulus cards; (2) the definition of hostility; (3) the criteria for selecting subjects for group membership (e.g., clearly delinquent groups, teacher report of fighting, sociometric ratings); and (4) the scoring systems utilized. The nature of the aggression, how it is expressed, the inclusion of inhibiting factors such as external or internal punishment, the criterion to be predicted, the nature of the stimuli, and type of scoring system all contribute to the prediction.

Role of the Stimulus

Murstein (1963), citing the findings of previous research, concluded that the stimulus is by far the most important determinant of the T.A.T. response. There is some controversy about whether cards with medium or low stimulus pull for hostility, as opposed to unambiguous cards, are better at predicting aggressive behavior. Positive correlation with aggression is more likely if stimulus cards clearly suggest aggressive content (Bach, 1945; James & Mosher, 1967; Kagan, 1966) and have a single figure who looks clearly aggressive but is in an ambiguous situation (Kempler & Scott, 1970).

Given the provocation of an aggressive stimulus, it is important for the examiner to review the inhibitions against aggression such as anxiety or perceived consequences associated with expressing aggression (Gluck, 1955; Kagan, 1966). The message of the story includes not only aggressive behaviors but the rationale for and inhibitions against such actions.

James and Mosher (1967) compared aggressive responses of Boy Scouts (mean age 12.7) to high or low pull cards. Boys who told aggressive stories to high pull (but not low pull) cards engaged in more fighting, (according to a

319

sociometric procedure) than those who did not. Guilt over hostility was negatively related to aggressive stories told to cards with little aggressive pull. It should be noted that the cards that were described as having high stimulus pull were unstructured enough to allow individual variability.

Kaplan (1967) concluded that the level of self-reported hostility was best differentiated on cards that were relevant for aggression. The subjects (college females) with higher hostility told more aggressive stories to cards with high stimulus relevance. On the other hand, when groups of delinquent male adolescents were identified on the basis of their aggressive behavior, there was a tendency to find an inverse relationship (Matranga, 1976).

Murstein (1968) obtained two types of ratings of hostility: sociometric ratings of "friendliness" by fraternity, sorority, or dormitory members, and self-ratings of friendliness. T.A.T. cards were given with low, medium, and high relevance for hostility. Murstein argued that a trait such as hostility would not be expressed unless it was consistent with the self-concept. Thus, the average college student should be able to control the content of the T.A.T. responses to be in accord with the *perceived* self-concept rather than with the objective expression of the behavior. Furthermore, indices of inhibition of aggression were included on the basis of past arguments (e.g., Lesser, 1958; Mussen & Naylor, 1954; Purcell, 1956) that simply counting aggressive themes without considering factors that inhibit the expression of hostility (such as guilt, shame, remorse, punishment) were of little use. Murstein (1968) came to the following conclusions: By far the most important determinant of the response, accounting for half the total variability, was the nature of the stimulus. The second most important determinant was the self-concept. There were no significant differences between hostile and friendly persons determined by peer nominations. Those with friendly self-concepts made aggression more remote to distance the actor from the hostile behavior that presumably was inconsistent with self-perception. In addition, those with friendly self-concepts showed less discrepancy between the hostile stimulus and content than hostile self-concept persons.

Epstein (1962) hypothesized "that cards which have low cue relevance for a particular personality trait are more sensitive to indices of drive on that dimension, whereas cards with high cue relevance on the dimension are more suitable for measuring inhibition." A post hoc analysis of Murstein's (1968) findings supported Epstein's (1962) contention that low-relevant cards are more sensitive to measures of drive and that high-relevant cards are more sensitive to measures of inhibition.

The balance between measuring aggressive drive and control mechanisms depends on the stimulus material. Kempler and Scott (1970) reported that virtually all subjects gave aggressive responses to one of the cards that best distinguished delinquent from nondelinquent boys. The difference was found not in the amount of hostility but in the failure of the delinquent boys to include conciliatory behavior following the aggressive interaction, coupled with failure to explain the aggression in terms of beneficial or socially acceptable intent such as defending a younger brother. Thus, the aggressive card pulled a similar amount of hostility from both groups, but the intent of the action and its place in the larger interpersonal interaction differentiated the groups.

Kagan (1956) argued that "if an individual does not report an aggressive theme to a stimulus which regularly elicits aggressive content one might assume that anxiety over aggression has led to inhibition of an aggressive interpretation. It is assumed that such a subject is apt to inhibit overt aggressive acts in other interpersonal situations as well" (p. 390).

However, such a conclusion requires caution. Matranga (1976) reported that the more aggressive institutionalized male delinquents told less hostile T.A.T. stories. Since four of the six cards administered had high stimulus pull, it appeared the subjects were *avoiding* hostile content. A story that ignores or contradicts the stimulus pull represents an inappropriate response that may be motivated by (1) flagrant attempts to fake in an antisocial individual; (2) insensitivity to the features of the task (which may underlie other inappropriate behaviors); or (3) avoidance due to oversensitivity. The reason for the failure to deal with the stimulus has to be clarified before one can assume that an individual who does not report an aggressive theme to a high pull stimulus will ordinarily inhibit the expression of hostility or aggression.

Telling aggressive stories to nonaggressive cards is also an inappropriate response reflecting a generalized tendency to perceive aggression in relationships that may characterize everyday behavior in an ambiguous context. Weissman (1964) found evidence that delinquent boys told more aggressive stories to nonaggressive cards.

The stimulus can be considered as a provocation with the degree of stimulus pull being systematically varied. Kagan (1956) studied the frequency of fighting behaviors among young boys (ages 6–1 to 10–2 with a median age of 7–9). The teacher ratings were based on the following: (1) tendency to start fights at the slightest provocation and (2) tendency to hold in anger and not to express it overtly. He found support for a direct and positive relationship between fighting expressed in fantasy and in overt behavior with stimuli that suggest aggressive content. It is important to note that the pictures in this study did not depict fighting, and the children could tell nonaggressive stories without seriously distorting the stimulus. Kagan states, "There is a limit to the amount of structure that should be imposed on a fantasy stimulus in order to measure a subject's tendency to avoid aggressive interpretation. The non-psychotic child strives to be accurate in his interpretation of external stimuli" (p. 392).

The tendency to respond with content relating to fighting to such cards may be interpreted as an impulsive action provoked by the stimulus. If the stimulus is highly structured and pulls for aggressive themes, their absence must be explained. If it is neutral or provides no pull, then the reason for giving such themes must be questioned. The interpretation requires knowledge of the stimuli, and relevant units of interpretation may not remain constant across cards.

Measurement of Hostility and Delineation of Comparison Groups

Studies vary in scoring systems and in the criterion behaviors for designating comparison groups. The essential question to be answered concerns what scoring elements relate best to what criteria.

Behavior is multiply determined, and thematic content as a sample of behavior is also multiply determined. Aggressive activity is generally not socially sanctioned. Therefore, its direct expression is likely to be inhibited when it is inconsistent with the self-concept. The inhibition may occur on two levels. One is at the level of fantasy expression, and the other is in the behavioral manifestation. At the fantasy level, inhibition can occur in many ways: (1) avoidance of hostile content, even under conditions of high stimulus pull; (2) putting the hostile behavior into an *acceptable context* such as a socially approved intent or expressing shame, guilt, remorse, restitution, or punishment; (3) distancing the action from the character by positing a special circumstance or describing people as removed in time and place; and (4) distancing the story from the narrator by describing the characters as "bums," as unsavory, or as otherwise not acceptable to the story teller.

At the behavioral level, aggressive behavior could occur for any number of reasons: absence of controls, misperceiving situations as hostile and thus being confrontational, deliberate manipulation, or feeling of entitlement to immediate gratification. Aggression can be behaviorally expressed in various ways: verbal, physical, passive withholding, or active provocation. Aggressive behavior can be intentional or can stem from inability to inhibit reaction. Likewise, aggression can be direct or indirect (e.g., vandalism or theft versus personal violence). A child with a history of delinquency is different from one who is rated by his teacher as easily provoked to fight.

In the Kagan (1956) study, there was a match between the grouping (teacher reports of "tendency to start fights at the slightest provocation") and the scoring critera (depiction of fighting behavior to stimuli showing boy-boy interactions). Kagan (1956) suggests that there be a match between the prediction and the criterion. In his study, children rated as most likely to initiate fighting behavior produced significantly more fighting themes than boys rated as extremely nonaggressive. Possibly other categories of aggressive fantasy were not significantly related to the behavioral ratings.

It has been demonstrated (Davids, 1973; Henry, 1982; Lesser, 1958; Mussen & Naylor, 1954; Purcell, 1956) that simple content scores tallying aggression are of little use unless they consider the inhibitions present in the story that moderate their expression. These include both internal and external punishment. Mussen and Naylor (1954) found that lower-class boys (ages 9–0 to 15–8) who show a high level of fantasy aggression, coupled with a small degree of fear of punishment, engage in more aggressive behavior than those with a low level of fantasy expression and high fear of punishment related to aggressive themes.

The degree of correspondence between the criterion and the thematic elements is an important consideration for behavioral prediction. Karon (1981) indicated that thoughts predict thoughts, actions predict actions, and feelings predict feelings. Hafner and Kaplan (1960) differentiated overt and covert hostility, defining the former as the hostility that is manifest and direct, and the latter as the hostility that is insidious, indirect, disguised, or latent. They found the correlation between overt and covert scores on the T.A.T. to be significant and negative so that a person scoring high on one would score low on the other.

Some have argued that T.A.T. aggression would translate into overt behavior when there is cultural or familial support or encouragement for aggressive behavior. Under conditions of maternal encouragement of aggression, there was a greater correspondence between fantasy and overt expression in children (ages 10–0 to 13–2) (Lesser, 1958). However, inhibitions to aggression within the stories themselves were not measured.

The method of identifying groups is relevant for prediction. Studies using self-report such as Murstein (1968) or Kaplan (1967) have found a relationship with direct expression of aggressive themes to cards with aggressive pull. Perhaps such individuals do not inhibit the expression in fantasy. There is some evidence indicating that among college students hostile thematic content is related to self-concept but not to sociometric ratings (those extremely low on friendliness were assumed to be hostile) (Murstein, 1968).

Another issue with respect to delineating groups is in how extreme they are. Group comparisons have been based on the following: (1) subdivisions within groups of children in regular classes (Kagan, 1956); (2) sociometric ratings of Boy Scouts (James & Mosher, 1967); (3) subgroups of delinquents (Matranga, 1976); (4) ratings of "overall tendency to be aggressive"; (5) aggressive versus nonaggressive boys in a hospital setting (Davids, 1973); and (6) antisocial boys versus normal comparison (Kempler & Scott, 1970).

Weissman (1964) utilized subgroups and clear-cut comparison groups by including institutionalized acting-out boys subdivided into aggressive and less aggressive groups, as well as by contrasting noninstitutionalized aggressive and nonaggressive male adolescents. The major conclusion was that thematic content is most likely to differentiate between groups that are clearly different with respect to aggression. Nevertheless, an analysis of scoring elements that differentiate *behaviorally* distinct groups of children requires consideration of the *stimulus pull* of the picture cards.

Kempler and Scott (1970) compared antisocial boys ($N = 17$) who were selected by teachers for a study of delinquency on the basis of "serious and persistent antisocial characteristics" with a matched comparison group. They reported the following findings: The antisocial group perceived people as less nurturant, less conforming, and less conciliatory. They told fewer stories that included interaction among people and they elaborated less positive emotions and less guilt. The aggressive cards discriminated the best. All boys told aggressive stories, but the aggressive boys did not include conciliatory actions nor did they rationalize aggression in terms of beneficial intent. While *hostility* per se didn't differentiate the groups, the view of people did. People had less conformity, less remorse, and story figures were less helpful.

With regard to the stimulus, they concluded that a combination of cards that represented single figure, situational ambiguity and some cue relevance for aggression might be best suited for eliciting aggressive content in antisocial children.

Mussen and Naylor (1954) measured fantasy aggression and fear of punishment associated with aggression in lower-class boys (ages 9–0 to 15–8) who had been in conflict with school or court authorities. Among lower-class boys, a greater degree of fantasy aggression was associated with more behavioral aggression. However, those who exhibited a high level of fantasy aggression and a low degree of fear of punishment relative to the fantasy aggression were the most aggressive behaviorally.

James and Mosher (1967) looked at T.A.T. stories of Boy Scouts and found that the number of aggressive themes told to high stimulus cards differentiated between groups designated with a sociometric procedure. It should be noted that some of the "high pull" cards in this study would be seen in other studies as medium pull cards because they were not so highly structured that they consistently elicited aggressive themes. The authors stated with regard to the stimulus, "If the aggressive cues depicted thematically are too intense, too many subjects will report aggressive stories out of respect for the stimulus properties. Yet, some fairly specific cues must be depicted" (p. 66).

Davids (1973) did not find a strong relationship between aggressive content and ratings of aggression in boys (ages 7 to 12–5 with mean of 9–9) who were institutionalized for severe emotional disturbance.

Conclusions and Implications for Assessment

A multifaceted approach to the prediction of overt aggression is necessary. The folowing general conclusions are based on the foregoing literature review:

1. Prediction is best if there is a correspondence between predictor and behavioral criterion. Karon (1981), referring to Tomkins (1947) with regard to

prediction, emphasized the need to look at the level of expression in terms of thought, dream, feeling, or overt action. Covert and overt levels may be inversely related in thematic expression, and only the overt level is expected to be expressed in direct action.

2. Groups defined according to varying characteristics represent different aspects of the hostility/aggression dimension, and predictors must be in line with the characteristics of criterion groups that are best differentiated if they are clearly distinct with regard to aggression (Weissman, 1964).

3. Hostility that is consistent with the self-image or is encouraged in the environment may be more directly expressed in behavior. It has been argued that when aggressive behavior is consistent with self-concept, there may be less inhibitions to its direct expression in fantasy and in behavior.

4. Two major aspects to aggressive themes are the intensity and type of aggressive drive and mechanisms of control or inhibition. Little attention has been given to differentiating aggressive themes that are gruesome or sadistic from less extreme forms of interpersonal violence (Purcell, 1956). The amount of aggression/hostility per se may not distinguish the groups. The balance among content relating to aggression and its control, intent, and consequence must be considered. The likelihood of overt aggression depends, in part, on the perceived consequences of aggression that can be internal (feelings of remorse, guilt, shame, concern for the victim, desire to make restitution) or external (punishment, humiliation). External punishment was more frequently noted among the antisocial men, whereas the comparison group expressed more frequent internal punishment than external (Purcell, 1956). High expression of aggressive need, coupled with a low ratio of anticipation of punishment, was associated with a high amount of aggression among a group of lower-class preadolescent boys (Mussen & Naylor, 1954). Consideration of aggression, along with perceived consequences, appears more effective than a simple frequency count of aggressive themes. Other dimensions of story characteristics that have an indirect relationship to hostility (e.g., interpersonal relatedness) are highly relevant. Individuals can deliberately choose not to include aggressive content but it is harder to fake the depiction of genuine reciprocal interpersonal relationships.

5. The stimulus characteristics may elicit different aspects of hostility/aggression. Studies using cards with high-stimulus relevance to which subjects gave aggressive themes relied on characteristics that inhibited aggression, such as internal or external punishment or description of interpersonal qualities and relationships that are inconsistent with aggression. Aggressive themes told to ambiguous or low-cue relevance cards have different interpretive significance than those told to cards with high stimulus pull. When using high-relevance cards, it is best to look for indices of inhibition. If aggression is expressed to low-relevance cards, then it is more significant for acting-out behavior.

6. Mitigating circumstances of aggression should be considered. A reasonable explanation for aggression such as being drunk or subject to extreme

provocation suggests that it is not sanctioned under ordinary circumstances. Tomkins (1947) suggests that the remoteness of the condition under which antisocial wishes are expressed be considered. Remoteness relates to the use of time, place, and personal attributes in a way that suggests that the behavior does not occur under everyday conditions.

7. It may be important to consider the interpersonal context for aggression and essential attitudes toward people inferred from the stories. Mutual respect and empathy would probably preclude overt, willful aggression. Kempler and Scott (1970) found that acting-out boys attribute less conformity and remorse to their characters than a comparison group. Furthermore, story figures were portrayed as being less helpful than those of normal boys.

8. If there is satisfaction in work, relationships, and long-term goals (as opposed to control, dominance, immediate gains, material possessions), then these satisfactions are barriers to aggressive, antisocial acts that are for short-term gain.

It is important to note that factors other than aggression appear to be related to chronic delinquency and acting-out behavior. Other known characteristics of antisocial and delinquent populations have not been systematically related to elements of T.A.T. stories. Inaccurate perception of Rorschach stimuli is associated with greater likelihood of becoming involved in confrontational situations (Exner, 1986) but has not received much attention with regard to projective stories.

The foregoing review of the literature on predicting aggressive behavior suggests that such prediction requires integration of many contributing elements, as listed here:

1. *Appropriateness of Story Content to the Stimulus*   If there is high-cue relevance, is the aggression overly extreme or is aggression/hostility excluded? If there is low relevance, is there expression of aggression/hostility that is unprovoked by the stimulus?

2. *Intensity of Expression of Hostility/Aggression*   The centrality of aggression to story plot, including vividness and elaboration of aggression, needs to be considered, as well as the degree of violence or cruelty.

3. *Level of Expression of Hostility/Aggression*   Hostility can vary in its expression from being overt to covert and direct to indirect. Is the aggression manifested in direct action, threat, wish, or thought?

4. *Object of Aggression*   Aggression can be aimed at different targets such as property, person, society, or animal. What are the characteristics of victims? Are they weaker? Noncompliant? What are the relationships between victims and aggressors?

5. *Intent of Aggression*   Since hostility per se may be an appropriate response to the stimulus, its *intent* is important to gauge. Sometimes intent is not

stated as the content is directly provoked by the stimulus (e.g., "This is a gun so he must have shot someone"). Different types of intentions are as follows: (a) no intent—the story is a direct, unmodulated reaction to the emotional provocation of the stimulus; (b) the character is provoked by others in the story; (c) aggression is simply a way of life; (d) a socially acceptable intent such as defending self, others, or general principle; (e) the character is puzzled as to why such behavior occurred; there is a sense of accidental, impulsive action; and (f) the character gets gratification, gains material things, and subjugates others.

6. *Consequences of Aggression*   Both internal and external restraints that inhibit the expression of aggression are significant: (a) *Internal*—Is there remorse or guilt? Is remorse expressed after being caught? Does it prevent future occurrences? Is there genuine concern or attempts at restitution? (b) *External*—Is there punishment for wrongdoing? If so, what is the timing or severity? Is external punishment effective or does the behavior recur despite repeated punishment?

7. *Acceptability of Hostility/Aggression*   What is the attitude of the story teller to the aggressive content? Does the story teller attempt to distance the self from the aggressive theme by characterizing the action as remote in time, place, or location? Are there mitigating circumstances such as description of the offending character as operating under special circumstances such as being drunk, disturbed, confused, or facing extreme provocation? Is there any evidence of the narrator's disparagement of the aggressive behavior (e.g., a bum)?

Summary

Literature pertaining to the prediction of aggressive behavior based on the content of projective stories is reviewed to extract implications for assessment.

CHAPTER 22

Conduct Disorder

Classifications of childhood disorders based on empirical multivariate approaches have clearly distinguished the dimensions of conduct disorder from anxious-depressed withdrawal (Quay, 1986). In terms of associated emotions, the conduct disorder is characterized by chronic boredom, whereas affective symptoms of depression, anxiety, and suspicious apprehension are typically experienced as a consequence of getting into trouble.

Conduct-disordered youth express their experiences with extreme envy, grandiosity, as well as with inner emptiness and boredom (Gacono & Meloy, 1988). They fear being controlled and readily experience anger or frustration. They are quick to blame others, exhibit unstable control of affect or impulse, and have poor tolerance for frustration, all of which may result in hair-trigger responses. The routine of life offers little satisfaction because of the tendency to be bored without excitement.

DSM-III-R (APA, 1987) defines *conduct disorder* as belonging to the class of behavior disorders in which "socially disruptive" behaviors are often more distressing to others than to those who manifest the disorder. Disruptive behavior disorders include Attention-Deficit Hyperactivity Disorder, Oppositional Defiant Disorder, and Conduct Disorder. The symptoms of these disorders covary to a great degree, and the behaviors associated with these disorders have been referred to as *externalizing symptoms* (Achenbach, 1985).

According to DSM-III-R (APA, 1987), the essential feature of conduct disorder "is a persistent pattern of conduct in which the basic rights of others and major age-appropriate societal norms or rules are violated" (p. 53). The behaviors are not isolated acts but continue for a period of six months and represent a "repetitive and persistent" pattern. Conduct and oppositional disorders are qualitatively similar (Anderson et al., 1987; Werry, Reeves, & Elkind, 1987). Oppositional, defiant disorders include some of the features of conduct disorder (CD), such as disobedience and defiance of authority, but the basic rights of others and major age-appropriate societal norms are not violated. The behaviors characteristic of CD are theft, running away from home, lying, deliberate destruction of property, truancy, physical aggression, and cruelty against others.

Associated features described in DSM-III-R (APA, 1987) are early use of alcohol or drugs and precocious sexual behaviors; disregard for the feelings, wishes, or well-being of others; and failure to experience appropriate empathy, guilt, or remorse. Furthermore, there may be symptoms consistent with additional diagnoses. Such individuals usually have low self-esteem despite the presentation of outward toughness. There is poor frustration tolerance, irritability, temper outbursts, and impulsive risk taking, as well as learning or attentional difficulties.

Conners (1970) factor-analyzed parent ratings or symptom patterns in hyperkinetic, neurotic, and normal children. He found that of five factors, only the factor of aggressive conduct disorder discriminated between hyperactives and neurotics. Robinson, Eyberg, and Ross (1980) administered the 36-item Eyberg Child Behavior Inventory (ECBI) to parents of 512 children ages 2 to 12. On the basis of the relative consistency of scores across ages, they suggested that a conduct disorder is independent of stages in the child's development and, therefore, is unlikely to be resolved by maturation alone.

Conduct Disorder and Emotional Disorder

Within the educational system, Conduct Disorder and Serious Emotional Disturbance represent two distinct but overlapping syndromes. Public Law 94-142 requires a distinction between serious emotional disturbance (SED) and social maladjustment (SM). The latter corresponds to the description of conduct disorder in the DSM. The intent was to exclude from eligibility for special educational services individuals who may require the intervention of the juvenile justice system and, therefore, may not be best served in the schools (Center, 1989; Weinberg & Weinberg, 1990).

Difficulty arises when the diagnostic criteria in the educational system exclude an entity that is viewed clinically as a disturbance. The distinction is made more difficult when the child is not under legal jurisdiction, and practical issues of placement availability confound purely diagnostic considerations. Both SED and SM are associated with poor school achievement and interfere with functioning in a normal classroom, albeit in different ways. It makes sense to distinguish SM from SED in the educational system because there are implications for intervention, program planning, and the delivery of educational services.

Emotional disturbance is an entity in which emotions interfere with thought organization and behavioral modulation. The elements are (1) thought disturbance and (2) distressing emotions such as incapacitating fears, disorienting anxieties, pervasive depressed mood, or extreme lability.

Public Law 94-142, the Education for all Handicapped Children Act, which delineates the rules and regulations for the operation of special education, defines the seriously emotionally disturbed individual as:

exhibiting one or more of the following characteristics over a long period of time and to a marked degree, which adversely affects educational performance: (a) an inability to learn which cannot be explained by intellectual, sensory, or health factors; (b) an inability to build or maintain satisfactory relationships with peers and teachers; (c) inappropriate types of behavior or feelings under normal circumstances; (d) a general pervasive mood of unhappiness or depression; or (e) a tendency to develop symptoms or fears associated with personal or school problems. (Federal Register, *Aug. 23, 1977, p. 42478)*

Learning

Youth who exhibit patterns of conduct disorder have been characterized as aggressive, impulsive, reward oriented, and stimulus seeking (see Binder, 1988, for a review). They have low tolerance for frustration; they simply tune out information that is not immediately and personally relevant. On the other hand, those classified as emotionally disturbed exhibit low-stress tolerance and vulnerability to cognitive disorganization. The learning environment needs to be structured and supportive. Such children need reduction of arousal, stimulation, and stress, and benefit from feedback and structure that simplifies the processing demands of the environment. Their thought processes worsen in unstructured situations or when dealing with affectively loaded information. Such individuals may become aggressive when disorganized in thinking.

Those classified as SM also need structure; they respond to clear rewards and punishments, not sentimentality. They are most likely to learn when material to be mastered has immediate relevance. Complicating factors for educational intervention are the frequent association of conduct disorder with learning disability and attentional deficits.

Interpersonal Relationships

Children labeled as SED typically have no friends or they play with younger children. Thought disorders impair interpersonal relationships. Difficulty with perceiving patterns of behavior over time and with making inferences about these patterns, as well as problems modulating behavior to changing cues in the immediate situation, interfere with forming relationships. Difficulties making and keeping friends are inevitable if the child cannot (1) coordinate different perspectives or separate fantasy from reality, (2) cannot back away from details or from preoccupations to focus on the main idea, (3) cannot coordinate task and interpersonal elements of a situation, and (4) cannot reconcile discrepancies or draw inferences about different levels of experience.

Reconciling discrepant messages (Reilly & Muzekari, 1986) is particularly difficult for emotionally disturbed children.

Conduct-disordered children are seen as incapable of genuine interpersonal warmth and enduring relationships. They form short-term alliances for self-serving purposes. Ruthlessness, impulsivity, egocentricity, and remorseless disregard for the rights of others preclude the formation of relationships beyond short-term ties for mutual gain. Fear of being controlled or victimized or simply lack of perspective leads often to assuming a grandiose role.

Differences between boys considered aggressive and nonaggressive by teachers and peers have been found in the interpretation of social situations (reviewed by Whalen & Henker, 1985): (1) aggressive boys are more likely to infer hostile intent in the behavior of their peers (Dodge, 1980; Dodge & Frame, 1982; Nasby, Hayden, & DePaulo, 1980); (2) aggressive boys process less information in a situation (Dodge & Newman, 1981; and (3) aggressive boys are more likely to generate aggressive and inept solutions when presented with real-life or hypothetical problem situations (Dodge, 1980; Richard & Dodge, 1982).

Whalen and Henker (1985) concluded that these differences are apparent primarily in ambiguous situations. Furthermore, regardless of measured intelligence, middle class disturbed and antisocial adolescents were substantially deficient in interpersonal problem-solving skills when compared with normal youth (Spivak & Levine, 1963). Deficiency in "means-end" thinking was particularly pronounced.

Ideation

Yochelson and Samenow (1977a; 1977b) defined conduct disorders in terms of cognitive-behavioral style such as irresponsibility, specific thinking errors, and general thinking patterns. They indicated that a key aspect of the sociopath's thinking pattern is the exclusion from awareness those aspects of personality that would diminish grandiose self-perceptions or lead to questioning their exploitive and ruthless behavior toward others. The externalization of responsibility manifested by sociopaths is viewed by Gacono and Meloy (1988) as attributable to the defense mechanism of splitting (Kohut, 1971), which at its most primitive is denial and at its most advanced is rationalization. The lack of integration of experiences of good and bad affect makes possible the simultaneous presence of grandiosity (unrealistic, overvalued self-representation) and of inner emptiness and boredom. These two states are kept separate and not synthesized into a cohesive self-unit. The acting-out behavior and grandiosity of conduct-disordered youth prevent the experience of emptiness and boredom (Gacono & Meloy, 1988).

Concrete thinking and "fragmentation" (Yochelson & Samenow, 1977a) also characterize this population. Concrete thinking is manifested in vacillating views of people over time, in failure to learn from experience, and in drawing conclusions from a few concrete clues. Fragmentation or lack of integration can be seen in the contradictions in thinking such as the discrepancies between stated intentions and actual behavior, and between behavior and self-perceptions. With this population, one is likely to find noticeable differences between self-report (e.g., the Sentence Completion) and projective measures (e.g., T.A.T.), as well as numerous inconsistencies within the self-report measures.

The conduct-disordered individual does not reconsider a response in terms of internal standards, long-term self-interests, or the welfare of the community. Events are not placed into a broader context, so the individual does not coordinate various facets of an experience as indicated by inadequate connections: (1) among past, present, and future time frames; (2) between actions and consequences; (3) between judgments about possibility and probability; (4) among needs and welfare of more than one person; (5) between self and social system; and (6) between experience and emotion. When an event is viewed in isolation from a meaningful pattern of events, the individual does not see the necessity to delay action but responds immediately to perceived provocation.

Two other reasons for antisocial behavior are worth noting: Wishful thinking and the inability to refrain from responding to immediacy may result in being taken in by others to go along with antisocial actions. Such "passive" antisocial behavior may be spurred by the desire to take the easy way out or to get "something for nothing." Second, poor judgment, which is not due to wishful thinking or excitement seeking, results from an inability to meet information-processing demands of interpersonal relationships.

Conduct Disorder and Projective Stories

The characteristics of conduct disorders reviewed above are evident in projective stories.

Immediate Gratification   Stories reflect a view of the world at large as providing opportunities for exploitation and self-gratification. Characters cannot delay desire for gratification; their awareness is dominated by what is of immediate relevance for the self. Selective processing of information according to its immediate relevance for the self is indicated by (1) wishful thinking that confuses remote possibility with probability; (2) satisfaction of immediate personal needs; characters may focus on possible rewards to the self without interpersonal connection or interests besides immediate gain; (3) intolerance of boredom; (4) intolerance of sustained effort or work; and (5) search for stimulation.

Characters are devoid of values and interests that do not contribute to immediate gratification when (1) there is an absence of internalized values or principles that guide and regulate behavior; (2) interests are limited to that which is immediately gratifying; thus, work and study are considered boring (story teller may yawn frequently); emphasis is on outcome or success with disinterest in the process; and (3) self-regulation of affect, ideation, and behavior is in terms of immediate satisfaction. Characters do not utilize ideation but resort to action that is impulsive, shortsighted, and fails to anticipate consequences.

Absence of Insight and Foresight   Lack of insight is due to the absence of an internal framework to guide action. Lack of foresight is due to the absence of internal goals or long-term purposes to guide action. Without such an internal context, behaviors are shallow, superficial, stereotyped, and serve trivial purposes or immediate external demands. Character's actions are not planned, and consequences are not anticipated. Characters do not reflect on their actions, and behaviors are not guided by long-term purposes. Analogously, the narrative unfolds without a preconceived plan, made up in small details rather than conceptual steps. Story elements are provoked by the stimulus, whim, or previous idea.

Absence of Internal Responsibility   Characters blame the external environment or other people for their problems or failures and display an absence of remorse or guilt for their malicious acts. Their primary regret is getting caught.

Poor Control of Behavior under Provocation   Characters' behaviors are provoked rather than planned. They are prone to anger and hypersensitivity to betrayal and tend to become overwhelmed by deeply felt angers and resentments.

Flouting of Conventional Authority, Rules, and Established Social Customs   Open and undisguised expression of unacceptable content suggests a disregard of convention or inability to monitor self-presentation. People are portrayed either as ruthless or as victims of others' ruthlessness. Characters resort to violence to resolve disagreements. The story teller does not feel that conventions, even the laws of nature, apply to the self. Relationships are depicted as cruel, destructive, and sadistic.

Unidimensional View of Relationships   The view of relationships is not governed by insight, empathy, or enduring connection. The characteristics of relationships are described below:

1. *Superficial Relationships*   Stories are not based on real experience but portray phony sentimentality or stereotyped interactions. People are viewed in terms of external trappings, status, power, and possessions. Since ideations and

emotions lack meaning beyond the moment, responses may be appropriate to the circumstance but are divorced from a sense of enduring reality. Similarly, efforts of characters are lackadaisical and not persistent because they have momentary meaning. There is no empathy, interest, connection, or investment in relationships or principles that provide coherence to subjective experience due to a lack of internalization and inner structure to the personality.

2. *Manipulative/Exploitive Relationships*   There is little regard for the well-being or safety of others, and people are used as means to ends or to satisfy needs. One character may be described as a victim of ruthless circumstances and may exhibit self-pity. However, for one person to be a victim, others must be devious, controlling, punitive, mistrustful, vengeful, or hostile. Attitudes and actions toward others are justified by projection, which is the prime defense mechanism. The presentation of the self as victim or as indignant bystander subjected to unjust persecution and hostility is an excuse to mistrust others.

3. *Dichotomous Relationships*   People are weak or strong, superior or inferior, victim or persecutor, winner or loser. Sensitivity to being betrayed, manipulated, victimized, or controlled leads to the fear that strong people force others to do their will. There is a demanding quality of relationships where people are available on demand to help a family member or loved one. One person is the hero, whereas another is helpless or remains ill defined. Relationships have unequal power, and devaluation of others is fostered by lack of empathy and the conviction that "might makes right."

4. *Extremely Cruel or Sadistic Relationships*   Characters take pleasure in usurping the rights, privileges, and property of others. They take revenge and feel vindicated when other people are demeaned. The search for power (not autonomy) springs from an expectancy of a dog-eat-dog environment, along with a deep well of hate and desire for retribution or vindication.

Case Illustrations

Case One
Jimmy, age 10–11, had been retained in the third grade and was referred because teachers were concerned about his behavior and suspected that he was not achieving in a manner commensurate with his ability. His Full-Scale IQ score was 91 according to the WISC-R. Jimmy was described as resistant to authority, disruptive to ongoing activities, and manipulative of teachers and peers. When conversing with the examiner, he related stories about how he had lost two of three girlfriends by deliberately humiliating them in public. Then he indicated that he can easily get other girlfriends. Jimmy also described how he and his friends would go into a laundromat, turn off the lights, and kiss some of the women. Then they would laugh at the ones who were "rejected." His stories told to T.A.T. cards exemplify the criteria described above.

Card 1: Ricky looks bored. Looks like the violin is broken or he doesn't know how to play. Can I throw it away? Looks at sheets, says this is beautiful. I wish I would play. Then he plays "I have a dream that I'll play this some day." That's it.

The expression of boredom and frustration is glibly followed by a phony but socially acceptable response where the boy plays simply by wishing it.

Card 2: This girl Susan has a bible and a notebook; she is looking at her mother who is having her 58th child and at father who is dragging his 112th horse. He is very tired. Mother is looking at sunset, wishing the baby was a boy cause she had 57 girls. She would name him Jonathan Leigh Junior, and when Susan has her baby, she'll name it after her husband, Joseph Franklin Pasinski. Susan's gonna be a lawyer, and her husband will be a doctor. Susan will live a very good life and have 42 kids.

The routine of life on the farm is absurd and tiresome. A young woman can do better than her parents by becoming a lawyer and by marrying a doctor (without any interest or effort).

Card 3BM: One day, Joseph Lee Mayers was walking down the street of Brooklyn, New York, and he met Maniey's best friend, Millicent. He started talking to her, and then the Brooklyn beast came around and they were looking for Joseph. Joseph ran to his house and he locked the door. All of a sudden, it got foggy and the fog came in and the Brooklyn beast came in and now he's dead on the couch. (Jimmy laughed and said he was the Brooklyn beast.)

The story characters are grandiose and base vindictive actions on initial impression without regard for context or intention. Actions are not modulated to the constraints of social conventions or internal principles.

Card 4: It's Friday night in Hollywood, California. It's Brooke Shields and Chevy Chase. They were walking down the street together; they stopped and saw Maniey, the Cool. Brooke saw Maniey then started going for Chevy Chase. She knew she was Maniey's lover and she tried to make Maniey jealous. Maniey couldn't stand for it, he pulled out a gun and said "Chevy, you've been waiting for this." Shot in the air four times. Chevy said, "She's not my type." Humphrey Bogart walks down the street. Maniey shot both of them. They were dead.

Relationships are manipulative, and the story teller expresses the conviction that might makes right.

Card 5: Mother walked into the room and yelled at Eunice. Eunice said, "Mamma, shut up," and mamma said, "Some weirdo is looking out here for you." Eunice says, "Let him in, probably Clyde." Eunice's husband says, "Who's Clyde?" Eunice says, "Clyde is the baddest dude in town. If he doesn't like someone, he kills 'em." Clyde comes in and throws a knife. His magnetic hand brings it back. Eunice's husband got killed, then it was Eunice and Clyde.

Again, relationships are devalued and brutal; people are interchangeable.

Card 6BM: Yesterday the Congress said to Reagan, "We have to leave the office." Reagan said, "You gotta bite me before you leave." At once they all bit him. Then Reagan said, "You have to hit me," so one at a time they all hit him. Then he said, "You'd have to kill me," which they have no guts to do. So one at a time they did it, then that's the end of Reagan.

The message of the story is as follows: Famous people bluff and dare others, thinking they won't follow through, but there are those ruthless enough to carry out that deed. Those who are least constrained by moral considerations emerge as the victor. The lack of concern with external constraints is also indicated by the fact that the story is unrelated to the stimulus.

Card 7BM: Boy named Jonathan said to his father, "You have to learn the ways of life." "I'll teach you my son," Poppa says, "I'm the best shooter in town, but you have to stand up and fight and shoot the ignorant, ugly, and mean Maniey." He (Jonathan) said, "I'll do it." (Q) That's how all of us got to live, first to kill Maniey and be first again. Jonathan will be best critter we ever had. Jonathan says, "You're dead, Maniey!" They shoot it out. Maniey wins and the town rejoices 'cause Jonathan was the baddest guy in town.

Again, the message of this story is that might makes right.

Card 8BM: Once upon a time, there was a boy named Ricky and so his best friend Derek, he used his talent. I'm making up any old stupid thing. We're surgeons . . . one day we were messing with gangsters. Derek got caught and he gets cut open, on the side. Gangsters ate Derek for dinner. Ha, ha, ha.

The story was told for the narrator's amusement and obviously flouted social convention. There is a suggestion of ruthless lack of concern and an absence of empathic interpersonal connection.

Card 9BM: Sylvester Stallone who was the baddest boldest green beret fighter. These army guys started shooting at him. He got an M-14 and started turning the whole city, shootin' it up. His wife said, "Stop." Son said, "Go ahead, Daddy, show 'em what it's like." He did, bullied 'em, and shot 'em. When getting ready to go to jail, everyone came back to life. Now he's in jail for life.

The consequences of one's actions aren't really that serious because they are based on fantasy. The story is shallow, superficial, and power oriented.

Card 10: Benjy and Laverne were the best couple that ever got married. At the wedding Maniey watched them kiss, when preacher said, "You may kiss the bride," he said, "Hold it." They said, "What's the matter with you kid?" "I want a girlfriend, bring in a little midget 35 years old." They walked down the aisle together. Maniey and Sylvia lived happily ever after.

The characters are absorbed in their self-centered wishes and mock others.

Case Two
According to records, Dwayne, age 11–2, IQ = 99, has had difficulty adjusting to school since first grade. His behavior during the past three years was marked by physically and verbally aggressive attacks on peers and teachers. This behavior occurred despite the fact that he received individual and group psychotherapy and placement in a special education program, which provided individual and small-group resource room instruction, classroom behavioral reinforcement programs, and frequent use of school crisis-intervention services. With these supports, Dwayne's behavior fluctuated from total rage to very controlled and appropriate behavior. During periods of loss of control, he assaulted both peers and authority figures, primarily by biting and kicking. These incidents were typically followed by prolonged feelings of revenge. When it was to his advantage, he has been reported to demonstrate controlled behavior. He seems unaffected by peer pressure, and his inability to maintain adequate interpersonal relationships with peers or adults has continued without change despite numerous interventions. In the classroom, Dwayne exhibits low frustration tolerance, disruptiveness, and defiant behaviors. At school, the only effective reinforcer is food.

During testing, Dwayne was cooperative until items started to become difficult for him, at which point he became negativistic and oppositional in what appeared to be an attempt to mask anxiety and exposure of weakness. At other times, he repeatedly walked around his chair while answering test items. When he was assured that there was no specific right or wrong answers, as on the projective tests, cooperation increased. He generally tended to respond quickly and to give up quickly.

To assess the effects of external sources of motivation, Dwayne was retested after an initially poor performance on the Bender Gestalt Test. With the promise of a candy bar if he tried his best, the number of scorable errors decreased significantly. Within a year of the present testing, Dwayne came under the auspices of the juvenile criminal justice system for having repeatedly robbed the apartments in the complex in which his mother was custodian.

Dwayne told the following stories to T.A.T. cards:

> Card 1: A little boy sitting there looking at his violin. He can't do it. He got mad at his violin because he couldn't play it very good. (Next?) He looked down at the table and said, "I quit." And that's it. (End?) He quits his music band for good. (Feel?) Mad. (Thinking?) That he don't want to play violin.

The inability to do something leads to anger, frustration, quitting and rationalization of disinterest.

> Card 2: A lady standing there looking at something. (Q) Man is teaching his horse to ride English saddle. Someone just got done plowing the field. (Next?) A lady is standing there. (Q) Just standing there. (Before?) Don't know (End?) Just keeps on standing there and working with the horse. (Feel?) OK, I guess. (Does he like working with his horse?) Yes, he likes it. (Others feel?) Good. (Thinking?) Going to die soon. (Who?) All of them. I even think I'm going to die sooner or later. And you will too.

The child needed prodding to generate the story, which was primarily descriptive of the stimulus until provoked by the examiner's queries. The theme of death is a convenient way to end the story, which is really not going anywhere.

> Card 3BM: A man. (Doing?) He's mad, sitting on the step. (Why is he mad?) The same reason I'd be mad at my mom. (Q) Not cleaning my room and she told me to and I didn't want to. (Next?) He goes outside and sits on the stairs. (Thinking?) His mom telling him to clean his room—about his argument—how he's going to argue. (Feel?) Mad. (End?) He don't clean his room; he plays outside just like I would do. (Mother?) Yells at him.

A child is angry and defiant when his mother tells him to work when he'd rather play. There is no relatedness, cooperation, concern, or effort at reconciliation. Characters react without any consideration for one another.

Card 4: Man and lady. Guy got shot. Wife ran over and grabbed him and she got shot in front of a barber shop, Safeway, and Sheriff's office. (Next?) Both get killed, buried, and put in the grave. (Feel?) Like they're dead. (Thinking?) Nothing, they're dead.

The story is a dramatic, movie-like scene with no context or reason for the shooting. If a wife tries to comfort her husband, even in a public place and in front of authorities, she too gets killed.

Card 5: A lady is opening the door and looking at her plants to see if they're OK. Her husband is sitting on the sofa with a knife in his hand, bullet in his stomach and slit down his leg and the guy that killed her husband comes up and stabs her in the back and she dies instantly from a broken spinal cord. (Feel?) Family hasn't found out yet. (When they find out, what happens?) Have them buried in the ground and what was on their will be handed out.

Violence is a way of life. No one grieves but takes another's possessions.

Card 6BM: Her son and old lady standing next to her and his wife got killed in a car accident. Broke her spinal cord and died instantly. In the picture they're talking about it, making up a will and the husband is being greedy. (Feel?) Unhappy. (What about?) About his wife being killed. (Thinking?) About his wife being killed, about her accident and what she looked like. (End?) She gets buried and everything from her will gets handed out.

Elements from the previous story are perseveratively included. Again, there is an emphasis on the will rather than on the value of life.

Card 8BM: Someone in the hospital getting operated on because they were in a car accident. There's a surgeon and the guy's wife (foreground). (Next?) He's in the hospital getting ready to die. Got to get his blood pressure up. (End?) He dies. She feels unhappy. (Thinking?) About all the good times they had since they got married.

The story is superficial, expressing the simplistic message that when her husband dies, a wife thinks about the good times.

Card 17BM: Looks like the Incredible Hulk climbing up the rope. (Q) To save somebody. Saves somebody. (Q) Don't know. (Feel?) Good. (Thinking?) Don't know.

A grandiose character saves somebody with little regard for the appropriate means or for the identity or circumstance of the other person. The message of the story is that a superhero like the Incredible Hunk is capable of saving people.

Summary

Characteristics of conduct disorder are described and applied to the interpretation of projective stories. Two case illustrations are provided.

CHAPTER 23

Report of the Assessment

To this point, a variety of approaches to the interpretation of projective stories has been provided. It is not necessary to use all of the approaches or to scrutinize all aspects of the personality. Rather, the professional focuses on the attributes relevant to a particular individual and gears the assessment toward clarifying the presenting problems and dealing with the practical issues at hand.

A systematic approach to story interpretation would include the synthesis of process and formal analysis of the narrative with content interpretation, and the integration of conclusions with other sources of data.

Integration of Process and Formal Analysis with Content Interpretation

What a story means is revealed by *how* it is told as well as by *what* is told. When interpreting projective stories, what is relevant is not the perspective of the characters but what the story means for the narrator. The professional does not take the viewpoints expressed by characters at face value but translates them into their implications for the subjective experiences and objective competencies of the narrator. Content may be so meager or disorganized that the interpreter's inferences are guided primarily by consideration of the story telling process and narrative structure. If ideas are random associations or fleeting reactions to the stimuli, the interpretation may pertain only to the narrator's approach to the task. When sufficient content is produced, story details are carefully scrutinized to decipher the overall meaning rather than attributing significance to isolated parts. In doing so, the interpreter also considers what is not there, given the stimulus, instructions, and age-appropriate expectations.

The interpreter's translation of what the story suggests about the narrator's phenomenology is the *import* (Arnold, 1962), which is formulated by recasting the story content into a general statement representing the narrator's convictions or attitudes. The import of the story is virtually identical with Bellak's (1975; 1986) interpretive level, both of which encapsulate the attitudes and convictions of the respondent.

The interpreter also formulates *explanatory hypotheses,* which go beyond the import by (1) explaining the reasons for the attitudes or convictions expressed in the story and (2) fostering an understanding of the presenting problems. The explanatory hypotheses resemble Bellak's diagnostic level in the sense that the focus is on the interpreter's conclusions, rather than on the narrator's perspective. The professional's theoretical orientation, skill, and knowledge base influence the systematic selection and interpretation of the available information.

The import simply states the conviction expressed by the story teller as inferred by the professional, whereas the explanatory conclusions clarify the import. A protocol that repeatedly expresses the conviction that failure is inevitable despite active effort is scrutinized for possible reasons for the development and maintenance of such an expectation. If an examination of the story telling effort reveals that ideas ramble and that characters' actions are shortsighted and occur without reflection, then these qualities would serve as the explanatory concepts that underlie the narrator's anticipation of failure. The interpreter might examine other relevant concerns such as the nature of the goals and the meaning of the failure for the narrator.

The following story told by a boy, aged 9–3, with very superior intelligence, illustrates the relationship between the import and explanatory hypotheses.

Card 2: Harvesting crops when the horse kicks me. I fall on my back and horse runs over me. I decided to do it with the oxen and he charged me. I decided to do it with the mule and when I put on plow he kicked my fingers. I decided to pull my plow myself when there was a flood. Stormy winds came together and there was a whirlpool and that was the end of one farm. And we lived horribly ever after.

Import   Despite a series of singlehanded, almost heroic efforts, outside forces keep you from getting your work done and you fail.

Explanatory Hypotheses   The interpreter's conclusions must incorporate the following: (1) efforts are perseverative; seemingly different actions are taken without conceptual change in strategy; (2) the story begins by association to the stimulus; subsequent ideas are elaborations triggered by previous story elements; there is no overall context to the sequence of events; (3) absence of reflection and integration of thinking or feeling; the narrative is an action-packed response to external forces with a notable absence of goals or deliberate planning; (4) a lack of distance is evident as the narrative proceeds in the first person; (5) efforts are singlehanded, emphasizing one character, while others are virtually ignored; and (6) the focus is restricted to the background features of the stimulus.

In general, there is inadequate coordination of inner-outer states, time, characters, and stimulus qualities. There is one track of thinking where action leads to obstacles, which lead to further actions and more obstacles. The explanatory hypotheses that clarify the import are as follows: The child's inability to step back, reflect, and organize behavior according to the clues presented leads to action without reflection and results in the perception that efforts are useless. Furthermore, the tendency to quick action in response to partial information may lead to impulsive behavior.

Integration with Other Sources of Data

Explanatory concepts that are derived from projective stories are systematically related to other test patterns and to the presenting concerns. The focus of such explanatory concepts may be on selected attributes such as *ego functions* (reality testing, judgment, self-regulation, or object relations) or *thought processes* (attention, concentration, memory, abstraction, logic, differentiation, or integration). These attributes are expressed differently according to circumstances, and a comprehensive evaluation is possible by considering multiple sources of information and by examining the data from a variety of perspectives. The import of the stories suggests how certain attributes are reflected in subjective experiences. For instance, the frustrations and lack of confidence expressed toward learning tasks in projective stories may stem from affective or cognitive processes evident from a careful analysis of the stories themselves, as well as from other sources of information. The explanatory concepts gleaned from story analysis are systematically related to conclusions based on other data.

The following stories were told by Denise, age 14, with low-average IQ, placed in a residential setting for emotionally disturbed youngsters. They illustrate how conclusions from various stories might be compared with each other and with behavior during the administration.

> Card 1: He's doing his homework and he's pissed off. (End?) He stays pissed off and doesn't do it.

Interpretive Considerations The child reacts to immediacy of events: first to the stimulus ("child doing homework and pissed off"), then to the anger that is evoked by the demands of the story telling task (query about an ending).

Import If doing school work gets you angry, you just stay angry and refuse to do it.

Explanatory Hypotheses The child is easily frustrated and readily provoked to anger; she reacts to these feelings with hostile rebellion. Her anger and frustration are in direct response to perceived external demand or provocation. Once in the grip of these feelings, she lashes out without self-control.

Card 2: She's going to school. She's thinking about something and she comes home and everything's done and so she doesn't have to do anything. (Feeling?) I don't know, how am I supposed to know? (In your story, how does she feel?) I don't know.

Interpretive Considerations   The focus is on the young woman in the foreground whose primary motivation is relief from the tedium of burdensome demands. The character is preoccupied only with her feelings and does not consider the perspectives of others. Likewise, Denise cannot take in the needs, viewpoints, or intentions of others but evaluates situations in terms of the amount of frustration or demand that is imposed.

Import   The demands of school are difficult, and you wish that other family members would do the household tasks and release you from these burdens.

Explanatory Hypotheses   The child is primarily aware of her own feelings and oriented to minimize her own frustration and anger; she has difficulty incorporating the feelings and views of others. She does not rely on long-term goals or purposes to guide her actions and thoughts; her behaviors are provoked by externally imposed elements.

During the administration, Denise was angry and resentful that she was being tested and openly expressed these feelings by yelling and cursing at the examiner. When tasks were difficult, her snappishness increased. She treated all of the tests as aversive, regardless of how much they resembled school work. When offered concrete rewards during the second session, she became more friendly and cooperative and showed efforts to control her anger even when tasks were difficult. Denise is ruled by her anger, and her momentary reaction to a task determines the degree of her effort, which results in uneven performance (evident in IQ and achievement tests). In Card 1, school work itself is a source of anger, whereas in Card 2, the character wishes to be relieved from burdensome chores. The story below jives with Denise's admission during the interview that she does not know how to resolve conflicts when she is angry.

Card 3GF: She just got dumped and she's angry at him. (End?) They never talk to each other again.

Interpretive Considerations   The anger is in response to being rejected. Neither the preceding circumstances nor subsequent resolution is processed.

Import   When people are angry with each other, the relationship just dissolves.

Explanatory Hypotheses   People don't read one another's intentions but react to each other's provocations with anger rather than constructive efforts to understand one another. When Denise is upset, she feels that others do not understand. The story to Card 7GF suggests that she feels children are left with their negative emotions (anger and upset), whereas adults (mother) remain cheerful and happy.

> Card 7GF: She's being lectured by her mother and she doesn't want to hear it and she walks out. (Feeling?) She feels disgusted and her mother's feeling cheerful and happy.

Interpretive Considerations   The formulation of the explanatory concepts seeks to clarify the reasons for the discord between mother and daughter. To some extent, these inferences can be made solely on the basis of this story. However, conclusions have more utility when they are reconsidered in the context of other stories. Furthermore, the youngster's relationship with the examiner, background, history, and performance on other tests in the battery contribute to the refinement of explanatory concepts. The interpretation of the above story is consistent with previous explanations.

The story is characterized by a general vagueness. There is no indication of the topic of the mom's lecture and no destination when the girl walks out. The content is limited to the scene presented, without a context, without a resolution to the dilemma, and without inner or outer direction that guides action. People do what suits them in the moment, without a goal or plan and without coordinating their reaction or effort to the interpersonal context (e.g., people's feelings are not influenced by each other's condition). Behavior is provoked by angry reactions to external demands and reflects extremely limited tolerance for frustration.

Import   If a girl doesn't want to be lectured at by her mother, she walks out in disgust, but the mother is cheerful and happy.

Explanatory Hypotheses   The child does not view events in a larger context and is easily overcome by anger and frustration. She feels misunderstood and rejects parental (societal) demands.

The following example illustrates how conclusions drawn from stylistic elements of responses to other tests converge with T.A.T. interpretation. Jack, also age 14, with low-average intelligence, was referred for testing by his mother who was concerned about the disorganized quality of his school work, as well as about his lack of interest in and resistance to academic tasks. For the past several years, Jack's mother has provided a great deal of structure and pressure to complete homework. During this assessment, Jack scored poorly on the Vocabulary subtest of the WISC-R (first percentile). An examination of several of his responses provides clues about the nature of his disorganization: *knife*—gun; *umbrella*—raincoat; *clock*—radio; *nail*—hammer; *alphabet*—soup; *thief*—crook; *join*—membership; *brave*—strong; *diamond*—earring. These responses are clearly associative, each representing the word that immediately came to mind. There is an obvious lack of organizational effort to define the meaning of the words conceptually, despite the examiner's attempts to redirect him to tell what the words mean.

Jack's attitude toward work is reflected in the following two scenarios given to T.A.T. pictures:

> Card 1: The little kid looks at the violin cause he doesn't want to play it so at the end his mom forces him to play and so he gets reprimanded. He looks sad, he looks mad.

Interpretive Considerations   A similar lack of investment in the task indicated in the response to the vocabulary items is shown in this story. Jack starts out with a literal reading of the stimulus—"The little kid looks at the violin"—which is followed by the next thought—"because he doesn't want to play it." The next association is to external pressure imposed by Mom—"forces him to play." The story does not delve inward to deal with possible effects of task engagement but moves to the next association—"he gets reprimanded." Finally, the boy ends up with the emotions as depicted in the stimulus (he looks sad, mad). Although his thinking is neither illogical nor disorganized, the process of narrating the story is unidimensional. Thoughts are provoked in a linear, associative fashion without imposing an organizational framework. The initial reaction to the stimulus is followed by piecemeal reactions to previous story elements. The boy in the story simply doesn't want to play. No alternatives are given, no context is set, and no explanations are offered about the meaning of playing the violin or about the reasons for the parental demand. The boy passively and unhappily complies with external pressure. The content, structure, and process of story telling suggest that Jack is not invested in the task and takes the quickest, most expedient route to meeting imposed demands.

Import   If a child doesn't want to do his work, his mom will force him to do it, but he gets reprimanded and feels sad and mad.

Explanatory Hypotheses   The child has no intrinsic interest in accomplishments but expects to be forced to do work by authorities (mother). His feelings are tied concretely to the immediate external circumstance (looks sad and mad) rather than resulting from inner-directed effort or satisfaction.

Card 2: The girl is waiting for the bus to go to school and her dad is working at the farm with the crops and when the bus comes, she just goes to school and when she gets home, she just does her chores. (T/F?) They got to do their work.

Interpretive Considerations   The story evolves in a similar manner to the previous one. Again, the initial response is close to a literal reading of the stimulus. The details of the story are simply evoked by the stimulus and preceding ideas. Events proceed in sequence, as triggered by prior events: waiting for the bus, going to school on the bus, coming home, doing chores. There are no goals, aims, or larger purposes to behavior.

Import   Life is humdrum, and everyone must do their own work.

Explanatory Hypotheses   The child reacts to ongoing demands without putting them into a larger context and without intrinsic interest. His attempts to integrate the various elements of his experience are superficial.

The sequence of ideas and the juxtaposition of events reveal an associative process akin to Jack's responses to the vocabulary items. This cognitive approach precludes the type of organization required of high academic performance and is not compatible with investment in such activities. The concerns of both mother and son are understandable in this light. Jack's mother has acted on the impression that her son was not exerting sufficient effort. Jack's attitudes toward work as reflected in the T.A.T. imports were outgrowths of his cognitive style and reaction to external demands.

Report of the Assessment

The conclusions derived from the assessment procedure are communicated to others orally via conferences and in writing by the psychological report. The emphasis is on conveying explanatory concepts that meaningfully relate to the presenting problems. Increased parent or teacher understanding of the youngster in relation to environmental demands and opportunities provides the framework for making decisions on behalf of the child. When appropriate, the youngster might benefit from discussions with the examiner.

The report incorporates the point of view of the youngster and the examiner's explanations. The following is an illustration of a judgmental flavor that results from not including the child's subjective experience: "Child wishes to be the center of attention and is excessively demanding." In contrast, a more child-oriented approach evokes empathy for the youngster's struggle: "When the child is not receiving feedback, she assumes that she has done something wrong and, therefore, seeks reassurance." The report that incorporates the child's perspective helps diffuse anger on the part of parents and teachers and provides them with a basis for gearing their demands to the child's adaptive capacities.

Recommendations are based on an understanding of what the child needs to function optimally and may focus, as appropriate, on what can be done at home, at school, by the therapist, and so forth. The report should also include a summary of how conclusions and recommendations were received by relevant parties (parents, teachers, the child, therapist, school system). Inclusion of the steps to be taken to implement recommendations and plans for follow-up serve the client and the professional. Such information acts as documentation for the record, provides a vehicle for continued contact as needed, and furnishes feedback for the professional to gauge the efficacy of the recommendations and of the interventions.

Topics Included in the Personality Test Report

In writing a report based on projective stories, the material is not self-contained but systematically related to other sources of information (e.g., self-report, observations, and performance on various tasks). Topics should not be presented mechanically one at a time but as interwoven concepts that reflect their interplay in relation to the presenting problems. The following topics should be covered, though not necessarily in any particular order. Emphasis should be given to the areas most pertinent to the individual being assessed.

1. *Cognitions*   Characteristics of thinking are manifested differently on tasks that have discrepant demands. Personality test results are not used to substitute for or to verify the intelligence test scores but to get an indication of whether functioning on the projectives is on a level expected from intelligence test patterns and conclusions from other data. Predominant cognitive styles are noted (e.g., concrete versus abstract, original versus stereotyped, organized versus loose, perceptual versus conceptual, realistic versus wishful, conforming versus bizarre); impairments (aphasia, attention, or memory disturbance) are described. The manner in which cognitive processes influence the organization of life experiences helps clarify the convictions and attitudes expressed in the projective stories. Thus, it is important to note the quality of integration in thinking, as well as the regulation of cognitive and attentional processes.

2. *Quality of Affect*   The role of affect in processing information and organizing experiences is addressed; ways of interpreting events as prompted by emotions are described. Affect-laden information may be processed differently

than purely factual material. The coordination of the affective-cognitive components of experience are clarified by noting the interplay of perceptual, conceptual, and affective elements of responses.

3. *Interests or Motives* That which is of interest captures attention and thereby dominates awareness. Interests and motives guide the delineation of the central dilemma or theme of the story. They relate to goals, aspirations, needs, values, and expectations. It is important to consider (a) whether interests or aspirations are realistic in comparison to ability or other resources, (b) whether interests are focused on activities or outcomes, and (c) whether aims of behaviors reflect immediate reactions or long-term interests.

4. *Means to Goals* The degree of volitional, planful, realistic, or resourceful effort to overcome obstacles or attain goals (e.g., quality of planning, foresight, initiative, or persistence) is described along with methods of dealing with challenge (e.g., reliance upon self, others, legal authorities, higher powers, luck, or various combinations). The relationship of means to ends (actions to outcomes) is an important consideration.

5. *Self-Regulation* The degree of self-monitoring, self-direction, and self-determination employed in handling social situations or task demands is described because such functions constitute the resources and organizational capabilities for self-control and deliberate, planful effort. Situational influences on self-regulation are clarified.

6. *Self-Evaluation* The nature of self-awareness is described in terms of the kind and extent of self-concern and degree of introspection or insight. Under what circumstances does the respondent see the self as adequate or competent as opposed to dependent, inadequate, a pawn of others, or victim of fate? What makes the person happy or miserable? What are the bases for self-acceptance? Is the individual self-critical or unaware of inconsistencies in self and behavior? How severe is the yardstick for self-evaluation in various circumstances?

7. *Relationships* The characteristic ways of relating to others such as parents, siblings, other relatives, peers, authorities, or subordinates are described (e.g., dependence, dominance, mutuality). What is the yardstick for evaluating others (e.g., what functions they provide, superficial appearances, etc.)? How do emotions and cognitions contribute to the processing of interpersonal information?

8. *Areas of Conflict or Concern* Current problems are described in the context of typical modes of experiencing conflict or stress. Internal as well as external sources of conflict are delineated. Inner sources of conflict relate to self-esteem enhancement and self-consistency as follows: (a) aspiration versus ability or effort to reach goals, (b) belief system or standards versus behavior, and (c) dependence versus independence. External source of conflict may stem from demands versus ability or inclination, and social standards versus self-interest or comfort.

Case Illustrations

Two cases that emphasize story telling techniques are presented. Names have been changed and identifying details omitted to protect the privacy of the families involved. Test administration, interpretation, and report writing were done by graduate students enrolled in an assessment practicum under the author's supervision. The conclusions and bases for interpretations follow each story. The manner in which these interpretations are integrated with each other and with other assessment information is shown in the complete psychological report that follows each case. The reports differ in length and style to convey the impression that there is no uniform standard or model for an ideal report. The format, style, and content of the report can vary according to its purpose and the author's framework. The criterion for judging the report should be the usefulness of the content and the clarity of communication.

Case One

The following set of stories was told by Trudie, a 14-year-old youngster of average intelligence.

> Card 1: What's he looking at? (Up to you). Looks like a kid who was taking violin lessons and he wasn't very good at it and he decided to give it up and his parents were very disappointed and the kid is deciding whether he should take it up again to make his parents proud. (What?) He probably decided to take it up again and he works at it every day and he finally improves himself.

Interpretive Considerations   Self-direction is problematic because the child takes action (decides to give up the violin) to avoid an aversive task without anticipating parental reaction (disappointment). Self-evaluation is based on external approval; despite an absence of intrinsic interest or sense of efficacy, parental disappointment leads to a reevaluation of the decision. In response to a query, the narrator indicates that the child works hard to improve himself. However, given the lack of interest in the task and unrealistic quality of the effort, it is doubtful that the child can sustain independent, goal-directed activity under frustrating circumstances.

Import   If a child is not good at his work, he gives it up, but upon realizing that his parents are disappointed, he is persuaded to continue his efforts to make his parents proud despite lack of interest.

Explanatory Hypotheses   Frustration and lack of investment make rigorous effort difficult to sustain unless the child is provided with strong external guidance, support, and motivation.

Card 2: Looks like a farm girl who's unhappy being on a farm and has had an argument with her mom about moving to the city 'cause she wants to experience a different life and she's holding books in her hand, books about cities, people who live in the city. And her mom finally gives in and lets her move to the city. When she gets to the city, she gets a job and she buys an apartment and I don't know. This isn't an easy one. She gets married (that's good enough).

Interpretive Considerations The following characteristics of the girl in the story are considered in deciphering the overall meaning: (1) the girl wants to leave her present circumstances to get away from an unhappy situation, (2) she wishes to experience more variety and stimulation rather than to seek something specific, (3) her mother does not approve but gives in to the child's argument, and (4) the youngster shows poor planning by getting to the city first, then getting a job and apartment. At this point, the story teller is stuck for an ending and continues with "she gets married." As in the previous story, the character acts on her wishes as they arise without anticipating the eventual complications.

Import When a young woman is unhappy, she leaves home for a more interesting place, only to find out that she must get an apartment and a job, unless she gets married.

Explanatory Hypotheses The demands of home and routine are not satisfying or exciting. In her desire to get away, the child is likely to seek supportive friends because she feels that she cannot rely on her own resources.

Card 3BM: This is a picture of me. Looks like a person who, looks like a gun in background, had argument with her husband. Husband tried to beat her and she shot him with the gun. She notified the police, and she's very upset, she's depressing. She afterwards, after the police leave, she takes the gun and she shoots herself.

Interpretive Considerations The following points are considered: (1) the self-reference (personalization) indicates that the narrator has difficulty taking distance from the pull of immediate circumstance; (2) her impulsive reaction to the presence of the "gun" provoked the violent theme; and (3) analogously, the character acts on her impulse (shoots husband) and later regrets the impulsive action (upset). Nevertheless, the story ends with another impulsive act (character shoots herself). In the previous story, marrying off the character is an "easy out" on two levels. First, the character no longer has to be alone in the city. Second, it is a stock ending that serves the purpose of concluding the story. Similarly, killing off the character in this story precludes any further demand to deal with the task.

Import   If a wife is provoked by the violence of her husband, she shoots him and subsequently shoots herself because she's depressed.

Explanatory Hypotheses   Rather than taking a long-term view, the youngster is easily provoked by external pressure to engage in impulsive actions that are destructive to self and others. She gets caught up in the moment and cannot think of problem resolutions other than an immediate reaction.

Card 4: This looks like a couple who were stranded out on the road and they found this restaurant on a country road and the guy starts to pick on the girl. The guy that the girl is with starts a fight with the other guy. The girl is telling him not to go and to just walk away. Umm . . . He listens to her and they both leave. How old are these cards? (about 50 years old).

Interpretive Considerations   Again, the issue concerns the character's reaction to external provocation. Yet this time, another person who is a peer has a constructive influence.

Import   If someone close to you is antagonized, you have enough perspective to dissuade him from being provoked to impulsive action.

Explanatory Hypotheses   As part of a couple or close relationship, the youngster can be persuaded to withstand provocation.

Card 5: (long pause) I can't even make up a story for this. Lady looks like she's looking for something. She's been looking for a long time and she's getting upset that she can't find it. (Yawn) Umm . . . (long pause) Don't know. (What's she gonna do?) (long pause) (hard breathing) Don't know.

Interpretive Considerations   The response shows the narrator's extreme reaction to frustration. A story doesn't come easily, and the youngster reacts by becoming visibly upset. Likewise, the woman in the story gets upset because she can't find what she wants. However, what she wants is not specified. In fact, the story content is limited to what appears on the card. As with previous stories, the narrator does not elaborate intentions or describe inner-directed action without cues provided in the stimulus.

Import   If a woman becomes upset when she cannot find "something" she's vaguely looking for, she becomes immobilized.

Explanatory Hypotheses   The youngster has little commitment or investment to a course of action and has difficulty directing her effort. She tries to take cues from the environment and complies when the task demands are clear and appear manageable. Knowing that she should do something but not knowing exactly what to do leaves her upset and frustrated.

> Card 6BM: This looks like a very rich young man who inherited his father's business and he's having to lay off one of the maids since the business has gone down since he's inherited it. And the lady is real upset. And . . . he promises her that he'd find her another job. (stares) (Is that the end?) (shrugs).

Interpretive Considerations   The man's inherited business is unsuccessful. Therefore, he is forced to lay off an employee. He offers to find her another job only after he observes that she's upset. Again, the response is to an immediate provocation (lady is upset) rather than to the anticipation that the maid would need another job. Given that the character's promise was in response to the momentary demand, one gets the impression that the narrator introduced this element (granting a promise) to get by the difficult moment and that she would tend not to follow through on her word.

Import   When a man's inherited business fails, he's forced to lay off an employee with an empty promise of finding her another job.

Explanatory Hypotheses   Good intentions are difficult to put into effect because the youngster gets caught up in the immediate situational pull. She may respond to the interpersonal tugs in the moment but may not anticipate others' needs.

> Card 7GF: This looks like a little girl who's having to listen to a tutor read to her about English and she's wishing she could go outside and play with her friends 'cause she can see them through the window. . . . And she finally waits through her tutoring and gets to go outside to be with her friends. (Yawn)

Interpretive Considerations   A child wishes to be with her friends rather than listen to a tutor. The immediate pull of her friends is intensified by the fact that she can see them through the window. Her solution is to pretend to comply until she gets to go outside. Thus, she exhibits no investment in learning and maintains a superficial relationship with the tutor.

Import   When a child would rather play with her friends than attend to her lessons, she just waits for the lesson to end so she can go outside.

Explanatory Hypotheses The youngster feels caught between the demands for learning and social expectations and the more exciting world of peers. If she is receiving one-to-one attention (e.g., from a tutor), she complies superficially and bides her time so she can do what she really wants.

> Card 8BM: This looks like a boy, a son, thinking about his father's having an operation and he's considering whether he's going to live or not. He waits for several hours and finally the doctor comes out and tells him that his father is going to live 'cause the operation was successful.

Interpretive Considerations The story is in line with the stimulus and appropriate to the scene depicted. However, there is no context for the surgery and no reflection on the relationship between father and son. The story is superficial and vague, with a highly constricted time frame.

Import When a child is worried about the outcome of an event (surgery), he simply waits to be told the good news.

Explanatory Hypotheses Tasks and situations are dealt with as simply as possible.

> Card 12M: Reminds me of the book I just read. It looks like a woman who has just died from a very serious illness and a priest has come to bless her, and don't know, there's not much you can do after you're dead. It's hard to give it an ending. Does it have to have an ending? (It'd be nice.) (Laughs) I can't think of an ending.

Interpretive Considerations The narrator gives a description of the scene (borrowed from a book) but puts herself into a "trap" by initially declaring the woman dead and then realizing that it's hard to generate an ending. The message in terms of the convictions being expressed by the narrator is difficult to decipher when there is meager content beyond stimulus description. In this case, the message is formulated in terms of the child's approach to the task.

Import If you react without sizing up the whole situation, you cannot change your strategy as you become more aware.

Explanatory Hypotheses The child reacts with the most obvious response without anticipating subsequent steps. When the child gets into difficulty by not looking ahead, she wishes to be relieved of responsibility ("Does it have to have an ending?").

Psychological Report

Name: Trudie X   Date(s) of Testing:
Age: Date of Birth:
Grade: School:
                          Examiner:

Reason for Referral

Trudie's mother, Mrs. X, was concerned about recent incidents of stealing, running away from home, and academic difficulties. Since Trudie is easily influenced by peers, there is added concern that her new friends may have an adverse influence.

Background Information

Trudie had a great deal of difficulty last year getting through the eighth grade but did pass with daily assistance from her mother who reported that Trudie did not have academic difficulties during the earlier grades.

Tests Administered

Wechsler Intelligence Scale for Children—Revised
Bender-Gestalt
Thematic Apperception Test
Interview

Behavioral Observations During Testing and Interview

Trudie appeared to be highly cooperative but generally bored by the interview and testing procedures. She yawned constantly throughout the sessions. Nevertheless, she attempted all tasks and worked as hard as she could. She was quick to give up when a task was difficult but responded well to encouragement. When she felt she was doing well, she seemed very proud. However, there was the sense that she was trying so hard to maintain her effort that she felt drained and probably disliked the testing process. Her perception of her "problems" was that others such as teachers and parents expect too much. She perceives herself as a fair person and expressed concern that her parents do not trust her (i.e., her mom asks questions and sets limits, which imply a lack of confidence and trust). When asked whether anything had happened that might have made her parent worry, she readily acknowledged that there were "incidents." Nevertheless, she had several suggestions for how her mother might approach her differently with regard to helping with homework or with limit setting. Trudie indicated that she finds school frustrating and when the suggestion of tutorial help was raised, she insisted that this would just increase the hours she has to be burdened with school.

Test Results

On the Wechsler Intelligence Scale for Children—Revised, Trudie obtained a verbal score of 91 and performance score of 105. Her total IQ score of 97 placed her at the 42nd percentile and in the average range. The subtest scale scores (with a mean of 10) were as follows:

Information	5	Picture Completion	9
Similarities	13	Picture Arrangement	12
Arithmetic	8	Block Design	11
Vocabulary	9	Object Assembly	12
Comprehen-sion	8	Coding	10
(Digit Span)	12		

Trudie's general fund of information is significantly below her other verbal subtest scores because she tends to tune out information that is not of immediate relevance to her. When she is motivated as, for example, in the digit span subtest, a measure of short-term memory, she was able to concentrate on the material and obtained an above-average score. Nevertheless, although Trudie did well on this rote recall task, she protested that she "couldn't do it." The strain of the effort was evident and it is unlikely that she could maintain this level of energy and persistence over the long haul. Generally, if Trudie knew the answers, she gave them quickly; otherwise, she needed encouragement to persist. In the structured one-to-one testing session, Trudie performed at the average to above-average levels on tasks that did not require prior knowledge. On such tasks she was able to concentrate well and apply appropriate strategies. Subtests that were based on previously acquired knowledge ranged from average to well below average.

Trudie's drawings of the Bender-Gestalt figures were well organized and executed. However, her low tolerance for frustration was evident in the increasing size of the designs. Even within each design, she would start off relatively well, but indications of impulsivity were apparent (e.g., dots that grew bigger and darker, finally becoming circles as the design progressed). Her ability to recall the Bender figures was as expected (6).

Personality testing with the Thematic Apperception Test indicates that in unstructured situations Trudie is likely to make decisions before she evaluates her options or weighs the likely consequences. She may exercise poor judgment because she doesn't pause to reflect on possible alternatives. Once involved in a situation, Trudie doesn't have the resources to back away. She may even recognize that her actions may lead to undesirable consequences, but seems to get "lost" in the sequence of events and is unable to take constructive action. The recent incident of stealing involved just such poor judgment. Trudie wanted the items and took them without realizing how easily she would be caught.

Trudie's low tolerance for frustration, impulsivity, absence of long-range goals, and lack of intrinsic satisfaction with school work contribute to a general feeling of being overburdened. She feels that enormous efforts are required to please others and meet their standards. Therefore, it is unlikely that she can persist in these endeavors (especially if she keeps falling behind academically).

Normal expectations of teachers and parents to persist on tasks and follow routines are experienced as overly demanding. At this point, she is caught in the dilemma of finding the routine of school and academic demands to be meaningless and frustrating, while at the same time her friends bring her acceptance and good feelings. Trudie is highly influenced by peers and by the immediacy of what is happening in the moment. She does respond to the feelings and concerns of other people when such feelings are directly expressed. Although she really doesn't want to disappoint others, she is now caught up in a stream of events and is feeling very much out of control.

Recommendations

Trudie is currently caught up in a cycle of oppositionalism and rejection of authorities, which is fueled by her disinterest in and frustration with academic and other demands. She has sought refuge in a peer group, which not only provides acceptance and support but also provides places to stay when she runs away from home. Additionally, the group supplies companionship while she is truant from school. It is important to break the cycle of truancy and of running away with the aim of establishing a new start, which recognizes Trudie's low tolerance for frustration and her impulsivity. She needs a great deal of structure, supervision, and firm limits. However, if she is expected to do work that brings no intrinsic satisfaction, it is important to maintain interpersonal "closeness" and support as motivating factors. It may also be necessary to lower expectations somewhat to minimize frustration. Peer support and feeling of belonging on a team will facilitate her efforts. As long as limits are firm, discussions and explanations of concerns would be helpful.

Presently, her primary concern is to get away from the drudgery and demands of school and home. A new beginning would have to consider Trudie's impulsivity and need for supervision, along with the necessity to reduce the frustration she feels. Hobbies and activities that she enjoys and that could lead to feelings of competence and commitment should be encouraged.

Parent Conference

There were several parent conferences where various strategies were discussed. After continued episodes of running away, Trudie was enrolled in a private boarding school designed to meet her needs. A year later, it was reported that she had made a good adjustment to this intervention.

Case Two

The following stories were told by Albert, a 6-year-old (6–2) kindergarten student with low-average IQ, as measured by the Stanford-Binet.

Card 1: Is it wrong about something? (What?) Is it a wrong picture? (Instructions repeated) . . . I'm thinking . . . I know something for it. Want me to tell? (Happening?) Once upon a time there was a little boy, and he loved to play a violin, and he's just worried about guitars and all that stuff. And also, his best friends were teenage-mutant ninja turtles and sometimes he went to play with them but he had to knock on the sewer until the ninja turtles said to come in. The end. (To?) He went out to play.

Interpretive Considerations   Having previously been administered picture absurdities requiring him to indicate what is "not right" or "funny" about the picture, the child wondered if the same principle applied. He finally begins ("loved to play violin") but cannot develop his idea and tries to start a different way ("worried about guitars and all that stuff"). At this point he is stuck again because he is not able to go beyond a description of the scene. He retreats into fantasy by aimlessly describing ninja turtles, popular cartoon characters, as the boy's best friends.

Import   If the task is hard, you try to see if it's like something you did before but you cannot figure it out. You think about TV characters being your friends.

Explanatory Hypotheses   The child is too disorganized to deal with the task beyond a description of the scene and weaves fantasy and reality together as he verbalizes content from fictional TV characters that dominate his awareness.

Card 2: Once upon a time there was a poor lady. They lived in . . . a house that was made out of wood . . . b . . . They had to find beans, buy the beans to plant. They always knew how to make farms but the problem was they . . . had to find . . . beans to plant so there could be a whole lot of plants to grow. The end. And in the end they found some ninja turtles. And after they found the ninja turtles, the ninja turtles found the seeds for them to plant. The end. (Thinking? Feeling?) Sad.

Interpretive Considerations   The initial sentence is focused on "the lady" and the scene. The focus shifts momentarily to their house, made of wood, then to the need to find beans to plant. The narrator did not integrate these elements but focused on one feature of the stimulus at a time. Having said "something" about the various areas of the picture, he feels that he has exhausted his "options," and again retreats into a fantasy ending where the ninja turtles find the beans for them.

Import   If it's hard to meet the demands of life, one fantasizes about being rescued by fictional characters.

Explanatory Hypotheses   It's difficult for the child to grasp the relationships of the characters or events. He cannot find a strategy for telling this story and cannot think of a way for the characters to solve their problem. Therefore, he provides a magical ending where fictional characters save the day.

Card 3BM: Is he crying? He's crying. When people hurt his feelings, he always cries and throws pine cones at them. (Albert had a small pine cone in his hand when he came for the testing.) So after that he stops crying. And some people hurt his feelings again and again and the end and the end. And in the end, he's dead. All the other people live. (How did they hurt his feelings?) By calling him names.

Interpretive Considerations   The story teller identifies the character in the picture as crying. He continues by indicating that when people hurt the boy's feelings, he always cries and throws pine cones at them. Throwing pine cones relates to the fact that Albert had them with him during testing. Thus, the narrator and the character retaliate by whatever means are immediately available. The character's action has no impact as people continue to hurt his feelings again and again. At this point, the narrator needs to get out of the perseverative loop and kills off the character to produce an ending.

Import   When people hurt your feelings, you cry and retaliate but they continue to hurt you until you die.

Explanatory Hypotheses   The child is vulnerable to feeling hurt and, besides crying or blind retaliation, has no resources to understand or cope with his feelings or circumstances.

Card 4: A stranger took a lady away . . . but . . . but . . . the lady thought he wasn't somebody he wasn't a real stranger. The end. (To?) They're dead. (Thinking? Feeling?) I don't know how they're feeling. (Before?) I finished that story.

Interpretive Considerations   The content is about a woman who was abducted because she realized too late that the man was a stranger. The lady's confusion about the man's identity reflects the narrator's disorientation. He has probably been warned against trusting strangers and superimposed this fragment of his experience in a way that did not quite fit the stimulus. When pressed to give an ending, he states that the characters are dead. Killing the characters was effective in ending the previous story and is used again for that purpose.

Import   Someone (a woman) who trusts the wrong person (stranger) could get hurt.

Explanatory Hypotheses   The child reacts to isolated pieces of information that are viewed out of context and are inappropriately interpreted. The child has difficulty applying previously acquired knowledge and perseveratively tries whatever seems to have worked before.

Card 5: She was so surprised when she opened the door because her son was gone because somebody killed the son. The end. (Before?) I don't know. I don't know. (To?) Fine.

Interpretive Considerations   The story starts out with the woman being surprised when she opens the door. So far, this is in keeping with the stimulus. She is surprised because her son was gone and instantly realizes that somebody killed him. The mother is helpless in the face of this recognition. As in previous stories, killing the son is Albert's way to end the story and be done with a confusing task. Albert is so disorganized that he cannot set a context or realistic time frame nor can he attribute competent action or appropriate emotions to any characters.

Import   A mother is surprised when her son is gone and immediately concludes that somebody killed him but she doesn't know how to feel or what to do.

Explanatory Hypotheses   The child struggles to deal with the task by grasping at approaches that seemed to work in the past. The results are fragmented and disorganized efforts that reflect his confusion and helplessness.

Card 6BM: She's looking out the window b . . . because she must missed . . . missed her ch . . . chance to go on the bus to go home. And the dad was worried. The end. (Before?) I don't know. (End?) Repeats. (To?) Fine . . . You're silly, you know that. When school's over and you're going somewhere else, will you listen to all the stories? . . . You could ask a lot of kids to come and have a whole lot of stories, day and night and day and night.

Interpretive Considerations   Again, the child attempts to deal with the "concrete" facts provided in the stimulus cues. Yet, something is amiss in relation to the perception of the characters and quality of thinking. The woman is looking out the window because she missed her chance to go on the bus to go home. Having told something about the woman in front of the window, Albert shifts his attention to the man looking down, which triggers the idea of "and the dad is worried." But if "the dad" is physically present, why is he worried? Thus, the stimulus is not logically related to the story. Furthermore, given the respective ages of the characters, the man is unlikely to be the woman's father. Concepts of time and space, cause and effect, and intentions and actions are not understood. The story teller is aware of details of his experiences without integrating them into coherent patterns. Past experience does not form a context that can be meaningfully applied to the interpretation of current circumstances. Rather, Albert grasps at fragments of experiences that are applied haphazardly without aim, organization, or deliberate purpose. Albert focuses sequentially on one area of the picture at a time and fails to integrate the pieces as he associates to each part. When he is stuck, he declares, "the end," retreats into fantasy, or engages in off-task chatter.

Import   When a child misses the bus, he loses his chance to get home and causes others to worry.

Explanatory Hypotheses   The child is superimposing fragments of previous experience but does not apply them appropriately and is stranded in his confusion with a vague sense that others are worried. He seems to have acquired some stereotypic adages (e.g., don't trust strangers, people worry if you miss the bus) in the course of socialization but cannot integrate them into his experience.

Card 7GF: They're happy because . . . she had a little baby but the baby's starting to cry because the girl isn't holding it right. The end. (Thinking? Feeling?) Sad. (You know why?) (Repeats story) Well, because the head's leaning back. (To?) Fine, it turns out fine . . . fine . . . fine. (How?) It's fine, I like it that way.

Interpretive Considerations   The story begins by describing the characters as happy because they have a baby. Albert cannot develop this idea further and focuses back on the picture. His description of the baby as crying "because the girl isn't holding it right" is a literal reading of an isolated part of the stimulus. As in the previous stories, Albert has difficulty responding to the entire gestalt of the picture. When pressed to continue beyond the first sentence where Albert wanted to end the story, he indicated that they felt "sad." In a departure from the usual practice, the examiner asked why they were sad. Albert could not relate this feeling to the content of the story but justified it by referring to the stimulus ("head's leaning back"). Evidently, he is not able to monitor the events of the unfolding story or meaningfully relate feelings, thoughts, actions, and outcomes. He seems aware that the examiner is not entirely pleased with his product and seems annoyed with queries that he cannot handle.

Import   If you try very hard to do what others want by following the cues literally, they may not be satisifed but you insist, nevertheless, that things are fine.

Explanatory Hypotheses   The child has difficulty going beyond the concrete clues provided. He focuses on isolated stimulus elements, one at a time, and when he cannot fathom the examiner's queries, he insists that things are fine. He has difficulty seeing relationships between people or making connections between events. Likewise, he cannot grasp people's feelings or intentions. The defiant behaviors that were among the referral issues may be his way of responding to demands that he cannot handle.

Card 8BM: He sticked a needle in him . . . to kill him. That guy is. Is it bad? Look at it. (Shows card) I think it's bad because they poked it in him. (Happening?) He died. (Before?) I don't know, I don't know. (Q?) I don't know. I think they're killing him. (Why?) They're bad guys. (To?) Bad.

Interpretive Considerations   Again, there is an inability to take in the entire scene, and the child's attention is riveted on part of the background. The story begins by a reaction to the threatening element ("he sticked a needle in him . . . to kill him."). Albert perceives that the picture is "bad," but cannot explain what is going on other than to describe the stimulus literally ("sticked a needle") and to characterize the aggressors as "bad guys."

Import   If you are not sure if bad things are happening, you ask others, but when they ask you to decide, you just tell what you see.

Explanatory Hypotheses   Events are misinterpreted because the child cannot integrate all the available information and cannot make the inferences required by this task. Rather, the child makes assumptions on the basis of isolated details.

Card 7BM: They're happy because . . . they met each other again. The end. (Happening?) I'm finished with the story.

Interpretive Considerations   This is simply an interpretive description of the stimulus. As with the previous responses, this is as far as Albert can go. He doesn't have the resources to describe external context or inner life.

Import   One is happy when good things happen.

Explanatory Hypotheses   People's feelings are determined by whatever is happening to them without any attempt to influence events or to understand relationships.

Card 12: He's sleeping and somebody's knocking to his room. (Then what?) (Repeats) He's sleeping and somebody is sneaking in his room. (Go on) I don't know (To?) Fine. (Fine?) Because he didn't wake him up. That's what's fine. Real fine. When I talk in there the light goes on (tape recorder).

Interpretive Considerations   Again, the handling of the stimulus is amiss. His initial description referred to someone "knocking to his room," but the stimulus portrays someone as leaning over a reclining figure. When pressed to continue the story, Albert focuses back on the picture and changes his description to "someone sneaking in his room." Everything's fine because the person is not awakened. Since Albert could not elaborate on the character he introduced as knocking, he redefines the scene as someone sneaking past a person to keep from waking him. The story teller may have been told not to wake someone (e.g., a parent) and associated that fragment of his experience to part of the stimulus presented.

Import   When it's hard to understand the situation, you are fine if you figure out something you're supposed to do.

Explanatory Hypotheses   The child can deal with an obvious behavioral limit if it is very clear but can't generalize it to another context. He retains isolated restrictions and stereotyped strictures (e.g., don't trust strangers; be quiet when someone is sleeping).

Card 13B: He was real worried because he . . . wanted to live in the world where there is grass and trees and friends. (sings) (To?) Fine. (Feeling?) He was so happy he changed his mind he didn't want to move, mooove.

Interpretive Considerations   The narrator is superimposing words that come to mind (the picture has no trees, grass, or other people) without any idea of constructive action to ameliorate his worries, which are simply transformed to their opposites. And he's happy.

Import   If you are worried, fantasies can make you happy.

Explanatory Hypotheses   Again, fragments of experience are not tied together. Feelings exist in the moment and worries about grass, trees, and friends vanish when one is happy.

Card 14: When you hear all my voices, will you think you're still in the same room? He wanted to jump out the window. He's looking at the sky. And he didn't want to jump in, from the window, but it was real dark in the room because somebody turned out the lights. He was happy. (Happy?) Well, I just told you happy, I don't know all of it.

Interpretive Considerations   The opening sentence (after chatting about the tape recorder) is about wanting to jump out the window; it is a wish with no particular purpose or context, pulled by the proximity of the silouette and the open window. We can infer how vulnerable Albert is to the cues in the environment to which he responds directly without reflection or logical thought process. In the story, Albert has some sort of time continuum—he wanted to jump out the window; he's looking at the sky. Then he didn't want to jump in. (Do we assume that he jumped out?) Throughout the narrative, he sticks close to the card (it was dark, and someone turned out the lights), but cannot impose meaningful relationships among stimulus elements or story events.

Import   If you don't fully understand what's going on around you, you can still be happy as long as nothing bad seems to be happening.

Explanatory Hypotheses   The child formulates one thought at a time without relating each to another and, therefore, reacts only to the immediate, most obvious nuance of the situation.

General Comments

Throughout the stories, the narrator cannot shift from one logical idea to another. He takes cues directly from stimuli and stays on the descriptive level or drifts into fantasy. When required to interpret the more complex stimuli, he focuses on isolated detail without grasping the gist of the entire scene. Albert cannot identify the tension or dilemma depicted by the pictures and cannot develop concepts beyond his initial associations. Happiness is expressed when stimuli are less complex and less negative.

The overriding consideration is Albert's impaired capacity to integrate various components of experience. The narratives are fraught with confusion and misinterpretation and are characterized by a general lack of understanding of cause-effect relationships. Stories are devoid of purposeful or intentional action and are marked by absence of connections between events and between external reality and inner life.

Psychological Report

Name: Albert X   Date(s) of Testing:
Age: Date of Birth:
Grade: School:
                        Examiner:

Reason for Referral and Relevant Background Information

Albert was referred for testing by his parents at the suggestion of his kindergarten teacher. Concerns were expressed by both teacher and parents over the child's high activity level, short attention span, inconsistent performance in school activities, poor social skills, and, at times, outwardly defiant behavior. His teacher reportedly sees Albert's behaviors as indicative of ADHD and, according to his parents, has suggested consideration of medication. However, Albert's pediatrician questions the ADHD diagnosis. Testing was requested to help define the nature of Albert's difficulty in responding to the structure of school and to suggest avenues of intervention.

Developmentally, Mrs. X described Albert as an active child, walking at age 9 months. Language appeared late in development, with Albert seldom speaking at 25 months when in daycare. His learning was described as occurring in spurts. When he did begin speaking, it was in complete sentences. This seemed to coincide with a change in his daycare placement. Toilet training was also accomplished late (52 months) due to resistance on Albert's part.

At home, his parents see Albert as having many friends in the neighborhood and as normal in his after-school play activity. Contrary to this, his mother did note that Albert often lacks the social skills necessary to involve himself in other children's play. After school and on weekends, his mother described him as constantly seeking the companionship of other children in the neighborhood. At school, Albert appears to have more difficulty controlling his activity and interacting. His teacher indicates that some children are fearful of interacting with him because of his boisterous activity and reports that Albert is frequently off task and moving about the classroom.

Behavioral Observations

Albert was observed to be an appealing 6-year-old of average stature, though less mature than his age peers in both language and social skills. From the outset, Albert was a difficult child to assess. The examiner observed many of those behaviors and interactive patterns that were of concern to parents and teacher. The more sensitive and controlled side of Albert reported by his parents was also evident. The process by which Albert responded to the testing and interacted with the examiner was as informative as the test results themselves.

Albert responded to the strangeness of the testing situation with resistance to and avoidance of the various activities presented. He had to be cajoled into the testing room for each of the four sessions while respecting his desire not to verbally interact or make eye contact. Comprehending task demands, sustaining interest and effort, and monitoring the appropriateness of his actions were all observed to be difficult for Albert. The combination of these factors appeared to significantly limit his ability to meet the minimal requirements of many tasks. At times, what initially appeared to be willful opposition to an activity turned out to be his means of coping with his inability to coordinate all the aspects of the task.

His attention span was often fleeting, particularly when the task was new, did not provide sufficient direction, and was subsequently threatening to him. When presented with an activity, Albert's attention was often drawn to some peripheral aspect, such as the obscure watermark on a sheet of bond paper.

Often, when the examiner asked Albert questions about his activity, such as drawings or play, he did not answer and seemed puzzled or stressed by the simple probe. It almost appeared that he could not coordinate the question with the activity before him. After some time he would initiate a new topic, as if recognizing the need to respond socially but unable to reply to the specific request. There was an unusual quality to Albert's expressive language, including frequent whole-word repetitions and many pauses as he struggled to find the words to express himself. He enjoyed singing and repeating cartoon themes over and over, often interjecting these songs into the activity at hand.

When proceeding with a task, Albert sometimes became distracted and incorporated some association into the activity. For example, his Kinetic Family Drawing became an elaborate hidden picture puzzle. Across all activities, Albert's thinking was repeatedly drawn to cartoon characters such as Ninja Turtles and Ghost Busters, and he would incorporate these characters into his test responses. At times, when attending and appropriately responding, he would creep his fingers across the table and make facial grimaces as if still preoccupied with these fantasy characters.

Assessing Albert required the examiner to allow him control over the proceedings by providing him with choices, alternating periods of work with periods of play, and responding to his actions in an accepting manner. Albert appeared highly sensitive to any tone of displeasure with his actions on the examiner's part, yet appeared to behaviorally test the limits to see how the examiner would respond to him. Any response other than accepting his behavior and verbalizing for him the seeming intent of his actions appeared only to intensify acting-out behavior. Before the examiner took such a nondirective, tolerant approach to Albert's behavior, little was accomplished. During this time, he refused to attempt many of the test components, was often destructive with the test materials (banging, throwing, collapsing easel books), was dis-respectful to the examiner (including throwing pencils at her and calling her names—usually "stupid" and immature toileting vocabulary), and was up and about the room (including under the table, removing vent door panels, and reaching up to touch the dials on the wall clock). This was in stark contrast to his compliance and approval seeking during the final two sessions. During this time he cooperatively attempted everything asked of him, verbalized to the examiner when he was getting tired of an activity, helped the examiner with the test materials, and complied with the scheduled work and play times. He expressed a desire to give his free-time drawings to the examiner and, on several occasions, asked the examiner whether she would review his activities in the summer when there were no children present. Despite Albert's greater investment in his relationship with the examiner and his more controlled behavior in the final sessions, the same sorts of processing issues were observed.

Evaluation Results

A battery of tests was administered to assess Albert's intellectual functioning, cognitive strengths and weaknesses, academic achievement, and aspects of social/emotional functioning.

The Stanford-Binet Intelligence Scale—Revised (SB:FE) provided the primary assessment of intellectual functioning. On the SB:FE, Albert achieved a test composite score of 84 ± 5, which places his overall functioning in the low-average range of intelligence (16th percentile). The SB:FE also provides scores for four cognitive ability areas, each of which impacts on learning. Albert's standard scores in each of the areas were as follows:

Verbal Reasoning	98 (45th percentile)
Abstract/Visual Reasoning	95 (37th percentile)
Quantitative Reasoning	80 (9th percentile)
Short-Term Memory	72 (3rd percentile)

It should be noted that an individually administered intelligence test such as the SB:FE often provides an optimal level of functioning given the degree of direction and support available. Performance in everyday situations where this structure is absent can be considerably lower.

Significant variability was observed among Albert's scores on the SB:FE. This variability appears due to the manner in which he processes information and responds to task demands. He was most successful on tasks that required simple rote recall of facts or definitions. Though this would appear inconsistent with his lowest scale score on the SB:FE Memory cluster of tests, this cluster score was unduly depressed by one extremely low score (1st percentile) on a subtest within the cluster that demanded more than rote recall. This is to be discussed more fully later in this report. When simply required to draw on rote auditory memory skills, Albert scored at the 24th and 38th percentiles, which appears commensurate with his overall ability level. His functional capabilities became much more limited when he had to go beyond rote processing of information. He encountered inordinate difficulty on tasks that required him to generalize information, to apply principles or concepts to new situations, or to break down information into its constituent parts. In these instances, he does not appear able to simultaneously attend to what is most critical, to maintain cognitive focus as he attempts to manipulate information, and to monitor his mental activity toward a given goal. These difficulties are evident in both verbal and nonverbal areas assessed by the SB:FE.

The Bead Memory subtest represented the isolated low score on the SB:FE Memory Cluster. This subtest involves simultaneous attention to bead color, shape, and sequence. The child must simultaneously keep track of and integrate numerous attributes of the stimulus in problem solving. Albert could not consistently complete even the single-bead memory item. He would attend either to the color or shape of the bead but not both. If shown a white, round bead, he would respond with a red round bead. Similarly, if shown a two-bead pattern, he would remember the appropriate shapes but not color.

Additional assessment of his skill in conceptually grouping and shifting focus in this manner was conducted informally with the Conceptual Grouping subtest of the McCarthy Scales of Children's Abilities. This test assesses similar skills in simultaneously attending to shape, color, and size without the added memory component seen in the Bead Memory subtest. It often serves as an indicator of early skill in classification and generalization. Albert was able to simultaneously attend to the three stimulus dimensions, but only momentarily. He would initially correctly classify the materials presented to him, but then would lose the underlying concept by which he had proceeded and become random and disorganized in what he was doing. These observations suggest that with considerable structure and direction, as was provided by the Conceptual Grouping subtest, Albert can attend to and relate critical elements of a problem. However, he is unable to selectively attend and make these discriminations for himself when individual guidance is not provided for him. And, even with such assistance, Albert cannot sustain his focus or the quality of his performance.

Analysis of Albert's responses to those areas of the SB:FE that did not place him significantly below children his age revealed many qualitative indicators of his difficulty in integrating information and perceiving critical elements of a task. On a test that assessed number concepts, Albert could count and match sets of six or fewer items, but could not grasp the concept of combining sets. For example, when shown three dice, each with one spot, and asked how many there were all together, he responded with "one-one-one." He was unable to shift his thinking to combine the discrete elements into a unitary concept, even with additional prompting. In other contexts, Albert was observed to be able to engage in simple addition and subtraction. His ability to apply his skills and concepts appear very much influenced by the specific stimulus features of a task that draw his attention.

It was the examiner's impression that Albert was most prone to behavior inappropriate to the situation when he was not able to comprehend the task and appeared to act out his frustration in not being able to perform. For example, when unable to remember the words on a memory test requiring repetition of sentences of increasing complexity, Albert substituted such words as *pee* or *pig* with an antagonistic look at the examiner. Throughout the testing, imprecision was observed in Albert's language usage, suggesting difficulty in retrieving and matching vocabulary to the task. He identified a stamp on a letter as a sticker and referred to sweeping with a broom as *brooming*. Lengthy pauses were frequent as he struggled to express his thoughts.

Academic achievement was assessed through the Peabody Individual Achievement Test—Revised (PIAT—R) and supplemental informal assessment of basic kindergarten skills. Albert's performance on the PIAT—R suggests relative strengths in general information and learning stemming from having a variety of experiences and cultural opportunities. His general information score on the PIAT was firmly in the average range. Again, this is a test that assesses rote recall of facts. Albert scored considerably lower on tests that assess knowledge and skills typically acquired through formal instruction in school (e.g., early reading and mathematics).

Adequate visual-motor development plays an important role in early writing and readiness skills in school, and Albert demonstrates age-appropriate visual-motor skills per se, corresponding with teacher and parent reports of excellent drawing and handwriting skill. His score on the Developmental Test of Visual Motor Integration placed him firmly in the average range. However, consistent with the difficulties observed in other tasks, Albert had a hard time sustaining cognitive focus and organizing himself in writing or drawing activities. His attention would be drawn to some peripheral aspect of the task or his drawing would trigger an idea that would then become the focus of his activity. For example, on the SB:FE Copying subtest, each of the geometric forms to be drawn reminded Albert of some object. Rather than simply drawing the model, he took considerable time to illustrate an elaborate scene for each item. Albert became so engrossed in these peripheral aspects of the drawing that he did not respond to redirection. The end result was a series of creative drawings, but far removed from the task at hand. Similarly, in his Kinetic Family Drawing, he thought of making a snow scene and became locked into filling the sky with a series of snowballs, which then triggered the thought of the need for an umbrella, and then a Ninja Turtle holding the umbrella, and then concluding by making the drawing into the hidden object activity noted in the behavioral observations. Thus, it appears that while visual-motor skills are an area of strength for Albert, he gets locked into repetitive actions and associative thought patterns that limit his ability to conform to the constraints of the task. He often cannot let go of this thought activity to respond to redirection and his outward behavior can be interpreted as willful opposition.

Projective tests (Thematic Apperception Test and the Rorschach Inkblot Technique) were administered to assess social, emotional, and cognitive functioning with less structured tasks. There are indications across projective testing that Albert very much wants to please and to conform to others' expectations. He does attempt to deal with his environment in a reality-oriented manner but cannot maintain the cognitive processes necessary for this. His thinking is drawn to isolated thoughts and associations due to his inability to organize his experiences. The manner in which he interprets situations appears to result in inappropriate types of behavior or expressions of feeling under normal circumstances and a serious deficit in his ability to build or maintain satisfactory interpersonal relationships with peers and adults. These deficits in capacity to organize his perception and behaviors appear to adversely affect Albert's learning capability and personal development under normal circumstances. His difficulties are intensified when confronted with unfamiliar, unstructured, or stressful situations.

In responding to the Thematic Apperception Test, Albert was unable to develop coherent ideas beyond description of isolated stimulus features because (1) he could not impose meaningful relationships among the stimulus elements, (2) he could not organize story events in a logical manner, and (3) he could not grasp the inner life of characters to infer motives and intentions.

Albert did not make connections between causes and their effects and did not incorporate organizing concepts in the narratives. He responded to isolated elements of the picture in a sequential manner without grasping the idea conveyed by the whole scene. At best, he could associate bits of his previous experiences to parts of the stimulus presented. When pressed for other parts of the story, Albert would retreat back to the stimulus to get an idea. When he was feeling particularly pressed, he proceeded to respond with associations to the Ninja Turtles and similar images of TV characters. The association to Ninja Turtles seemed to occur most frequently during the beginning of a new activity, including his initial interaction with the examiner, suggesting that the association is a means by which Albert copes with overwhelming or threatening situations. To him, the Ninja Turtles appear to serve a protecting and empowering function.

Albert appears to feel quite vulnerable within his environment as a result of his impaired ability to integrate himself meaningfully with his surroundings. He responds to isolated pieces of information that are viewed out of context. His attempts to incorporate fragments of experiences are often perseverative and inappropriate to the situation. His actions are often misunderstood and elicit a punitive response from adults and rejection from his peers. Therefore, Albert feels a sense of badness and anticipates being rebuffed. School appears to be a place where these feelings about himself are intensified. Albert concluded nearly every testing session by some play activity in which he assumed a role of authority over the examiner. In this spontaneously initiated play, he would verbalize repeatedly that he was going to punish the examiner, that she would sit in the office and would get notes written home. This, combined with his shared perceptions during structured interview techniques, suggests that he perceives school as a punitive place where few emotional supports are available. His Kinetic School Drawing consisted of several of the interesting elements of his classroom but no people. It is difficult for Albert to put disciplinary action in proper perspective, given the manner in which he processes experiences. Punishment from significant others can easily instill a sense of rejection and fears of abandonment. His inability to respond to the demands of a regular classroom elicits redirection, frustration, and anger from peers and adults, which create a vicious cycle for Albert of being punished and rejected without being able to benefit from these experiences. He requires a highly structured and supportive environment where he is not constantly faced with situations he cannot handle.

Summary and Recommendations

Albert has inordinate difficulty selectively attending to critical aspects of his environment, meaningfully relating what he experiences, and monitoring the appropriateness of his thoughts and actions to the situation. His overall intellectual functioning as evaluated by the SB:FE was in the low-average range; however, Albert appears to require a highly structured, nurturing environment for him to meet the minimal performance demands placed on him. Without this support, he is easily threatened and disorganized by experiences to which most other children quickly adapt. In less structured situations in testing, Albert did not seem able to monitor the course of his thinking. His thoughts were repeatedly drawn to idiosyncratic associations to the activity before him or to ideas that seemed to pervade his thinking. He could not easily shift his thoughts and actions from those ideas that capture his attention, making him often resistant to external redirection. His actions are easily misinterpreted as defiance, while they are actually a function of his inability to integrate the expectations of the situations with his own feelings, reactions, and cognitions. There are indications that Albert does strive to interact with his environment in a conforming, reality-oriented manner but just cannot maintain the cognitive processes to do so. He tends to see his environment as rejecting and punitive and experiences feelings of considerable social isolation and vulnerability.

Albert's distractibility, his difficulty in shifting attention and discriminating relevant information within his environment, and his inability to integrate various facets of a task are consistent with characteristics of children with an attention deficit disorder; however, they appear qualitatively more extreme. Additionally, there appears to be significant emotional overlay in response to these impairments in efficient cognitive functioning. Albert is intensely frustrated with not being able to meet expectations or to understand what people want, and he proceeds with a diffuse awareness that people are angry and upset with him. Interventions for Albert will have to be developed in light of the interplay of cognitive and emotional factors that appear to be directing his behavior.

Based on the results of this evaluation, the following recommendations are offered. These suggestions may give some direction in working with Albert but will not correct the multitude of difficulties he experiences.

1. Albert's learning and social/emotional needs appear to be more than can be met in a traditional classroom. A therapeutic learning program is recommended. His parents are strongly encouraged to seek an educational environment that is highly structured, offers a low student-to-teacher ratio, and individualizes

instruction to meet specific learning and social/emotional needs. His parents may wish to explore services available through public special education.

2. Albert's problems demand more than the usual degree of parenting skills. His parents are encouraged to continue with counseling to help them with management issues. The added understanding of Albert's functional capabilities provided through this assessment should be considered in the counseling process. Furthermore, this counseling can help Albert's parents to become an advocate for his needs within the schools.

3. Albert will need to be instructed in many basic interpersonal skills and routine classroom behaviors and patiently retaught as each new situation presents itself. Everyday situations to which other children easily adapt can be threatening and will require more preparation and guidance for Albert to feel secure and be in more control of his thoughts and actions.

4. Albert is acutely sensitive to anger and frustration in those who interact with him. Adults need to be keenly aware of how their own reactions to his behavior increase his sense of instability and exacerbate the problematic behavior patterns.

5. Given the extent to which Albert becomes absorbed with the compelling images and actions of cartoons, his parents may want to limit his exposure, especially if the cartoons are gruesome or violent. Ideas easily intrude upon his thoughts, and limiting such content might be beneficial.

Parent Conference

Albert's mother and father attended the interpretive conference and felt that the results were consistent with many of their own observations. Given the complexity of the problems presented, the examiner and supervising psychologist felt that a specific diagnosis would not be made solely on the basis of testing. A more lengthy period of interaction and observation, combined with the information provided through testing, would most likely be necessary for this purpose. Both parents concurred with the recommendation for a special school placement and viewed this course as the most immediate intervention needed. The parents were to meet with the school referral team the following morning to initiate the special education referral process. It was strongly agreed that placement should be confirmed before the start of the next school year. Albert's continued participation in a highly structured, therapeutic play group, such as the one in which he participated briefly this past spring, was encouraged in addition to adjunct family counseling.

References

Achenbach, T. M. (1985). Assessment and taxonomy of child and adolescent psychopathology. In A. E. Kazdin (Ed.), *Developmental clinical psychology and psychiatry series, Volume 3*. Beverly Hills: Sage.

Ackerman, P. T., Oglesby, M. D., & Dykman, R. A. (1981). A contrast of hyperactive, learning disabled, and hyperactive-learning disabled boys. *Journal of Clinical Child Psychology, 10*, 168–172.

Adler, G. (1980). A treatment framework for adult patients with borderline and narcissistic personality disorders. *Bulletin of the Menninger Clinic, 44*, 171–180.

Allport, G. W. (1937). *Personality: A psychological interpretation*. New York: Holt.

Allport, G. W. (1960). The open system in personality theory. *Journal of Abnormal Psychology, 61*, 301–311.

Allport, G. W. (1961). *Pattern and growth in personality*. New York: Holt, Rinehart, and Winston.

American Educational Research Association. (1985). *Standards for educational and psychological testing*. Washington, DC: American Psychological Association.

American Psychiatric Association. (1968). *Diagnostic and Statistical Manual of Mental Disorders, II*. Washington, D. C.

American Psychiatric Association. (1980). *Diagnostic and Statistical Manual of Mental Disorders, III*. Washington, D. C.

American Psychiatric Association. (1987). *Diagnostic and Statistical Manual of Mental Disorders, III-R*. Washington, D. C.

Anderson, J. C., Williams, S., McGee, R., & Silva, P. A. (1987). DSM-III disorders in pre-adolescent children: Prevalence in a large sample from the general population. *Archives of General Psychiatry, 44*, 69–76.

Anderson, R. C., Shirey, L. L., Wilson, P. T., & Fielding, L. G. (1987). Interestingness of children's reading material. In R. E. Snow & M. J. Farr (Eds.), *Aptitude, learning, and instruction: Vol. 3. Cognitive and affective process analyses* (pp. 287–299). Hillsdale, NJ: Erlbaum.

Armstrong, M. A. S. (1954). Children's responses to animal and human figures in thematic pictures. *Journal of Consulting Psychology, 18*, 67–70.

Arnold, M. B. (1962). *Story sequence analysis: A new method of measuring motivation and predicting achievement*. New York: Columbia University Press.

Asher, S. R., & Coie, J. D. (Eds.) (1990). *Peer rejection in childhood*. New York: Cambridge University Press.

Atkinson, J. W. (1957). Motivational determinants of risk-taking behavior. *Psychological Review, 64*, 359–372.

Atkinson, J. W. (1958). *Motives in fantasy, action, and society*. Princeton: Van Nostrand.

Atkinson, J. W. (1964). *An introduction to motivation*. Princeton: Van Nostrand.

Atkinson, J. W. (1974). Strength of motivation and efficiency in performance. In J. W. Atkinson & J. O. Raynor (Eds.), *Motivation and achievement* (pp. 117–142). New York: Winston.

Atkinson, J. W. (1981). Studying personality in the context of an advanced motivational psychology. *American Psychologist, 36,* 117–128.

August, G. J. (1987). Production deficiencies in free recall: A comparison of hyperactive, learning disabled, and normal children. *Journal of Abnormal Child Psychology, 15(3),* 429–440.

Bach, G. R. (1945). Young children's play fantasies. *Psychological Monographs, 59,* Vol. 2 (Whole No. 272).

Bachtold, L. M. (1975). Perceptions of emotionally disturbed male adolescents on the Thematic Apperception Test. *Perceptual and Motor Skills, 40,* 867–871.

Bacon, S. J. (1974). Arousal and the range of cue utilization. *Journal of Experimental Psychology, 102,* 81–87.

Bahrick, L. E., & Watson, J. S. (1985). Detection of intermodal proprioceptive-visual contingency as a potential basis of self-perception in infancy. *Developmental Psychology, 21(6),* 963–973.

Bailey, B. E., & Green, J. (1977). Black thematic apperception test stimulus material. *Journal of Personality Assessment, 41,* 25–32.

Bandura, A. (1977). Self-efficacy: Toward a unifying theory of behavioral change. *Psychological Review, 84,* 191–215.

Bandura, A. (1982). The self and mechanisms of agency. In J. Suls (Ed.), *Psychological perspectives on the self* (Vol. 3, pp. 38–49). Hillsdale, NJ: Erlbaum.

Bandura, A. (1986). *The social foundations of thought and action: A social cognitive theory.* Englewood Cliffs, NJ: Prentice-Hall.

Bandura, A. (1988). Self-regulation of motivation and action through goal systems. In V. Hamilton, G. H. Bower, & N. H. Frijda (Eds.), *Cognitive perspectives on emotion and motivation* (pp. 37–61). Dordrecht, Netherlands: Kluwer Academic Publishers.

Bandura, A. (1989). Human agency in social cognitive theory. *American Psychologist, 44(9),* 1175–1184.

Bandura, A., Reese, L., & Adams, N. E. (1982). Microanalysis of action and fear of arousal as a function of differential levels of perceived self-efficacy. *Journal of Personality and Social Psychology, 43,* 5–21.

Bandura, A., Taylor, C. B., Williams, S. L., Mefford, I. N., & Barchas, J. D. (1985). Catecholamine secretion as a function of perceived coping self-efficacy. *Journal of Consulting and Clinical Psychology, 53,* 406–414.

Bandura, A., & Wood, R. E. (1989). Effect of perceived controllability and performance standards on self-regulation of complex decision-making. *Journal of Personality and Social Psychology, 56,* 805–814.

Barkley, R. A. (1981). The use of psychopharmacology to study reciprocal influences in parent-child interaction. *Journal of Abnormal Child Psychology, 9,* 303–310.

Barkley, R. A. (1990). *Attention deficit hyperactivity disorder.* New York: Guilford.

Barnett, M. A., Howard, J. A., Melton, E. M., & Dino, G. A. (1982). Effect of inducing sadness about self or other on helping behavior in high and low-empathic children. *Child Development, 53(4),* 920–923.

Baron, J. (1985). *Rationality and intelligence.* New York: Cambridge University Press.

Barrat, E. S. (1985). Impulsiveness subtraits: Arousal and information processing. In J. T. Spence & C. E. Izard (Eds.), *Motivation, emotion and personality* (pp. 137–146). North-Holland: Oxford.

Barron, A. P., & Earls, F. (1984). The relation of temperament and social factors to behavior problems in three-year-old children. *Journal of Child Psychology and Psychiatry, 25,* 23–33.

Bates, J. E., Maslin, C. A., & Frankel, K. A. (1985). Attachment security, mother-child interaction, and temperament as predictors of behavior-problem ratings at age three years. In I. Bretherton & E. Waters (Eds.), Growing points of attachment theory and research. *Monographs of the Society for Research in Child Development, 50,* Serial No. 209.

Beck, A. T. (1967). Depression: *Clinical, experimental and theoretical aspects.* New York: Harper & Row.

Beck, A. T. (1976). *Cognitive therapy and the emotional disorders.* New York: International Universities Press.

Beebe, B., & Lachmann, F. M. (1988). The contribution of mother-infant mutual influence to the origins of self and object representations. *Psychoanalytic Psychology, 5,* 305–337.

Beery, K. E. (1982). *Revised administration, scoring and teaching manual for the Developmental Test of Visual-Motor Integration.* Toronto: Modern Curriculum Press.

Bell, J. E. (1948). *Projective techniques: A dynamic approach to the study of personality.* New York: Longmans, Green.

Bell, R. Q. (1968). A reinterpretation of the direction of effects in studies of socialization. *Psychological Review, 75,* 81–95.

Bell, R. Q. (1979). Parent, child, and reciprocal influences. *American Psychologist, 34,* 821–826.

Bell, R. Q., & Harper, L. V. (1977). *The effect of children on parents.* Hillsdale, NJ: Erlbaum.

Bellak, L. (1954). *The TAT and CAT in clinical use.* New York: Grune & Stratton.

Bellak, L. (1975). *The Thematic Apperception Test, the Children's Apperception Test and the Senior Apperception Test in clinical use.* New York: Grune & Stratton.

Bellak, L. (1986). *The TAT, CAT, and SAT in clinical use* (4th ed.). Orlando, FL: Grune & Stratton. Discusses CAT, CAT-H

Bellak, L., & Bellak, S. (1949). *The CAT-H: A human modification.* Larchmont, NY: CPS.

Bellak, L., & Bellak, S. (1965). *The Children's Apperception test.* Larchmont, NY: CPS.

Bellak, L., & Bellak, S. (1973). *Manual: Senior Apperception Test.* Larchmont, NY: CPS.

Bellak, L., & Hurvich, M. S. (1966). A human modification of the Children's Apperception Test (C.A.T.-H). *Journal of Projective Techniques and Personality Assessment, 30,* 228–242.

Bellak, L., & Loeb, L. (1969). *The schizophrenic syndrome.* New York: Grune & Stratton.

Bender, W. N. (1986). Teachability and behavior of learning disabled children. *Psychological Reports, 59,* 471–476.

Bender, W. N. (1987). Behavioral indicators of temperament and personality in the inactive learner. *Journal of Learning Disabilities, 20(5),* 301–305.

Berg, M. (1986). Diagnostic use of the Rorschach with adolescents. In A. I. Rabin (Ed.). *Projective techniques for adolescents and children.* New York; Springer.

Berger, M. (1985). Temperament and individual differences. In M. Rutter & L. Hersov (Eds.). *Child and adolescent psychiatry: Modern approaches (2nd Edition).* Oxford: Blackwell Scientific.

Berkowitz, L. (1990). On the formation and regulation of anger and aggression. *American Psychologist, 45(4),* 494–503.

Berlyne, D. E. (1960). *Conflict, arousal and curiosity.* New York: McGraw-Hill.

Berlyne, D. E. (1965). *Structure and direction in thinking.* New York: McGraw-Hill.

Berlyne, D. E. (1966). Curiosity and exploration. *Science, 153,* 25–33.

Bieri, J. (1968). Cognitive complexity and judgment of inconsistent information. In R. B. Abelson, E. Aronson, W. J. McGurie, T. M. Newcombe, M. J. Rosenberg, & P. E. Tannenbaum (Eds.), *Theories of cognitive consistency: A source book.* Chicago: Rand McNally.

Bieri, J. (1971). Cognitive structures in personality. In H. M. Schroeder & P. Suefeld (Eds.), *Personality theory and information processing* (pp. 178–208). New York: Ronald Press.

Biersdorf, K. R., & Marcuse, F. L. (1953). Response of children to human and to animal pictures. *Journal of Projective Techniques, 17,* 455–459.

Biggs, J. B. (1979). Individual differences in study processes and the quality of learning outcomes. *Higher Education, 8,* 381–394.

Binder, A. (1988). Juvenile delinquency. *Annual Review of Psychology, 39,* 253–282.

Blashfield, R. K., & Draguns, J. G. (1976). Toward a taxonomy of psychopathology: The purpose of psychiatric classification. *British Journal of Psychiatry, 128,* 574–583.

Blatt, S. J., & Lerner H. D. (1983). The psychological assessment of object representation. *Journal of Personality Assessment, 47,* 7–28.

Blum, G. S. (1950). *The Blacky Pictures.* New York: Psychological Corporation.

Borkowski, J. G., Carr, M., & Pressley, M. (1987). "Spontaneous" strategy use: Perspectives from metacognitive theory. *Intelligence, 11,* 61–75.

Bower, G., & Cohen, P. (1982). Emotional influences in memory and thinking: Data and theory. In M. Clarke & S. Fiske (Eds.), *Affect and cognition* (pp 291–331). Hillsdale, NJ: Erlbaum.

Boyd, N. A., & Mandler, G. (1955). Children's responses to human and animal stories and pictures. *Journal of Consulting Psychology, 19,* 367–371.

Bransford, J. D., & Stein, B. S. (1984). *The IDEAL problem solver.* New York: W. H. Freeman.

Bransford, J. D., Stein, B. S., Vye, N. J., Franks, J. J., Auble, P. M., Mezynski, K. J., & Perfetto, G. A. (1982). Differences in approaches to learning: An overview. *Journal of Experimental Psychology: General III,* 390–398.

Breckler, S. J., & Greenwald, A. G. (1986). Motivational facets of the self. In R. M. Sorrentino & E. T. Higgins (Eds.), *Handbook of motivation and cognition: Foundations of social behavior* (pp. 145–164). New York: Guilford Press.

Brewin, C. R. (1988). *Cognitive Foundations of Clinical Psychology.* Hillsdale, NJ: Erlbaum.

Brimer, E., & Levine, F. M. (1983). Stimulus-seeking behavior in hyperactive and nonhyperactive children. *Journal of Abnormal Child Psychology, 11,* 131–139.

Brown, A. (1980). Metacognitive development and reading. In R. Spiro, B. Bruce, & W. Brewer (Eds.), *Theoretical issues in reading comprehension* (pp. 453–481). Hillsdale, NJ: Erlbaum.

Brown, A. L., Bransford, J. D., Ferrara, R. A., & Campione, J. C. (1983). Learning, remembering, and understanding. In J. H. Flavell & E. M. Markman (Eds.), *Carmichael's manual of child psychology* (Vol. 1, pp. 77–166). New York: Wiley.

Brown, A. L., & Campione, J. C. (1981). Inducing flexible thinking: A problem of access. In M. Friedman, J. P. Das, & N. O'Connor (Eds.), *Intelligence and learning* (pp. 515–530). New York: Plenum.

Brown, A. L., Campione, J. C., & Day, J. D. (1981). Learning to learn: On training students to learn from texts. *Education Researcher, 10,* 14–21.

Bruner, J. S. (1966). On cognitive growth. In J. S. Bruner, R. R. Oliver, & P. M. Grunfield (Eds.), *Studies in cognitive growth.* New York: Wiley.

Bryant, B. K. (1982). An index of empathy for children and adolescents. *Child Development, 53,* 413–425.

Bryant, B. K. (1987). Mental health, temperament, family, and friends: perspectives on children's empathy and social perspective taking. In N. Eisenberg & J. Strayer (Eds.), *Empathy and its development* (pp. 245–270). Cambridge: Cambridge University Press.

Buchsbaum, M. S., & Haier, R. J. (1983). Psychopathology: Biological approaches. *Annual Review of Psychology, 34,* 401–430.

Budoff, M. (1960). The relative utility of animal and human figures in a picture-story test for young children. *Journal of Projective Techniques, 24,* 347–352.

Buss, A. H., & Plomin, R. (1975). *A temperament theory of personality.* New York: Wiley.

Buss, A. H., & Plomin, R. (1984). *Temperament: Early developing personality traits.* Hillsdale, NJ: Erlbaum.

Cameron, J. R. (1977). Parental treatment, children's temperament and the risk of childhood behavioral problems. *American Journal of Orthopsychiatry, 47,* 568–576.

Campbell, D. T., & Fiske, D. W. (1959). Convergent and discriminant validation by the multitrait-multimethod matrix. *Psychological Bulletin, 56,* 81–105.

Campbell, S. B., Douglas, V. I., & Morgenstern, G. (1971). Cognitive styles in hyperactive children and the effect of methyphenidate. *Journal of Child Psychology and Psychiatry, 12,* 55–67.

Campione, J. C., & Brown, A. L. (1977). Memory and metamemory development in educable retarded children. In R. V. Kail & J. W. Hagen (Eds.), *Perspectives on the development of memory and cognition* (pp. 367–406). Hillsdale, NJ: Erlbaum.

Campione, M. A., & Lord, R. G. (1982). A control systems conceptualization of the goal-setting and changing process. *Organizational Behavior and Human Performance, 30,* 265–287.

Campos, J. J., & Barrett, K. C. (1984). A new understanding of emotions and their development. In C. E. Izard, J. Kagan, & R. B. Zajonc (Eds.), *Emotions, cognition, and behavior* (pp. 229–263). Cambridge: Cambridge University Press.

Campos, J. J., Barrett, K. C., Lamb, M. E., Goldsmith, H. H., & Stenberg, C. (1983). Socioemotional development. In M. M. Haith & J. J. Campos (Eds.), *Handbook of child psychology, Vol. 2 Infancy and developmental psychobiology.* New York: Wiley.

Campus, N. (1976). A measure of needs to assess the stimulus characteristics of TAT cards. *Journal of Personality Assessment, 40,* 248–258.

Cantor, N., Markus, H., Niedenthal, P., & Nurius, P. (1986). On motivation and the self-concept. In R. M. Sorrentino & E. T. Higgins (Eds.), *Handbook of motivation and cognition: Foundations of social behavior* (pp. 96–121). New York: Guilford Press.

Cardell, C. D., & Parmar, R. S. (1988). Teacher perceptions of temperament characteristics of children classified as learning disabled. *Journal of Learning Disabilities, 8,* 497–502.

Carey, W. B. (1985). Clinical use of temperamental data in pediatrics. *Developmental and Behavioral Pediatrics, 6,* 137–142.

Carey, W. B. (1990). Temperament risk factors in children: A conference report. *Developmental and Behavioral Pediatrics, 11,* 28–34.

Center, D. B. (1989). Social maladjustment: Definition, identification, and programming. *Focus on Exceptional Children, 22,* 1–12.

Chess, S., & Thomas, A. (1984). *Origins and evolution of behavior disorders from infancy to early adult life.* New York: Brunner/Mazel.

Chi, M., Glaser, R., & Reese, E. (1982). Expertise in problem solving. In R. Sternberg (Ed.), *Advances in the psychology of human intelligence* (Vol. 1, pp. 7–75), Hillsdale, NJ: Erlbaum.

Clark, R. (1952). The projective measurement of experimentally induced levels of sexual motivation. *Journal of Experimental Psychology, 44,* 391–399.

Clark, M. S., & Reis, H. T. (1988). Interpersonal processes in close relationships. *Annual Reviews in Psychology, 39,* 609–672.

Clements, S. D. (1966). *Task Force One: Minimal brain dysfunction in children.* National Institute of Neurology Diseases and Blindness Monograph, No. 3. Rockville, MD: U.S. Department of Health, Education and Welfare.

Cohen, H., & Weil, G. R. (1975). *Tasks of emotional development: A projective test for children and adolescents.* Boston: T.E.D. Associates.

Cohen, N. J., & Douglas, V. I. (1972). Characteristics of the orienting response in hyperactive and normal children. *Psychophysiology, 9,* 238–245.

Cohen-Sandler, R., Berman, A. L., & King, R. A. (1982). A follow-up study of hospitalized suicidal children. *Journal of the American Academy of Child Psychiatry, 21,* 398–403.

Conners, C. K. (1970). Symptom patterns in hyperkinetic, neurotic, and normal children. *Child Development, 41,* 667–682.

Constantino, G., Colon-Malgady, G., Malgady, R. G., & Perez, A. (1991). Assessment of Attention Deficit Disorder using a Thematic Apperception Technique, *Journal of Personality Assessment, 57,* 87–95.

Constantino, G., & Malgady, R. G. (1983). Verbal fluency of Hispanic, Black and White children on TAT and TEMAS, a new thematic apperception test. *Hispanic Journal of Behavioral Sciences, 5,* 199–206.

Constantino, G., Malgady, R. G., & Rogler, L. H. (1988). *Tell-Me-A-Story, Manual.* Los Angeles: Western Psychological Services.

Constantino, G., Malgady, R. G., Rogler, L. H., & Tsui, E. C. (1988). Discriminant analysis of clinical outpatients and public school children by TEMAS: A Thematic apperception test for Hispanic and Black children. *Journal of Personality Assessment, 52,* 670–678.

Cooper, A. (1981). A basic TAT set for adolescent males. *Journal of Clinical Psychology, 37,* 411–415.

Cowan, P. A. (1982). The relationship between emotional and cognitive development. In D. Cicchetti, & P. Hesse (Eds.), *New directions for child development, Vol. 16, Emotional Development* (pp. 49–81). San Francisco: Jossey-Bass.

Cox, B., & Sargent, H. (1950). TAT responses of emotionally disturbed and emotionally stable children: Clinical judgment versus normative data. *Journal of Projective Techniques, 14,* 61–74.

Crockenberg, S. (1986). Are temperamental differences in babies associated with predictable differences in caregiving? In J. V. Lerner & R. M. Lerner (Eds.), *Temperament and child development: New directions for child development* (pp. 53–73). San Francisco: Jossey-Bass.

Crockett, D., Klonoff, H., & Clark, C. (1976). The effects of marijuana on verbalization and thought processes. *Journal of Personality Assessment, 40,* 582–587.

Cronbach, L. J. (1970). *Essentials of psychological testing* (3rd ed.). New York: Harper and Row.

Cronbach, L. J. (1988). Five perspectives on validity argument. In H. Wainer & H. I. Braun (Eds.), *Test validity* (pp. 3–17). Hillsdale, NJ: Erlbaum.

Cronbach, L. J., & Meehl, P. E. (1955). Construct validity in psychological tests. *Psychological Bulletin, 52,* 281–302.

Dana, R. H. (1959). Proposal for objective scoring of the TAT. *Perceptual and Motor Skills, 9,* 27–43.

Dana, R. H. (1982). *A human science model for personality assessment with projective techniques.* Springfield, IL: Charles C. Thomas.

Davids, A. (1973). Aggression in thought and action of emotionally disturbed boys. *Journal of Consulting and Clinical Psychology, 40,* 322–327.

Deardoff, P. A., Kendall, P. C., Finch, A. J., Jr., & Sitarz, A. M. (1977). Empathy, locus of control, and anxiety in college students. *Psychological Reports, 40,* 1236–1238.

DeCharms, R. (1976). *Enhancing motivation: Change in the classroom.* New York: Irvington.

Deci, E. L. (1975). *Instrinsic motivation.* New York: Plenum.

Deci, E. L. (1981). *The psychology of self-determination.* Lexington, MA: Heath.

Deci, E. L., & Ryan, R. M. (1980). The empirical exploration of intrinsic motivational processes. In L. Berkowitz (Ed.), *Advances in experimental social psychology* (Vol. 13). New York: Academic Press.

Derryberry, D. (1987). Incentive and feedback effects on target detection: A chronometric analysis of Gray's model of temperament. *Personality and Individual Differences, 6,* 855–866.

Derryberry, D., & Rothbart, M. K. (1984). Emotion, attention, and temperament. In C. E. Izard, J. Kagan, & R. Zajonc (Eds.), *Emotion, cognition and behavior* (pp. 132–166). Cambridge: Cambridge University Press.

Derryberry, D., & Rothbart, M. K. (1988). Arousal, affect, and attention as components of temperament. *Journal of Personality and Social Psychology, 55,* 958–966.

DeVries, M. (1984). Temperament and infant mortality among the Masai of East Africa. *American Journal of Psychiatry, 141,* 1189–1194.

Diener, E., & Larsen, R. J. (1984). Temporal stability and cross-situational consistency of affective, behavioral and cognitive responses. *Journal of Personality and Social Psychology, 47,* 871–883.

Dodge, K. A. (1980). Social cognition and children's aggressive behavior. *Child Development, 51,* 162–170.

Dodge, K. A., & Frame, C. L. (1982). Social cognitive biases and deficits in aggressive boys. *Child Development, 53,* 620–635.

Dodge, K. A., & Newman, J. P. (1981). Biased decision-making process in aggressive boys. *Journal of Abnormal Psychology, 90,* 375–379.

Douglas, V. (1972). Stop, look, and listen: The problem of sustained attention and impulse control in hyperactive and normal children. *Canadian Journal of Behavioral Science, 4,* 159–182.

Douglas, V. (1980). Treatment and training approaches to hyperactivity: Establishing internal or external control. In C. Whalen & B. Henker (Eds.), *Hyperactive children: The social ecology of identification and treatment.* New York: Academic Press.

Douglas, V. I. (1983). Attentional and cognitive problems. In M. Rutter (Ed.), *Developmental Neuropsychiatry* (pp. 280–329). New York: Guilford Press.

Douglas, V. I., & Parry, P. A. (1983). Effects of reward on delayed reaction time task performance of hyperactive children. *Journal of Abnormal Child Psychology, 11,* 313–326.

Douglas, V. I., & Peters, K. G. (1979). Toward a clearer definition of the attentional deficit of hyperactive children. In G. A. Hale & M. Lewis (Eds.), *Attention and the development of cognitive skills.* New York: Plenum Press.

Dunn, J. (1988). *The beginnings of social understanding.* Cambridge: Harvard University Press.

Dunn, J., & Kendrick, C. (1982). *Siblings: Love, envy and understanding.* London: Grant McIntyre.

Dweck, C. S. (1986). Motivational processes affecting learning. *American Psychologist, 41(10),* 1040–1048.

Dweck, C. S., & Goetz, T. E. (1978). Attributions and learned helplessness. In J. H. Harvey, W. Ickes, & R. F. Kidd (Eds.), *New directions in attribution research* (Vol. 2). Hillsdale, NJ: Erlbaum.

Dweck, C. S., & Licht, G. G. (1980). Learned helplessness and intellectual achievement. In J. Garber & M. E. P. Seligman (Eds.), *Human helplessness: Theory and applications.* New York: Academic Press.

Dykman, R. A., Ackerman, P. T., & Oglesby, D. M. (1979). Selective and sustained attention in hyperactive, learning, disabled, and normal boys. *Journal of Nervous and Mental Disease, 167,* 288–297.

Dymond, R. (1954). Adjustment changes over therapy from TAT ratings. In C. R. Rogers & R. Dymond (Eds.), *Psychotherapy and personality change.* Chicago: University of Chicago Press.

Elias, M. J., Rothbaum, P. A., & Gara, M. (1986). Social-cognitive problem-solving in children: Assessing the knowledge and application of skills. *Journal of Applied Developmental Psychology, 1,* 77–94.

Ellis, A. (1962). *Reason and emotion in psychotherapy.* New York: Stuart.

Emmons, R. A., & Diener, E. (1985). Personality correlates of subjective well-being. *Personality and Social Psychology Bulletin, 11,* 89–97.

Emmons, R. A., & Diener, E. (1986). An interactional approach to the study of personality and emotion. *Journal of Personality, 54,* 371–384.

Endler, N. S., & Magnusson, D. (1976). *Interactional psychology and personality.* Washington, DC: Hemisphere.

Entwisle, D. (1972). To dispel fantasies about fantasy-based measures of achievement motivation. *Psychological Bulletin, 77,* 377–391.

Entwisle, D. (1988). Motivational factors in students' approaches in learning. In R. R. Schmeck (Ed.), *Learning strategies and learning styles* (pp. 21–51). New York: Plenum.

Entwistle, N., Hanley, M., & Hounsell, D. J. (1979). Identifying distinctive approaches to studying. *Higher Education, 8,* 365–380.

Epstein, S. (1962). The measurement of drive and conflict in humans: Theory and experiment. In M. R. Jones (Ed.), *Nebraska symposium on motivation* (pp. 127–206). Lincoln: University of Nebraska Press.

Epstein, S. (1966). Some considerations on the nature of ambiguity and the use of stimulus dimensions in projective techniques. *Journal of Consulting Psychology, 30,* 183–192.

Epstein, S. (1979). The stability of behavior: On predicting most of the people much of the time. *Journal of Personality and Social Psychology, 37,* 1097–1126.

Eron, L. D. (1950). A normative study of the Thematic Apperception Test. *Psychological Monographs, 64(9),* Whole #315.

Frequencies of themes both various cards.

Eron, L. D., & Huesmann, L. R. (1984). The control of aggressive behavior by changes in attitudes, values, and the conditions of learning. In R. J. Blanchard & D. C. Blanchard (Eds.), *Advances in the study of aggression* (pp. 139–173). New York: Academic Press.

Escalona, S. K. (1968). *The roots of individuality: Normal patterns of development in infancy*. Chicago: Aldine.

Exner, J. E. (1986). *The Rorschach: A comprehensive system, Vol. 1: Basic Foundations*. New York: Wiley.

Eysenck, H. J. (1967). *The biological basis of personality*. Springfield: C. C. Thomas.

Eysenck, H. J. (1981). Learning, memory and personality. In H. J. Eysenck (Ed.), *A model for personality*. Berlin: Springer-Verlag.

Eysenck, H. J. (1982). *Attention and arousal: Cognition and performance*. Berlin: Springer-Verlag.

Eysenck, H. J. (1983). Human learning and individual differences: The genetic dimension. *Educational Psychology, 3(3 & 4)*, 169–188.

Fairbairn, W. R. D. (1952). *Psychoanalytic studies of the personality*. New York: Basic Books.

Fairbairn, W. R. D. (1954). *An object-relations theory of the personality*. New York: Basic Books.

Farr, M. J. (1987). Cognition, affect and motivation: Issues, perspectives and directions toward unity. In R. E. Snow & M. J. Farr (Eds.), *Aptitude, learning and instruction: Conative and affective process analyses* (Vol. 3, pp. 347–354). Hillsdale, NJ: Erlbaum.

Feagans, L. (1983). A current view of learning disabilities. *Journal of Pediatrics, 102*, 487–493.

Feldman, H., Levine, M. D., & Fenton, T. (1986). Estimating personal performance: A problem for children with school dysfunction. *Developmental and Behavioral Pediatrics, 7*, 281–287.

Feshbach, N. D. (1978). Studies of empathic behavior in children. In B. A. Maher (Ed.), *Progress in experimental personality research* (Vol. 8, pp. 1–47). New York: Academic Press.

Firestone, P., & Douglas, V. I. (1975). The effects of reward and punishment on reaction times and autonomic activity in hyperactive and normal children. *Journal of Abnormal Child Psychology, 3*, 201–216.

Fiske, S. T., & Pavelchak, M. A. (1986). Category-based versus piecemeal-based affective responses: Developments in schema-triggered affect. In R. M. Sorrentino & E. T. Higgins (Eds.), *Handbook of motivation and cognition: Foundations of social behavior*. (pp. 167–203). New York: Guilford Press.

Fitzgerald, B. J., Pasewark, R. A., & Fleisher, S. (1974). Responses of an aged population on the Gerontological and Thematic Apperception Tests. *Journal of Personality Assessment, 38*, 234–235.

Flavell, J. H. (1963). *The developmental psychology of Jean Piaget*. Princeton: Van Nostrand.

Flavell, J. H. (1979). Metacognition and cognitive monitoring: A new area of cognitive-developmental inquiry. *American Psychologist, 34*, 906–911.

Flavell, J. H. (1985). *Cognitive development (2nd ed.)*. Englewood Cliffs, NJ: Prentice-Hall.

Forgus, R., & Shulman, B. (1979). *Personality: A cognitive view*. Englewood Cliffs, NJ: Prentice-Hall.

Forrest-Pressley, D. L., & Waller, T. G. (1984). Knowledge and monitoring abilities of poor readers. *Topics in Learning & Learning Disabilities, 3*, 73–80.

Fox, N. A., & Davidson, R. J. (1984). Hemispheric substrates of affect: A developmental model. In N. A. Fox & R. J. Davidson (Eds.), *The psychology of affective development* (pp. 353–381). Hillsdale, NJ: Erlbaum.

Frank, L. D. (1939). Projective methods for the study of personality. *Journal of Psychology, 8,* 389–413.

Fransson, A. (1977). On qualitative differences in learning, IV. Effects of motivation and test anxiety on process and outcome. *British Journal of Educational Psychology, 47,* 244–257.

Frederiksen, N. (1986). Toward a broader conception of human intelligence. *American Psychologist, 41,* 445–452.

Freud, S. (1923). *The ego and the id.* New York: Norton.

Furuya, K. (1957). Responses of school children to human and animal pictures. *Journal of Projective Techniques, 21,* 248–252.

Gacono, C. B., & Meloy, J. R. (1988). The relationship between cognitive style and defensive process in the psychopath. *Criminal Justice and Behavior, 15,* 472–483.

Garber, J., & Seligman, M. E. P. (1980). *Human helplessness: Theory and applications.* New York: Academic Press.

Gardner, H. (1983). *Frames of mind.* New York: Basic Books.

Gardner, J. M., & Karmel, B. Z. (1983). Attention and arousal in pre-term and full term neonates. In T. Field & A. Sostek (Eds.), *Infants born at risk* (pp. 69–98). New York: Grune & Stratton.

Garfield, S. L., & Eron, L. D. (1948). Interpreting mood and activity in TAT stories. *Journal of Abnormal and Social Psychology, 43,* 338–345.

Garmezy, N., & Rutter, M. (1983). *Stress, coping, and development in children.* New York: McGraw-Hill.

Gedo, J. (1988). *The mind in disorder: Psychoanalytic models of pathology.* Hillsdale, NJ: Erlbaum.

Geen, R. G. (1984). Preferred stimulation levels in introverts and extroverts: Effects on arousal and performance. *Journal of Personality and Social Psychology, 46,* 1303–1312.

Gelman, R., & Baillargeon, R. (1983). A review of some Piagetian concepts. In J. H. Flavell & E. M. Markman (Eds.), *Carmichael's manual of child psychology* (Vol. 3). New York: Wiley.

Getzels, J. W. (1966). The problem of interests: A reconsideration. In H. A. Robinson (Ed.), *Reading: Seventy-five years of progress* (Supplementary Education Monographs, 66).

Gitomer, D. H., & Glaser, R. (1987). If you don't know it, work on it: Knowledge, self-regulation and instruction. In R. E. Snow & M. J. Farr (Eds.), *Aptitude, learning and instruction: Conative and affective process analyses* (Vol. 3, pp. 301–326). Hillsdale, NJ: Erlbaum.

Gluck, M. R. (1955). The relationship between hostility in the TAT and behavioral hostility. *Journal of Projective Techniques, 19,* 21–26.

Goldsmith, H. H., & Campos, J. J. (1986). Fundamental issues in the study of early temperament: The Denver Twin Temperament Study. *Annual Progress in Child Development,* 231–283.

Graham, P., Rutter, M., & George, S. (1973). Temperamental characteristics as predictors of behavior disorders in children. *American Journal of Orthopsychiatry, 43,* 328–339.

Gray, J. A. (1981). A critique of Eysenck's theory of personality. In H. J. Eysenck (Ed.), *A model for personality.* Berlin: Springer-Verlag.

Gray, J. A. (1982). *The neuropsychology of anxiety.* Oxford: Oxford University Press.

Gresham, F. M. (1985). Behavior disorder assessment: Conceptual, definitional, and practical consideration. *School Psychology Review, 14(4)*, 495–509.

Grinder, R. E. (1985). The gifted in our midst: By their divine deeds, neuroses, and mental test scores we have known them. In F. D. Horowitz & M. O'Brien (Eds.), *The gifted and talented: Developmental perspectives* (pp. 5–35). Washington, DC: American Psychological Association.

Guntrip, H. J. S. (1968). *Schizoid Phenomena, object-relations, and the self*. New York: International Universities Press.

Guntrip, H. J. S. (1974). Psychoanalytic object relations theory: The Fairbairn-Guntrip approach. In Silvano Arieti (Ed.), *American Handbook of Psychiatry* (Vol. 1, pp. 828–842). New York: Basic Books.

Gurel, L., & Ullmann, L. P. (1958). Quantitative differences in response to TAT cards: The relationship between transcendence score and number of emotional words. *Journal of Projective Techniques, 22*, 432–439.

Gurevitz, S., & Klapper, Z. S. (1951). Techniques for and evaluation of the responses of schizophrenic and cerebral palsied children to the Children's Apperception Test (C.A.T.). *The Quarterly Journal of Child Behavior, 3*, 38–65.

Hafner, A. J., & Kaplan, A. M. (1960). Hostility content analysis of the Rorschach and TAT. *Journal of Projective Techniques, 24*, 137–143.

Hamilton, N. G., & Allsbrook, L. (1986). Thirty cases of "schizophrenia" reexamined. *Bulletin of the Menninger Clinic, 50*, 323–340.

Hamsher, J. H., & Farina, A. (1967). "Openness" as a dimension of projective test responses. *Journal of Consulting Psychology, 31*, 525–528.

Harris, R. (1981). Conceptual complexity and preferred coping strategies in anticipation of temporally predictable and unpredictable threat. *Journal of Personality and Social Psychology, 41*, 380–390.

Harter, S. (1978). Pleasure derived from optimal challenge and the effects of extrinsic rewards on children's difficulty level choices. *Child Development, 49*, 788–799.

Hartman, A. A. (1949). An experimental examination of the thematic apperceptive techniques in clinical diagnosis. In H. S. Conrad (Ed.), *Psychological Monographs* (Vol. 63, Whole #303). Washington, DC: American Psychological Association.

Hartman, A. A. (1970). A basic TAT set. *Journal of Projective Techniques and Personality Assessment, 34*, 391–396.

Hartmann, H. (1939). *Ego psychology and the problem of adaptation*. New York: International Universities Press.

Hartmann, H. (1950). Comments on the psychoanalytic theory of the ego. In H. Hartmann (Ed.), *Essays in ego psychology: Selected problems in psychoanalytic theory* (pp. 113–141). New York: International Universities Press.

Hartmann, H. (1951). Ego psychology and the problem of adaptation. In D. Rapaport (Ed.), *Organization and pathology of thought*. New York: Columbia University Press.

Hartmann, H. (1956). The development of the ego concept in Freud's work. In *Essays on ego psychology* (pp. 37–68). New York: International Universities Press.

Hayes, S. C., Nelson, R. O., & Jarrett, R. B. (1987). The treatment utility of assessment: A functional approach to evaluating assessment quality. *American Psychologist, 42*, 963–974.

Haynes, J. P., & Peltier, J. (1985). Patterns of practice with the TAT in juvenile forensic settings. *Journal of Personality Assessment, 49*, 26–29.

Hebb, D. D. (1955). Drives and the C.N.S. (Conceptual Nervous System). *Psychological Review, 62*, 243–255.

Hechtman, L., Weiss, G., & Perlman, T. (1980). Hyperactives as young adults: Initial predictors of adult outcome. *Journal of the American Academy of Child Psychiatry, 23*, 250–260.

Heckhausen, H. (1967). *The anatomy of achievement motivation.* New York: Academic Press.

Heckhausen, H., & Gollwitzer, P. M. (1987). Thought contents and cognitive functioning in motivational versus volitional states of mind. *Motivation and Emotion, 11,* 101–120.

Heckhausen, H., & Krug, S. (1982). Motive modification. In A. J. Stewart (Ed.), *Motivation and society.* San Francisco: Jossey-Bass.

Heider, F. (1958). *Psychology of interpersonal relations.* New York: Wiley.

Henker, B., & Whalen, C. K. (1989). Hyperactivity and attention deficits, *American Psychologist, 44*, 216–223.

Henry, R. M. (1981). Validation of a projective measure of aggression-anxiety for five-year old boys. *Journal of Personality Assessment, 45*, 359–369.

Henry, R. M. (1982). The socialization of aggression in five-year-old boys. *Journal of Genetic Psychology, 141,* 105–113.

Henry, W. E. (1951). The thematic apperception technique in the study of group and cultural problems. In H. H. Anderson & G. L. Anderson (Eds.), *An introduction to projective techniques* (pp. 230–278). Englewood Cliffs, NJ: Prentice Hall.

Henry, W. E. (1956). *The analysis of fantasy.* New York: Wiley.

Hidi, S. (1990). Interest and its contribution as a mental resource for learning. *Review of Educational Research, 60*, 549–571.

Hinshaw, S. P. (1987). On the distinction between attentional deficits/hyperactivity and conduct problems/aggression in child psychopathology. *Psychological Bulletin, 101,* 443–463.

Hockey, R. (1979). Stress and the cognitive components of skilled performance. In V. Hamilton & D. M. Warbarton (Eds.), *Human stress and cognition: An information processing approach.* New York: Wiley.

Hoffman, M. L. (1982). Affect and moral development. In D. Cicchetti, & P. Hesse (Eds.), *Emotional Development* (pp. 83–103). San Francisco: Jossey-Bass.

Hoffman, M. L. (1986). Affect, cognition and motivation. In R. M. Sorrentino & E. T. Higgins (Eds.), *Handbook of motivation and cognition: Foundations of social behavior* (pp. 244–280). New York: Guilford Press.

Hogan, R. (1969). Development of an empathy scale. *Journal of Consulting and Clinical Psychology, 33*, 307–316.

Hogan, R., & Nicholson, R. A. (1988). The meaning of personality test scores. *American Psychologist, 43*, 621–626.

Holmes, D. S. (1974). The conscious control of thematic projection. *Journal of Consulting and Clinical Psychology, 42*, 323–329.

Holmstrom, R. W., Silber, D. E., & Karp, S. A. (1990). Development of the Apperceptive Personality Test. *Journal of Personality Assessment, 54*, 252–264.

Holt, R. R. (1956). Gauging primary and secondary processes in Rorschach responses. *Journal of Projective Techniques, 20*, 14–25.

Holt, R. R. (1958). Formal aspects of the TAT—A neglected resource. *Journal of Projective Techniques, 22*, 163–172.

Holt, R. R. (1960). Recent developments in psychoanalytic ego psychology and their implications for diagnostic testing. *Journal of Projective Techniques, 24*, 254–266.

Holt, R. R. (1961). The nature of TAT stories as cognitive products: A psychoanalytic approach. In J. Kagan & G. Lesser (Eds.), *Contemporary issues in thematic apperceptive methods* (pp. 3–40). Springfield, IL: Charles C. Thomas.

Honor, S. H., & Vane, J. R. (1972). Comparison of Thematic Apperception Test and Questionnaire methods to obtain achievement attitudes of high school boys. *Journal of Clinical Psychology, 28,* 81–83.

Horney, K. (1950). *Neurosis and human growth.* New York: Norton.

Howard, G. S. (1991). Cultural tales: A narrative approach to thinking, cross-cultural psychology and psychotherapy. *American Psychologist, 46(3),* 187–197.

Humphries, M. S., & Revelle, W. (1984). Personality, motivation, and performance: A theory of the relationship between individual differences and information processing. *Psychological Review, 91,* 153–184.

Hunt, E. B. (1978). Mechanics of verbal ability. *Psychological Review, 85,* 109–130.

Hunt, E. B. (1983). On the nature of intelligence, *Science, 219,* 141–146.

Hunt, J. McV. (1961). *Intelligence and experience.* New York: Ronald Press.

Hunt, J. McV. (1965). Intrinsic motivation and its role in psychological development. In D. Levine (Ed.), *Nebraska Symposium on Motivation* (Vol. 13, pp. 189–282). Lincoln: University of Nebraska Press.

Hynd, G. W., Hern, K. L., Voeller, K. K., & Marshall, R. M. (1991). Neurobiological basis of attention-deficit hyperactivity disorder (ADHD). *School Psychology Review, 20,* 174–186.

Irvin, F., & Vander Woude, K. V. (1971). Empirical support for a basic TAT set. *Journal of Clinical Psychology, 27,* 514–516.

Isen, A. M., Daubman, K. A., & Gorgoglione, J. M. (1987). The influence of positive affect on cognitive organization: Implications for education. In R. E. Snow & M. J. Farr (Eds.), *Aptitude, learning and instruction: Conative and affective process analyses* (Vol. 3, pp. 143–164). Hillsdale, NJ: Erlbaum.

Isen, A. M., & Means, B. (1983). Positive affect as a variable in decision-making. *Social Cognition, 2,* 18–31.

Izard, C. (1977). *Human emotions.* New York: Plenum Press.

Izard, C. E. (1984). Emotion-cognition relationships and human development. In C. E. Izard, J. Kagan, & R. B. Zajonc (Eds.), *Emotion, cognition, and behavior* (pp. 17–37). New York: Cambridge University Press.

Jacobson, E. (1964). *The self and the object world.* New York: International Universities Press.

James, P. B., & Mosher, D. L. (1967). Thematic aggression, hostility, guilt and aggressive behavior. *Journal of Projective Techniques and Personality Assessment, 31,* 61–67.

Johnson, J. A., Cheek, J. M., & Smither, R. (1983). The structure of empathy. *Journal of Personality and Social Psychology, 45,* 1299–1312.

Johnston, Jr., H. R. (1974). Some personality correlates of the relationships between individuals and organizations. *Journal of Applied Psychology, 59,* 623–632.

Kagan, J. (1956). The measurement of overt aggression from fantasy. *Journal of Abnormal and Social Psychology, 52,* 390–393.

Kagan, J. (1966). Reflection-impulsivity: The generality and dynamics of conceptual tempo. *Journal of Abnormal Psychology, 71,* 17–24.

Kagan, J. (1989). Temperamental contributions to social behavior. *American Psychologist, 44,* 668–674.

Kagan, J., Reznick, J. S., & Snidman, N. (1987). The physiology and psychology of behavioral inhibition in children. *Child Development, 58,* 1459–1473.

Kagan, J., Rosman, B. L., Day, D., Albert, J., & Phillips, W. (1964). Information processing in the child: Significance of analytic and reflective attitudes. *Psychological Monographs, 78,* (1, Whole #578).

Kaplan, M. F. (1967). The effect of cue relevance, ambiguity, and self-reported hostility on TAT responses. *Journal of Projective Techniques and Personality Assessment, 31,* 45–50.

Karon, B. P. (1981). The Thematic Apperception Test. In A. I. Rabin (Ed.), *Assessment with projective techniques: A concise introduction* (pp. 85–120). New York: Springer.

Karp, S. A., Banks, V., Silber, D. E., Holmstrom, R. W., & Karp, J. (1989). Outcomes of Apperceptive Personality Test (APT) and Thematic Apperceptive Test (TAT) stories. *IDS Monograph Series (Whole No. 3).* Chicago: International Diagnostic Systems.

Karp, S. A., Holmstrom, R. W., & Silber, D. E. (1989). *Apperceptive Personality Test Manual.* Chicago: International Diagnostic Systems.

Kavanagh, D. J., & Bower, G. H. (1985). Mood and self-efficacy: Impact of joy and sadness on perceived capabilities. *Cognitive Therapy and Research, 9,* 507–525.

Kegan, R., Noam, G. G., & Rogers, L. (1982). The psychology of emotion: A neo-Piagetian view. In D. Cicchetti & P. Hesse (Eds.), *Emotional Development* (pp. 105–128). San Francisco: Jossey-Bass.

Kellerman, H. (1980). A structural model of emotion and personality: Psychoanalytic and sociobiological implications. In R. Plutchik & H. Kellerman (Eds.), *Emotion: Theory, research, and experience* (pp. 349–384). New York: Academic Press.

Kelly, G. A. (1963). *A theory of personality.* New York: Norton.

Kempler, H. L., & Scott, V. (1970). Can systematically scored thematic stories reflect the attributes of the antisocial child syndrome? *Journal of Projective Techniques and Personality Assessment, 34,* 204–211.

Kenny, D. T., & Bijou, S. W. (1953). Ambiguity of pictures and the extent of personality factors in fantasy responses. *Journal of Consulting Psychology, 17,* 283–288.

Kent, G. (1987). Self-efficacious control over reported physiological, cognitive and behavioural symptoms of dental anxiety. *Behaviour Research and Therapy, 25,* 341–347.

Kent, G., & Gibbons, R. (1987). Self-efficacy and the control of anxious cognitions. *Journal of Behavior Therapy & Experimental Psychiatry, 18,* 33–40.

Keogh, B. K., & Margolis, J. (1976). Learn to labor and to wait: Attentional problems of children with learning disorders. *Journal of Learning Disabilities, 9,* 276–286.

Kernberg, O. (1970). A psychoanalytic classification of character pathology. *Journal of the American Psychoanalytic Association, 19,* 595–635.

Kernberg, O. (1975). *Borderline conditions and pathological narcissism.* New York: Jason Aronson.

Kernberg, O. (1976). *Object relations theory and clinical psychoanalysis.* New York: Jason Aronson.

Kihlstrom, J. F., & Cantor, N. (1984). Mental representations of the self. In L. Berkowitz (Ed.), *Advances in experimental social psychology* (Vol. 15, pp. 1–47). New York: Academic Press.

King, C. A., & Young, R. D. (1981). Peer popularity and peer communication patterns: Hyperactive versus active but normal boys. *Journal of Abnormal Child Psychology, 9,* 465–482.

Kistner, J. A. (1985). Attentional deficits of learning disabled children: Effects of rewards and practice. *Journal of Abnormal Child Psychology, 13(1),* 19–31.

Klein, M. (1932). *The psychoanalysis of children.* New York: Grove Press.

Klein, M. (1948). *Contributions to psychoanalysis, 1921–1945.* London: Hogarth Press.

Kohlberg, L. (1976). Moral stages and moralization: The cognitive development. In T. Lickona (Ed.), *Moral development and behavior: Theory, research, and social issues.* New York: Holt, Rinehart and Winston.

Kohut, H. (1971). *The analysis of the self: Psychoanalysis of the child.* New York: International Universities Press.

Kohut, H. (1977). *The restoration of the self.* New York: International Universities Press.

Kohut, H. (1978a). *The search for the self. Selected writings of Henry Kohut: 1950–1978* (Vol. 1). New York: International Universities Press.

Kohut, H. (1978b). *The search for the self.* (Vol. 2). New York: International Universities Press.

Kuhl, J. (1984). Volitional aspects of achievement motivation and learned helplessness: Toward a comprehensive theory of action control. In B. A. Maher & W. B. Maher (Eds.), *Progress in experimental personality research* (Vol. 12, pp. 100–171). Orlando, FL: Academic Press.

Kuhl, J. (1986). Motivation and information processing: A new look at decision making, dynamic change, and action control. In R. M. Sorrentino & E. T. Higgins (Eds.), *Handbook of motivation and cognition: Foundations of social behavior.* (pp. 404–434). New York: Guilford Press.

Lahey, B. B., Green, K. D., & Forehand, R. (1980). On the independence of ratings of hyperactivity, conduct problems, and attention deficits in children: A multiple regression analysis. *Journal of Consulting and Clinical Psychology, 48,* 566–574.

Lahey, B. B., Schaughency, E. A., Hynd, G., Carlson, C. L., & Nieves, N. (1987). Attention deficit disorder with and without hyperactivity: Comparison of behavioral characteristics of clinic-referred children. *Journal of the American Academy of Child and Adolescent Psychiatry, 26,* 718–723.

Lahey, B. B., Schaughency, E., Strauss, C., & Frame, C. (1984). Are attention deficit disorders with and without hyperactivity similar or dissimilar disorders? *Journal of American Academy of Child and Adolescent Psychiatry, 23,* 302–309.

Lamb, M. E. (1981). The development of social expectations in the first year of life. In M. E. Lamb & L. R. Sherrod (Eds.), *Infant social cognition.* Hillsdale, NJ: Erlbaum.

Landau, S., & Moore, L. A. (1991). Social skill deficits in children with attention-deficit hyperactivity disorder. *School Psychology Review, 20,* 235–251.

Landy, F. J. (1986). Stamp collecting versus science: Validation as hypotheses testing. *American Psychologist, 41,* 1183–1192.

Lang, P. J. (1987). Fear and anxiety: Cognition, memory and behavior. In D. Magnusson & A. Ohman (Eds.), *Psychopathology: An interactional perspective* (pp. 159–176). Orlando, FL: Academic Press.

Larsen, R. J., & Diener, E. (1987). Affect intensity as an individual difference characteristic: A review. *Journal of Research in Personality, 21,* 1–39.

Larsen, R. J., Diener, E., & Emmons, R. A. (1986). Affect intensity and reactions to daily life events. *Journal of Personality and Social Psychology, 51,* 803–814.

Lazarus, R. S. (1991). Progress on a cognitive-motivational-relational theory of emotion. *American Psychologist, 46,* 819–834.

Lazarus, R. S., & Folkman, S. (1984). *Stress, appraisal, and coping.* New York: Springer.

Lee, C. L., & Bates, J. E. (1985). Mother-child interaction at age two years and perceived difficult temperament. *Child Development, 56,* 1314–1325.

Leight, K. A., & Ellis, H. C. (1981). Emotional mood states, strategies, and state dependency in memory. *Journal of Verbal Learning and Verbal Behavior, 20(3),* 251–266.

Leitch, M., & Schafer, S. (1947). A study of the thematic apperception tests of psychotic children. *American Journal of Orthopsychiatry, 17,* 337–342.

Leon, M. R., & Revelle, W. (1985). The effects of anxiety on analogical reasoning: A test of three theoretical models. *Journal of Personality and Social Psychology, 49,* 1302–1315.

Lerner, J. V., & Lerner, R. M. (1983). Temperament and adaptation across life: Theoretical and empirical issues. In P. B. Bates & O. G. Brim, Jr. (Eds.), *Life-span development and behavior* (Vol. 5). New York: Academic Press.

Lerner, R. M., & East, P. L. (1984). The role of temperament in stress, coping, and socioemotional functioning in early development. *Infant Mental Health Journal, 5,* 148–159.

Lesser, G. S. (1958). Conflict analyses of fantasy aggression. *Journal of Personality, 26,* 29–41.

Leventhal, H., & Tomarken, A. J. (1986). Emotion: Today's problems. *Annual Review of Psychology, 37,* 565–610.

Levine, D. (1981). Why and when to test: The social context of psychological testing. In A. I. Rabin (Ed.), *Assessment with projective techniques* (pp. 553–580). New York: Springer.

LeVine, R. A. (1984). Properties of culture: An ethnographic view. In R. Shweder & R. LeVine (Eds.), *Culture theory: Essays in mind, theory and emotion* (pp. 67–87). Cambridge: Cambridge University Press.

Levinson, D. J. (1978). *The seasons of a man's life.* New York: Ballantine.

Lewin, K. (1935). *A dynamic theory of personality.* New York: McGraw-Hill.

Lewinsohn, P. M., Mischel, W., Chaplain, W., & Barton, R. (1980). Social competence and depression: The role of illusory self-perceptions? *Journal of Abnormal Psychology, 89,* 203–212.

Lewis, M., & Michaelson, L. (1983). *Children's emotions and moods: Developmental theory and measurement.* New York: Plenum Press.

Lezak, M. D. (1982). The problem of assessing executive functions. *International Journal of Psychology, 17,* 281–297.

Light, B. H. (1954). Comparative study of a series of TAT and CAT cards. *Journal of Clinical Psychology, 10,* 179–181.

Lindzey, G. (1952). Thematic Apperception Test: Interpretive assumptions and related empirical evidence. *Psychological Bulletin, 49,* 1–25.

Lindzey, G. (1961). *Projective techniques and cross-cultural research.* New York: Appleton-Century-Crofts.

Locraft, C. A. (1988). *Validation of a projective measure of empathy with children.* Unpublished doctoral dissertation, University of Maryland.

Loeber, R., & Dishion, T. (1983). Early predictors of male delinquency: A review. *Psychological Bulletin, 94,* 68–99.

Loevinger, J. (1979). Construct validity of the Sentence Completion Test of Ego Development. *Applied Psychological Measurement, 3,* 281–311.

Loevinger, J., & Wessler, R. (1970). *Measuring ego development I: Construction and use of a sentence completion test.* San Francisco: Jossey-Bass.

Loney, J., & Milich, R. (1982). Hyperactivity, inattention, and aggression in clinical practice. In M. Wolraich & D. K. Routh (Eds.), *Advances in behavioral pediatrics* (Vol. 2, pp. 113–147). Greenwich, CT: JAI Press.

Luk, S. (1985). Direct observational studies of hyperactive behaviors. *Journal of the American Academy of Child Psychiatry, 24,* 338–344.

Lundy, A. (1985). The reliability of the Thematic Apperception Test. *Journal of Personality Assessment, 49(2),* 141–145.

MacLeod, C. M., Hunt, E. B., & Mathews, N. N. (1978). Individual differences in the verification of sentence-structure relationships. *Journal of Verbal Learning and Verbal Behavior, 17,* 493–507.

MacLeod, C. M., Mathews, A., & Tata, P. (1986). Attentional bias in emotional disorders. *Journal of Abnormal Psychology, 95,* 15–20.

Magnusson, D. (1987). Individual development from an interactional perspective. In D. Magnusson (Ed.), *Paths through life* (Vol. 1). Hillsdale, NJ: Erlbaum.

Magnusson, D., & Endler, N. S. (1977). *Personality at the crossroads: Current issues in interactional psychology.* Hillsdale, NJ: Erlbaum.

Magnusson, D., & Ohman, A. (1987). *Psychopathology: An interactional perspective. Personality, psychopathology, and psychotherapy.* Orlando, FL: Academic Press.

Mahler, M. (1966). Notes on the development of basic moods: The depressive affect. In R. M. Loewenstein, L. M. Newman, M. Schur, & A. J. Solnit (Eds.), *Psychoanalysis-A general psychology* (pp. 152–168). New York: International Universities Press.

Mahler, M. (1968). *On human symbiosis and the viccissitudes of individuation, Vol. 1. Infantile psychoses.* New York: International Universities Press.

Mahler, M. (1971). A study of the separation-individuation process: And its possible application to borderline phenomena in the psychoanalytic situation. *The Psychoanalytic Study of the Child, 26,* 403–424.

Mahler, M., Pine, F., & Bergman, A. (1975). *The psychological birth of the human infant.* New York: Basic Books.

Mainord, F. R., & Marcuse, F. L. (1954). Responses of disturbed children to human and to animal pictures. *Journal of Projective Techniques, 18,* 475–477.

Malgady, R. G., Constantino, G., & Rogler, L. H. (1984). Development of a thematic apperception test (TEMAS) for urban Hispanic children. *Journal of Consulting and Clinical Psychology, 52,* 986–996.

Malgady, R. G., Rogler, L. H., & Constantino, G. (1984). Ethnocultural and linguistic bias in mental health evaluation of Hispanics. *American Psychologist, 42,* 228–234.

Malone, T. W., & Lepper, M. R. (1987). Making learning fun: A taxonomy of intrinsic motivations for learning. In R. E. Snow & M. J. Farr (Eds.), *Aptitude, learning and instruction: Conative and affective process analyses* (Vol. 3, pp. 223–254). Hillsdale, NJ: Erlbaum.

Maloney, M. P., & Ward, M. P. (1976). *Psychological assessment: A conceptual approach.* New York: Oxford University Press.

Mandler, G. (1975). *Mind and emotion.* New York: Wiley.

Mandler, G. (1990). Interruption discrepancy theory: Review and extensions. In S. Fisher and C. L. Cooper (Eds.), *On the Move: The Psychology of Change and Transition* (pp. 13–32). New York: Wiley.

Mandler, G., & Watson, D. L. (1966). Anxiety and the interruption of behavior. In C. C. Spielberger (Ed.), *Anxiety and behavior* (pp. 263–288). New York: Academic Press.

Markus, H. (1980). The self in thought and memory. In D. M. Wegner & R. R. Vallacher (Eds.), *The self in social psychology* (pp. 102–130). New York: Oxford University Press.

Markus, H., & Sentis, K. (1982). The self in social information processing. In J. Suls (Ed.), *Psychological perspectives on the self.* Hillsdale, NJ: Erlbaum.

Marsh, H. W., & Parker, J. W. (1984). Determinants of student self-concept. *Journal of Personality and Social Psychology, 47,* 213–231.

Marshall, G. D., & Zimbardo, P. G. (1979). Affective consequences of inadequately explained physiological arousal. *Journal of Personality and Social Psychology, 37,* 970–988.

Maslach, C. (1979). Negative emotional biasing of unexplained events. *Journal of Personality and Social Psychology, 37(6),* 953–969.

Masters, J. C., Barden, R. C., & Fard, M. E. (1979). Affective states, expressive behavior, and learning in children. *Journal of Personality and Social Psychology, 37,* 380–390.

Mathews, A. (1986). Cognitive processes in anxiety and depression: A discussion paper. *Journal of the Royal Society of Medicine, 79,* 158–161.

Mathews, A., May, J., Mogg, K., & Eysenck, M. (1990). Attentional bias in anxiety: Selective search of defective filtering. *Journal of Abnormal Psychology, 99,* 166–173.

Matranga, J. (1976). The relationship between behavioral indices of aggression and hostile content on the TAT. *Journal of Personality Assessment, 40,* 130–134.

Maziade, M., Caperaa, P., Laplante, D., Boudreault, M., Thivierge, J., Cote, R., & Boutin, P. (1985). Value of difficult temperament among 7-year-olds in the general population for predicting psychiatric diagnosis at age 12. *American Journal of Psychiatry, 142,* 943–946.

Maziade, M., Caron, C., Cote, R., Boutin, P., & Thivierge, J. (1990). Extreme temperament and diagnosis: A study in a psychiatric sample of consecutive children. *Archives of General Psychiatry, 47,* 477–484.

McArthur, D. S., & Roberts, G. E. (1982). *Roberts Apperception Test for Children Manual.* Los Angeles: Western Psychological Services.

McClelland, D. C. (1972). Opinions predict opinions: So what else is new? *Journal of Consulting and Clinical Psychology, 38(3),* 325–326.

McClelland, D. C. (1987). *Human motivation.* New York: Cambridge University Press.

McClelland, D. C., & Atkinson, J. W. (1948). The projective expression needs: I. The effects of different intensities of the hunger drive on perception. *Journal of Psychology, 25,* 205–232.

McClelland, D. C., Atkinson, J. W., Clark, L. A., & Lowell, E. L. (1953). *The achievement motive.* New York: Appleton-Century Crofts.

McGrew, M. W. (1987). *The TAT responses of disturbed and normal boys using an integrated scoring system.* Unpublished doctoral dissertation, University of Maryland.

McGrew, M. W., & Teglasi, H. (1990). Formal characteristics of thematic apperception test stories as indices of emotional disturbance in children. *Journal of Personality Assessment, 54,* 639–655.

Meichenbaum, D. (1977). *Cognitive-behavior modification: An integrative approach.* New York: Plenum Press.

Meichenbaum, D., & Asarnow, J. (1979). Cognitive-behavior modification and metacognitive development: Implications for the classroom. In P. Kendall & S. Hollon (Eds.), *Cognitive-behavioral interventions* (pp. 11–35). New York: Academic.

Meissner, W. W. (1971). Notes on identification, II. Clarification of related concepts. *Psychoanalytic Quarterly, 40,* 277–302.

Meissner, W. W. (1972). Notes on identification, III. The concept of identification. *Psychoanalytic Quarterly, 41,* 224–260.

Meissner, W. W. (1974). Differentiation and integration of learning and identification in the developmental process. *Annual of Psychoanalysis, 2,* 181–196.

Meissner, W. W. (1981). *Internalization in psychoanalysis.* Psychological Issues Monograph 50. New York: International Universities Press.

Messick, S. (1965). Personality measurement and the ethics of assessment. *American Psychologist, 20,* 136–142.

Messick, S. (1976). Personality consistencies in cognition and creativity. In S. Messick (Ed.), *Individuality in learning* (pp. 4–33). San Francisco: Jossey-Bass.

Messick, S. (1979). Potential uses of non-cognitive measurement in education. *Journal of Educational Psychology, 71,* 281–292.

Messick, S. (1987). Structural relationships across cognition. In R. E. Snow & M. J. Farr (Eds.), *Aptitude, learning, and instruction* (Vol. 3, pp. 35–68). Hillsdale, NJ: Erlbaum.

Messick, S. (1984). The nature of cognitive styles: Problems and promise in educational practice. *Educational Psychologist, 19,* 59–74.

Messick, S. (1989). Validity. In R. Linn (Ed.), *Educational Measurement* (pp. 13–103). New York: Macmillan.

Messick, S., & Kogan, N. (1966). Personality consistencies in judgment: Dimensions of role constructs. *Multivariate Behavioral Research, 1,* 165–175.

Milich, R., & Dodge, K. A. (1984). Social information processing in child psychiatric populations. *Journal of Abnormal Child Psychology, 12,* 471–489.

Milich, R., & Landau, S. (1982). Socialization and peer relations in hyperactive children. In K. D. Gadow & I. Bialer (Eds.), *Advances in learning and behavioral disabilities: A research annual, Vol. 1.* Greenwich, CT: JAI Press.

Milich, R., Loney, J., & Landau, S. (1982). Independent dimensions of hyperactivity and aggression. A validation with playroom observation data. *Journal of Abnormal Psychology, 91,* 183–198.

Millon, T. (1981). *Disorders of personality: DSM III Axis II.* New York: Wiley.

Mischel, W. (1968). *Personality and assessment.* New York: Wiley.

Mischel, W. (1973). Toward a cognitive social learning reconceptualization of personality. *Psychological Review, 80,* 253–283.

Mischel, W. (1979). On the interface of cognition and personality: Beyond the person-situation debate. *American Psychologist, 34,* 740–754.

Mischel, W. (1984). Processes in delay of gratification. In L. Berkowitz (Ed.), *Advances in Experimental Social Psychology* (Vol. 7). Orlando: Academic Press.

Mischel, W. (1986). *Introduction to personality: A new look.* New York: Holt, Rinehart, and Winston.

Morgan, C. D., & Murray, H. A. (1935). A method for investigating fantasies: The Thematic Apperception Test. *Archives of Neurology and Psychiatry, 34,* 289–306.

Morris, W. N., & Reilly, N. P. (1987). Toward the self-regulation of mood: Theory and research. *Motivation and Emotion, 11(3),* 215–249.

Murray, H. A. (1938). *Explorations of personality.* New York: Oxford.

Murray, H. A. (1943). *Thematic apperception test manual.* Cambridge: Harvard University Press.

Murray, H. A. (1951). Uses of the Thematic Apperception Test. *American Journal of Orthopsychiatry, 21,* 577–581.

Murray, H. A., & Kluckhohn, C. (1953). Outline of a conception of personality. In C. Kluckhohn, H. A. Murray, & D. Schneider (Eds.), *Society and culture.* New York: Knopf.

Murstein, B. I. (1958). The relationship of stimulus ambiguity on the TAT to productivity of themes. *Journal of Consulting Psychology, 22,* 348.

Murstein, B. I. (1963). *Theory and research in projective techniques (emphasizing the TAT).* New York: Wiley. ᶜ Many references to this text.

Murstein, B. I. (1965). The stimulus. In B. Murstein (Ed.), *Handbook of projective techniques.* New York: Basic Books.

Murstein, B. I. (1968). The effect of stimulus, background, personality and scoring system on the manifestation of hostility on the TAT. *Journal of Consulting and Clinical Psychology, 32*, 355–365.

Murstein, B. I., & Pryer, R. S. (1959). The concept of projection: A review. *Psychological Bulletin, 56*, 353–374.

Mussen, P. H., & Naylor, H. K. (1954). The relationship between overt and fantasy aggression. *Journal of Abnormal and Social Psychology, 49*, 235–240.

Myers, M., & Paris, S. G. (1978). Children's metacognitive knowledge about reading. *Journal of Educational Psychology, 70*, 680–690.

Nasby, W., Hayden, B., & DePaulo, B. M. (1980). Attributional bias among aggressive boys to interpret unambiguous social stimuli as displays of hostility. *Journal of Abnormal Psychology, 89*, 459–468.

Nawas, M. M. (1965). Objective scoring of the TAT: Further validation. *Journal of Projective Techniques and Personality Assessment, 29*, 456–460.

Neman, R., Brown, T., & Sells, S. (1973). *Language and adjustment scales for the TAT for children 6–11 years.* Rockville, MD: U.S. Dept. of Health, Education and Welfare. HRA 74-1332.

Newmark, C. S., & Flouranzano, R. (1973). Replication of an empirically derived TAT set with hospitalized psychiatric patients. *Journal of Personality Assessment, 37*, 340–341.

Newmark, C. S., Hetzel, W., & Frerking, R. A. (1974). The effects of personality tests on state and trait anxiety. *Journal of Personality Assessment, 38*, 17–20.

Newmark, C. S., Wheeler, D., Newmark, L., & Stabler, B. (1975). Test-induced anxiety with children. *Journal of Personality Assessment, 39*, 409–413.

Nolen, S. B. (1988). Reasons for studying: Motivational orientations and study strategies. *Cognition and Instruction, 5*, 269–287,

Oatley, K., & Jenkins, J. M. (1992). Human emotions: Function and dysfunction. *Annual Review of Psychology, 43*, 55–85.

Obrzut, J. E., & Cummings, J. A. (1983). The projective approach to personality assessment: An analysis of thematic picture techniques. *School Psychology Review, 12*, 29–35.

Ohman, A., & Magnusson, D. (1987). An interactional paradigm for research on psychopathology. In D. Magnusson & A. Ohman (Eds.), *Psychopathology, an interactional perspective* (pp. 3–24). Orlando, FL: Academic Press.

Olweus, D. (1979). Stability of aggressive reaction patterns in males: A review. *Psychological Bulletin, 86*, 852–875.

Orris, J. (1969). Visual monitoring of performance in three subgroups of male delinquents. *Journal of Abnormal Psychology, 74*, 227–229.

Owings, R. A., Peterson, G. A., Bransford, J. D., Morris, C. D., & Stein, B. S. (1980). Spontaneous monitoring and regulation of learning: A comparison of successful and less successful fifth graders. *Journal of Educational Psychology, 72*, 250–256.

Palisin, H. (1986). Preschool temperament and performance on achievement tests. *Developmental Psychology, 22(6)*, 766–770.

Palmer, J. O. (1983). *The psychological assessment of children* (2nd ed.). New York: Wiley.

Paris, S. G., Lipson, M. Y., & Wixson, K. K. (1983). Becoming a strategic reader. *Contemporary Educational Psychology, 8*, 293–316.

Parry, P. A., & Douglas, V. I. (1983). Effects of reinforcement on concept identification in hyperactive children. *Journal of Abnormal Child Psychology, 11*, 327–340.

Parsons, J. E. (1981). Attributions, learned helplessness and sex differences in achievement. In S. R. Yussen (Ed.), *The development of achievement.* New York: Academic Press.

Parsons, J. E. (1982). Expectancies, values and academic behaviors. In J. T. Spence (Ed.), *Assessing achievement*. San Francisco: W. H. Freeman.

Pasewark, R. A., Fitzgerald, B. J., Dexter, V., & Cangemi. (1976). Responses of adolescent, middle-aged, and aged females on the Gerontological and Thematic Apperception Tests. *Journal of Personality Assessment, 40*, 588–591.

Pearson, P. D., Hansen, J., & Gordon, G. (1979). The effect of background knowledge on young children's comprehension of explicit and implicit information. *Journal of Reading Behavior, 11*, 201–210.

Pelham, W. E., & Bender, M. E. (1982). Peer relationships in hyperactive children: Description and treatment. In K. D. Gadow & I. Bialer (Eds.), *Advances in learning and behavior disabilities: A research annual* (Vol. 1, pp. 365–436). Greenwich, CT: JAI Press.

Pervin, L. A. (1985). Personality: Current controversies, issues, and directions. *Annual Review in Psychology, 36*, 83–114.

Pervin, L. A., & Lewis, M. (1978). *Perspectives in interactional psychology*. New York: Plenum.

Peterson, C. A. (1990). Administration of the Thematic Apperception Test: Contributions of psychoanalytic psychotherapy. *Journal of Contemporary Psychotherapy, 20*, 191–200.

Phillips, D. (1984). The illusion of incompetence among academically competent children. *Child Development, 55*, 2000–2016.

Piaget, J. (1952). *The origins of intelligence in children*. New York: International Universities Press.

Piaget, J. (1954). *The construction of reality in the child*. New York: Basic Books.

Piaget, J. (1981). *Intelligence and affectivity: Their relationship during child development*. Annual Reviews Monograph. Palo Alto: Annual Reviews, Inc.

Plomin, R. (1983). Developmental behavioral genetics. *Child Development, 54*, 253–259.

Plomin, R., & Daniels, D. (1987). Why are children in the same family so different from one another? *The Behavioral and Brain Sciences, 10*, 1–59.

Polyson, J., Norris, D., & Ott, E. (1985). The recent decline in TAT research. *Professional Psychology: Research and Practice, 16*, 26–28.

Porges, S. W., Walker, G. F., Korb, R. J., & Sprague, R. L. (1975). The influence of methylphenidate on heart rate and behavioral measures of attention in hyperactive children. *Child Development, 46*, 727–733.

Procidano, M. E., & Guinta, D. M. (1989). Object representations and symptomatology: Preliminary findings in young adult psychiatric inpatients. *Journal of Clinical Psychology, 45*, 309–316.

Purcell, K. (1956). The TAT and antisocial behavior. *Journal of Consulting Psychology, 20*, 449–456.

Quay, H. C. (1965). Psychopathic personality as pathological stimulation-seeking. *American Journal of Psychiatry, 122(2)*, 180–183.

Quay, H. C. (1977). Measuring dimensions of deviant behavior: The behavior problem checklist. *Journal of Abnormal Child Psychology, 5*, 277–287.

Quay, H. C. (1979). Classification. In H. C. Quay & J. Werry (Eds.), *Psychopathological disorders in childhood* (pp. 3–24). New York: Wiley.

Quay, H. C. (1986). A critical analysis of DSM-III as a taxonomy of psychopathology in childhood and adolescence. In T. Millon & G. Klerman (Eds.). *Contemporary directions in psychopathology: Toward DSM-IV* (pp. 151–165). New York: Guilford.

Quay, H. C. (1988). Attention deficit disorder and the behavioral inhibition system: The relevance of the neuropsychological theory of Jeffrey A. Gray. In L. Bloomingdale & J. Sergeant (Eds.), *Attention deficit disorder: Criteria, cognition, and intervention* (pp. 117–126). New York: Pergamon Press.

Rabin, A. I. (1981). *Assessment with projective techniques: A concise introduction.* New York: Springer.

Rabin, A. I. (1986). Concerning projective techniques. In A. I. Rabin (Ed.), *Projective techniques for adolescents and children* (pp. 3–11). New York: Springer.

Rabin, A. I., & Haworth, M. R. (1960). *Projective techniques with children.* New York: Grune and Stratton.

Radomski, L. (1986). Need of stimulation and motivational determinants of job choice. *Polish Psychological Bulletin, 17,* 27–38.

Rangell, L. (1986). The executive functions of the ego: An extension of the concept of ego autonomy. *Psychoanalytic Study of the Child, 4,* 1–37.

Rapaport, D. (1947). The scoring and analysis of the Thematic Apperception Test. *Journal of Psychology, 24,* 319–330.

Rapaport, D. (1952). Projective techniques and the theory of thinking. *Journal of Projective Techniques, 16,* 269–275.

Rapaport, D., Gill, M. M., & Schafer, R. (1975). *Diagnostic psychological testing* (revised edition by R. R. Holt). New York: International Universities Press.

Raynor, J. D. (1982). Self-possessions of attributes, self-evaluation, and future orientation: A theory of adult competence motivation. In J. D. Raynor & E. E. Entin (Eds.), *Motivation, career striving and aging* (pp. 207–226). Washington, DC: Hemisphere.

Raynor, J. D., & McFarlin, D. B. (1986). Motivation and the self-system. In R. M. Sorrentino & E. T. Higgins (Eds.), *Handbook of motivation and cognition: Foundations of social behavior.* (pp. 315–349). New York: Guilford Press.

Rehm, L. P., & Plakosh, P. (1975). Preference for immediate reinforcement in depression. *Journal of Behavior Therapy and Experimental Psychiatry, 6,* 101–103.

Reilly, S. S., & Muzekari, L. H. (1986). Effects of emotional illness and age upon the resolution of discrepant messages. *Perceptual and Motor Skills, 62,* 823–829.

Resnick, L. B., & Glaser, R. (1976). Problem solving and intelligence. In L. B. Resnick (Ed.), *The nature of intelligence.* Hillsdale, NJ: Erlbaum.

Revelle, W. (1987). Personality and motivation: Sources of inefficiency in cognitive performance. *Journal of Research in Personality, 21,* 436–452.

Richard, B. A., & Dodge, K. A. (1982). Social maladjustment and problem solving in school-aged children. *Journal of Consulting and Clinical Psychology, 50(2),* 226–233.

Rinsley, D. B. (1980). The developmental etiology of borderline and narcissistic disorders. *Bulletin of the Menninger Clinic, 44,* 127–134.

Ritter, A., & Eron, L. D. (1952). The use of the Thematic Apperception Test to differentiate normal from abnormal groups. *Journal of Abnormal and Social Psychology, 47,* 147–158.

Ritzler, B. A., Sharkey, K. J., & Chudy, J. F. (1980). A comprehensive projective alternative to the TAT. *Journal of Personality Assessment, 44,* 358–362.

Robins, L. N. (1979). Follow up studies. In H. C. Quay & J. S. Werry (Eds.), *Psychopathological disorders of children* (pp. 483–513). New York: Wiley.

Robins, L. N., & Helzer, J. E. (1986). Diagnosis and clinical assessment: The current state of psychiatric diagnosis. *Annual Review of Psychology, 37,* 409–432.

Robinson, E. A., Eyberg, S. M., & Ross, A. W. (1980). The standardization of an inventory of child conduct problem behaviors. *Journal of Clinical Child Psychology, 22–28.*

Rogers, R. W., & Deckner, C. (1975). Effects of fear appeals and physiological arousal upon emotions, attitudes, and cigarette smoking. *Journal of Personality and Social Psychology, 32,* 222–230.

Rokeach, M. (1973). *The nature of human values*. New York: Free Press.

Rosenthal, R. H., & Allen, T. W. (1978). An examination of attention, arousal, and learning dysfunctions of hyperkinetic children. *Psychological Bulletin, 85,* 689–715.

Ross, D. M., & Ross, S. A. (1982). *Hyperactivity: Current issues, research, and theory* (2nd ed.). New York: Wiley.

Rosvold, H. E., Mirsky, A. F., Sarason, I., Bransome, E. D., & Beck, L. H. (1956). A continuous performance test of brain damage. *Journal of Consulting Psychology, 20,* 343–350.

Rothbart, M. K., & Derryberry, D. (1981). Development of individual differences in temperament. In M. E. Lamb & A. L. Brown (Eds.), *Advances in developmental psychology* (Vol. 1, pp. 37–86). Hillsdale, NJ: Erlbaum.

Rotter, J. B. (1946). Thematic Apperception tests: Suggestions for administration and interpretation. *Journal of Personality, 15,* 70–92.

Rowe, D. C. (1983). A biometrical analysis of perceptions of family environment: A study of twin and singleton sibling kinships. *Child Development, 54,* 416–423.

Rushton, J. P., Fulker, D. W., Neale, M. C., Nias, D. K. B., & Eysenck, H. J. (1986). Altruism and aggression: The heritability of individual differences. *Journal of Personality and Social Psychology, 50,* 1192–1198.

Rust, L. W. (1977). Interests. In S. Ball (Ed.), *Motivation in education*. New York: Academic Press.

Rutter, M. (1978). Early sources of security and competence. In J. S. Bruner & A. Garten (Eds.), *Human growth and development*. London: Oxford University Press.

Rutter, M. (1987). Temperament, personality and personality disorder. *British Journal of Psychiatry, 150,* 443–458.

Rutter, M., & Giller, H. (1983). *Juvenile delinquency: Trends and perspectives*. Harmondsworth, England: Penguin Books.

Sackett, P. R., Zedeck, S., & Fogli, L. (1988). Relations between measures of typical and maximum job performance. *Journal of Applied Psychology, 73,* 482–486.

Salkovskis, P. M., & Harrison, J. (1984). Abnormal and normal obsessions—A replication. *Behaviour Research and Therapy, 22,* 549–552.

Sameroff, A. J. (1975). Early influences on development: Fact or fancy? *Merrill Palmer Quarterly, 20,* 275–301.

Samuels, S. J., & Edwall, G. (1981). The role of attention in reading with implications for the learning disabled student. *Journal of Learning Disabilities, 14,* 353–368.

Sandberg, S. T., Rutter, M., & Taylor, E. (1978). Hyperkinetic disorder in psychiatric clinic attenders. *Developmental Medicine and Child Neurology, 20,* 279–299.

Sandler, J. (1960). On the concept of the superego. *The Psychoanalytic Study of the Child, 15,* 128–162.

Sandler, J. (1981). Character traits and object relationships. *Contemporary Psychoanalysis, 17,* 180–196.

Sandler, J., & Rosenblatt, B. (1962). The concept of the representational world. *The Psychoanalytic Study of the Child, 17,* 128–145.

Sarason, I. G. (1975). Anxiety and self-preoccupation. In I. G. Sarason & D. C. Spielberger (Eds.), *Stress and Anxiety* (Vol. 2., pp. 27–44). Washington, DC: Hemisphere.

Sarason, I. G. (Ed.) (1980). *Test anxiety: Theory, research and application*. Hillsdale, NJ: Erlbaum.

Satterfield, J. H., Hoppe, C. M., & Schell, A. M. (1982). A prospective study of delinquency in 110 adolescent boys with attention deficit disorder and 88 normal adolescent boys. *American Journal of Psychiatry, 139,* 795–798.

Scardamalia, M., & Bereiter, C. (1985). Fostering the development of self-regulation in children's knowledge processing. In S. F. Chipman, J. W. Segal, & R. Glaser

(Eds.), *Thinking and learning skills: Research and open questions* (Vol. 2, pp. 563–577). Hillsdale, NJ: Erlbaum.

Scarr, S., & Kidd, K. K. (1983). Developmental behavior genetics. In M. M. Haith & J. J. Campos (Eds.), *Handbook of Child Psychology, Vol. 2: Infancy and Developmental Psychobiology.* New York: Wiley.

Scarr, S., & McCartney, K. (1983). How people make their own environments: A theory of genotype environment effects. *Child Development, 54,* 424–435.

Schachar, R., Logan, G., Wachsmuth, R., & Chajczyk, D. (1988). Attaining and maintaining preparation: A comparison of attention in hyperactive, normal, and disturbed control children. *Journal of Abnormal Child Psychology, 16(4),* 361–378.

Schafer, R. (1968). *Aspects of internalization.* New York: International Universities Press.

Schaughency, E. A., & Rothlind, J. (1991). Assessment and classification of attention deficit hyperactive disorders. *School Psychology Review, 20,* 187–202.

Schneider, M. F. (1989). *Children's Apperceptive Story-Telling Test.* Austin: Pro-Ed.

Schoenfeld, A. H. (1983). Beyond the purely cognitive: Belief systems, social cognitions and metacognitions as driving forces in intellectual performance. *Cognitive Science, 7,* 329–363.

Schroeder, H., Driver, M., & Streufert, S. (1986). *Human information processing.* New York: Holt, Rinehart and Winston.

Schroth, M. L. (1977). The use of the associative elaboration and integration scales for evaluating CAT protocols. *The Journal of Psychology, 97,* 29–35.

Schwartz, J. C., & Pollack, P. R. (1977). Affect and delay of gratification. *Journal of Research in Personality, 7,* 384–394.

Schwartz, J. C., & Shaver, P. (1987). Emotions and emotion knowledge in interpersonal relations. In W. Jones & D. Perlman (Eds.), *Advances in personal relationships* (pp. 197–241). Greenwich, CT: JAI Press.

Seligman, M. E. P. (1975). *Helplessness: On depression, development and death.* San Francisco: Freeman.

Shabad, P., Worland, J., Lander, H., & Dietrich, D. (1979). A retrospective analysis of the TATs of children at risk who subsequently broke down. *Child Psychiatry and Human Development, 10,* 49–59.

Shapiro, D. (1965). *Neurotic styles.* (The Austen Riggs Center Monograph Series Number 5.) New York: Basic Books.

Shapiro, S., & Garfinkel, B. (1986). The occurrence of behavior disorders in children: The interdependence of Attention Deficit Disorder and Conduct Disorder. *Journal of the American Academy of Child Psychiatry, 25,* 809–819.

Shaver, P., Schwartz, J., Kirson, D., & O'Connor, C. (1987). Emotion knowledge: Further exploration of a prototype approach. *Journal of Personality and Social Psychology, 52,* 1061–1086.

Shepard, R. N. (1984). Ecological constraints on internal representation: Resonant kinematics of perceiving, imaging, thinking, and dreaming. *Psychological Review, 91,* 417–447.

Sherwood, E. T. (1957). On the designing of TAT pictures with special reference to a set for an African people assimilating Western culture. *Journal of Social Psychology, 45,* 161–190.

Slemon, A. G., Holzwarth, E. J., Lewis, J., & Sitko, M. (1976). Associative elaboration and integration scales for evaluating TAT protocols. *Journal of Personality Assessment, 40,* 365–369.

Snow, R. E. (1982). Education and intelligence. In R. J. Sternberg (Ed.), *Handbook of human intelligence* (pp. 493–585). New York: Cambridge University Press.

Snow, R. E. (1987). Aptitude complexities. In R. E. Snow & M. J. Farr (Eds.), *Aptitude, learning and instruction: Conative and affective process analyses* (Vol. 3, pp. 11–34). Hillsdale, NJ: Erlbaum.

Snow, R. E., & Lohman, D. F. (1984). Toward a theory of cognitive aptitude for learning from instruction. *Journal of Educational Psychology, 76,* 347–376.

Sobel, H. J. (1981). Projective methods of cognitive analysis. In T. Merluzzi, C. Glass, & M. Genest (Eds.), *Cognitive assessment* (pp. 127–148). New York: Guilford Press.

Solomon, I. L., & Starr, B. (1968). *School Apperception Method (SAM).* New York: Springer.

Sorrentino, R. M., & Higgins, E. T. (Eds.) (1986). *Handbook of motivation and cognition: Foundations of social behavior.* New York: Guilford.

Sorrentino, R. M., & Short, J. C. (1986). Uncertainty orientation, motivation, and cognition. In R. M. Sorrentino & E. T. Higgins (Eds.), *Handbook of motivation and cognition: Foundations of social behavior* (pp. 379–403). New York: Guilford.

Spear, W. E., & Lapidus, L. B. (1981). Qualitative differences in manifest object representations: Implications for a multidimensional model of psychological functioning. *Journal of Abnormal Psychology, 90(2),* 157–187.

Speers, R. W., McFarland, M. B., Arnaud, S. H., & Curry, N. E. (1971). Recapitulation of separation individuation processes when the normal three-year-old enters nursery school. In J. B. McDevitt & C. F. Settlage (Eds.), *Separation-Individuation: Essays in honor of Margaret Mahler* (pp. 297–321). New York: International Universities Press.

Spielberger, C. D., Gorsuch, R. L., & Lushene, R. E. (1970). *Manual for the State-Trait Anxiety Inventory.* Palo Alto: Consulting Psychologists Press.

Spivak, G., & Levine, M. (1963). *Self-regulation in acting-out and normal adolescents* (Report M-4531). Washington, DC: National Institute of Mental Health.

Spring, C., Greenberg, L., Scott, J., & Hopwood, J. (1974). Electrodermal activity in hyperactive boys who are methylphenidate responders. *Psychophysiology, 11,* 436–442.

Sroufe, L. A. (1979). The coherence of individual development. *American Psychologist, 34,* 834–841.

Sroufe, L. A. (1985). Attachment classification from the perspective of infant-caregiver relationships and infant temperament. *Child Development, 56,* 1–14.

Sroufe, L. A., Schork, E., Motti, F., Lawroski, N., & LaFreniere, P. (1984). The role of affect in social competence. In C. E. Izard, J. Kagan, & R. B. Zajonc (Eds.), *Emotions, cognition and behavior* (pp. 289–319). Cambridge: Cambridge University Press.

Srull, T. K., & Wyer, R. S. (1986). The role of chronic and temporary goals in social information processing. In R. M. Sorrentino & E. T. Higgins (Eds.), *Handbook of motivation and cognition: Foundations of social behavior* (pp. 503–549). New York: Guilford.

Stein, M. I. (1948). *The Thematic Apperception Test.* Cambridge: Addison Wesley.

Stein, M. I. (1955). *The Thematic Apperception Test* (rev. ed.). Cambridge: Addison Wesley.

Stein, M. L., & Stone, G. L. (1978). Effects of conceptual level and structure on initial interview behavior. *Journal of Counseling Psychology, 25,* 96–102.

Stenberg, C. R., & Campos, J. J. (1990). The development of anger expressions in infancy. In N. Stein, B. Leventhal, & T. Trabasso (Eds.), *Psychological and biological approaches to emotion* (pp. 247–282). Hillsdale, NJ: Erlbaum.

Sternberg, R. J. (1984). Toward a triarchic theory of human intelligence. *Behavioral and Brain Sciences, 7,* 269–315.

Sternberg, R. J. (1985). *Beyond IQ: A triarchic theory of human intelligence.* New York: Cambridge University Press.

Sternberg, R. J., & Powell, J. S. (1983). Comprehending verbal comprehension. *American Psychologist, 38,* 878–893.

Sternberg, R. J., & Weil, E. M. (1980). An aptitude-strategy interaction in linear syllogistic reasoning. *Journal of Educational Psychology, 72,* 226–234.

Stevenson-Hinde, J., & Hinde, R. A. (1986). Changes in associations between characteristics. In R. Plomin & J. Dunn (Eds.), *The study of temperament: Changes, continuities and challenges.* Hillsdale, NJ: Erlbaum.

Stewart, M. A., Cummings, C., Singer, S., & DeBlois, C. S. (1981). The overlap between hyperactive and unsocialized aggressive children. *Journal of Child Psychology and Psychiatry, 22,* 35–45.

Stolorow, R. D., & Lachmann, F. M. (1980). *Psychoanalysis of developmental arrests.* New York: International Universities Press.

Strelau, J. (1983). *Temperament—Personality—Activity.* London: Academic Press.

Strelau, J. (1987). Emotion as a key concept in temperament research. *Journal of Research in Personality, 21,* 510–528.

Streufert, S., & Streufert, S. C. (1978). *Behavior in the complex environment.* Toronto: Wiley.

Sullivan, H. S. (1953). *The interpersonal theory of psychiatry.* New York: Norton.

Suomi, S. J. (1981). The perception of contingency and social development. In M. E. Lamb & L. R. Sherrod (Eds.), *Infant social cognition.* Hillsdale, NJ: Erlbaum.

 Sutton, P. M., & Swensen, C. H. (1983). The reliability and concurrent validity of alternative methods for assessing ego development. *Journal of Personality Assessment, 47(5),* 468–475.

Symonds, P. (1939). Criteria for the selection of pictures for the investigation of adolescent phantasies. *Journal of Abnormal and Social Psychology, 34,* 271–274.

Tarvin, N. (1989). *Identifying emotional disturbance in children with projective stories.* Unpublished Master's Thesis.

Teglasi, H., & MacMahon, B. H. (1990). Temperament and common problem behaviors of children. *Journal of Applied Developmental Psychology, 11,* 331–349.

Tesser, A. (1987). Toward a self-evaluation maintenance model of social behavior. In L. Berkowitz (Ed.), *Advances in experimental social psychology* (Vol. 20). New York: Academic Press.

Thoits, P. A. (1984). Coping, social support, and psychological outcomes: The central role of emotion. In P. Shaver (Ed.), *Review of personality and social psychology* (Vol. 5, pp. 219–238). Beverly Hills: Sage.

Thomas, A., & Chess, S. (1977). *Temperament and development.* New York: Brunner/Mazel.

Thomas, A., & Chess, S. (1980). *The dynamics of psychological development.* New York: Brunner/Mazel.

Thomas, A., & Chess, S. (1981). The role of temperament in the contributions of individuals to their development. In R. M. Lerner & N. A. Busch-Rossnagel (Eds.), *Individuals as producers of their own development: A life span perspective* (pp. 231–255). New York: Academic Press.

Thomas, A., Chess, S., & Birch, H. (1968). *Temperament and behavior disorders in children.* New York: New York University Press.

Thomas, A., Chess, S., Birch, H., Hertzig, M., & Korn, S. (1963). *Behavioral individuality in early childhood.* New York: New York University Press.

Thompson, A. E. (1986). An object relational theory of affect maturity: Applications to the Thematic Apperception Test. In M. Kissen (Ed.), *Assessing Object Relations Phenomena* (pp. 207–224). New York: International Universities Press.

Thompson, C. E. (1949). The Thompson modification of the Thematic Apperception Test. *Rorschach Research Exchange and Journal of Projective Techniques, 13,* 469–478. *Used A·F·A·M Characters .*

Thompson, J. M., & Sones, R. A. (1973). *Education Apperception Test.* Los Angeles: Western Psychological Services.

Thompson, R. A. (1986). Temperament, emotionality, and infant social cognition. In J. V. Lerner and R. M. Lerner (Eds.), *Temperament and social interaction during infancy and childhood.* New Directions for Child Development, no. 31 (pp. 35–52). San Francisco: Jossey-Bass.

Tomkins, S. S. (1947). *The Thematic Apperception Test.* New York: Grune and Stratton.

Tomkins, S. S. (1962). *Affect, imagery, consciousness: 1. The positive affects.* New York: Springer Verlag.

Torgesen, J., & Goldman, T. (1977). Verbal rehearsal and short-term memory in reading-disabled children. *Child Development, 48,* 56–60.

Torgesen, J. K. (1977). The role of non-specific factors in task performance of learning disabled children: A theoretical assessment. *Journal of Learning Disabilities, 10,* 27–35.

Torgesen, J. K. (1980). Conceptual and educational implications of the use of efficient task strategies by learning disabled children. *Journal of Learning Disabilities, 13,* 19–26.

Torgesen, J. K., & Licht, B. G. (1983). The learning disabled child as an inactive learner: Retrospects and prospects. In J. D. McKinney & L. Feagans (Eds.), *Current topics in learning disabilities* (Vol. 1, pp. 3–31). Norwood, NJ: Ablex.

Triandis, H. C. (1972). *The analysis of subjective culture.* New York: Wiley.

Trites, R. L., & LaPrade, K. (1983). Evidence for an independent syndrome of hyperactivity. *Journal of Child Psychology and Psychiatry, 24,* 573–586.

Trope, Y. (1986). Seeking information about one's own ability as a determinant of choice among tasks. *Journal of Personality Assessment and Social Psychology, 32,* 1004–1013.

Tucker, D. M., & Williamson, P. A. (1984). Asymmetric neural control in human self-regulation. *Psychological Review, 91,* 185–215.

Tuckman, B. (1966). Integrative complexity: Its measurement and relation to creativity. *Educational and Psychological Measurement,* 369–382.

Ullmann, L. P. (1957). Productivity and the clinical use of TAT cards. *Journal of Projective Techniques, 21,* 399–402.

Urist, J. (1980). Object relations. In R. H. Woody (Ed.), *Encyclopedia of clinical assessment* (Vol. 2, pp. 821–833). San Francisco: Jossey-Bass.

Vane, J. R. (1981). The Thematic Apperception Test: A review. Clinical *Psychology Review, 1,* 319–336.

Veroff, J. (1969). Social comparison and the development of achievement motivation. In C. P. Smith (Ed.), *Achievement-related motives in children* (pp. 46–101). New York: Russell Sage Foundation.

Veroff, J., Wilcox, S., & Atkinson, J. W. (1953). The achievement motive in high school and college-age women. *Journal of Abnormal and Social Psychology, 48,* 108–119.

Waddell, K. J. (1984). The self-concept and social adaptation of hyperactive children in adolescence. *Journal of Clinical Child Psychology, 13,* 50–55.

Wallander, J. L., & Hubert, N. C. (1987). Peer social dysfunction in children with developmental disabilities: Empirical basis and a conceptual model. *Clinical Psychology Review, 7,* 205–221.

Weinberg, L. A., & Weinberg, C. (1990). Seriously emotionally disturbed or socially maladjusted? A critique of interpretations. *Behavioral Disorders, 15,* 149–158.

Weiner, B. (1972). *Theories of motivation: From mechanism to cognition.* Chicago: Markham.

Weiner, B. (1980). *Human motivation.* New York: Holt, Rinehart, & Winston.

Weisskopf, E. A. (1950). A transcendence index as a proposed measure of the TAT. *Journal of Psychology, 29,* 379–390.

Weisskopf, E. A., & Dieppa, J. J. (1951). Experimentally induced faking of TAT responses. *Journal of Consulting Psychology, 15,* 469–474.

Weisskopf-Joelson, E. A., & Foster, H. C. (1962). An experimental study of stimulus variation upon projection. *Journal of Projective Techniques, 26,* 366–370.

Weisskopf-Joelson, E. A., Zimmerman, J., & McDaniel, M. (1970). Similarity between subject and stimulus as an influence on projection. *Journal of Projective Techniques and Personality Assessment, 34,* 328–331.

Weissman, S. (1964). Some indicators of acting out behavior from the Thematic Apperception Test. *Journal of Projective Techniques, 28,* 366–375.

Werry, J. S. (1988). Differential diagnosis of attention deficits and conduct disorders. In L. Bloomingdale & J. Sergeant (Eds.), *Attention deficit disorder: Criteria, cognition, and intervention* (pp. 83–96). New York: Pergammon Press.

Werry, J. S., Reeves, J. C., & Elkind, G. S. (1987). Attention deficit, conduct, oppositional, and anxiety disorders in children: I. A review of research on differentiating characteristics. *Journal of the American Academy of Child and Adolescent Psychiatry, 26,* 133–143.

Wertheim, E. H., & Schwartz, J. C. (1983). Depression, guilt, and self-management of pleasant and unpleasant events. *Journal of Personality and Social Psychology, 45,* 884–889.

West, A., Martindale, C., Hines, D., & Roth, W. T. (1983). *Marijuana induced primary process content in the TAT, 47,* 466–467.

Westen, D., Lohr, N., Silk, K. R., Gold, R. & Kerber, K. (1990). Object relations and social cognition in borderlines, major depressives, and normals: A Thematic Apperception Test Analysis. *Psychological Assessment: A Journal of Consulting and Clinical Psychology, 2,* 355–364.

Whalen, C. K., & Henker, B. (1985). The social worlds of hyperactive (ADDH) children. *Clinical Psychology Review, 5,* 1–32.

Whalen, C. K., Henker, B., Collins, B. E., McCaullife, S., & Vaux, A. (1979). Peer interaction in a structured communication task: Comparisons of normal hyperactive boys and of methylphenidate (Ritalin) and placebo effects. *Child Development, 48,* 388–401.

White, R. W. (1959). Motivation reconsidered: The concept of competence. *Psychological Review, 66,* 297–333.

Whitely, J. M. (1966). A method for assessing adaptive ego functioning using the Thematic Apperception Test. *Journal of Experimental Education, 34,* 1–21.

Widiger, T. A., Knudson, R. M., & Rorer, L. G. (1980). Convergent and discriminant validity of measures of cognitive styles and abilities. *Journal of Personality and Social Psychology, 39,* 116–129.

Wilson, T. D., Hull, J. G., & Johnson, J. (1981). Awareness and self-perception: Verbal reports on internal states. *Journal of Personality and Social Psychology, 40,* 53–71.

Winnicott, D. W. (1958). *Collected papers: Through pediatrics to psychoanalysis.* New York: Basic Books.

Winnicott, D. W. (1965). *The motivational process and the facilitating environment.* New York: International Universities Press.

Winnicott, D. W. (1971). Transitional objects and transitional phenomena. In *Playing and reality.* New York: Basic Books.

Witkin, H. A. (1965). Psychological differentiation and forms of pathology. *Journal of Abnormal Psychology, 70,* 317–336.

Witkin, H. A. (1976). Cognitive style in academic performance and in teacher-student selections. In S. Messick (Ed.), *Individuality in learning* (pp. 38–72). San Francisco: Jossey-Bass.

Witkin,, H. A., & Berry, J. W. (1975). Psychological differentiation in cross-cultural perspective. *Journal of Cross-Cultural Psychology, 6,* 4–87.

Witkin, H. A., Moore, C. A., Goodenough, D. R., & Cox, P. W. (1977). Field-dependent cognitive styles and their educational implications. *Review of Educational Research, 47,* 1–64.

Wolk, R. L., & Wolk, R. B. (1971). *The Gerontological Apperception Test.* New York: Behavioral Publications.

Wood, R. E., & Bandura, A. (1989). Impact of conceptions of ability on self-regulatory mechanisms and complex decision-making. *Journal of Personality and Social Psychology, 56,* 407–415.

Wyatt, F. (1947). The scoring and analysis of the Thematic Apperception Test. *Journal of Psychology, 24,* 319–330.

Wyatt, F. (1958). A principle for the interpretatoon of fantasy. *Journal of Projective Techniques, 22,* 173–180.

Wyer, R. S., & Srull, T. K. (1981). Category accessibility: Some theoretical and empirical issues concerning the processing of social stimulus information. In E. T. Higgins, C. P. Herman & M. P. Zanna (Eds.), *Social cognition: The Ontario symposium* (Vol. 1, pp. 161–197). Hillsdale, NJ: Erlbaum.

Yerkes, R. M., & Dodson, J. D. (1908). The relation of strength of stimuli to rapidity of habit-information. *Journal of Comparative Neurology and Psychology, 18,* 459–482.

Yochelson, S., & Samenow, S. (1977a). *The criminal personality: A profile for change* (Vol. 1). New York: Jason Aronson.

Yochelson, S., & Samenow, S. (1977b). *The criminal personality: The change process* (Vol. 2). New York: Jason Aronson.

Zajonc, R. B. (1980). Feeling and thinking: Preferences need no inferences. *American Psychologist, 35,* 151–175.

Zajonc, R. B. (1984). On the primacy of affect. *American Psychologist, 39,* 117–123.

Zimring, F. M., & Balcombe, J. K. (1974). Cognitive operations in two measures of handling emotionaly relevant material. *Psychotherapy: Theory, Research and Practice, 11,* 226–228.

Zubin, J., Eron, L. D., & Schumer, F. (1965). *An experimental approach to projective techniques.* New York: Wiley.

Zuckerman, M. (1974). The sensation seeking motive. In B. A. Maher (Ed.), *Progress in experimental personality research* (Vol. 7). New York: Academic Press.

Zuckerman, M. (1979). *Sensation seeking: Beyond the optimal level of arousal.* Hillsdale, NJ: Erlbaum.

Index